THE ART OF THE CITY

THE ART
OF THE CITY

Views and Versions of New York

PETER CONRAD

New York   OXFORD UNIVERSITY PRESS   Oxford
1984

Library of Congress Cataloging in Publication Data
Conrad, Peter.
The art of the city.
Includes index.
1. Arts, American—New York (N.Y.)   2. Arts—New York (N.Y.)
3. Arts, Modern—20th century—New York (N.Y.)   I. Title.
NX511.N4C66   1984   700′.9747′1   83-24935
ISBN 0-19-503408-2

Printing (last digit): 9 8 7 6 5 4 3 2 1
Printed in the United States of America

For
Jorge Calado

Preface

I first visited New York in the summer of 1969 and don't think I have been the same since. It exhilarated and alarmed me in about equal parts. I mostly remember myself in panicking flight—from slumped winos on the Bowery who uncoiled to growl and bark curses as I scuttled past, from a bright-eyed loon on a bench beside the lake in Central Park who had conceived an intimate interest in my boots, from the reception clerks in the 23rd Street Y where I had slunk in, without being registered, to take a shower. But I remember too the open-handedness and open-heartedness of people, the generosity behind the wary gruffness and time-saving laconicism. The perils of the place breed mutuality: we are all in it together and had better help one another. And though the streets are often bruising, there are always, in compensation, the heights. The skyline and the dazzling sky pardon and transfigure all.

Since 1969, the alarm has diminished—I now have the means of holding it at bay, with a door to (double-) lock and a window to look out at the city through—while the exhilaration and astonishment have continued to grow, until they become obsessive enough to be written down. After all, New York is, as John Russell has said, "one of the supreme subjects of our century."

This book is about New York's intimidation and elation of people, about how art tries to cope with its physical magnitude and the profusion of its possibilities. More generally, it is about all cities and their human challenge to us, for in reacting to them we are expressing ourselves about the fellow creatures with whom we share them. Dare we embrace the crowd? Can we tolerate the city's reminder—writ large on the signs of the cheaper New York hotels with their "transient rates"—of our own temporariness in it and on earth? I begin with Whitman's epic anchoring of New York in earth, and end with a generation of artists who don't need to consider it rooted and are happy to see it and everything it contains as a concatenation of idle chances.

Beyond this, the book intrudes on two larger objects. One of them is artistic modernity. Since New York is the capital of the modern world, the development of modern literature and art can be studied by observing responses to it. For many of the artists discussed here, the city itself *is* modern art. The other subject is the relation between life and art. If insular New York constitutes a closed field of reality, then this book looks at the ways art performs within that delimited arena, reflecting, deforming, rearranging, hoping to humanize the given data—the city's objects, institutions, and other people—upon which it works.

Still, the book's most urgent reason for being is its simplest. It is an attempt to understand a place that fascinates me, and to understand my own fascination.

I could not have managed it without the assistance of many people— first among them, my editor Curtis Church, who supported the project so energetically and imaginatively. I am grateful as well to Natalie Tutt for her countless letters and telephone calls to museums, to Kim Lewis for the pains she took in copyediting, and to Stephen Koss for helping me gain access to the libraries of Columbia University. As I was about to begin writing the book, an invitation came to lecture at Williams College in Massachusetts. I tried out some of my ideas on my audience there; its response was vitally encouraging. For making possible this boost to my morale, and for the generosity of their welcome, I must thank Charles and Johanna Karelis. Dobson Books have allowed me to quote from their edition of Mayakovsky's poems in Herbert Marshall's translation. My final debt is to two artists of the city. The designs above the chapter titles were made by Joaquin Vaquero for the 1930 translation of Paul Morand's book on New York. He has not only consented to their reproduction here, but has supplied four additional blocks—those to Chapters 4, 7, 8, and 15—not used in 1930. They are seen here for the first time. And I am proud that my book has on its jacket a photograph by Arthur Tress.

Christ Church, Oxford P.C.
November, 1983

Contents

THE ART OF THE CITY

1

The Epic City

A city's founding is an epic act. The deed immortalizes the founder and confers a term of solidity and permanence on all men who will live there. Our existences rescued from perishable time, blockaded inside the city from the depredations of nature, we can adhere to and hope to partake of the durability of architecture. By building a city, the vagrant human tribe has manifested a new, concerted strength, fortifying itself with walls against the imminence of death. The city's bequest to us is to collectivize us. Compounding our bodies, it melds them into a statue, a giant whose flesh is resistant brick or marble or iron or steel. It is the collaborative perfection of human effort, since it overcomes on our combined behalf the suspicion that our lives are an errant transit through the world, of which no record will remain. In the city, we all enjoy a proxy immortality. This is why we all long to inscribe our names on it, whether in commemoration or defacement. It is a habitation and a sociable grave to us, first sheltering us, then interring us in the company of our fellows.

The city's foundation (in the *Aeneid*) or its defense (in the *Iliad*) is the inevitable subject of epic, the literary form which celebrates the human leveling of nature and the settling of community. The epic hero's sturdy battle-scarred body, like the city's ramparts, guards the tribe. His is the body statufied, the human life reprieved from its brevity and magnified into architecture. The city itself, as much as the hero who founds or defends it, is a fabrication of myth. We need to know why we are on an earth that seems reluctant to house or own us, and we devise myths to explain our origins to us by first explaining the creation and purpose of the world. Specifically, we need to know why we are *where* we are on this inhospitable planet. To the indiscriminate expanses of geography, the city is a calculated human affront. Establishing ourselves in this place rather than any other, we declare it to be central, rearranging geography around it, like New York promulgating its self-centered world view in Saul Steinberg's cartoon, or George M. Cohan declaring that when you're away from Broadway, you're only camping out. Every city requires its own myth to justify this presumption of centrality. The city isn't a natural association like the tribe. It's constituted by an exertion of will, impelled by fear. Yet we must pretend to ourselves that this chance asylum has some logical necessity. We have to agree on the invention of gods or heroes who will patrol the city's bounds. The first urban act is an imaginative one, the making of a myth to supply the city with a heredity and guarantee its legitimacy. Religious mythologies justify the ways of gods to their subjects, men; urban mythologies justify the rapacious ways of men to the nature which they have decided they may treat as their subject.

But because the city is a studied self-deception—our delusion that we're central on the earth, that we can outlast nature—the myths which consecrate that city are frauds, rationalization of randomness. Their task is to sanctify the appropriation or extermination which precedes human settlement. The epic does so by telling grandiose untruths, licensing the city's robbery of terrain and devising for it the glorious past it feels it deserves.

The literary invention of New York occurs in a work that does exactly this, deviously unsettling the city and doubting its legitimacy while purportedly toiling to supply it with a worthy lineage—a joking epic which admits the dishonesty of its own means. It is the *History of New York*, which Washington Irving published in 1809 and attributed to Diedrich Knickerbocker. Irving's chronicler establishes the divine right of the city to occupy the space it has wheedled away from the natives and extols the social priority of its Dutch citizens. But he does so by hieratic overstatement and verbal bluster, and gives New York a mock-epic before it has acquired an epic. Irving begins New York's literary history by proposing it as a problem only evasion or mendacity can solve: is our sense of connection with the city anything more than bravado? aren't our claims for it stratagems of self-interest? isn't the place a mere literary illusion, sustained by municipal rhetoric? In succession to Irving—doing in earnest what Knickerbocker does in jest—Walt Whitman volunteers himself as the center of New York's existence and the source of its legitimacy. It becomes an extension of his body, its thronging traffic and burgeoning commerce an overflow from his clamorous, multitude-containing egotism. Irving is New York's mock-epic unfounder, Whitman its belated epic founder.

Knickerbocker's epic disappears into myth, reaching "from the Beginning of the World to the End of the Dutch Dynasty," because he can only explain to New Yorkers how they happen in the world by explaining how the world itself is constructed. But his activity soon becomes self-referring and self-congratulatory. The composition of his own epic qualifies, for Knickerbocker, as the epic feat that the actual founders of the city omitted to perform. Milton in *Paradise Lost* opposes to the martial swagger of the mock-epic Satan his own epic intellectual heroism, which enables him to comprehend and assist God's design; Knickerbocker correspondingly sees that his subject demands from him a brave, reckless sophistry, which he compares with the physical hardihood of previous epic heroes. Those forebears confronted material obstructions. For Milton, however, the trials of his courage were theological conundrums; for Knickerbocker they're legal embarrassments. Admiring himself as "an adventurous knight" embarked on "a perilous enterprise, by way of establishing his fame"—the epic project of self-deification— he announces that his ennobling labor will be to grapple with the question of by what right the discoverers of New York claimed it for their own and dispossessed the aboriginal residents, and his own brand of heroic forbearance will be to abide the reproaches of latter-day Yankees whom he may have offended: "I shall need the tough hide of an Achilles or an Orlando Furioso to protect me from their stings." Founding the city was an act of piracy; writing about it requires an equal brazenness and a defiant insensitivity.

Knickerbocker is the tribal memory. He protests against the forgetfulness of the present, which will erase the city from recollection. However, in remembering a past for New York, he is astutely protecting his own investment in it and propping up the Dutch hegemony. His great-great-grandfather, he says, served as a cabin boy on Hudson's ship in 1609, so details of that voyage are "traditionary in our family." New York to the Knickerbockers is an ancestral heirloom. The dress of the original settlers at Communipaw—broad-brimmed hat, broad-skirted coat, broad-bottomed breeches with silver knee-buckles—has been transmitted paternalistically, "handed down inviolate, from father to son." History, like this costume, is an observance of filial duty. Knickerbocker writes the chronicle to discharge the debt New York owes to Communipaw as its begetter, the "mother settlement." His concern for the genealogy of actions assures his patrimony, seeing to it that epic deeds—the initiatives of colonization—aren't misattributed and permitted to leave the family. He worries because he can't be certain about the antecedents of the four adventurers who made the exploratory canoe trip from Communipaw to Hell Gate, but history's failure is made good by the convenient fabulation of myth: he solves the problem by likening them to those antediluvian heroes who claimed their parentage from the gods.

Because the history he rigs up for New York is merely verbal—a forgery of deeds and titles, a faking of evidence to support an appropriation—there's an analogy between the family trees he patriarchally cultivates for people and those he fancifully concocts for words. Etymology is a verbal genealogy. A word's derivation is its pedigree. Manhattan, Knickerbocker pretends, takes its name from a sartorial habit of its squaws, who liked to wear men's hats. His whimsy asserts ownership. Since the place named after the word belongs to him and his kin, he can make it mean whatever he pleases. He's exhibiting in language the same proprietorial effrontery the first settlers displayed in commandeering the land. Accordingly, in his urban epic, the only conceivable valor is linguistic. Though Knickerbocker describes the history of armaments, in his own epic the technology of destruction—the battering rams of the Homeric siege, the gunpowder invented by Milton's devils—has been supplanted by oratorical flyting or by bellicose eructation. The savages were first frightened away not by any deed of arms but by the fearful noise of the Low Dutch language. Governor Kieft's mode of epic detonation is to sneeze. He prefaces his address to his council with a nasal blast, which serves as a "signal trumpet." When crossed by a band of Yankees at Fort Good Hope, his broadsides are the firing of anathematic curses. Linguistic weapons—"huge, mis-shapen, nine-cornered Dutch oaths"—explode from his gullet. Wilhelm the Testy admonishes his refractory subjects with literary instruments, dispatching proclamations "piping-hot," and Peter Stuyvesant intimidates by reverberation: he is, "as Plutarch describes Coriolanus, not only terrible for the force of his arm, but likewise of his voice, which sounded as though it came out of a barrel." Heroism is a matter of nomenclature. A petition from Rhode Island signed by one Alicxsander Partridg is cited as a dangerous document, for "the name of Alexander, however misspelt, has been war-like in every age," even though mitigated by attachment to "the gentle cognomen of Partridge."

The epic history a city writes for itself is, as Knickerbocker demonstrates, an exercise in self-flattery. Events are banal. Hudson, discovering New York, can only point and say "See! There!" The historian's job is to aggrandize, promoting accident to inevitability and innocuous circumstance to portent, as one of the mariners does when, whirled in a vortex off the Long Island shore, he imagines he sees specters and hears hobgoblins howling and therefore names the place Hell Gate. Knickerbocker apologizes for an actuality as yet unredeemed by rhetoric when his explorers encounter a shoal of porpoises headed into "the strait vulgarly called the East River." Rather than physical puissance, epic belligerency now connotes a braggart proficiency in language and gesture. Promenading on the Battery in 1804, Knickerbocker recalls the bulwark of Fort Amsterdam, which used to threaten the city's foes. Now, "like many a whiskered warrior and gallant militia captain," the installation is past performing valiant deeds and contents itself with "frowns alone." He looks over at Governors Island and sees it too as an epic imposter. Once bucolic, now fortified, it flourishes its incongruous ordnance like "a fierce little warrior in a big cocked hat." The Battery can't keep up the posture of aggression, and subsides from warfaring epic to idolent pastoral. Stuyvesant's fort, overgrown with moss and planted with sycamores, is the resort of dallying lovers and pipe-puffing elders. "Ostensibly devoted to the purpose of war," it has surrendered to "the sweet delights of peace," and its lapse from strenuous epic to vegetative pastoral is the destiny too of Knickerbocker's New York. The city which prides itself on its ancient enmities and political contentions is in truth placid, smug, pastorally bovine. Knickerbocker is at first dismayed by its pusillanimity. He asks forgiveness from readers who expect epic and who—as if they were, in reading, epic activists, just as he in his sedentary occupation of writing can pretend to be one—would like to be "continually storming forts, sacking cities, springing mines, marching up to the muzzles of cannon, charging bayonet through every page, and revelling in gunpowder and carnage," for the dull peace of Governor Van Twiller's reign. New Amsterdam then, he explains, was a rural place where all the burghers had to do was supervise their livestock.

Still, there's a pastoral as well as an epic heroism: an idyllic self-satisfaction, which Knickerbocker sets against the fretful ambition of the warrior. Though his New Yorkers affect to possess the mettlesome energy of epic, theirs is a cozy pastoral valor which, like Falstaff's, discreetly attends to the protection of its fleshly sovereignty—the defense of an imperially bloated body. Knickerbocker's epic grows from verbal surfeit; the heroism of his characters is measured by their corpulence.

Whatever they do ministers to an appetite. Stuyvesant's "hunger for martial glory" is compared with an alderman's salivation at a corporation dinner when he begins to guzzle his turtle soup. The capture of Oyster Bay is resented because it attacks the stomachs of the rotund New Amsterdam burgomasters. The victory over the Yankees here is a culinary triumph. The conquering hero returns with "fifty cart loads of oysters, five hundred bushels of Weathersfield onions, a hundred quintals of cod fish, two hogsheads of molasses." For Stuyvesant too, military honors assume corporeal form. He treasures his wooden leg as a trophy, "the only prize he had gained, in bravely fighting the battles of his country." Epic toil and strife succumb to a pastoral ethic of physical satiety. Van Twiller passes for a sage because he smokes pensively, says little, and has a body "like Dutch statuary." Knickerbocker approves of orbicular aldermen, considering that the body's bulk testifies to the mind's sober torpor. These well-fed officials "sit for hours dozing and smoking over public affairs." The variant etymologies of Knickerbocker's own name sum up the city's choice between epic and pastoral. In one version, he says, the name means "Knicker Becker," which is to shake a goblet, "indicating . . . that they were sturdy tosspots of yore"; another possibility is "Knicker Boeken," or nod book, "meaning that they were great nodders or dozers over books." Though Knickerbocker tries to represent his clan as warriors, they're actually peaceable pastoral feeders, and the city he's lauding turns out to be a slumberous village. New York, he implies, has no history and is the happier and the plumper for it.

Whitman's tactics for the constitution of an urban epic follow from those of Knickerbocker. The city for the Dutch burghers is an outgrowth from their adipose bodies. Whitman too—bequeathing to the city and the nation his life, which he sees as an epic poem, its often uneventful specimen days a democratic answer to the crises and combats of the epic hero—derives the city from his body. He generates the crowd, potentiates the city, incorporates its masses into himself. The athletic, ecstatic body inside which he thrives is a body politic. His fellow citizens on Broadway or the Brooklyn ferry are members, literally physical components, of Whitman, partaking of his transcendentally capitalized, polymorphous, and prolific egotism. "The proof of a poet," he said, "is that his country absorbs him as affectionately as he absorbs it," and he makes poetry by enumerating the inhabitants of city or country and enrolling them in his own existence, until *Leaves of Grass* resembles, as he claimed, "a great city." Whitman is New York's epic hero—the individual who procreates and protects his tribe, the compound being in whose capacious "Me myself" we're housed and shielded.

8

English romanticism flinches from the city. Wordsworth can cope with London only if, as in the sonnet about Westminster Bridge, its mercenary life has been stilled, its heart prevented from beating. The "thickening hubbub" of its streets alarms the contemplative solitary who decides, without regret, that "The face of every one / That passes by me is a mystery!" American romanticism isn't an individual retrenchment from the indifferent many but the individual's dilation to beget or contain the many, and even when Whitman surveys the empty western plains he sees them, like the city, as congested—infinitudes, not vacancies, "that vast Something, stretching out on its own unbounded scale, unconfined." Whitman declared in the Brooklyn *Standard* in 1862 that "the child is already born, and is now living, stout and hearty, who will see Brooklyn number one million inhabitants!" This is an urban and literal revision of a Wordsworthian faith. The child is not merely father of the man, recalling him to a private past. He germinates all men, replenishing the city with a million likenesses of himself. For Whitman the poetic faculty is a means of self-reproduction and a way of founding and building a place: hence his trade as a carpenter, his involvement in the Brooklyn property boom of the early 1850s, and his discovery of an analogy between his own emotional growth and the city's economic boom as it matured from a rural outpost, increasing and multiplying. His own life is cognate with Brooklyn's. He remembers the laying of the cornerstone of the Apprentice's Library in 1825, when he was seven; Lafayette's visit made it "a historical event." For the bardic Whitman, history consists in what he can remember. It solemnizes a physical bondage to the past. Thus, during the ceremony, the young Whitman was "touched by the hands, and taken a moment to the breast of the immortal old Frenchman." Contact with a tribal god has granted Whitman a share in that immortality, since he can now enter a remoter past, predating his own existence. This was the last of Lafayette's American tours. The first had been during the Revolutionary War, so Whitman, in that laying on of hands, is personally conjoined with the birth of the nation in 1776.

The municipal reminiscences Whitman collated during his years as a journalist in Brooklyn are his attempt to graft onto the city a memory as dilated—as acquainted with its own pre-existence—as his own. He worried about the city's negligent obliteration of its past. A symbol of this amnesia was the profiteering fad of incendiarism, and Whitman demands indignantly how the first fire bell, procured by the villagers of Brooklyn in the 1790s, can have been recently mislaid. Single-handedly constructing a history of Brooklyn, he relies first on the epic method of oral transmission, then passes to the bureaucratic technique of documentation

—inventories of records, a roll call of local stalwarts—because these paper relics are all the future will have to rely on when personal ties with the past have been sundered. The child is at once regenerating his distant paternity and securing his posterity, making sure that Brooklyn will remain biologically rooted, during its metropolitan future, in its rustic past. Whitman is the Wordsworthian infant constituting from the exercise of memory and foresight an entire urban world. The limits of that world are the periphery of life itself, and Whitman who, via Lafayette, has remembered back to the origins of his tribe and the nativity of America, superstitiously treats the railroad tunnel at South Ferry—the means of transit from Brooklyn to Manhattan—as an orifice where, hurtled out of the world we know, we re-enact the birth or death trauma. This "passage of Acheron-like solemnity and darkness" seems "dark as the grave," and leaving it is resurrection: "How beautiful look Earth and Heaven again, as we emerge from the gloom!"

Whitman's choice of a newspaper, the weekly Brooklyn *Standard*, as the form through which to disseminate this collective memory is itself epically significant. Breeding the race, stocking the city with comradely look-alikes, he posits himself—in the poem "Ma femme! for the brood beyond us and of us"—as patriarch and mother at once; and to his prophetic self-propagation or self-publication the newspaper's mechanical reproduction acts as a corollary. The paper assembles the community and unifies it. Its duplication of itself is a model of our birth in equality. It's a bardic agency for the modern city. P. T. Barnum remarked that "he who is without a newspaper is cut off from his species." The paper is what city dwellers have in common. Whitman during his term on the Long Island *Star* argued that newspapers forge "intellectual and moral association" and "maintain civilization." He likened his own creativity to the cloning of "the many-cylinder'd steam printing-press," and found in typesetting a process similar to that whereby he postulated the democratic city of New York and filled it with self-images. Mechanically, type is eugenic: "the Hoe press whirling its cylinders, shedding the printed leaves," guarantees that each copy will be as perfect as the original. The press has achieved the future of self-regeneration that Whitman predicts for the slave at auction, who is "not only one man" but "the father of those who shall be fathers in their turns" and who, like Whitman, will be the founder and biological supplier of cities, "the start of populous states and rich republics." In "A Font of Type" Whitman describes the mechanical letters as a seedbed, each with a voice latent in it. As an individual, Whitman himself is a species; as a single man, he holds within him a germinal city. In furnishing that city, he's running off copies of himself, in a typographic feat of self-renewal. The newspaper is both an appropriate medium for and a symbol of the urban epic, communalizing and equating (or typing) those to whom it's distributed.

The newspapers orally alerted Whitman to the beginning of the Civil War. He had left the opera and was walking down Broadway when in the distance he heard the newsboys declaiming a headline. Their cries diffused the event in the air, just as Whitman himself had bawled Shakespeare from a bus on the same thoroughfare, duetting with the city's "heavy, dense, uninterrupted street-bass." Now he bought a paper and hurried to the Metropolitan Hotel to join a crowd: the two acts complement one another, since the paper is his passport to the community. Because epic history can be accredited only if announced orally and oratorically, in the hotel the telegram about the outbreak of hostilities is read aloud "for the benefit of some who had no papers." During the war the papers bardically exhort the city they have convened. Like military music, their reports coerce New Yorkers into an optimistic unity, reviving morale after Bull Run "with leaders that rang out over the land with the loudest, most reverberating ring of clearest bugles." Grief for Whitman expresses itself in silent reading—not declamation—of a paper. After Lincoln's murder, "we got every newspaper morning and evening, and the frequent extras of that period, and pass'd them silently to each other." As tribal scribe, Whitman helped others to publish and pass on their experiences. In Washington hospitals in 1863 he wrote and posted letters for recuperating soldiers or issued them paper, pencils, and stamped envelopes, providing them with the means for a self-duplication like his own.

New York's history doubles as Whitman's autobiography. He's concerned, like Knickerbocker, with genealogy and etymology, perceiving an alliance between the city's emergence and his own, between the retrieval of its native name and his own epic reanimation of that name in poetry. He writes the lines about his ancestors in *Specimen Days and Collect* (1882) while "seated on an old grave . . . on the burial hill of the Whitmans of many generations" on Long Island. His own life begins in that earth and has been spent in growth back into it. The imaginative act he performs is an incorporation—the interembodiment of the city or of nature. He feels he has ingested Long Island, having walked all over Paumanok. His walking isn't a leisurely divagation inside the mind, as were the digressive hikes of Wordsworth and Coleridge. Whitman's heroism is physical, and walking over Paumanok is an epic campaign, a one-man army's subjugation of a territory that belongs to him. Strolling down Broadway is his education and apprenticeship as epic hero, for this is the arena where he sees the city's forefathers on patrol. James Fenimore Cooper and John Jacob Astor are remembered at various locations on it, and he first glimpsed Lincoln there in February 1861, when Lincoln arrived at the Astor House as Whitman passed by on the top of a bus. Unlike the walking of the English romantics, Whitman's is never an induction into solitude. Whether sauntering on Broadway or in a landscape, he dispenses sociability. His "communion with the waters" while crossing on the Camden ferry is a communalizing of those waters, and to him the prairies are as congested with comrades as urban streets, since on his journeys there he has been accompanied "by a pleasant floricultural friend, or rather millions of friends"—by which he means wildflowers.

Whitman establishes an official religion for New York: a metropolitan pantheism. His urban enjoyments involve not the self's extinction—which the English romantics feared in the city—but its expansive merger with a collective life. He loved New York's ferries because they conferred on him membership of the human crowd and of the elemental crowd of nature. Crossing the bay, they equate the "oceanic currents, eddies underneath" with the teeming, tidal humanity of their passengers. Whitman insists on the water-borne status of New York because the city's an incident in a life spawned and supported by the elements. He sees its places of amusement "bubbling and whirling and moving like its own environment of waters" and thinks of its streets as fluctuant and riverine: he calls Fifth Avenue in 1879 "a Mississippi of horses and rich vehicles." Since he refuses to distinguish between the city's vital plenum and the profusion of nature, urban occupations can be mistaken for a romantic relapse into landscape. A policeman to whom Whitman talks near 90th Street squints into the distance, "moving where he can get full views of the vistas" near Central Park, like a visionary scrutinizing a natural prospect, not an officer on the lookout for traffic misdemeanors; the maritime economy of "tall-top't, ship-hemm'd" New York thrills him because it's a communion with the ocean. Whitman liked to watch the docking or departure of steamers, and often accompanied them as far as the Narrows. He rejoiced in the transformation of water—as on his Mississippian Fifth Avenue—into a highway spanning the globe, rhapsodized over the laying of the transatlantic cable, and argued that the St. Lawrence River should be a channel, not a frontier, between the United States and Canada.

His analogy for these communicative outgrowths is always the body's integration of itself: the epic hero's triumphant occupancy of physical space. In a telegraph office on the prairies he considered it wonderful that "you could send a message by electricity anywhere around the world!" Singing the body electric, he was proposing an electrification of the body so that, infusing the air with its energy, it galvanizes others into an excited union. He refers to the "personal electricity" of the orator Father Taylor, who preached to Boston sailors; and just as his own exponentiation of himself resembles the printing press with its mechanization of birth, so cities are to Whitman turbines for the generation of "human electricity," ignited by the tindery conjunction of bodies. In Washington during the summer, he speculates that the population contributes the sparky, fulgural heat of the place. Thus energetically inspirited or electrically vivified, New York's ambition—like that of the epic hero in training for feats of arms—must be the attainment of bodily wholeness. Whitman urged the incorporation of Brooklyn and New York into a municipality to be known as Manhattan. In 1898 this corporeal union was accomplished. New York City gathered to itself the boroughs which were, in Whitman's view, its natural physical extremities, adding Brooklyn, Queens, Staten Island, and part of the Bronx to Manhattan.

The commonality of experience in a city makes us all parts of one another, like the limbs or nerves of a single polymorph. On this necessary sharing, Whitman founds a metaphysical faith. In "Crossing Brooklyn Ferry" he claims to participate in the existence of all those who have traveled this way before and all who will do so in the future. Sectors of time overlap on the ferry as they do for Wordsworth revisiting Tintern Abbey. But in Wordsworth the chronology works out a desacralizing loss. Each time the initial feeling returns to him, it's further diminished until only poetry remains as a funereal consolation for the robbery of time, since in verse you can at least remember experiences you can no longer have. Whitman, in contrast, abolishes time. The ferry plies through a perpetual present. The English romantic lyric is inured to failure. It's the elegy for a feeling that is forfeited in being written about, admitting (as when Keats's nightingale absconds) the fallacy of its own too trusting pathos. Whitman in the city confidently collectivizes and universalizes impressions that the English poets can't prevail on anyone else, not even a bird or an urn, to share. The serial repetitions in "Crossing Brooklyn Ferry"—"Just as," "Saw," or "Look'd"—originate in Whitman's senses but are analogically imputed to everyone else, allocated in turn to past, present, and future. Rhetoric acts out the individual's procreation of a species or his populating of a city, and the same metaphysical enlargement elasticizes Whitman's lines so they can accommodate more and more words as the denominators of more and more existences contained in the poet:

13

Fifty years hence, others will see them as they cross, the sun half an hour high,
A hundred years hence, or ever so many hundred years hence, others will see
    them, . . .

Whitman's city promotes lyric from helpless plaint to epic coercion
by altering the rhetoric of invocation. When the English romantics use
this, there's a qualifying helplessness to their appeal. A god who's not
there is being invoked. Whitman's exclamations—"Flow on, river! . . .
Stand up, tall masts of Mannahatta! Stand up, beautiful hills of Brooklyn!"—are commandments, not vain supplications. He boldly selects
physical states that have no need of human intervention, like the lunar
motions of the tide or the stability of the Brooklyn hills, and addresses
them as if they were subject to his behest, co-opting them as tributaries
for his energy and accomplices of his will. Language to the epic poet
is a power. When he speaks, he acts, imposing himself on the world,
like Milton in *Paradise Lost* recapitulating the primary epic fiat of God,
who spoke the world into existence. And the throb and surge of words
in him is reciprocated by the collectivity of phenomena outside: the
flooding tide, the marching crowd respond to the poetic pneuma. This
is why Whitman likened poetry to singing. It's the generous expenditure
of a breath which you have inhaled from the air and must, exhaling,
render up. Similarly, he receives life from the city and returns life to it.
His bardic remonstrances are—literally, not metaphorically—an in-
spiration to it, actuating it as if divinely, prompting it by directing into
it his own vitality, as he does in "First O Songs for a Prelude" or in
"City of Ships," where the energy with which he has quickened New
York turns bellicose and swaggering and the city at his orders arms
itself, in a ceremony of weapons like that performed by the epic hero,
for the Civil War. Martially unifying New York by singing to it, Whitman proposes himself as a poetic avatar of the hero of political epic,
Lincoln. The accord that Lincoln defends politically is proclaimed meta-
physically by Whitman and owes its warranty to him, since he is the
archetypal self of whom all other democratic citizens are offprints. "I
will make the continent indissoluble," he promises. He can do so because he holds its society, as he has enfolded the city, within himself,
recalling the masses which are his offspring to their phylogenetic source
in his own being: "who except myself has yet conceiv'd what your children en-masse really are?" Together, Whitman and Lincoln battle for
the preservation of a body politic, and Whitman's poetry is emphatic
about the physiological meaning of that abstract notion. His political
edicts are issued to guard the bodily integrity which the epic hero

armors. He advises the states to "resist much, obey little," not to submit even to partial abrogation because freedom consists in retaining the use of your body, which the slave has had to forego. America's "athletic Democracy" depends on and delights in physique because it prides itself on the physical equality of all those who are its members.

Corporeally, the city means a congregation of bodies—not an antagonistic rabble of disparate selves but a common identity, for all its creatures share the same physical form. Poetry's mission in the city is to overcome a protective individuation and reunite that generic crowd. Whitman, who imagines nature as a crowd (watching the swarming of bees, he reflects that "Nature marches in procession, in sections, like the corps of an army," as if parading on Broadway), sees in it a retreat from the fission of individuality: the subject's return to the serene, unanxious strength of the object. He admires trees, which incarnate the undifferentiated solemn stability of being, like the "all-basis, the nerve, the great-sympathetic" which is the common denominator of our fractious, fractionalized humanity; they possess a heroism epic in its impersonality. Poetry addresses this collectivity that is the city or the race. "To You" asks why we shouldn't speak to strangers and they to us, since we're all fellows in the same biological or metropolitan crowd. On the streets of Whitman's New York, a Wordsworthian definition of poetry is tested: a man emboldens himself to speak to other men, sturdily defying them to cower inside their alarmed individuality. This ecstatic invasion of the lives of passersby makes the city a place of alluring sexual possibility. Whitman has generated New York by the self-fertilizing "need of comrades," and they defer to their parentage in "City of Orgies," returning his glances and offering themselves to him as potential lovers. The idling sensual appraisal of the flaneur is his presumptive incorporation of himself with all those he passes. Pantheism incites a bacchanal, with one man twined round, rooted in, contained by, or containing multitudinous others. The poetry which describes this rampant congregation already possesses its own collective life, beyond mere individuality, for Whitman writes chorally, not lyrically. His voice duplicates itself in an orotund echo chamber. "I hear the chorus, it is a grand opera," he declares in *Song of Myself*. Opera elated him because it achieved this choral impersonalizing of the plangent single voice: a sonic transcendence. Listening to Donizetti's *La Favorita* on a summer evening in 1851 at Castle Garden in the Battery, he hears the voices oceanically welling out of individual bodies or aerially drifting over the city until they resound through the universe, supported by "a sublime orchestra of a myriad orchestras—a colossal volume of harmony."

Opera singers in their own way performed the physical feat Whitman set for himself and which the city too had achieved. By strenuous physical exertion they manage an expansion of body into spirit, and at the same time they overcome the physical separateness of those who listen to them, eliciting "the living soul" in each of us and chorally compounding all our small vocal plaints. From a litter of human individualities they forge a mass (as Whitman's singing hopes to do); they then return that mass to the superhuman individuality which is its fount, "the vast pure Tenor,—identity of the Creative Power itself." It's this which O. Henry, in succession to Whitman, will hear as "the voice of the city."

Whitman's conviction that the city's history is a biography, the annals of an epic career analogous to his own, makes him concerned for its name. This is an epic scruple. The epic hero rages to consecrate his name and wrathfully challenges anyone who dares trifle with it. But because his fury is individual, it can, like that of Achilles, seem no more than titanic pique. The city has outgrown such murderous petulance, for its name—like the self which it defends—is collective. That name, however, cries out for restitution against those who have misrepresented it, and only poetry can grant it reparation. Whitman believed that poetic justice demanded a salutary renaming of Long Island and New York. The former, he argued, should revert to its original name of Paumanok. Long Island is an unloving label; Paumanok—which means, as Whitman explains, "the island with its breast long drawn out, and laid against the sea"—recorporealizes geography and makes the place a nurturing maternal home. He proposed that New York should be restored to its Algonquin name of Mannahatta (meaning "the place encircled by many swift tides and sparkling waters"), and in poems addressed to the city in 1860 and 1888 he officiates at this rebaptism. He prefers the Indian name because it's latently metaphoric and thus can be true to the indwelling spirit of the place. Its original reference is to the river-girt situation of the city; Whitman in the 1860 poem "Mannahatta" adapts it to characterize the cascading, buoyant life of the city itself. He sets himself to "see that word" and to meditate on etymology as the nesting or homing of words: he imagines the name "nested in nests of water-bays," borne on and born from the water. And this meditation on "what there is in a name" draws the qualities of that name into the poem. Whitman first utters the word by placing it at the head of the poem as its title, then goes on to effect the word's reconquest of its lost realm. He does so in a catalogue of impressions; but that catalogue, epically active, not lyrically inert, is itself a freshet, a gush, a torrent of images (most of them watery: the city's shipping, steamers, lighters, ferries, its icy rivers) driven by an urge as unanswerable as that which speeds the waters.

"Mannahatta" is an urban ode. Rather than dedicating itself to a god or to a human demigod, it prays to a place, or to the etymological god inhabiting that place. As an ode must, it begins with a reverent act of naming, the evocation of a sacred vocable: "lo! upsprung the aboriginal name." Almost too potent for inclusion in the poem, the name waits just outside it as the title, a text to be both revolved in the mind and physically traversed. Then, in its prolific catalogue, the poem paraphrases that name. It ends by advancing from evocation ("I was asking for something specific and perfect for my city") to invocation:

> City of hurried and sparkling waters! city of spires and masts!
> City nested in bays! my city!

Those exclamations and that final pronoun are Whitman's victorious arrogation of the name and thereby of the place. He inherits the word from its aboriginal users, extends its meaning to cover the new urban torrent of the place, and then imprints it again on the city to certify his ownership. "Mannahatta" duplicates that magic act of naming undertaken by Adam, who, attaching words to plants and animals in Eden, begat poetry. Whitman first superstitiously conjures up the name as a spirit or gene that implants identity; this titling issues at last in a possessive or animistic naming. Between these two acts, Whitman's list epically tours the city and animates things by naming or noticing them. Because the sportive, reckless, ambitious objects outside himself—swift tides, trundling carts, sailing clouds, clustering immigrants—correspond to the élan within the poet, they attest to his parentage of "my city!" The poem has made itself a conduit or a place of transit for life—

> See, steamers steaming through my poems,
> See, in my poems immigrants continually coming and landing

—as the streets are, or as the womb and rocking cradle are, and in its language it subsumes the city's hubbub, "the blab of the pave, . . . talk of the promenaders, . . . the clank of the shod horses on the granite floor, . . . shouted jokes, . . . the hurrahs for popular favorites."

The city's individuated people are reconciled and made one in Whitman. Sensing an affinity between his own compendious egotism and the "many-item'd Union" or this "million-headed city," he works imaginatively on the city as New York was expected to do on those it had recruited. In the melting pot of New York, ethnically incompatible arrivals would be compounded into the new composite race of Americans.

Within Whitman, people undergo the same alteration. Deprived of an old, divisive identity—as they have been initiated into the new loyalties of their new citizenship—they emerge as an idyllically healthy, eugenic mass. The ranks of the parading army in Washington during the war persuaded Whitman, as did the urban crushes on Broadway, of "the majesty and reality of the American people *en masse*." Observing, he doesn't bother to individualize them, since his epic concern is the democratic average: the hero is just a random sampling of his race. Everyone on the streets of New York seemed to Whitman, when he returned to visit the city in 1878, good-natured and upstanding, an epic brave in embryo. His taking of the mass into himself works architectonically as well as biologically. Housing the city, he resembles those containers of multitudes built in New York during the nineteenth century—the department stores, which agglomerated all commodities under a single roof; or Franconi's Hippodrome, which opened in 1853 with room for ten thousand people, "a dense mass of human beings, exceeding in number" (in the opinion of the *Herald*) "any assemblage . . . ever seen inside a building in this city." The panoramas popular at the same time are models of Whitman's all-embracing urban pantheism, his capacity to comprehend the city in a single omniscient survey. Burckhardt's panorama wrapped New York into a sectional circle and placed the viewer at its midpoint, while in E. Porter Belden's you looked down on it, seeing it all at once like Whitman in "Mannahatta."

Compressing masses, New York had, however, created a new likelihood of panic and riot. The nineteenth-century city is beset by the trauma of congestion. The engravings in *Harper's Weekly* register political disturbance or economic mischance as mob frenzies, a consequence of the city's dangerous overloading or overfeeding of itself. Mobs maraud in the streets of New York during the protests against the draft in 1863 or the bank failure in 1884 or the transport strikes in 1886 and 1889. In the city's clogged thoroughfares, hearsay can provoke a stampede. One such mad emergency occurred among the crowds milling across the Brooklyn Bridge on Memorial Day in 1883. A woman cried out as she fell, people nearby jostled to see what was happening, and others farther off assumed from the agitation that the bridge was toppling. The crowd multiplied one person's mishap into a collective catastrophe: there were a dozen deaths in the rush to safety. The massiveness that exhilarated Whitman can easily turn into mayhem. He therefore pacifies it, drilling and disciplining an urban mob into a corps, epically choreographing its movements as if exercising an army. In a series of articles on "New York Dissected" for *Life Illustrated* in 1856 he mar-

John Bachman's panorama of "New York & Environs" (1859). Eno Collection, New York Public Library, Astor, Lenox, and Tilden Foundations.

shals the crowd into a legion, or sees in its flux the orderly operation of a natural rhythm. On the Fourth of July the city erupts with the banging of jubilant artillery, yet its pandemonium is for Whitman restrained by the military parade down Broadway. The march embodies his epic urban democracy. With the interincorporation of the phalanx, each soldier is attuned and adherent to all his fellows. The clumsiness of the first ranks—stumbling and scrambling, dragging along their breastworks—dismays Whitman. He's offended by the messiness of individuation and by lapses from the divine average of physique. Some

marchers are round-shouldered, and "the cavalry ride like bags of sand."
But with the arrival of the Seventh Regiment he can applaud an exact,
epic coordination. "That is real marching—close, straight, every musket
sloped true, steadily, and with a front as even as a wall." The simile
compliments an epic interenforcement of men, who collectivize their
bodies and make from the sum an object as impenetrable as architecture:
their walking wall is the rampart that defends the city. Though he deplores the city's listless failure to behave in a manner befitting this
march, he is able, in another of these articles, to interpret the traffic
on Broadway processionally. Early in the morning he watches the "industrial regiments" (a phrase which in Whitman's city is no dead metaphor, since its people are his conscripts, ordered as members of his
one-man army) traipsing to work, followed by troops of shopgirls,
scampering clerks, then solid blocks of burghers who bring the street
to "high tide" between 11 a.m. and 3 p.m. Between 4 and 5 p.m. there's
grace for an interlude of leisured promenade. Then the waters recede
in symmetrical reverse: "the successive waves of the morning tide now
begin to roll backward in an inverse order—merchants, brokers, law-
yers, first; clerks next; shop-girls and laborers last." This life-stream
surges into supernature, for as well as noting demographic data, Whitman perceives "spirits walking amid the crowd," cozening devils or
solicitous angels "among or above the hurrying mass." In a third article,
"Street Yarn," Whitman analyzes the passersby taxonomically. He
glimpses faces which he at once assigns to categories. By guessing rank
and occupation, he can symbolically militarize the crowd, for as he says
"soldiers and militiamen are not the only people who wear uniforms."
Clothes and demeanor enable him to identify types—an Episcopalian
deacon, a Wall Street broker, a harlot, a gambler. These people wear
syndical uniforms so as to advertise their incorporation into a group,
"to assimiliate them to each other," like the physically overlapping men
of the Seventh Regiment. Sometimes, as with the huddle of villainous
short-boys, they have formed a team and hunt in packs. Having assigned people to trades, Whitman goes on to name and individualize
some of those he spots—the editor Charles Dana, the beautiful Ada
Clare, the scholarly Dr. Francis. But these too are only members of or
extrusions from Whitman, who is the human totality and who therefore
ventures to see himself in the crowd. He spies a "tall, large, rough-
looking man, in a journeyman carpenter's uniform." This, he discloses,
is "Walt Whitman, the sturdy, self-conscious microcosmic, prose-
poetical author of that incongruous hash of mud and gold—'Leaves of
Grass.'" His placement of himself in his own essay is the furthest reach,

egotistic and altruistic at once, of Whitman's urban vision. He has filled the city with the clamoring infinity of selves he contains; he may have generated the crowd, but he is content to see himself—anonymously, almost dismissively—as a member of that crowd.

Whitman the carpenter and house-builder, for whom poetry was an act of making, erected the city. Whitman the typesetter, for whom poetry was the mechanically aided replication of yourself, filled it with fraternal similacra. New York is his work, a monument to the collaboration in America of epic (the song of heroic individual force) and industrialism (the technological harnessing and collectivizing of that force). To him, the city's durability ensured the continuity of the race. In 1849 he imagined New York after the passage of a century: "you and I . . . ," he assured his readers, "won't be much thought of then," but the city will still exist, its sun shining, its rivers flowing. Despite his exclusion of himself from the city's posterity, he lives on in it with the eternality of the epic hero. He will therefore extend and proliferate through this book—as a rebuke to Edith Wharton and Henry James, who retreat from his injunction to embrace the city; as a model for the painters of New York in the teachings of Robert Henri, who said Whitman might have been an ideal art student because he put his deepest life on record, and who presented John Sloan (another prophet of the urban body) with a copy of *Leaves of Grass* as an earnest of discipleship; as a ruddy sunbather at Coney Island in a painting by Reginald Marsh and as "a white aeroplane of help" for Joseph Stella, a hovering mechanical angel who directed Stella's efforts to depict the city as "a harmonic whole of vibrating love"; as a lost cause for Hart Crane and Garcia Lorca, who implore his aid in their own desperate poetic redemptions of materialistic New York; as a slangy spokesman for the urban vernacular in the paintings of Stuart Davis and as the case-hardened voice of the city's worldly wisdom on the sound track of Jules Dassin's film *The Naked City*. He will be abstractly reduced to angular precision by Charles Sheeler and Paul Strand and will find his epic catalogues spilling over into litter bins in the work of Claes Oldenburg. He is present at the 1939 World's Fair as a statue in Perylon Court, briskly named "Afoot and Light-Hearted," and he accompanies Judy Holliday when, in obedience to the admonition of "To You," she greets a stranger while crossing West 45th Street in Vincente Minnelli's *Bells Are Ringing*. He is the genius loci of this book, as he is of New York.

2

Houses of Fiction

Whitman's epic, democratic city is at once debarred by the novelists. The New York of Henry James, W. D. Howells, and Edith Wharton enforces social distinctions that Whitman's city abolishes; theirs is reclusive, ambuscaded indoors, whereas his exults in the life of the streets. The novel constructs its own indoor New York for characters whose vocation is introversion. True, Whitman has a spectral walk-on in one of the stories Edith Wharton collected in 1924 as a chronicle of *Old New York*, and here, returning in spirit to the changed, rigidly proper city of the novelists, he sponsors an act of social amelioration. Hayley Delayne in "The Spark" dimly recalls the hospital visits of a heathen backwoodsman in Washington after Bull Run. Now he learns that the kind creature was Whitman, who "wrote all that rubbish." Despite his distaste for the poetry, Whitman's shade encourages Delayne to perform his own work of charity, caring for the alcoholic father of his unfaithful wife, even in the face of the wife's disapproval and society's scorn. In Whitman's urban epic, the individual dilates to embrace the city; Henry James cautions the individual against a collectivity which he can't absorb but which instead threatens to absorb him. In a review of Whitman's *Drum-Taps*, James—who later regretted his juvenile impudence—reproved the poet's omnivorous egotism: "In one place you threaten to absorb Canada. In another you call upon the city of New

York to incarnate you, as you have incarnated it." For James the ambition is rudely greedy, absurdly carnal. His own imaginative tactic was to disincarnate New York, to remove it beyond barricades as he does in *Washington Square* (1880); or else to incarnate it belittlingly as he does in *The American Scene*, personifying its portents so as to scold and disarm them.

Defensively, he names *Washington Square* after the place, not the characters. There's an analogy between the square, an enclave of obdurate gentility in the vulgar commercial city, and the enforced domesticity of Catherine Sloper, incarcerated for life with her fancywork. Washington Square has turned its back on New York, as Catherine is required to turn her back on the enticements of life. Both character and place are images of immovable retirement, and the story is James's delimitation of terrain, his prescription of the borders of a novelistic New York. *Washington Square* means its title: it is a fable of urban development and an act of determined resistance to that development. New York's progress up the island becomes a confident self-reproduction, in which Catherine is prevented from joining and in which James himself also refused to join, declining to marry because—as he put it —that would have implied a higher estimation of life than he was prepared to admit. In 1820, when Sloper married, his bride had been a luminary of "the small but promising capital which clustered about the Battery and overlooked the Bay, and of which the uppermost boundary was indicated by the grassy waysides of Canal Street." But as the city slithers north, Sloper continues stubbornly to face this obsolete center. Having begun in a red-brick house near City Hall, he has compromised with change by moving as far as Washington Square, but there he remains, cherishing it as a haven of repose in the "long, shrill city."

James abets this denial of the city. The square constitutes one of those jealously closed fields which, bounded by a taboo (like the house in "The Turn of the Screw," from which communications have been compulsorily but causelessly suspended) or else (as in Sloper's case) by a cordon of genteel suspicion, are the arenas of fiction. Closure means that within the intense and limited space available, psychological reactions or social developments can be studied as inexorable processes, immune from outside interference. What James disliked about New York was its coincidental detours and deflections. He felt its abundance to be aimless and feckless. A city is by definition a place where anything can happen, a device for the multiplying of possibility. But the Jamesian novel can only exist by denying to itself this fertile freedom. *Washington Square* finds a formula for that renunciation in the geography of

New York. The island itself insists on a rigorous necessity. James notes that "the tide of fashion began to set steadily northward, as, indeed, in New York, thanks to the narrow channel in which it flows, it is obliged to do." Unlike Whitman, who in calling Broadway tidal pays tribute to its overwhelming and confluent liveliness, James intends the metaphor restrictively. His tide doesn't flood; it moves implacably, in obedience to strict limits. New York's street plan reduces the city to a parallelogram of social impulses and economic motives. Development occurs diagonally, following Broadway up and across the island. But as settlement mounts this imperative, initiatory vertical, other horizontal ventures complicate the theorem: "the great hum of traffic rolled farther to the right and left of Broadway," colonizing the empty space to east and west. Commercial causality instigates changes which illustrate another theorem. Edith Wharton's decorative schemes for houses are the working out of a social law and an aesthetic formulation, winning over the city from crass utilitarianism to the connoisseurship of beauty. Art is therefore defined as beauty's proud repudiation of use. But in Sloper's old downtown neighborhood this evolution has gone into shaming reverse, retreating from beauty (or domestic retirement) to use. Private houses in the street where he lived have, since he left, been converted into offices, warehouses, and shipping agencies.

Society in James's New York doesn't randomly and naturally grow. It is constituted, theoretically anticipated. Already, at its base around Washington Square, Fifth Avenue trusts in the "high destinies" which await it uptown. The grid symbolizes this presumptive faith, foreknowing a social history. New Yorkers who have moved north translate themselves into a region of arithmetical abstraction. They have gone to reside in a future that is immaterial and perhaps nonexistent. Mrs. Almond, for instance, lives far uptown "in an embryonic street, with a high number." The northern migration, though it has fond hopes of the metropolitan future, is actually a regression to the rustic past which precedes the city, for as New York unravels ahead along "the great longitudinal thoroughfare," it grows backward into nature. At least Washington Square looks as if it possesses a social history, suggesting reveries about one's ancestors and outings with one's nursemaid; in Mrs. Almond's precinct, pigs and chickens root and peck in the gutters. The proximity of this uncultivated anarchy in New York disinters the past of its socially aspiring citizens. James, writing three decades after the period in which the novel is set, remarks that though the livestock no longer sports in the streets, it did so "within the memory of middle-aged persons in quarters which would now blush to be reminded" of this muddy disgrace. While the inquisitive, acquisitive line of Broadway is reaching higher, it's also controverting itself, doubling back to plumb a depth of suppressed, embarrassed recollection.

On James's closed field of social forces, the northern trek of Broadway recapitulates inside the city the western trajectory of settlement across the continent. Arthur Townsend, cousin of the unscrupulous Morris, suggests to his prospective wife that they should go at once to the top of the island and smugly wait for New York to catch up with them. Proposing this, he's acting as an allegory of his name, graduating to the wilderness which is the town's end. But she doesn't want to be an urban pioneer and declares that "if she's got to be the first settler she had better go out to Minnesota." They therefore agree to "move up little by little; when we get tired of one street we'll go higher." This was the impetus of the frontiersman, decamping for the unknown as soon as settlement entrammeled him. In the city this pioneering intrepidity turns—since it now thrusts north not west, up not across—into a discontented social mobility. Arthur sees the grid as a ladder of affluent advancement. The further up it he scrambles, the more mod cons he'll have. For him, Broadway tilts into a sky of limitless self-betterment. But for Sloper, who refuses to credit the city with this extension into dreamy, wealthy infinity, the grid is a mental instrument, a map enabling you to place and therefore to judge a person. To locate an address is to ascertain a social station. When he discovers that Morris's sister lives on Second Avenue, he ingests the information studiously, with ruminative repetitions, for it tells him in advance all he needs to know: " 'Did you say the Second Avenue?' He made a note of the Second Avenue." He deploys the definite article as a sanitary precaution, as if Second Avenue were too noxious a notion to be uttered without that small denotative and distancing word to preface it. Conjectural exploration of the city—imagining its possibilities, experimenting with its worlds elsewhere—is in *Washington Square* a stratagem of the untrustworthy and the concupiscent, who make the obliging empty spaces of an unsettled New York into theaters of fantasy. The officious intriguer Mrs. Penniman delights in the mental liberty of the city, and in organizing a tryst with Morris ponders recondite locations (Greenwood Cemetery, the Battery) before appointing an oyster saloon on Seventh Avenue. Then, for no better reason than to maximize the city's supply of flirtatious sites and to aggrandize its potentiality, she lies to Catherine and says they met in the Bowery at a confectioner's.

The irony of New York's closure of field is that, for James, it delineates not inexhaustible possibility but exhausted vacancy. Morris is glad of excuses to call at Washington Square because "thirty years ago, in New York, a young man of leisure had reason to be thankful for aids to self-oblivion." While Sloper and his daughter are in Europe, their house is overtaken by the idle vacuity of the surrounding society, occupied by the unoccupied Mrs. Penniman (enjoying "dominion in the empty house") and the shiftless Morris (who treats it as a "castle of indolence" or "a club with a single member"). New York is a bored and refractory absence, a blank diagram waiting for something to be inscribed on it. Even the Seventh Avenue pavement outside the oyster bar is more absent than not, scarred with dents and dangerous emptinesses: "cavities and fissures played a disproportionate part" in it. The nonexistence of New York permits Morris to invent a spurious existence for himself within it, at a pair of coordinates which can't be checked on. He alleges that he works for a commission merchant on Duane Street, but represents the place as "peculiarly and unnaturally difficult to find." He partakes of the city's enigmatic nonentity. Places in it are unreal because no social history attaches to them; Morris too is unreal and unreliable because unattached to society. All his attributes are negative: an "absence of means, of a profession, of visible resources or prospects." And the grid likewise is tainted with confidence trickery, gesturing—on its northern forays—toward a future it can't actualize, making promises it can't keep.

Catherine's renunciation of Morris is her reprobation of the city. Hers is the novelistic fate of an enforced and enclosed meditation. She exempts herself from the city's continuing life and from the epic magnification of self the place granted to Whitman. She permits New York to pass her by. At the beginning of the novel, Washington Square still upholds gentility in the mercenary city. By the end, it has been superseded. Sloper's residence is dismissed as an "old house," and Catherine is recommended to quit it for one of the new brownstones which "adorn the transverse thoroughfares in the upper part of the town." She chooses to stay. The fortitude of novelistic character is its resistance to the blandishments of action, its sequestration. Hence its mistrust of the city, which it claustrally introverts.

This occlusion of the city and the sanctification of an interior to shelter the private life continue in W. D. Howells's *A Hazard of New Fortunes* (1890). When Basil March proposes leaving Boston for New York, his wife protests because the city is "so *big*, and *so* hideous!" She declares it inimical to her "inner quiet," that refined privacy which Howells presents as a conventual incarceration: in Boston she ventures out seldom, remaining "shut up in [their house's] refinement." She is genteelly incapable of Whitman's crowd-embracing urban pantheism. She imagines New York contains four or five million people, and when Basil says there are scarcely more than two, she pleads that "I couldn't make my sympathies go round two million people."

Howells's account of their search for a place to live in New York is a study in the novelistic exclusion of the city, the cushioning of privacy against a relentless publicity. They begin by employing the grid as a device for delimitation, anathematizing the city with solemn, fearful taboos. Their approved area is "not to be above Twentieth Street nor below Washington Square." They apply the same vertical prohibitions to the houses they consider: their apartment "must not be higher than the third floor." Their requirement of a space that is cellulated and cerebral—a catacomb of nervous privacies—makes Mrs. March stipulate at first a minimum of ten rooms, so that each member of the household can have a personal hermitage. The space they inhabit will be consecrated by their repose in it, and they eventually decide that New York flats are impious because so inescapably public, so averse to that holy inwardness which is the religion of the Jamesian novel (and indeed of all novels, from the novel-reading solitariness of Fanny Price in *Mansfield Park* to Virginia Woolf's demand for "a room of one's own"). No child raised in a flat, the Marches believe, can have any conception of home because the ground plan, which allows for drawing and dining rooms but no living room, favors exhibitionistic socializing at the cost of family congregation. In New York, the congested poor have the monopoly of domestic retirement. At least in the tenements, where a family lives squashed together in the kitchen, there can be a communion which the flat grandiosely impedes. The same irony warps urban vision: intimacy with others can be attained only by espionage, the casual, transitory empathy of the voyeur. Mrs. March enjoys the Third Avenue El because of the "domestic intimacy" and "perfect repose" she glimpses in second- or third-floor interiors, dissociated from the chaotic streets below.

Beneath the genteel fastidiousness of James's Sloper or Howells's Marches lurks a superstitious dread of the city. Edith Wharton's fashionable New Yorkers are primitively obsequious. Their social customs serve as tribal rites of propitiation. Newland Archer in *The Age of Innocence* (1920) subjects himself to a series of primeval decrees— arrival at the opera must be timed with the precise degree of nonchalant tardiness, two monogrammed brushes must be used to part one's hair— as potent as "the inscrutable totem terrors that had ruled the destinies of his forefathers thousands of years ago." The social calendar sacramentalizes the year: the tribe denominates the dates which are auspicious for it. Every year on October 15, Fifth Avenue "opened its shutters, unrolled its carpets and hung up its triple layer of window-curtains"; by November 1, social engagements have resumed. Primitive time is ritualized and thus made comfortingly repetitious. Each year is guaranteed to be a recapitulation of its predecessor. *The Age of Innocence* begins with Christine Nilsson singing *Faust* at the Academy of Music, which she does again near the end. The same people go to the same operas every year. In between, they eat the same meals. Mrs. Archer always serves canvasbacks, and her cook can be relied on always to scorch the roes of shad. But far from craving novelty, these characters primitively and cyclically hold it at bay.

New York reduces Howells's civilized Bostonians to scuttling, terrified creatures, whose house-hunting is their harried quest for a propitious cave to hide in, where they can install as sentinels their household gods. "Here we are, looking for shelter, and a little anxious about the disposition of the natives," says Basil. The city unnerves them by its indifference. So, originally, did the world, which is why we have to invent a god to assure us of its kind intentions toward us, and the Marches admit the religiosity of their search—for the city makes lost souls of us all—when they pause in Grace Church. It briefly persuades them that they are "rapt far from New York, if not from earth." Their well-bred mistrust of the city is a primitive instinct, sniffing along the perimeters of tribal safety: "they came to excel in the sad knowledge of the line at which respectability distinguishes itself from shabbiness." Alert to signals of danger, Mrs. March learns to decipher the traces of the enemy's presence. She recoils from houses advertising "Modes." Like the savage, she codifies the external world as a system of warnings and baleful auguries. She "refused to stop at any door where there were more than six bell ratchets." Then, with the numinous logic of primitive classification, rigging up rules for excommunication, she decides "against ratchets altogether and confined herself to knobs neatly set in the door trim." The need to own and be safe within a personal domain teaches the Marches disapproval of those who traffic in these sacred allocations of space—profiteering house agents or snide janitors who treat the collective space they regiment as if it were theirs and not an individual solace—as well as of social occasions that don't respect the binary decree separating public from private: the crush at New York receptions is "the spirit of the street transferred to the drawing room."

This savage conviction of hostility beyond the genteel stockade leads to a worshipful belief in the loyalty of known interiors and in the fidelity of furniture. Their accustomed New York hotel seems to the Marches "to have been waiting for them in a clean, quiet, patient disoccupation ever since they left it two years ago." It exists, like Catherine Sloper, in a clean, quiet, patient,. meditative stasis, a disoccupied calm. A room, like the city, is a camp set up in an alien world and fortified in fear, placed under the aegis of friendly deities. Decor functions fetishistically, as an offering to these gods. The interior is a shrine, a tabernacle where every surface must be devoutly layered, commemorated by concealment. This impulse justifies the gimcrackery of Mrs. Grosvenor Green's apartment, where, as Howells describes it, this decorative carapace is doubled and trebled in an effort to swaddle and soothe the invisible indigenous god: "the floors were covered with fillings, and then rugs, and then skins; the easy chairs all had tidies, Armenian and Turkish and Persian; the lounges and sofas had embroidered cushions hidden under tidies." The motive is a sacred prudery, which abhors the profaning of the interior. Thus "the radiator was concealed by a Jap screen, and over the top of this some Arab scarfs were flung. . . . China pugs guarded the hearth." Yet despite the defensive posture of those pugs, the room intimates its own temporariness. Things in it are flung, scattered, negligently disposed; it's as unstable as an Arab tent in the desert.

The interiors photographed by Joseph Byron, who established a business in New York in 1888, perfect this decorative hallowing. The purpose of decor is mollification: the beautiful contravention of use; the suffocation of objects with adornment. Chairs in Byron's pictures are fringed or tasseled, fireplaces draped, mirrors wear shawls and tables festoons, windows are provided with three sets of curtains. Space has been stifled and padded, floors carpeted, tables clad with velvet. Every object has its pudic outer case. A bed in the Lauterbach house has a baldachin, which doesn't qualify it as a setting for courtly receptions but instead cocoons it. Such plenitude breeds its own paranoia. In Mrs. Astor's art gallery every inch of wall is covered by canvases, each wearing a heavy gilt frame. The display of wealth and possessions admits to an underlying anxiety: the crowding, with its horror of blank space, implies that there's something being hidden. This room of Mrs. Astor made itself the measure of social exclusivity. It held no more than four hundred, so New York society, regulated by spatial paranoia, consisted only of that select Four Hundred. The room wasn't a Whitmanesque container but a convenient machine for elimination. At times this use of decor as defense, flimsily forbidding entry to the city, becomes preposterous in its bad faith. The Seton studio and the Lauterbach billiard room, both photographed by Byron in 1899, suspend Oriental parasols from a corner of the ceiling, as if they might be needed inside: these insecure enclosures don't even consider themselves weatherproof. The people Byron includes look exhausted, debilitated by a decor that commits them to idleness. At their most overrefined, these interiors cease to be rooms and turn into humid conservatories, where people are growths as tropically rare and tenuous as the ferns by which they're surrounded. Often the rooms quote from the outdoors, or from the exposed temporariness they're supposed to be belying. The reception room of the Halls, for instance, is a fabric tent inside the unseen shell of the actual room, and the Turkish corner in Mrs. Hughes's drawing room with its bear skins, cushions, and tented drapes refers, almost confessionally, to the most makeshift of lean-tos. The Seton studio is littered with animal pelts and antlers, unable to decide whether to be an arbor (as the parasol suggests) or a minaret (in its Turkish corner) or a primal lair. Its eclecticism gives away its unease about its purpose, and about its success in excluding the city.

The interior hopes to shut itself off from the city. Decor solemnizes this renunciation by making a room take holy orders. Mrs. Hazeldean in *Old New York* declares that the room in which her husband proposed to her is "sacred to me," and when her adopted daughter Tina is married, Mrs. Rawlston chooses a house wedding for her, despite Episcopalian objections. "The greater privacy of a marriage in the house made up for its more secular character," she reasons (though privacy is by now no longer secular but an anchoritic cult), and the drawing room is reoutfitted as a chapel. Mrs. Peniston's October housecleaning in Edith Wharton's *The House of Mirth* (1905) is like a religious retreat. She swathes her dwelling in penitential white and deluges it in expiatory soapsuds; she inspects her linen and blankets as if examining her conscience. When the architect Stanford White remodeled the Whitney mansion on Fifth Avenue at 67th Street, he intended a similar enshrining. He used items of decor sanctified in earlier incarnations, by religion or art or aristocracy—a corridor and stained glass from French monasteries, a ballroom from a chateau in Bordeaux, gates and ceilings from Roman palazzi. But the assembly, being so inconsistent, reneges on itself. Instead of a hermitage, it builds a museum of extracts from other cultures, and those objects are deconsecrated by their domestication. Poe in his essay "The Philosophy of Furniture" senses the troubled conscience of a decor that has as its purpose evasion and retreat. His people confide their culpability to their furnishings. A room is a monologue

Joseph Byron, "Ernest Thompson Seton Studio, 144 Fifth Avenue" (1899). Byron Collection, Museum of the City of New York.

overheard. We eavesdrop there on the inhabitant's conversation with himself and can deduce his moral nature from his choice of carpet. The houses of Edith Wharton's characters are guiltily retentive. Mrs. Peniston rages when a glimmer of light escapes from her battened-down interior—"I saw a streak of light under one of the blinds as I drove up: it's extraordinary that I can never teach that woman to draw them down evenly."

The interior harbors the specters which are our fears and suppressed desires. James called fiction a house; but because it's a house that repels the city and isolates us inside ourselves, it soon becomes haunted. Edith Wharton both campaigned for the house's dissociation from the city, and—in her ghost stories—studied the psychological consequences of that separation. In 1897, with Ogden Codman, Jr., she published a treatise, *The Decoration of Houses*, complaining that the modern house and its interior have been dissevered. The architect is responsible for one, the upholsterer for the other. She pleads that decoration must be an adjunct of architecture and, turning the house inside out, she calls it an "interior architecture." American houses strain to be palatial and neglect to cater to the "modern private life." For Edith Wharton the purpose of architecture was a novelistic contrivance of division, with every partition protecting a soliloquy. Newland Archer in *The Age of Innocence* is offended, when he calls on the ailing Mrs. Manson Mingott (who has moved to the ground floor of her house), to catch sight of a bedroom. He recalls the "architectural incentives to immorality" of the French flat, with its "indecent propinquities" of living and sleeping areas. The moral error is the failure to conduct different functions hierarchically on different floors, the refusal to separate public reception from private reclusion. Edith Wharton is for this reason vigilant about doors, the battlements of privacy. American architects have either slid them into walls or replaced them with portières or abolished them altogether, so that new houses have "doorways *without* doors." The front door, the house's protection against the street, has been made penetrable and transparent, supplanted by "a wrought-iron gateway lined with plate glass." Edith Wharton—who made her social debut at a ball in a private house on Fifth Avenue rather than at Delmonico's because her mother wouldn't permit her to appear "in a public room"— seals the interior against such brazen candor.

Excavating the house of fiction, she turns a habitation into a cranial alcove of conscience or consciousness. The novelist, foregoing the streets of the city, must prize open the locked doors of these covert people. Edith Wharton's iconography of character is architectural. The body is the façade the house shows to the street, its extroverted occupation; the mind hides behind the front door. Hayley Delayne in "The Spark" is a "finished monument," an architecturally accomplished fact "like Trinity Church, the Reservoir or the Knickerbocker Club," and, as exclusive as these, the guardian of his own interior—"a shut-up fellow." Mrs. Hazeldean in "New Year's Day," desperate to know whether her husband suspects her infidelity, sees his white forehead as "a locked door. I shall dash my brains out against it some day!" In her cast-off lover, the same architectural fortitude of brow is obtuseness, not reserve: his face "was so ostensibly a solid building, and not a nomad's tent" that he can't cope with the rapid succession of her thoughts. Mrs. Hazeldean's disposition of decor fusses to obscure her misdemeanors. The "scraps of lace and ribbon and muslin" on her dressing table have been economically purchased, her husband imagines, with the aid of a meager check from her stepmother. Actually, they're testimonials to her truancy, if he only knew how to decipher them: the subsidy came from her lover. When the widowed Mrs. Hazeldean becomes an enchantress, the narrator of *Old New York*, recalling the seductive comforts of her house, suggests that "the most perilous coquetry may not be in a woman's way of arranging her dress but in her way of arranging her drawing room." Outmoded furniture is a moral embarrassment to the owner. Like an ignoble past, it must be either forcibly expunged or discreetly forgotten. Because it's shamingly beyond reclamation, the old Lovell place on Long Island Sound in "The Old Maid" has been permitted to keep its incriminating "slender settees, . . . Sheraton consoles and cabinets." The neighborhood is unrespectable now, and until the place can be sold, the furniture is allowed to live on there in penitential obscurity, like an assortment of disgraced or derelict relatives. Vance in Edith Wharton's *Hudson River Bracketed* (1929) undergoes indictment by architecture. The squalor of his married life is broadcast by the "leprous brownstone" in which he lives, too far over on the West Side. Edith Wharton thought brownstones had been "cursed with universal chocolate-coloured coating of the most hideous stone ever quarried." Their gooey integument excites in her a culinary revulsion: the house seems to be made of confectionery, with an exterior which is viscous, not stern and stony. Inside, Vance's brownstone is a bottler-up of odors, leakages from lives whose privacy has been insufficiently insulated. The hall is greasy, and "a smell of canned soup and stale coffee told him that dinner had begun." Smells are this house's guilty secrets, by which it is haunted.

Vance's career—in a novel named after a category of architectural decoration—proceeds as an architectural parable. He imagines New York in advance as a citadel of solitude and ascesis; when he gets there, he finds it to be grubby, chaotic, unsacrosanct. His imagination awakens architecturally. On the first visit to the decaying mansion in the Hudson River bracketed style, he reads "Kubla Khan" in the library. Thereafter, poetry is to him a city as airily fragile as the Khan's, "arcane, aloof, and secret as the soul." A library is a room where these dreams of other insubstantial, cerebral rooms are stored; it symbolizes a building's sacredness to meditation, as against its sociable purpose. When Vance reaches New York, he doesn't recognize the Public Library on Fifth Avenue because its façade, so pompous and rhetorical, contradicts its true nature as "a haunt of studious peace." That word "haunt" points to the ghostliness of Edith Wharton's New York. Its buildings are infested by revenants: the unquiet thoughts of their inhabitants. She herself, internalizing the city in her recollections of her childhood, dismisses the "mean monotonous streets" and identifies "old New York" with "my father's library." For Vance, the library is a cemetery for the interring of poetic dreams and for ghoulish communion with the dead.

At Trinity Church he browses among the tombs and senses "a heart beating through the grave-wrappings of one of the mummies he had seen in the Museum." Instead of re-enlivening the past, quickening into contemporaneity all of one's precedessors in the city, as Whitman does on Brooklyn ferry, Edith Wharton's characters seek to make New York a storied necropolis, meditatively willing themselves into company with the omnipresent dead.

This is the phantasmal meaning of the New York houses in her ghost stories. Charlotte Ashby in "Pomegranate Seed" has backed even farther than Catherine Sloper into reclusiveness, and thence into nervous terror. She lives at a tangent to life, with the latchkey as her protection against the city she dreads. From inside her house, she watches the city's reflections or hears its echoes. Down her deserted cross street she can see "the great thoroughfare beyond," which is illuminated and crowded; looking up, she sees "the sky already aflare with the city's nocturnal life." But the house that she has detached from the brawling city becomes polluted by fear, invaded by ghosts of guilty association. The haunted house is a mind turned in on itself and terrorized by a causeless anxiety. As "Pomegranate Seed" begins, Charlottes hesitates on the boundary between the heedless uproarious public domain and the distraught psychological solitude of her privacy. She is standing on the doorstep of her house, about to quit "the grinding, rasping street life" of New York for "this veiled sanctuary called home." But she is reluctant to enter because this means a reassumption of her perturbed inner life. The house that ought to be her genteel fastness has been rendered out of bounds to her. She wavers in the vestibule and has to force herself to proceed. Living in a house you believe to be haunted means, for Edith Wharton, being the tenant of a mind which has become a stranger to you, its putative owner. This is the neurotic penalty of withdrawal from the commonality of the city. Charlotte contrasts the normality of the streets with her private distress, separating the technological rationality outside from the trauma and mystery within: "outside there, skyscrapers, advertisements, telephone, wireless, airplanes, movies, motors, and all the rest of the twentieth century; and on the other side of the door something I can't explain, can't relate to them." Dissociation from New York becomes in her a psychological ailment.

All Edith Wharton's New Yorkers are, like Charlotte, superstitious. They have traced in the air a magic cordon within which they live. Outside that ring, they know demons abound. They vigilantly patrol the borders of their sacred circle. The old lady in "Mrs. Manstey's View" dies policing it. She has been driven to despair by a backyard extension,

34

which will block the view from her boardinghouse window. (Hers is, incidentally, a novelistic invigilation of the privacies of others: because she has a rear room, she looks into other peoples' back windows and, like the novelist, can report on their hidden lives. She notices that a slatternly housemaid has for two days forgotten to feed the parrot of one of her neighbors.) Mrs. Manstey catches pneumonia when she goes out at night to set fire to the building works. Her death achieves a modest victory, for the arson halts construction for a day. The ancestral New York remembered in Edith Wharton's autobiography *A Backward Glance* (1934) is a genteel society which—like Howells's house-hunters placating the natives as they pitch their tent in the no-man's-land of the city—defends itself with rites of exorcism and exclusion. It's impelled by the same spatial paranoia that covers every inch of wall in Mrs. Astor's gallery. Beyond the integrity of the magic circle, that arbitrary portion of terrain the tribe has annexed as its living room, space suddenly becomes meaningless and for that reason demonic. Edith Wharton's New York is constituted not by inclusion but by expulsion. It's a city of barriers, not, like Whitman's, of bridges. It professes, for instance, to have exiled sin. A disreputable relative whirls in a hell "somewhere outside the safe boundaries of our old New York." Immediately outside the circle, limbo begins. Edith Wharton's old New York is therefore cautious of expansion, which entails a raid on space still untamed. In her youth, the city extends only "between the Battery and Union Square"; later it summons the courage for a colonial expedition and now stretches "between Washington Square and Central Park," though it still crouches inside a narrow vertical channel, frightened of the alien areas to either side; and Edith Wharton's own parents are considered intrepid when they settle in Gramercy Park, "then just within the built-on limits of New York." To those quarantined inside the boundaries the tribe has ordained, straying outside is an act of folly. An old New Yorker, asked why he never travels abroad, replies, "Because I can't bear to cross Murray Street," the lowly road leading to the docks.

Facing the city, Henry James's house of fiction admonishes it. The house is form's rebuke to the teeming, ungovernable content of the city. A novel for James resembles a house in being well run, balancing means and ends. The kind of novel he doesn't wish to write is like a city—loose, baggy, monstrous, abounding in irrelevances. What he flinched from in New York was this multitudinousness of content. Edith Wharton remembers him castigating its "noisy irrelevance." In *A Hazard of New Fortunes*, the city is criticized, according to this Jamesian standard, for lacking a center or a directing intelligence. Uncontrolled by form, it is

—like the art of Whitman as James described it in that early review—
a rampant self-expression, the laissez-faire of content. Traveling on the
Third Avenue El to Chatham Square, Howells's hero is amused by the
ethnic diversity of physiognomic types and "the gay ugliness—the
shapeless, graceless, reckless picturesqueness of the Bowery." Art's duty
is to impose shape on that amorphous havoc. March discerns in New
York the same garrulous profusion James criticized in Dickens and in
Whitman. He laments "the absence of intelligent, comprehensive purpose in the huge disorder and . . . the chaos to which the individual
selfishness must always lead." Many of the photographs James commissioned from Alvin Langdon Coburn in 1906–7 as frontispieces to the
collected edition of his novels are images of the mind's closure against
the distracting city, of templed intelligence turning the key on its secrets
—the shut door of the doctor for *The Wings of the Dove*, a shut gate
on the Faubourg St. Germain for *The American*, a reflexive shop window for *The Golden Bowl*. The door that prohibits the city and, as in
Charlotte Ashby's case, sequesters the mind with its specters, eventually
becomes synonymous with the commission of a crime. The shuttered
consciousness is confined with its guilt: the classic conundrum of the
detective story is therefore the murder in a locked room.

In 1927 Ford Madox Ford, still influenced by James's aesthetic judgment of the city, accused New York of lacking "corporate self-consciousness." It has no idea of itself, no capacity for the self-interrogation
which is the vocation of James's characters. Returning to New York in
1904, James had attempted to implant self-consciousness in the city by
the Socratic method. In *The American Scene* (1907) he cross-questions
the arrogant skyscrapers and demands that they justify themselves; he
hears what he calls the "testimony" of Central Park. The questions he
asks, since they are rhetorical, can have no answers, but the intention
is to equip the unreflective city with the means of self-inspection.
Rhetoric is for James, as decor was for Edith Wharton, a defense against
the city: it allows him to expostulate with New York or comically patronize it, and in doing so to lessen the shock of its hectoring presence.
He needs to keep a hesitant visual distance. The first sight of New York
he permits is during a circumnavigation, from a train-bearing barge
between Jersey City and Harlem, where he has a connection to make
for Boston. His rhetoric is as circuitous as his agenda, calculating what
he calls "my relation to New York." Style for him is a manner, archly
mediating or mitigating that too brutal relationship.

He cows the city by personifying it. Addressing it as a character, he
can chide it into conformity with his code of prevarication and refine-

ment, which it so carelessly flouts. To call the breezes on the bay inso-
lent, as he does, is to translate them from natural impetuosity to
incivility. Gusts of wind have to be suffered; but the bad manners of
these overfamiliar breezes, blusteringly vulgar, can be criticized and
corrected. James's style knows itself to be futile. After all, disapproving
of the wind in the harbor won't still it. Yet from this incapacity of style
to subdue a refractory, clamoring, commercial reality, James retrieves
an ironic compensation. Between himself and New York he interposes
metaphors, which tease the city by pretending to anthropomorphize it.
Rather than reuniting the city with the nature it has outgrown, his
imagery mocks it as blowsily domestic, homely, and slangy. Metaphors
miniaturize objects which are trying hard to stretch into hyperbole. Thus
the skyscrapers become a congested pincushion or a toothless hair-comb
seen in profile, which relocates them on an untidy dressing table. Or
the city's geography is envisaged as a squalid sexual arrangement, with
New York "held in the easy embrace of its great good-natured rivers"
like a superannuated courtesan sustained by the open arms of an un-
fastidious gallant. No respecter of persons, the city is a place of indiscriminate herding and jostling. James shames it by extending to it the
deference it has refused to him, as when he apologizes to the Hudson
for his discourtesy for having viewed it from a railway car, whereas "a
decent respect" for the river "would confine us to the use of a boat."
Metaphors fend off the city's promiscuity by seeing it as mere greed
(Ellis Island, ingurgitating human provender, is compared with a sword-
or fire-swallower at the circus, gobbling food which is unnutritious
and possibly fatal) or else as sad self-deception (the marine glare of the
light, matching the stark cold mercenariness of the buildings on which
it's trained, "has the abundance of some ample childless mother who
consoles herself for her sterility by an unbridled course of adoption").
In both cases, James withdraws the customary gift of metaphor, which
is to invest a human or natural motive in nonhuman objects. The city
doesn't merit such vivification, since its food is inorganic and its lucent
love is a symptom of infertility. New York itself has already devalued
metaphor by travestying nature in Central Park. James personifies the
harassed park—burdened with the responsibility of representing country
in the city, it needs to be encouraged with little pats on the back—only
to find that it has in advance personified itself, simulating something
that it's not. His metaphor therefore fixes on its inauthenticity. Its
contradictory samplings of different landscapes remind him of an actress
in a repertory company obliged to play every role "from the tragedy
queen to the singing chambermaid."

Personification was at first the pride of the skyscrapers. The architect Louis Sullivan saw them as virilely upright, with the columnar rectitude (as he remarked of the Marshall Field warehouse in Chicago) of "a man. that walks on two legs." For James this ambition of personification is their downfall, since it enables him to treat them as if they were people, to deal with structure as deportment and with decoration as manners. He compliments buildings for their modesty. The Tiffany headquarters is praised for its self-denial in not aspiring to twenty-five storeys, though it's warned never to forget that it's still only "a great miscellaneous shop"; he admires the polite restraint of the new Public Library because it's sedately lateral and "presents itself as seated rather than standing." Since architecture has insisted on likening itself to physique, James can reprimand the buildings as outsize, "grossly tall and grossly ugly," and can expect them to have some justification of themselves at hand. They can't reply, of course, but their very muteness evinces the stupidity with which he's charging them. His rhetorical interrogation prosecutes the skyscrapers; elsewhere it engages in special pleading on behalf of buildings that can't defend themselves, as in his lament for Trinity Church, beleaguered and abashed by the heights of Wall Street. Because he employs metaphor in extenuation, seeing the city through it, he learns to mistrust the metaphors on which the city itself cynically relies. He therefore complains that the "money-making structure" above Trinity Church has "quite horribly, quite romantically justified itself" by evoking an alpine pinnacle. The metaphor is its sublime lie about itself. Sometimes, however, he concedes that there's nobility in this valiant, mendacious determination of buildings to keep up appearances. One of his finest rhetorical questions, saluting in architecture a stylistic fortitude like his own, concerns the demolished university building on Washington Square. "Wasn't it somehow," he inquires, "with a desperate bravery, both castellated and gabled?" Since the building is no longer there, he asks the question not of it but of himself, and answers it with his own undeterred stylistic courage, which still trusts (however desperately) in linguistic gabling and syntactic castellation.

James's New York is about form's attempted subjugation of content. The skyscrapers exemplify this process. They constitute a problem for art and for the aesthetic observer because they exist at a juncture between the values—which are to James inimical—of beauty and use. New York can't for him be a novelistically or pictorially beautiful society because it's remorselessly utilitarian, a place of work outlawing introspective reverie. In it the materiality of content overrules the preciosity of form. The skyscrapers are diagrams of this inevitable enmity. Howells in his *World of Chance* (1893) calls them "the necessity of commerce and the despair of art." They grow tall to maximize rents, not to be beautiful. Yet James sees in their upward striving another desperately brave stratagem of vertiginous style, disclaiming earthbound content. He interprets the height of the Waldorf-Astoria as the ingenious escape of form from mere horizontality. The ground in New York has been devastated as an arena for the exhibition of style because of the "absence of margin" and the impertinent intrusion of cross streets. Builders, deprived of courts or gardens or any honorific vacancy in which to place their structures, seek their reward vertically. The higher up they go, the freer the skyscrapers are to indulge in decor. Sullivan described the skyscraper as an elasticized column, with solid base, featureless shaft, and a florid capital on top. James too uses style as a means of manuevering around or out of restriction. New York's "primal topographic curse" of the pettifogging grid corresponds, in his own creative case, to plain speaking, crass factual statement, the horizontality of prose which style exists to complicate. Hence his silencing of the dinner partner who had begun to tell him the anecdote which became *The Spoils of Poynton*. His informant wanted to prolong the narrative horizontally; James, rescuing it from life for art, extended it vertically into conjecture. Imagination is the addition of chimerical upper tiers, an architecture spurning gravity. Style likewise means deviation and deviance, which the street plan of New York proscribes. For this reason James grudgingly admires the skyscrapers, since they're conspiring to attain the same liberty he wishes for his own art. He reads them as words, drably and laterally literal, which are trying to acquire style.

New York for him had assaulted the probity of language. He describes the cafés of the Lower East Side as places of polyglot debauchery, "torture-rooms of the living idiom." The skyscrapers are casualties of the same linguistic cheapening. They are words used mercantilely, as a means (like coinage) of currency and exchange, not words artistically and narcissistically preserved from use. Erecting buildings is a version of narrative, an accretion of storeys which resembles the telling of stories. James remarks that "one story is good until another is told, and the skyscrapers are the last words of economic ingenuity only till another word be written. This shall possibly be a word of still uglier meaning, but the vocabulary of thrift at any price shows boundless resources." His own writing about the skyscrapers—the personae he invents for them, the accounts he makes them give of themselves—are his creation for them of an alternative vocabulary, a language which is not thrifty and efficacious but beautiful in its extravagance, luxury, and gratuitousness. The city is an overloquacious narrator, running on into the future like James's confidant telling him about Poynton. James, telling New York stories about itself in *The American Scene*, is challenging its faith in narrative and teaching it the different mental discipline of retrospection, which is archaeology not architecture, excavation not the erection of additional storeys in the air. New York, he says, has forbidden commemorative tablets. Revisiting lower Fifth Avenue and Washington Square, he restores a vanished world by remembering how it was. Like Whitman in the *Brooklyniana*, he proposes himself as the parent of the city that bore him. The aging James, back in New York after two decades, *is* the past which the city has in the meantime obliterated.

The city recalled by retrospection has been evacuated by introspection. Making it into a house for fiction means emptying it of its teeming inhabitants. He dreads a compulsory publicity, symbolized by the packed gregariousness of New York's elevators; he searches for hermetic enclaves, areas kept apart in meditative quiet—the museums and libraries or, more neurasthenically, the Presbyterian Hospital, where the city has been hushed or clinically sedated. His need for these mystic pauses, cessations of the city's overbearing life, leads him to criticize the monotonous frequency of windows in New York buildings: no provision has been made for "quiet interspaces," just as there are no "blest breathing-spaces . . . in New York conversation." Whitman, booming Shakespeare on the Broadway bus, attempted to intone a duet with the roaring city; its din drives James to a continent silence.

Interiorizing the city, he also consigns it to the care of tutelary female deities. Its comforting presences are feminine—Central Park the weary hostess of the one inn in town; the Waldorf a coquette smiling from across the road, disclaiming responsibility for your safety if you venture across but implying that she's worth the risk—because whereas the city's economy is male, its society and culture must be female. Men toil in their treasuries, while women in their gardens spend the wealth their husbands have amassed and buy with it leisure and seclusion. The division between the sexes restates the problem of James's skyscrapers. It's another consequence of the incompatibility between use and beauty. The men are engrossed in their dreary usefulness; women, like those James saw at Saratoga in 1870 exhibiting diamonds and laces which were "the most substantial and beautiful result" of their husbands' labor, redeem money by transforming it into adornment and atone for the curse of work by using its profits to subsidize idleness. New York becomes a society, as the skyscrapers become works of art, by the concealment of mercenary motives. The superstructure, according to James's decadent economics, exists to lie about the money-making base. Edith Wharton in *Hudson River Bracketed* dedicates New York to surplus and sumptuary expenditure. Westerners conceive of the city as "a place a man went to when he'd made his pile; a place you took your family to for a week's blow-out when you'd been on the right side of the market." The alliance between luxury and art, also the decadent concomitant of surplus and a disparagement of money-grubbing work, is enforced when Fernside tells Vance that "poetry won't earn your keep. It's pure luxury. Like keeping a car."

For James, form's denial of function is the imperative that makes New York livable and art possible. Edith Wharton, more dubious, warns of the dangers attending this denial. Her New York society affects ignorance of the economy which supports it and is penalized for that disavowal. Mrs. Peniston belongs to the coterie of old New Yorkers "who have always lived well, dressed expensively, and done little else." Their affluence is itself hard work, since it enjoins a martyrdom to appearance and an ornamental disdain for the chores that support the show. Mrs. Beaufort in *The Age of Innocence* goes to the opera on the night of her ball, undertaking this extra duty to "emphasize her complete superiority to household cares," while her husband, who runs the house, takes care to seem elegantly incapable when in company. Selden in *The House of Mirth* values society as the repression of economy, "an escape from work," and a tribute to "the decorative side of life": hence the importance of interior decor, cushioning a recuperative privacy. But eventually economy demands reparation from society. Trenor in *The House of Mirth* complains about his wife's smug assumption that he only needs "to go downtown once a month and cut off coupons." Actually, he toils unrelentingly "to keep the machinery working," but has to do so out of sight downtown. Lucre is as much a guilty secret as sex. Society's prudish hypocrisy about the economy is resented by the Jewish financier Rosedale, who demands social recognition as the reward of economic success, and it is fatal to the heroine Lily Bart. She depends on "this vast mysterious Wall Street of 'tips' and 'deals'" to which she entrusts her money, but she has been fabricated for decoration only and is destroyed when, impoverished, she's exposed to the material mechanism of life. In her shabby lodging she's affronted by "the intimate domestic noises of the house and the cries and rumblings of the street." These are congruent nuisances because both should be screened off and muffled. Lily, however, no longer enjoys the upholstered ignorance of the luxurious world, where the "machinery is so carefully concealed that one scene flows into another without perceptible agency."

New York's urban plan images its fraudulence. Ellen in *The Age of Innocence* believes New York to be "straight up and down . . . with all the cross-streets numbered," but those two sets of lines engage in different processes of social adjudication. The avenues are triumphal courses for social exhibition, the cross streets refuges of obscurity and indignity. Edith Wharton's own first memory was of promenading up Fifth Avenue with her father: she dated the inception of her identity from her debut there. Her characters take over the avenue as an extended receiving room. Newland Archer strolls up it one evening from Waverly Place and can tell who is visiting whom by identifying carriages parked at the doors of his friends' houses. The carriage is a traveling vestibule. Through the windows of her brougham, Lily sees "familiar profiles bent above visiting-lists, . . . hurried hands dispensing cards and notes to attendant footmen." In choosing to appear on Fifth Avenue, people tender their lives for observation and for possible arraignment. When Newland sees Beaufort sneaking out of his house, he knows he must be off on some adulterous errand, since there is no opera or party that night; and the unrespectable Fanny Ring in the same novel causes a scandal by daring to show herself on Fifth Avenue at the fashionable hour. Disgrace decrees banishment from the avenue to one of the side streets, where New York impounds its rejects. Lily after her fall has to trudge west to her boardinghouse, across Sixth Avenue and along "the degradation of a New York street in the last stages of decline" (as she is herself) "from fashion to commerce."

The grid is a dual convenience for the novelists. Longitudinally, it permits social display; latitudinally, it provides for social exclusion. Architecture possesses the same dutiful disingenuousness. The mansions of Edith Wharton's New Yorkers have a "muddle of misapplied ornament over a thin steel shell of utility." Wall Street manufactures the skeleton, Fifth Avenue supplies the social garniture. The Marvell sisters in *The Custom of the Country* (1913) can remember a time when the two realms were at least neighbors: New York then "centered in the Battery and the Bowling Green," so society and economy overlapped. But commerce and fashion have since been estranged. Wall Street conscientiously begets wealth, which Fifth Avenue, pretending not to know where it's come from, disburses. Roseland's manipulative chicanery has placed Wall Street "under obligations which only Fifth Avenue" can discharge by conferring social recognition. He indignantly requires the city to tell the truth about itself. The paradox of New York for both James and Edith Wharton is that art colludes with the city's euphemizings. Language mimics the segregation which Roseland deplores. Wall Street is blunt prosaic calculation, while Fifth Avenue conducts its affairs in a fanciful, falsifying diction of affluence. In *The Custom of the Country* "every Wall Street term had its equivalent in the language of Fifth Avenue, and while he [Elmer] talked of building up railways she [Undine] was building up palaces." The language of Fifth Avenue, disingenuously "castellated and gabled," is that of art: it describes things as they are not. Art provides wealth with an alibi and a means of self-laundering. You disinfect money if you use it, like James's tycoons in Europe, to buy art or, like Undine, to raise a replica of the Pitti Palace on Fifth Avenue. New York itself is the supremest of fictions.

3

Knight Errantry

Whitman had two successors in the convening of an epic New York, a city of generous public inclusion, not psychological retreat, and both begin by enlarging the city genteelly constricted by Catherine Sloper and by Basil March and his wife. Edith Wharton raises decorative barricades against New York; Stephen Crane's stories, however, treat those who can't afford such padded detachment, who are unhoused and unaccommodated. The heroine of his *Maggie* (1893) is by social definition, not moral imputation, "a girl of the streets." The stories of O. Henry likewise contradict Mrs. Astor's restriction of New York society to a select Four Hundred. His city comprises, in the title of one of his collections, *The Four Million.* Crane and O. Henry inherit between them Whitman's ambition to embody the city. Crane makes its raucous streets a turf for the trial of heroic daring. His "experiments" in Bowery flophouses, his interviews with streetwalkers, and his defiance of the venal police are his epic exposure of himself to the city's perils. He undertakes an urban assay of his courage and questions his worthiness for its red badge. He becomes a warrior of the back alleys, a knight errant redressing wrongs in the Tenderloin. If Whitman's mettlesome, assertive "Me" devolves on Crane, then the alternative aspect of his identity— its parliamentarism and its polymorphousness; its representative nature, which enables him to extrapolate the city from himself—passes to

O. Henry, who welcomes all members of the urban mob as his brothers. Yet despite the bravery of the one and the benevolence of the other, Crane and O. Henry are hindered from equaling Whitman. The city itself, having changed, impedes them. Crane finds it to have declined from the armed valor of Whitman's "City of Ships" to a ruffianly mock-epic. On the battleground of its streets, heroism is manifested as bully-ing and bragging. O. Henry suffers a similar rebuff. Though he foster-ingly includes the crowd within himself, he must accept that these multitudinous siblings are unknowable, strangers to whose lives he can gain access only by yearning, futile conjecture. Crane's form betrays him, as his epic similes founder into mean parodies. O Henry's form too admits defeat. His stories stop short because urban acquaintanceships do; the city aborts them.

The city which James and Edith Wharton turn claustrally inside out violently extroverts itself again in Crane. Its interiors are unhallowed by domestic care. Maggie's mother scrubs Jimmie in an "unholy sink." Domesticity should make a shrine of the house, but Maggie's mother is a home-wrecker who dismantles any room which presumes to contain her, demolishing the furniture in her rages. The home is defined, mini-mally, as a cage you want to break out of, not repose within: "a lighted room in which a large woman was rampant." The mother batters down distinctions between inner and outer, treating the house as if it were a turbulent street ("she returned and stirred up the room until her children were bobbing about like bubbles") or a willful, frothy natural element like the ocean. A reversal of in- and outside ironically restores the con-ditions of Whitmanesque epic, where living is done on the streets. The house, citadel of the private life for the novelists, is declared enemy territory. Jimmie crawls home "with the caution of an invader of a panther's den." Houses don't shelter but extrude people, expelling them into the street like refuse. The doorways of Bowery tenements are "grue-some" because the traffic through them proceeds in the wrong direction: instead of places of safe ingress, they're vents for enforced egress which "gave up loads of babies to the street and the gutter." Maggie's mother guts her house and spills its contents into the dispose-all of the street. She punishes "the lighter articles of household use" by carting them to a pawnshop "where Hebrews chained them with chains of interest," jailing them for having offended or obstructed her, and she conducts a vendetta against contumacious architecture: when she taunts a neigh-bor, she delivers her challenge to the panels of the woman's door and invites her to do battle in the hall. The woman won't venture out, so she kicks the door instead.

Crane's malign buildings are dispensers, not containers. Everything that issues from them is an excretion: "two or three theatres emptied a crowd upon the stormswept sidewalks." They employ functionaries to accelerate this eviction, and among the floozies, waiters, and drunkards in a saloon Crane notes the presence of a bouncer. Sound seeping from a building on Crane's Bowery is an ironic donation—a jeering charitable handout—to the exterior. "A concert-hall," he says, "gave to the street faint sounds of swift, machine-like music." Even light escapes from an interior as an insanitary emission. In another of the Bowery stories, "George's Mother," the chapel with the red street-lamp in front sheds a light "like the death-stain of a spirit upon the wet pavements," while "a flare of uncertain, wavering crimson" dirties the slick sidewalks from druggists' windows or fire-alarm boxes. Light foolhardy enough to enter a building is resented and rejected. When Maggie's death is announced, "the inevitable sunlight came streaming in at the window and shed a ghastly cheerfulness upon the faded hues of the room." Unless intending to waylay or gobble up walkers, like the saloon whose "open mouth . . . called seductively to passersby," the buildings in Crane's New York repel entry because they violate the privacy they ought to guard. Crane calls a hall "hilarious"—promiscuous and heartless in its enjoyment of the catastrophes it witnesses—and when Maggie returns home penitent, her mother harangues her in a room as public as a theater, with children wandering in to gape and a "doorfull of eyes" as audience, while down the hall there are other "open doors framing more eyes." If doors, sacred to James and Edith Wharton because they can be closed, serve here as windows, then windows in these buildings are apertures through which to launch projectiles. A man's mottled face pokes out of one to hurl first a curse and then a bottle at the singing mother. Staircases trumpet vaunting summonses to combat—a German woman and a dress-maker yell execrations "up and down between the balusters"—and walls, like the armor of a war-weary epic hero, are seamed with the mementos of ancient scuffles: the woodwork in Bleecker's lodging has a chipped slit, "celebrating the time when a man had thrown a hatchet at his wife." James's houses of fiction are cranial; Crane too anthropomorphizes buildings, but only to demonstrate their incapacity to offer sympathy. The warehouses Maggie passes on her way to the river have their orifices blocked or averted: "The shutters of the tall buildings were closed like grim lips. The structures seemed to have eyes that looked over them, beyond them, at other things."

Maggie is condemned to the streets. Her brother, however, rejoices in his expulsion from the private life indoors, since the street is his epic com-bat zone. Crane's Bowery is a more aggressive version of Whitman's triumphal Broadway. It resounds with the threat of war, its wheels and bells menacing the austere and timid little chapel like "an approaching barbaric invasion." But urban clearance offers the glory of an epic death with honor, for the meek chapel has resolved to die, when its time comes, "with a fine illimitable scorn for its slayers." Chivalric status is accorded by the street. Maggie calls her boyfriend Pete a knight because of the cocky nonchalance with which he struts in it. So is epic sovereignty: Jimmie is eminent because he bestrides intersections and terrorizes pedestrians from his truck, refusing to comprehend "their desire to cross the streets" and, whenever he encounters a fire engine, driving onto the sidewalk. Like Whitman, he boisterously expands to encompass the street he rules. "At the corners," Crane says, "he was in and of life." The truck is his chariot, the machine which epically augments his power. In his journalism Crane describes the Broadway cable cars as epic engines of war and has a joking project to resurrect a corps of chain-mailed knights, squeeze them into a cable car, and send it round a bend. The result would be a mock-epic cacophony, "the wild clash of steel upon steel—the tumult of mailed heads striking together, the bitter grind of armored legs bending the wrong way." Crane's streets have their own definition of heroic puissance. Minetta Lane grants you a reputation only if you "commit a number of furious crimes, and no celebrity was more important than the man who had a good honest killing to his credit." The bandits of the "old gorgeous days" before the law subdued the lane are recalled as ancestral swaggerers, gored and scarred with misdeeds and distinguished lesions. Crane mock-epically catalogues toughs like Bloodthirsty or No Toe Charley or Black-Cat in order "of combative importance." The harridans of the lane conduct their disputes in exchanges of invective ammunition. Mammy Ross and Apple Mag "used to argue with paving stones, carving knives and bricks." The city reinvents epic, that antique hieratic chant of arms and the man, as a homicidal poem in praise of carnage: Crane calls Minetta Lane's past "the song of the razor." Even buildings can be epic carnivores. In an 1894 essay on Coney Island, Crane imagines the amusement arcades late in the season gauntly hungering for a sustenance they can't find, and he describes the hall of Mammy Ross's den as "blacker than a wolf's throat."

Crane's demotic toughs, like the liquor-fueled Kelsey and his gang in "George's Mother," brag with an epic militancy "like veterans with their wars," each anecdote the trophy of some violent campaign. Among them George feels "capable of heroisms." As epic ruffians they despise the pastoral sloth of "contemporaneous life" and long for some "riotous upheaval, a cloudburst of destruction." Indoors, warfare proceeds domestically. George's mother cleans house militaristically, poising her broom "lance-wise, at dust demons. There came clashings and clangings as she strove with her tireless foes." Homely routine is regimentation and reveille. "Like a soldier" at her post, she fights a daily "battle to arouse" George from his bed. Assault and battery, siege and demolition are the principles of urban living. The mother lays the table as "a white garden, growing the fruits of her labor"; as a pastoral preserve it's offensive to the epic warrior, so George sets himself to wreck it. Bleecker assembles his bottles into the likeness of "a primitive bar" which by morning he has reduced to "a decaying battlefield." The fortitude Crane requires of his street-smart heroes is demanded as well from architecture, and in a journalistic piece of 1894 about a tenement fire off Sixth Avenue he admires the incinerated building for stoically abiding the flames: "the house, in manifest heroic indifference to the fury that raged in its entrails, maintained a stolid and imperturbable exterior." Like the Spartan youth, it lets the beast gnaw its innards without complaint.

But in migrating from the Civil War battlefields to the streets of New York, epic risks decline into blustering mock-epic. Crane's language equivocates between the two modes: how far does he commend the vigor of the corner boys and how far condemn them as noisy cowards? His metaphors tend to twist into mockery. The epic simile supposedly associates that taut heroic will with the elemental willfulness of nature; yet Crane compliments the endurance of the burning tenement in vain. How can the house's demeanor be heroic when it has no choice but to suffer its torment unprotestingly? Resolving the mechanical into the organic, metaphor finds the city to be a parody of nature. Crane's journalism abounds in such ironically metaphoric perceptions of New York. Metaphor promises to restore childhood vision, to recapture the eye's innocence by making us see things anew, but in New York it merely cozens us to see things as they are not, making false correspondences between city and country. In a *Tribune* article in 1892 Crane notices furniture vans rumbling along a slum street with "impossible landscapes on their sides." Like those impossibilities, metaphor pays unavailing homage to a natural reality the city can't possess. The arboreal roof gardens of New York, Crane says, are satisfying only "if you have never seen the mountains nor heard, to your heart, the slow, sad song of the pines": they're metaphors unable to match their referents, obliged to be a deceptive second best, just as Minetta Lane is a "becobbled valley between hills of dingy brick." Metaphor in the city is the complaining voice of a longing to be elsewhere. In an 1894 story Crane describes the holiday of Mr. Binks the clerk, who sees Madison Square from a cable car and, used to its brown and white drabness, is disconcerted by its greenery. The shock makes him want to go to the country. Those who can't afford this liberty are taunted by the city, which camouflages itself as nature. In "The Landlady's Daughter" the riggings of ships "grew like grass" at the end of the slum street; the view from the tenement window in "George's Mother"—"chimneys growing thickly on roofs," with a workman clinging to one like a bee; washing strung on "vine-like lines," flapping "strange leaves of cloth"; funneling smoke from the brewery, extending sooty pinions "like a great bird, flying"—is another trompe-l'oeil, a succession of metaphors that don't reawaken in the city reminiscences of the lost country but parody that process by making the slum a matted, pterodactyl-haunted swamp, its squabbling denizens "like animals in a jungle." In the city, metaphor's gift of activation becomes perverse and endows the inanimate with an unnatural life. Chimneys aren't built on the roofs but grow there in a biologically thriving thicket.

Crane's own heroic outings in New York open themselves to misunderstanding. Are they as fraudulent as the city's makeshift metaphoric landscapes? His preparation for his study "The Men in the Storm" was to spend the night on a breadline during a blizzard, and for "An Experiment in Misery" he lodged in a Bowery flophouse. Passing himself off as one of his subjects, he is claiming a heroism they lack. He remarked that "An Experiment in Misery" is about cowardice—the abjectness of the indigent, who accept life's hardships instead of fighting back. In volunteering to suffer what they do, Crane is proving himself capable of valor, blooding himself like the protagonist of *The Red Badge of Courage*. Slumming is his urban rite of maturation. Yet a suspicion remains of amateurism and adventurism, of fashionable flirting with the derangement of the senses. The framing passages of "Experiment" in the 1894 New York *Press* version, later omitted, make the trial a charade. The young man impersonates a tramp in order to "discover his point of view," and kits himself out for the dare by borrowing a scruffy costume from an artist friend. The same ambiguity attaches to the Dora Clark affair of 1896. The corrupt policeman Charles Becker, who took protection money from brothels and streetwalkers, arrested Dora at 31st Street and Broadway and threatened to do the same to Crane, who was interviewing her for a journalistic study of the Tenderloin. Crane denied she had been soliciting and had her released. The police resented his accusations and allegedly persecuted him with hints that they'd expose his sexual delinquencies and brand him as an opium dealer. The case still looks dubious. It's hard to tell the difference between the artist's or the journalist's investigation of urban vices and his covert enthrallment with those vices. Was Crane really intending to engage Dora's services, and did he (as some papers suggested) invent the alibi about studying human nature when the police embarrassed him? As for the charge that he ran an opium den, Crane admitted to having an opium layout in his room, "but . . . tacked to a plaque hung on the wall"—another tool of research for a previous article. The brave social experimenter can seem a trifler, affecting poverty as a stunt, turning misery into copy; the epic avenger of injustice can seem indistinguishable from one of the lawbreakers to whom he offers succour.

Crane also foresees the problem that for O. Henry has complicated Whitman's city: the individual's submergence in the crowd and the need to rescue a single life from that compressing composite before you can tell a story. Whitman recognized no such difficulty. Since the crowd had been expounded from himself, he could fraternize with everyone in it. They were all portions of that philoprogenitive self. Instead of this procreative union with others, Crane's journalism notices that the crowd has expunged individuality and has thus made people unintelligible. He says of the homing men in the storm that "if one dared to speculate upon the destinations of those who came trooping, he lost himself in a maze of social calculation; he might fling a handful of sand and attempt to follow the path of each particular grain." The city equalizes and erases the diverse purposes of individuals. On the steps of the charitable house Crane tries to isolate groups—separate nationalities, the hard-working versus the shiftless—but "they were all mixed in one mass so thoroughly that one could not have discerned the different elements." An individuality first eroded by the city is then obscured by the snow, which makes of the men a heap with "a unanimous rhythmical motion" as it sways, and by their own pushing, which threatens to pulp them. Individuality extrudes from the crowd only if marked down for catastrophe. When this happens, as in Crane's "graphic study of New York heartlessness" in 1896, the crowd convenes to witness the anonymous tragedy of an individual expelled from its safe collectivity. An old man has collapsed on an East Side street. The watching crowd gels into a mob, a single rampaging body, "each member of which struggles for one thing." When the victim is carried off in an ambulance, the mob grumbles at the curtailment of its free show. The curtain has been brusquely lowered: "this impenetrable fabric . . . intervening between a suffering creature and their curiosity, seemed . . . to them . . . an injustice." No one sympathetically volunteers, as Whitman did, to *be* the man, to share his pain. Rather the choric crowd preserves its unity by the sacrifice of an individual. He dies on its behalf, while it relishes the spectacle.

Character in the city has a brief life. Its tenure of identity begins when it's expelled from the crowd's undifferentiation, but that singleness is soon revoked. In another of Crane's 1896 New York sketches, "A Detail," a little old lady with flinching timidity trusts herself to "the tempest of the Sixth Avenue," is caught "in the clutch of the impetuous river," whirls about disoriented, then steadies herself by fixing on two girls. She inquires apologetically if they know where she might get some work. Gently rebuffed, she resigns herself to disappear again into the crowd. The girls watch the small figure retreat until "at last, the crowd, the innumerable wagons, intermingling and changing with uproar and riot, suddenly engulfed it." Crane defers here to the conclusion of Dickens's *Little Dorrit*, where Clennam and Dorrit leave the prison and enter London's "roaring streets, inseparable and blessed; and as they passed along in sunshine and shade, the noisy and the eager, and the arrogant and the froward and the vain, fretted and chafed, and made their usual uproar." The mob questions the confidence of narrative in its definitive termini. Because the crowd's life is continuous, as automatically self-repeating as a machine's, it vetoes the cessation or ceremonious pause which a happy ending proposes. Private fates are powerless in this public compendium. As Dickens realizes, the metropolis discounts narrative: it germinates stories only to miscarry them as people wander off and are obliterated by the city. There are a million or—in O. Henry's calculation—four million stories in New York, but you're prevented from telling them because you can't extricate from the crowd the people to whom they're happening. The only stories that can be told with impunity are short ones, anecdotes like Crane's of an individual's ephemeral career outside the crowd: the old man's falling in a fit, the old woman's request for help. Such stories are unconsecutive. They frustrate narrative by leading nowhere or at best elsewhere. "The ambulance on its banging, clanging return journey . . . vanished into the golden haze"; the old woman is reabsorbed by Sixth Avenue. The sequel is beyond the reach even of speculation. Dickens's vast metropolitan novels embrace this condition of discontinuity by being anthologies of short stories manacled together by the city's own random connective device of coincidence.

For O. Henry the responsibility of narrative in the city is the retrieval of an individuality forfeited to the crowd. He assumes this as his Whitmanesque mission. To individuate the crowd means to bless it and welcome it into kinship with himself, as Blinker epiphanically does at Coney Island in "Brickdust Row" when "he no longer saw a rabble, but his brothers seeking the ideal." Yet Whitman's ambition to hail in the crowd "duplicates of myself" and to reclaim them as offspring falters in O. Henry, whose New York, already a modern city, is a place not of epic self-definition but of discreet self-loss.

O. Henry himself used New York for a salving self-erasure, vanishing both into its collectivity and behind a pseudonym. Born W. S. Porter in Greensboro, North Carolina, he came to New York in 1902 after serving three years in jail for a bank fraud. He relegated himself to untraceable membership of the crowd and further dispersed his identity in a paper chase of literary aliases, calling himself Sydney Porter, S. H. Peters, Olivier Henry, James L. Bliss, T. B. Dowd, and Howard Clark. When magazines to which he had submitted his stories tried to contact him, they found he enjoyed the privileged existential liberty of the missing person. Whitman in New York resumed everyone else's life in his own. O. Henry, by his self-camouflaging, achieved the opposite: rather than drawing others into himself, he fled into them. The recognition which for Whitman familially unified the crowd was O. Henry's special terror. He told a crony from the jail in Columbus that he lived in fear of being accosted in a public place by another ex-con. He dreaded coincidence, the revelatory but sinister manipulation of probabilities by which cities—with seeming arbitrariness, but actually in obedience to some arcane (and, in O. Henry's case, judicial) necessity—reconnect their scattered inhabitants. Some of the coincidences engineered by O. Henry's New York are benign, as when in "Squaring the Circle" the feudists from Kentucky meet by chance and shake hands "in the angles of Broadway, Fifth Avenue, and Twenty-third Street." But the city which you rely on to consume your past and obscure your identity may arraign you by returning them to you, and O. Henry's characters make cautious provision against this happening. Raggles, arriving on the ferry, costumes himself "with care to play the role of an 'unidentified man,'" and the lawyer Bellford, passing himself off as "Edward Pinkhammer" in a New York hotel, treats himself to an amnesiac adventure—the urban delight of a vacation from your self.

Because the city confiscates identity and enables you to evade the consequences of your actions simply by moving on, narrative, in order to discern a logic in the bewilderment of phenomena, has to invent a new kind of deductive narrator, who specializes in assembling the inconsistent clues distributed through the city. He is the detective. His profession is decipherment of the city. He unscrambles its evidential litter, interrogates its alibi that everything that happens in it is inanely contingent. O. Henry's New York contains one such professional, Shamrock Jones, and many eager amateurs, like the baker Miss Martha, who decides that her customer must be a penniless artist because he has stained fingers and buys only stale bread. Her effort at detection is disastrous. The man is an architectural draftsman, who uses the bread crumbs to rub out his pencil marks (a scruple privately dear to O. Henry, himself an astute coverer-up and rubber-out of the tracings he'd made in life). When the doting Miss Martha surreptitiously butters his loaves, he smears and ruins his diagrams. The anecdote's moral is the impropriety of such supposition. Accordingly, there's a nervous tact to O. Henry's choice of the short story as the form most apt for New York. It frustrates sequence and so prevents the arrival at or untying of the knot, the apportionment of just deserts, which is the legalistic longing of all narrative. By continuing, narrative desiderates a reckoning. Writing only short stories, O. Henry is extending to his characters the same amnesty he hopes for in his own case and which he believed he would attain by living in New York. The story's abbreviation is its omission of particulars, a reluctance to scrutinize evidence and to undertake the detective's course of following things up. O. Henry hastens, as he says, "to make a short story shorter," as if unwilling to say anything that might incriminate him or his characters. The girl in "The Shock of Doom" who's the cause of Vallance's pauperizing "comes not," he warns, "into the story." She's thus granted immunity from prosecution. In "Tommy's Burglar" O. Henry's necessary terseness abets a felony: "the burglar," he reports, "got into the house without much difficulty; because we must have action and not too much description in a 2,000 word story." The break-in is made easier by the shortage of space. Had the story been longer, O. Henry would have been obliged to devise obstacles to the entry.

O. Henry expects from the city that harbors him a secretiveness equal to his own. He applauds its topographic obliquity, the unknowability it shares with its inhabitants. In "The Elusive Tenderloin" he tries to locate that dubious region—the scene of Crane's interview with Dora Clark—but decides that it exists only in hearsay and rumor, as absconded as its own vices. 'Tonio's restaurant in "A Philistine in Bohemia" is stealthily reticent about publicizing itself: you can only track it down by asking people in the street, who will whisper instructions to you. O. Henry's directions to his readers aim to lose them in the city's uncharted terrain, dispatching them like befuddled detectives in quest of red herrings. He won't disclose the exact whereabouts of the pharmacy in which Ikey Schoenstein brews his love philter, saying only that it's at the point where the distance between the Bowery and First Avenue is shortest. New York is also permitted the unscrupulous freedom of false identities. W. S. Porter had his repertory of alternative selves;

New York in his stories has exotic aliases of its own—Little Old Bagdad or Wolfville on the Subway, Yaptown or Noisyville on the Hudson, Badville near Coney, Big City of Razzle Dazzle or of Bluff, City of Too Many Caliphs, City of Chameleon Changes. Whitman's aboriginal naming restored identity to the city. New York was an imitative caption deriving the place's reality from somewhere else; Manhattan imagistically evokes its islanded uniqueness. But in O. Henry the epic celebration of a name as a badge of tribal provenance turns into jocose perjury. He doesn't want to entitle New York, to award it the name it owns by right. He issues it instead with forged cards of identity, a deck of double-dealing nicknames. And a nickname approximates ignominy: it's the teasing mask for an illicit self. Nicknaming New York also permits O. Henry to not know it. He can speculate about it, as he says in "The Romance of a Busy Broker," in the professional guise of the anthropologist, interpreting its foreignness. As an urban anthropologist, he controverts his profession, for instead of explicating the quaint customs and arcane rites of other tribes, he renders strange those of his own. He exotically expatriates New York. He turns Fifth Avenue, in "New York by Camp Fire Light," into an array of society tepees and Broadway into a thoroughfare of decadent Rome, "devoted to Thespis, Thais, and Bacchus." He even interprets his fellow citizens as extraterrestrials: the city's rubbernecks, addicts of ogling, are "a tribe . . . wonderfully composed, like the Martians, solely of eyes and means of locomotion."

In renaming New York as a region of recondite wonders, O. Henry presides over a change from epic to romance. The hero of romance is a solitary quester, not an epic combatant; rather than defending his tribe or encouraging its expansion (as Whitman does), he travels bemused through a world from which he is estranged. The epic hero's aim is near to home: protection of his native place. The romance hero embarks on a more quixotic pursuit and follows an ideal which vanishes ahead of him. The epic hero builds the city. The romance hero can only conjure it up and hope for a visionary glimpse of it, glimmering out of reach in the distance. The epic hero arms the city. The romance hero, dreamier and more ineffectual, tilts at windmills. New York qualifies as O. Henry's local Arabia because it's a landscape of such whimsical chivalric escapades. People commit themselves to the city in a spirit of reckless experimentation, detaching themselves from their pasts to envision a chimerical future. All city dwellers are, like the romance hero, unappeased seekers. Though their ideal is inevitably inaccessible, they're undeterred, for arrival and conquest—demanded by epic—matter less than the associative intricacy of the chase. The chivalric city dweller delights in exploration, with all its hazards and false turnings; he doesn't, like the epic hero, insist on the appropriation of terrain. O. Henry maps such a fanciful itinerary in "Thimble, Thimble" when giving directions for finding an office in the financial district: "you follow the Broadway trail until you pass the Crosstown Line, the Bread Line and the Dead Line, and come to the Big Cañons of the Money Grubbing Tribe. Then you turn to the left, to the right, dodge a push cart . . . and hop, skip, and jump to a granite ledge on the side of a twenty-one story synthetic mountain of stone and iron." He's encouraging his readers to get lost in their own city. Like all who live there, Porter himself expected the city to perform marvels for him, commissioning it to materialize his wishes. Whitman appraised the strollers on Broadway as comrades and potential lovers. Porter, instead of this frank epic fraternization, arranges assignations under cover, appealing to the city—in the spirit of the chivalric hero—to supply him with the heroine he has invented in fantasy. In 1905 he inserted a classified ad in the *Herald*, requesting two artistic and unconventional ladies to reconnoiter with himself and his brother at the subway station at 125th Street and Lenox Avenue. He signed it "Omar."

"The Green Door" elaborates a protocol for the urban adventurer. He should not have a personal gain in view, as the epic hero militaristically does; like Rudolf in this story, he must abandon himself to the city's chances and opportunities and accept "what might lie just around the next corner." The city will reward him with the spoils of romance, "golden fleeces, holy grails, lady loves, treasure, crowns and fame." These are its trove of "unknown fates." The deities of "Romance and Adventure" worshipped by Rudolf have as their factotum in the city the genie of coincidence. Though Rudolf knocks at the girl's door by mistake, he's convinced that "it was the hand of Fate that doped out the way for me to find her." Like the city, the chivalric narrative is episodic —a fortuitous collection of inconsequential novelties. The spirit of romance requires the hero to keep faith with this randomness and treat it as a providence, hailing coincidences as charmed and ordained revelations. Life in romance is a story that never ends. Scheherezade is safe so long as she can keep narrating. In "A Madison Square Arabian Night," Plumer the tramp, being fed by the philanthropic Caliph (whom he addresses as Mr. Al Raschid), says "I'm your Scheherezade all the way to the toothpicks." If she narrates to stay alive, he does so in order to eat, which is the same thing.

Whitman on Broadway wishes that "thy flagstones, curbs, façades" could "tell their innumerable tales." In O. Henry they do so. He re-marked that he'd "got some of my best yarns from park benches, lamp posts, and newspaper stands." The poet oracularly implants a tongue in the dumb things of nature, permitting the elements to sing. O. Henry confers the same gift of articulacy on the muted objects of the city, transcribing the life history of a ten-dollar bill or eavesdropping on the gossip between the Statue of Liberty and her colleague Diana, poised on the tower of Madison Square Garden. In his Orphic New York even the streets share the absentminded loquacity of narrators like Scheherezade and lazily repeat themselves in order to keep talking: in "The Last Leaf" he comments on the grid's buckling into curves and angles west of Washington Square, where "one street crosses itself a time or two."

Whitman's epic and O. Henry's romance are primal forms revived by the city because it's inventing for itself a new literature, and this return to origins explains the oral nature of both—Whitman's bardic song or his assembly of an oral history for Brooklyn; O. Henry's praise of a generous, communing garrulity. Between them, however, a loss has intervened. Whitman speaks for all. But O. Henry's narratives have to be enticed out of hiding, elicited by bribes (like those he offered to tramps on the Lower East Side if they'd tell him their stories) and conjecturally embellished, since personal testimony is now not epic oration but whispered monologue, and "the voice of the city" proves—when O. Henry tries to hear it—to be silent. Shutting out the hubbub of the streets and the spieling of the citizens, he hears New York speak only when he sits for an unspeaking half hour with Aurelia on the stoop. Through "the city's labyrinths" the chivalric quester seeks a Grail which is connection with another human soul, a silent com-munion of love. His motive is a religious one: the consecration and safekeeping of an individual life which the city (as O. Henry remarks of the hunt for Mary Snyder in "The Sleuths") has snuffed out. As he nears his goal, he finds it has migrated to another world, and his quest has become memorial and elegiac. His narrative is the gravestone of a life the city has already claimed. Rather than opening outward novel-istically, the histories he tracks down contract and dwindle into short stories and, beyond that, into the obituary minimalism of a newspaper paragraph, acknowledging an existence only once it has been terminated. The newspaper was for Whitman an engine of the city's exponentiation of community. For O. Henry it symbolizes the city's condensation of human fates, foreclosing lives in its headlines. Matthew Arnold was appalled by the announcement that "Wragg is in custody." The news-paper had wracked a tragedy into a telegram. Balzac claimed that a newspaper paragraph about a young man jumping into the Seine was a great novel in capsule. For O. Henry all that can be salvaged from such a donnée is a short story, because the paragraph precisely measures the individual's meager allotment of space and significance in the city: it permits you a tiny and anonymous area to live in; it's prepared to allow you more room, for a day only, if you die spectacularly. The newspaper's columns are the filed and tiered compartments of an urban morgue, containing the remnants of lives that are over. The destiny of the girl in O. Henry's "The Skylight Room" is relegation to or internment within a paragraph. "That is all," O. Henry remarks after noting down his observations of her. "Is it a story? In the next morning's paper I saw a little news item, and the last sentence of it may help you . . . to weld the incidents together." The sentence reports on the admission of a starved girl to Bellevue.

The story's shortness institutionalizes the city's ruthless concision— its editing of existences. Streets in New York suffer the same cruel abbreviation. Their careers are aborted; like Balzac's young man in the Seine, they commit suicide. This is the case with Fourth Avenue in "A Bird of Bagdad." It strides forth from its roguish infancy in the Bowery, frolics in Union Square, then meets a sudden elderly debility as it crosses 14th Street. Unnerved by the "mortuary relics" of the antique shops bordering it, it can't recover and resolves to end it all. "With a shriek and a crash Fourth Avenue dives headlong into the tunnel at Thirty-fourth and is never seen again." O. Henry's characters are haunted by the brevity of their lives. They have a metaphysical terror of the short story which, in collaboration with the city, works on them like a vice. Madder is "Extradited from Bohemia"—a piece exiguously described by its narrator as "our little story"—reasons that "we are short, and Art is long." But O. Henry's art learns from the city a dismissive and funereal shortness. Occasionally he relents syntactically and makes un-wonted bequests of space. Mr. Coulson of Gramercy Park in "The Marry Month of May" is granted such a bonus. After listing his assets, O. Henry adds, "And he had a housekeeper. Mrs. Widdup. The fact and the name deserve a sentence each. They have it." Still, this gram-matical generosity defrauds Mrs. Widdup even as it offers her its circum-spection. Detaining her in a sentence of her own, unaccompanied by attributes, without a verb to act on her behalf or an object toward which to direct herself, she's locked in solitary confinement. The sentence has sentenced her first to isolation, then—for the name is all we know of her, and it's as unrevealing as a stranger's in an obituary column—to premature extinction. A short story is the novel's implosion. "Lost on

Dress Parade" makes this point about the clerk Chandler, who can afford to bedizen himself to play the dandy on Broadway only once every ten weeks. His sartorial outing is referred to by O. Henry—with a poignantly supernumerary doubling of adjectives—as "Chandler's short little day." Just before his death, the ailing W. S. Porter lapsed into sleep and dreamed a narrative which expanded to cover a lifetime. He woke up when it was over and found he'd been asleep for only two minutes. A life accelerated to last two minutes is the definition of a short story. He wrote up the experience in "The Dream," which was published after his death in 1910.

The story's begrudgement of space, in league with the city's cramping of lives, refuses a novelistic ampleness. The pier glass in "The Gift of the Magi" imposes similar visual strictures. Straitened between the windows of a cheap flat, it only renders an image of yourself if you're "very thin and agile" and can segment, abridge, and anthologize your body, "observing [your] reflection in a rapid sequence of longitudinal strips." Allocation of space is managed by a progressive reduction. The landlady in "The Skylight Room" begins by showing prospective lodgers the double parlors, then leads them through a series of ever smaller chambers until she comes to an attic seven feet by eight. Here you arrive, as always in the urban short story, at your surcease: the room is the size of a coffin. Joe in "Psyche and the Pskyscraper" keeps "the smallest store in New York" and is mocked by Daisy—who lives in "a little hall bedroom, five feet by eight"—as "Two-by-Four." The spatial restrictions to which O. Henry's New Yorkers are accustomed make them unable to conceive of an outsize, outlandish world elsewhere. When Carter in "A Lickpenny Lover" woos Maisie by describing to her a honeymoon in Venice, she thinks he's talking about a jaunt to Coney Island and spurns him for being cheap. Yet there's a creaturely snugness to the urban microcosm. Flat dwellers, O. Henry says in "A Service of Love," wear their paltry rooms like exoskeletons or cozy armor: "if a home is happy it cannot fit too close." The smallest room is a cell voluntarily inhabited because it's a haven of bodily comfort, and the tramp Soapy in "The Cop and the Anthem" pines to be arrested so he can spend the winter impounded at the city's expense on Blackwell's Island.

In a New York of flats, the house is no longer sacred to a single life. It therefore can't continue to be the plenum of privacy and introversion which Henry James and Edith Wharton upholster as "the house of fiction." Stephen Crane's houses evict their tenants. Maggie's mother, disowning her, tells her to eat the stones and dirt of the street and to sleep in the gutter. O. Henry's shopgirl Maisie also takes the house out of doors, declaring the street corner to be her parlor, the park her drawing room, and the avenue her garden promenade. Indoors, the house now congregates and compartmentalizes a multitude of different lives into proximity and simultaneity. It becomes anthological. A lodging house resembles not a novel but a volume of short stories, with lives vertically overlaid and horizontally walled off from one another, happening at the same time though unrelated. In the streets of Dickens's city, tragedy and comedy collide and commingle. In O. Henry's urban lodgings, tragedy and comedy go about their business under the same roof but on different floors, never intersecting. You can listen in on the existences of others, yet cannot penetrate the partition dividing you from them. Sarah in "Springtime à la Carte" knows her neighbors by the noises they make: "At 7.30 the couple in the next room began to quarrel; the man in the room above sought for A on his flute." The lodgings are themselves, like O. Henry, elegiac and nonconsequential narrators. In "The Furnished Room" each of the transient spaces on the lower West Side has "a thousand tales to tell." With weary promiscuity the rooms lend themselves to new tenants every few weeks and anthologically preserve traces—in this case, olfactory (the lingering odor of the dead girl's mignonette)—of those who were once alive in them. The anthological house is here a cemetery, the furnished room being a station, like the city, in life's progress to dissolution. The girl in the story has disappeared into the city, which is "like a monstrous quicksand, shifting its particles constantly, with no foundation." The room resembles the human body in being a temporary incarnation through which the migratory spirit passes, and, like that spirit, it undergoes reincarnation as it's revamped to fit a new occupant. Poe's deductive philosophy of furniture turns into an art of divination. As if at a séance, the bereft objects converse of their departed users: "the room, confused in speech as if it were an apartment in Babel, tried to discourse . . . of its divers tenantry." The tenanting souls dematerialize, leaving only the recycled exterior, the depleted physical form. Things in cities exist and acquire meaning serially, as they are shared or stolen or bequeathed or otherwise transmitted between people, so in choosing to write multiple short stories, not novels, O. Henry is enunciating a truth about New York. Serialism circulates objects (like the rubber plant which in one of his stories recites its successive ownerships) and also elements: the rooms of the lodgers in "A Philistine in Bohemia" are supplied with "clean towels and cracked pitchers of freshly laundered Croton," for the water from the Croton reservoir has a history as serial as that of the towels, having traveled over and through innumerable bodies before it arrives at its current and also temporary destination. The wind in "A Newspaper Story" is another serial narrator, a gossip and a procurer picking up the paper from the sidewalk and gusting it along until it flaps into the face of "the young man who had written to the heart-to-heart editor." As it continues on its way, the paper connects other individuals, who are related, as lives in a city must be, only by its mediation—the girl who has written to the beauty advisor, the labor leader (actually her father) who's the object of its editorial imprecations. Currency too exists serially, named after its reincarnability and charged, like the wind and the newspaper, with the task of mediating relations between the city's dissociated people; and seriality makes money loquacious. Each note is a narrator with its own anthology of tales about those who have, one after the other, coveted or squandered it. "Money talks" says O. Henry at the beginning of "The Tale of a Tainted Tenner," in which the easygoing note exults in its "lively and gorgeous circulation." O. Henry encourages commodities to reminisce because they are the permanent residents of a city where people are fugacious. If currency is garrulous, then garrulity, like currency, is a means of exchange, one life's transmission of its testimony to another. The venal and cynical landlady in "The Furnished Room," who wants to rent lodgings and is afraid of superstitious objections, ostracizes herself from the community of narrative. "Did ye tell him, then?" asks Mrs. McCord, to which Mrs. Purdy dolorously replies, "I did not tell him." She won't tell; the hair bow, which the girl who has killed herself left behind in the room, can't tell. The bow halts the man rummaging frantically through the room. But the collectivity of ownership frustrates him. It might be hers and might equally well be anyone else's. Unless O. Henry can graft a tongue into them, as he does with the blabbing tenner, commodities are unforthcoming: "the black satin hair bow . . . is femininity's demure, impersonal common ornament and tells no tales."

Romance doesn't, like epic, record and immortalize a single act of bravado, such as Whitman's constitution and fortification of New York. It's an accumulation of short stories pointing toward an end which is forever deferred, since the romance hero's exploration of the world or of the city is a journey into himself and there can be no definitive arrival. The city's economy mimics the anthological form. The department store, one of the novelties of late-nineteenth-century New York, is a structure like a lodging house or a volume of short stories: it contains everything (which is the city's Whitmanesque ambition) but segregates the things it contains, rather than compounding them. Nancy in "The Trimmed

Lamp" sells handkerchiefs in a department store and rates men according to the kind they buy. Reasoning from the part to the whole, she discounts them as possible suitors if she dislikes their choice. She collates a piecemeal personality for herself by studying her female customers until she too, like the store, is a compendium of specialisms, an anthology of quirks: "from one she would copy a practice or gesture, from another an eloquent lifting of an eyebrow, from others a manner of walking, of carrying a purse, of smiling, of greeting a friend." The city is Nancy writ large. Its aggregated voice is choral, "a composite vocal message of massed humanity," melding four million different plaints. Though the hero of epic is proudly singular, the heroes of romance are a committee, like the knights of the Round Table or, as in O. Henry's New York, a chorus. Not all of us are able to perform the epic hero's acts of derring-do; we can all, however, cherish and wistfully grope toward an ideal, as the romance hero does. This is why O. Henry can insist that everyone is a potential hero and every event a potential tale. The storyteller himself must be a chivalric quester, for his mission is the intuiting, not the mere relaying, of stories. A tale is made, as Wordsworth proposes in "Simon Lee," by empathetic inquiry, the impingement of one life on another. When Frank Norris argued that there were just three "story cities" in the United States—New York, New Orleans, and San Francisco—and denied that a novel could be written about Nashville, O. Henry volunteered to do just that, testing his faith that stories inhered everywhere if only you had the solicitude to overhear them. The result was "A Municipal Retort."

O. Henry's tactics for inveigling a story out of selfish silence—intended to rebuke the taciturnity of urban manners—contrast with those of his successor Damon Runyon. Whereas O. Henry goes foraging for stories, Runyon, truer to the city dweller's blasé policy, expects them to come to him. His tales characteristically begin with the narrator positioning himself in some place of preoccupation—in Mindy's on Broadway, eating goulash; in Bobby's Chop House, eating beef stew; on the steps of the bank at 47th Street and Seventh Avenue, lounging in the summer heat. There he practices a weary, knowing indifference. Of Fergus Appleton, the posturing muscleman, he remarks, "I see maybe a million guys like him in my time on Broadway." He narrates against his will or better judgment, prefacing a story about Harry the Horse and some cronies from Brooklyn with a disclaimer: "these are not such parties as I will care to have much truck with." Like stories, characters wait on his leisure ("if anybody sits around Mindy's restaurant for long enough, they are bound to see some interesting and unusual scenes") and will connect only if hurled at him by force. As "Situation Wanted" begins, he is strolling past Mindy's when "the night manager suddenly opens the door and throws a character in a brown suit at me." Runyon, miffed, congratulates himself that at least "the character just misses me" and dents the mudguard of a parked car instead. Then, however, the character picks itself up and tells Runyon its story. Runyon's stories are collisions of people who don't particularly wish to be related. He is gratified by that near miss; in O. Henry, though, the narrator's life converges for an epiphanic instant with that of his character. At the same time, the character enjoys a holiday from the ignominy of the mob, a "crowded hour of glorious life" which reconciles him (as in "The Romance of a Busy Broker") to the "age without a name" that he's subsisted in before and will inevitably return to. The "transients in Arcadia" save to spend a week pretending to be swells in the Hotel Lotus on Broadway; Towers Chandler can afford "one day in seventy" among the beau monde. For others, the revelation endures only a few dazing seconds—Ikey Snigglefritz, the tailor's apprentice, soars above the city in elation when he shakes the hand of a Tammany politician, and Corney Brannigan, posturing in glad rags, perceives, when a lady rewards his courtesy, that he is a gentleman after all. But the story's end summons them back to the stifled diurnal despair of routine, revoking the identity with which it has haloed them. Tilly, waitress in a chophouse on Eighth Avenue, adorns herself for the benefit of the beery Seeders, is rejected, and after her "brief début" remorsefully sees that romance is a delusion, the exorbitant hope of Quixote: it's her mistake to have interpreted the kiss "as that of a pioneer and prophetic prince who might have set the clocks going and the pages to running in fairyland. But . . . she must forevermore remain the Sleeping Beauty."

Porter's favored coign of vantage in the city sums up both the generosity and the pathos of his effort to individuate the crowd and to romantically redeem the city. In his lodging on Irving Place he sat on sentry duty at a floor-length window in the front room, watching out for the passersby who would be the chance participants in his stories. When he spotted a person of interest, he'd invent a life for them and (in imagination) follow them home. Looking out of the window, you are looking into people, rendering them as transparent as the pane through which you see them. Jack in "The Duel" interprets the windows cut into the city's skyscrapers—"myriads of brilliant parallelograms and circles and squares through which glowed many colored lights"—as the spirit's vents in the materialistic body. Ravenel in "Roses, Ruses and a Romance" reads the vases that a girl across the backyard has placed on her sill as an amorous invitation to him and gazes entranced at what O. Henry calls "the window of his hopes." The phrase is an eloquent one: not only are his hopes invested in that window; hope itself is window-like, a yearning to escape from confinement in oneself (and in one's room), a dream of reciprocation. The window for Porter is an emblem of realism. He said that the confessions of Rousseau, Zola, and George Moore were "supposed to be windowpanes in their breasts," yet he mistrusted the translucency of the glass and suspected these memoirists of arranging reflections of themselves in the mirror. Ideally the window, as well as granting access to another human soul, is an aperture opening onto everywhere, an individual raying out to take in all other selves. "The Skylight Room" is two dollars' worth of space, but its glassed roof frames "a square of blue infinity." In the hole, you have the fancied freedom of a sublime immensity.

People in Edith Wharton's *Old New York* are as vigilant at their windows as Porter was. They, however, scan the streets for evidence of misdemeanors, like Mrs. Hazeldean's flushed, adulterous exit from the burning Fifth Avenue hotel. New Year's Day is passed in "looking out of the window: a Dutch habit still extensively practiced in the best New York circles." Its purpose now is social supervision and censorship. The looking O. Henry's people do transfuses sympathy among them. The brides in "Sisters of the Golden Circle" recognize their common destiny and semaphore comfort to one another in "the glance of an eye." But while the window symbolizes O. Henry's desire to see into other people, it also impedes that desire, imposing itself between inner and outer; and sometimes, unlike that astral skylight, it discloses only a dead end. The window in "The Harbinger" is "open upon its outlook of brick walls and drab, barren back yards." As the iconography of the city develops, the view out the window—for surveillance in Edith Wharton, for episodic visual adventure in O. Henry—turns around into a view in through the window, which represents the sadly opposite kind of urban vision: alienated, ejected, hopelessly curious. In the photographs of Alfred Stieglitz and the paintings of Georgia O'Keeffe the window onto New York stands for the image, which, like a window, is the framing of a view. The window's new function is to disconnect you from the city, to see it, as the image does, subjectively. Edward Hopper's paintings are often views in through windows, glimpses in transit such as he had while traveling on the El through the tenement districts of New York. Far from penetrating a soul housed within, he is permitted, as he's shuttled headlong past, only a fleeting sight of people conducting lives which must remain unintelligible to him. Ultimately, the city declares it dangerous to look in windows. Those whose existences you intrude on won't thank you for your commiseration but will hound you for spying. Tommy in Cornell Woolrich's story "The Boy Cried Murder" (filmed in 1949 as *The Window*) sleeps on a fire escape during the New York dog days and, climbing up toward a breeze, sees some neighbors stab a man. He raises the alarm but isn't believed, and the murders make plans to kill him too. O. Henry's altruistic urban visionary ends as a guilt-ridden and impotent voyeur.

4

The Picturesque and the Photographic

The social New York of Henry James and Edith Wharton nervously mystifies the sources of its wealth. James spiritualizes money, making it a bequest to the imagination. The rapacity of his tycoons is exclusively mental. There's a heroic profligacy to the plutocrats of the late nineteenth century, who—smoking cigars wrapped in $100 bills or ordering, like Diamond Jim Brady, gold-plated and gem-encrusted bicycles from Tiffany's—are not so much flaunting wealth as purging themselves of it by whimsically wasting it. In a society pledged to the denial of its own economic origins, realism's reprisal is the attachment of price tags. Upton Sinclair can therefore in his novel *The Metropolis* (1908) confound New York's fictionalizing of itself and disprove its theory of leisured superfluity by the radical act of counting costs. Realism, ever since Defoe's first industrious capitalists, has been professionally astute about commodities and quantities, the tallying of expenses. The characters of James disown the vulgarity of inventory; Sinclair calls their bluff by the resumption of economic reckoning, turning the description of New York into computation—how many millionaires are there in the city? how much does land cost per square inch on Wall Street? what's the lucrative length of Fifth Avenue? how much did that woman pay for her pelts? The realist's qualification is that he knows not the value but the cost of things. For Sinclair, describing is a matter of measuring and pricing. Mrs. Winnie's mansion on Fifth Avenue "occupied half a block, and had cost two million to build and furnish." In it she has installed a green marble swimming pool, which, she complacently adds, "was fifty thousand dollars." Decor, treasured by Edith Wharton because it muffles and deters the utilitarian city, is subjected to instant realistic appraisal. When the Montagues are shown an apartment hotel, Sinclair notes that there's no one present "to mention that the furniture has cost eight thousand dollars per room, and that the wall covering has been imported from Paris at a cost of seventy dollars per yard." It's the realist's job to supply such data.

In doing so, Sinclair is reducing New York from a picture to a diagram. James's New York is pictorial because of its genteel lassitude (around Washington Square) or its meditative evacuation (it might be charming, he speculates in *The American Scene*, if only you could rid it of its inhabitants). The pictorial is to James—as it was to the Impressionists, who hedonistically represent people at play, boating, picnicking, dancing, but not at work—a concomitant of leisure. A painting has stilled time and thus prohibits exertion. "A society that does nothing," James remarks of Newport in 1870, "is decidedly more pictorial, more interesting to the eye of contemplation, than a society which is hard at work." Society can compose itself pictorially (or novelistically) for James only by laying down tools. Sinclair's graphic model for New York is not the picture with its indolent and decorative stasis but the diagram, a brisk functional decipherment of who owns what and how much things are worth. *The Metropolis* contains a number of such illustrative aids: the blackboard in the brokers' office, "with the initials of the most important stocks in columns, and yesterday's closing prices above," and a ticker in readiness; the catalogue which would be necessary "to list the establishments maintained by the Wallings"; the diagram of boxes and their holders printed in the opera program, enabling everyone to "tell who was who" and circulating among the audience a supplementary cast list, since the protagonists of the performance aren't the singers on stage but the moneyed patrons distributed around the diamond horseshoe. The picture laminates and euphemizes the social surface, the diagram renders that surface transparent to see how society works. In rejecting the novel as written by James, Sinclair is redeploying the epic, which Whitman used to rally society and which Sinclair now uses as a summons to revolutionary change. Epic indeed became a synonym and an acronym for the process of analyzing society in order to impel an alteration in it. When in 1934 Sinclair campaigned, without success, for the governorship of California, he named his local party EPIC after the slogan "End Poverty in California."

Picturesqueness tolerates the city's social inequities as a decorative enhancement. In *A Hazard of New Fortunes* the Jamesian enclave of Washington Square has been invaded by "the familiar picturesque poverty of southern Europe," which exists apparently for the delectation of its betters. Howells's hero justifies the El tracks because they render the grimy, pullulating streets picturesque by concealing them. The picturesque is thus defined as a decorative fiction, a lie about society. The bends in the El below the Cooper Institute are "perfectly atrocious, . . . but incomparably picturesque!" That exclamation sums up the desperate fraudulence in this view of the city. Howells's people don't use the El to explore the city but to achieve the disengagement from it that enables them to flatter it as picturesque. Up on its stilts, they can deny membership of or responsibility for New York and enjoy it touristically, as they do when behind the Greenwich Village tenements they notice "the picturesqueness of clotheslines fluttering far aloft, as in Florence." Stephen Crane in his "Experiment in Luxury" marks the distance between this artful, arty disorder, which only the rich can afford to patronize, and the oppressive litter of the poor, who haven't been blessed by the charity of metaphor and don't find their own conditions picturesque. Describing the messy room of the affluent young man, Crane sees its clutter as pictorially studied, lovingly contrived. "The effect was good, because the disorder was not necessary, and because there are some things that when flung down, look to have been flung by an artist." The squalor of the poor lacks this fanciful premeditation and can't be assuaged by the fantastications of metaphor: "it would require genius to deal with the piled up dishes in a Cherry Street sink." The appropriate way to deal with them would be, rather than composing them into a genre scene, to clean them and clear them away, abolishing the possibility of a picture.

In 1890—the year when Howells's characters were exchanging social compunction for aesthetic admiration and encouraging the city pictorially to misrepresent itself, its squat commercial edifices at nightfall "rescued by obscurity from all that was ignoble in them"—the city was also making a retributive and statistically accusatory diagram of itself, in Jacob Riis's investigation of the slums, *How the Other Half Lives*. Riis was a police reporter who became a social reformer, and a photographer whose camera wasn't a means of pictorial mediation but an instrument of inflammation and redress; for while the picturesque is a detached pacification of life, the camera's involvement in the reality to which it attests is literally explosive. Riis wielded the flash as a weapon. Fired from a revolver during his nocturnal patrols with the police, it roused the sleepers in overcrowded tenements and enabled him to gauge their numbers. It also achieved, by happy accident, the slum clearance for which Riis agitated: twice, in igniting the flashes, he set on fire the shanties he was photographing. The painter's profession acquiesces in the way things appear; the photographer compels an incendiary change in them.

Riis's title opposes his photographically exposed and enumerated census to the pictorial muffling of New York. James and Edith Wharton treat only one half of the city's society and sever the introspectively cloistered refinements of New York from the grubby labor which sustains them. Contending that "every man's experience ought to be worth something to the community from which he drew it," Riis redefines the city—as O. Henry did in his electoral expansion from Mrs. Astor's Four Hundred to his own four million—to comprise all its inhabitants, however neglected or invisible. The suppressed city, the Other Half, inverts the fortunate world above it. Riis's photographs are therefore derisions of pictorial plenitude. The genre paintings of the nineteenth century, like the photographs made by Byron's company, abound in detail because they celebrate ownership. In Riis, pictorial abundance turns into insanitary congestion, spilling from fetid rooms into rubbishy alleys. Objects which to the painter are images are to Riis evidence: an ash barrel on a sidewalk, dingy bedding draped on a fire escape, punctured sacks of refuse in Bottle Alley. These things, like the soiled crockery in Crane's Cherry Street sink, have not been pictorially composed, and their very randomness—by which the momentary art of photography is unperturbed—impugns the tidiness of painting. The tenements of the Other Half develop too as a parodic commentary on social evolution elsewhere in the city. As the rich move uptown, their dwellings on the previously fashionable East Side are bought by unscrupulous agents and rack-renting landlords, partitioned, and rented to the industrious poor. The tenements begin as an alternative city, hidden behind a façade of propriety. Rear houses are erected on back lots that once were bourgeois gardens, and an alley is carved out as a new street between them. This catacombed city in exile even burrows beneath the foundation of its upper half: thieves use the vaulted sewers as a runway for speedy escapes.

Riis's city mocks the sanctification of place which James achieves by seeking out havens of repose and Edith Wharton by the provision of cosseting, swathing furniture. Riis encounters an Arab entrepreneur in Washington Street "who peddles 'holy earth' from the Battery as a direct importation from Jerusalem." James and Edith Wharton are adamant about doors and their closure, about a regime of exclusion. But Riis defines the tenement by the openness of its doors. In the summer, windowsills, fire escapes, and parked vehicles in the street are annexed as dormitories. Children are ejected into the streets to fend for themselves, off-loaded as foundlings or loosed on the world as thieves or vagrants, delivered from the family to the street-corner gang. The failure of the domestic interior inducts them into an outdoor world of brazen publicity, where the aspiring criminal dreams of getting "his name in the papers as a murderous scoundrel." The decorative scruples which, in the city of the novelists, segregate Fifth Avenue from Wall Street or lock out the raucous streets, look to Riis like preparations for war. The mobs have forced the official city into a state of siege, and the Subtreasury has Gatling guns, stacks of hand grenades, and bulletproof shutters to protect it. The interior becomes a horde of gold, arming itself against assault from without.

Such a city can't be depicted. It must instead be starkly delineated. Riis scolds the Italian tenement dwellers for importing a Mediterranean picturesqueness, which may delight the artist in Europe but in America is a "danger and a reproach." His language is that of a defeated pictorialism. Giving an account of life in a tenement block, he asks, "Why complete the sketch?," for it is merely "the frame in which are set days, weeks, months, and years of unceasing toil." The frame, for the pictorial interpreter of the city, is a convenience for disengagement. The life on show has been bordered, its indignity kept at bay (as for Howells's characters on the El) by art. But to Riis the frame is shackling and "drearily familiar," a circumscription which the tenement dwellers can't evade. The photographic subject ought to be unframed, caught on the run, not pictorially becalmed for contemplation. Riis's subjects are too undisciplined to tolerate pictorial detention. He tries to photograph the boys in a lodging house while they are washing for supper, but "they were quite turbulent" and wouldn't pose. One of them apologized to Riis: "if they would only behave, sir!—you could make a good picture." Yet a picture, stilling and arranging them in orderly rows, would have sentimentally soothed them. Riis's problem as a photographer isn't this boisterous indifference to his camera. On the contrary, he worries when his subjects do choose to slow down for him because in doing so they're exploiting him for profit or publicity. A tramp agrees to be photographed for a five-cent fee but then reneges on the deal, shrewdly maintaining that his pipe wasn't included in the contract; the young toughs on the West 37th Street dock aren't chastened by the camera, "whose acquaintance they usually first make in handcuffs and the grip of a policeman," but impudently enjoy the chance to show off. Sometimes, in spite of itself, the camera can encourage a pictorial falsification. It should warn and reprove, giving notice to those in front of it that their images are being entered in evidence against them. If they smile at it and befriend it—as do an Italian ragpicker's wife cradling her infant and a boy on Jersey Street shyly grinning as he learns to write—they disempower it, appearing to be at ease and at home in surroundings Riis. has declared intolerable. His angry text is palliated by being pictorialized in the engravings for the first edition of How the Other Half Lives. Riis decries the frowsy merchandise and musty eatables of the Jewish market, yet the engraving that illustrates the point dissents: the scene looks bustling, genial, idyllically profuse. George Luks, one of the Ashcan painters who specialized in New York street scenes, declared that "a child of the slums will make a better painting than a drawing-room lady gone over by a beauty shop." Paint, however, can't help being a cosmetic. The slum child in the painting will probably come out looking rosy-cheeked and jocund. The appropriate disproof of the beautifying picture is the wartily, rudely truthful photograph.

Or the diagram, which dispenses with imagery altogether. The tenements, a "destroyer of individuality and character," have reduced persons to statistics. Within the undifferentiated crowd, the only residual individuality belongs to ethnic quotas, as in Riis's calculation of the nationalities of beggars—15 percent Irish, 12 percent native American, 2 percent Italian, 8 percent German. Riis is forever numbering, marshaling data and taking census. "I counted . . . nineteen murders in the one block," he says of Baxter Street, and in Battle Alley "I counted seventeen deeds of blood," ironically dignifying the crimes—in a phrase which clashes with his own bureaucratic idiom of enumeration—as chivalric vendettas. His tallying and reckonings don't, however, add up to plenitude. Their purpose is subtraction. Of room in which to live, for instance—in the triangular yard of a Bayard Street tenement, with walls (measured by Riis) "fourteen or fifteen feet long," 128 children are put out to air themselves; and the lodging station at Elizabeth Street, with cubic air space for ten men, crams in 48. Number means compression and finally extinction. The statistical mode is for Riis necrotic, an estimate of the odds against survival. In an 1894 lecture he determines the ratio of deaths from cholera in the two halves of his city: 16 or 17 to the thousand uptown and in the slums 195. As the slums have statis-

Jacob A. Riis, "Five Cents a Spot" (ca. 1889). Lodgers in a Bayard Street tenement. Jacob A. Riis Collection, Museum of the City of New York.

tically equalized and compounded people (prior to extinguishing them), so Riis insists on understanding the city diagrammatically, not pictorially. The social discriminations made within it are rectilinear. A "color line" is drawn through the tenements by landlords, "to give the picture," as Riis puts it, "its proper shading." Here his lapse into a pictorial idiom has a savage irony, for the tints and hues of picturesque shading stand in this case for an ostracized race. Another notional boundary line segments the Other Half by separating the flat (which has its own doorbell and can guard its privacy) from the tenements. The lines traced by Riis on the map of the city are moral boundaries as well as sociological indices. Fourteenth Street supposedly fences off the good from the bad, though Riis reports that vice has crossed over and is flourishing in Hell's Kitchen and in Battle Row on East 63rd Street. Thanks to the grid, New York disposes itself as a diagram. The tenements, however, mar this regularity, with dozens of rear houses huddled at odd angles on a single block. Whereas the diagrammatic grid should serve him as a compass,

Riis manages to get lost in one of the tenement blocks on the East Side. The moral confusion and debasement of the ghetto tends to blur a linear rectitude in conduct: the tenements, Riis says, have rubbed out the line which ought to divide honest poverty from pauperism. Unmixing the crowd, Riis proposes a polychrome diagram of New York denoting the concentration of nationalities in neighborhoods, with Irish green on the West Side, German blue to the east, and stripes of Italian red and French purple downtown; a black mark would signify the Negro advance, a dully gray smear the presence of the Jew, and a "sharp streak of yellow" would indicate Chinatown. Color is here assigned as an ethnic badge, and its purpose is to soil, not to beautify. Riis calls the Arabs near the Battery an inky oozing stain on "the West Side emerald." The amplitude of the picture decomposes into a chart of "dots and dashes," indexing small colonies of Finns, Greeks, and Swiss.

The diagram, in Riis or in Upton Sinclair's novel, is an analytic tool prescribing and enforcing change. Picturesqueness has an investment in maintaining the status quo. When the sanitary renovation for which Riis campaigned had been achieved, James Huneker in his *New Cosmopolis* (1915) bemoaned the reforms because they had tidied up a disarray he found picturesque. The Lower East Side has been cheated of its "dear old dirty, often disreputable" scenic slovenliness. Crossing Third Avenue at 72nd Street in quest of an outpost of picturesque indigence, Huneker declares "the prosperity of the neighborhood" to be "positively dispiriting." In 1940 Jerome Myers, another of the Ashcan painters, whose preferred subject was the street life of Little Italy and the Bowery, remembered the slums and lamented that, though "conditions are . . . better in the beautified and sanitary New York of today," children no longer play on the pavements "and I know that picturesque types are seen less often." Even so, the city has other chores of amelioration for the picturesque vision to perform. Having sentimentally mollified poverty, it proceeds to redeem the brutal commercial city. Sentimentality takes on a spiritual mission: the conversion of New York from gross matter to ethereal spirit, from lucrative use to ideal beauty. The picturesque now aims at sanctification. It still relies on darkness or distance to mute the harsh actuality. S. Parkes Cadman in 1918 recommends observing the financial district from the Brooklyn Bridge at dusk, when the "bold outlines" of the buildings will be softened. If you adopt the right point of vantage and if the weather concurs, the headquarters of Mammon can be seen evanescing into a New Jerusalem, purging itself of cupidity, casting off solidity. Parkes Cadman described the Woolworth Building, thus atmospherically gentled and pardoned, as a "Cathedral of Commerce," soaring "like a battlement of the paradise of God which St. John beheld." The detachment enjoined by the picturesque, which makes Howells's characters value the El, becomes a spiritual withdrawal, the body's exhalation of the soul. In 1931 Brooks Atkinson emphasized the need for perspective in viewing New York. Up close, the skyscrapers are crass and hectoring. From afar, they undergo a picturesque death as bodies to be reborn as spirits: "their material fabrication melted," Atkinson reports, "into a thing unreal." The transubstantiation can be observed from the Staten Island ferry. Atkinson sees Manhattan gleaming "like a mystic fantasy, the ideal image of a religious dream, the white fingers of the slender towers stretching in supplication towards the sky." The metaphor has cowed the commercial eminences. Rather than arrogantly scraping the sky, they prayerfully implore it.

Huneker's novel *Painted Veils* (1920) studies this picturesque transfiguration of the city and finds it sadly inadequate—art's protest against a reality it cannot alter but may briefly mitigate. The picturesque becomes a plaintive, pathetic fallacy. The metaphoric redemptions in *Painted Veils* remain in the eye of the beholder, who knows them to be illusions. Mona Milton, looking down on the electric luminosity of New York at midnight, sees its undulating stream of "blue and grey and frosty white" as the tonalities of Venice. But it's a Venice gone wrong, dessicated and petrified, "a Venice of receded seas, a spun-steel Venice, sans hope, sans faith, sans vision." In the absence of faith, hope, and vision, the sense of beauty—which persuades Mona to see the lamps warning of road repairs as crimson beacons or the trolleys as a "canary color"—is a vain solace. Another of Huneker's aesthetes, Ulick Invern, studying the nocturnal mutation from a balcony above Lexington Avenue, treats it musically, not pictorially. The city is silenced by "the softer and richer symphony of the night," its "racking noises" quelled. The purpose of Ulick's metaphoric seeing is a determined misreading of money-making structures as religious fanes. For him the city's light is votive offering, not commercial enticement. Tongues of flame crackle from Broadway, and the theater district is a scorching hell, while "the Synagogue across from the park . . . might have been mistaken for an Asiatic mosque as it lay sleeping in the moon-rays." The blanching moonlight cancels the function of buildings, consecrates and ages them. "At night, he mused, the city loses its New World aspect. It reveals the patina of Time. It is a city exotic, semi-barbaric, the fantasy of an Oriental sorcerer." Ulick is desperate to turn reality into art, which is now the only viable religion. Therefore, from his lookout he sees Central

Park as "a mezzo-tint," the picture of a park, and open spaces as theaters: "Battery Place and the Bay are operatic, the stage for a thrilling
fairy spectacle." But the metaphors expire in helplessness. Mona's end
in the perception that New York is a parched Venice, Ulick's in an image
of the city as a "cemetery of immemorial Titans," whose gravestones
are the "granite house-tops." These two demises mark the vision as a
self-deluding conjuration, a magic no one else will believe in. Both
Mona's reverie and Ulick's lead to petrification. Their fluid impressionism butts against the insentient actuality of stone. They have attempted
to give sensory life to New York, which means to moisten or inflame it.
Hence their attention to the incandescence of its lights or to a fancied
liquidity—Central Park for Ulick "flowed in plastic rhythm, a lake of
velvety foliage." Yet it remains immutable stone, uncombustible and
arid.

The early photographers developed this pictorial mis-seeing of New
York into a tricky smudging of sight. In their eagerness to render the
city impressionistically molten, they'd jolt their cameras during exposure
(according to the photographer Ralph Steiner) so the image trembled,
or they'd grease their lens. Atmosphere was applied from without, as a
shock or a lubricant smear. The illustrations of Joseph Pennell wishfully
ruin the city in order to make it pictorially appealing. Arriving in 1904,
Pennell regretted that his friend Whistler hadn't seen the new metropolis. His own depiction of it interprets it as Whistler might have done,
its obtuse facts mistily wavering into fantasy. He pleads for the mitigation of atmosphere, for a pictorial fictionalizing of the city. From the
harbor the vista is "finer than Claude ever imagined, or Turner ever
dreamed," not seen but fabulated, and one of his etchings titles New
York "The Unbelievable City," stressing its implausibility and ineffa-
bility. Pennell, watching New York reconstruct itself, extolled "the
wonder of work" and considered American engineering to be classic art,
yet there's a contradiction between the city's vitality and his atmospherically impotent style, as there is between the labor he praises and
his own impromptu and dilettantish creativity. Thus, while the engineers are building New York, Pennell is picturesquely demolishing it.
The engineers toil and strain to raise the city. Pennell, recording their
efforts, prides himself on his sketchy, effortless facility. During his first
sojourn in New York, he left a note for his wife saying, "it is so beautiful I must go out and make more immortal works": he opposes the hard
won, labored-over immortality of the skyscrapers he was drawing to
the momentary, dashed-off immortality of his own works, made without
labor. In 1909 Pennell illustrated John van Dyke's *The New New York*,

and though van Dyke acclaims the city's novelty, Pennell contrives to suggest its dilapidated age. He likened the New York skyline to that of San Gimignano. There's an irony here, for the towers of San Gimignano are the moldered remnant of the original fortress, and the aesthete who makes this comparison is (like Huneker with his Venetian analogy) wishing the same subsidence into picturesque wreckage on New York. In the very act of drawing New York's optimistic refabrication of itself, Pennell turns into the Piranesian elegist of its imagined decay. His "Bridge at Hell Gate" could as well be a ruin as a work in progress. The incomplete (or broken?) arch, the suspended cranes, the distant thicket of buildings make it look like a collapsed monument in rusting steel. A 1919 view of the Cortlandt Street ferry from the Jersey shore uses the interior of the ferry house with its chains and pulleys as a Piranesian vault, a carious, overgrown prison which consumes the Manhattan skyline across the river. Pennell drew the monument to Vittorio Emmanuele in Rome and relished its confrontation of the ruined Forum: new and old imperial cities, both perishable. The Piranesian conviction of the obsolescence of empires and the mortality of their architecture—as against the glib and instant immortality of the art which memorializes them—informs the railway etchings Pennell made in 1919. The association is apt because the concourse of Pennsylvania Station was modeled on the Baths of Caracalla. America's heroic engineers unwittingly predict the death of the structure they're erecting by imitating a ruin.

Riis had employed the camera as a means of indictment and social deliverance. In defiance of his example, it soon learned how to effect a metaphoric mitigation of the city, to confer on it a beauty which may not be there. Alfred Stieglitz returned to New York from Europe in 1890. Offended by the city's ugliness, morosely alone in it, he turned to photography as a recompense. The camera mechanically contrived a union between his suffering subjectivity and an uncaring objectivity. Romanticism had called this the wedding of the mind to nature: baptismal immersion in the one life within us and abroad. It creates the romantic image, for an image is an object to which we have married our subjective longings. Photography formalizes the capture of that elusive image. Stieglitz proclaims an emotional equivalence between himself and the urban incidents he photographs. His camera is an instrument of introversion: "I decided to photograph what was within me." The lens nominates as subjects and elects as symbols objects as defensively isolated as the dejected romantic is from his fellows and as Stieglitz was from New York—a dirigible in an empty sky, a sapling trying to

Joseph Pennell, "Not Naples, but New York" (1921). The view is of the anchorage to the Manhattan Bridge on Cherry Street on the Lower East Side. Picker Art Gallery, Colgate University.

grow on a wet pavement, the trolley-car horses in the 1902 photograph "The Terminal," which Stieglitz envied because they at least had a human being (the driver who is watering and rubbing them down) to care for them. Healingly restoring him to contact with the city, Stieglitz's early New York scenes also romantically reassimilate the city to the nature it denies or (in Stephen Crane's jesting metaphors) parodies. This is why they're concerned with weather—blizzards on Fifth Avenue, the spring showers that lash the sapling in its wire cage, the sleek wet pavement in "Night, New York" (1907). The elements alone are capable of subduing New York and recalling it to membership of nature. The city manufactures its own alternative seasons indoors. Stieglitz defies this insulation by obstinately abiding rain and snow to take the pictures. The electrified city also abolishes the difference between day and night. Stieglitz reverts to a natural order by making it a rule never to work with artificial light.

Photography for Stieglitz is a meditative act, an insight which, as he says, "brings what is not seen to the surface." What's not seen could be defined as the metaphor—an attributed identity, a perceived correspondence, which assists the particular's dilation into the universal; a visual salvation which, for instance, reclaims the Flatiron Building in Stieglitz's winter photograph of 1903. The Flatiron, derisively named after the triangle into which it was squeezed, already had an invidious symbolic tag attached to it. Its title announced its meager utilitarianism, subordinating form to function. One habit of aesthetic critics of New York in this period was to belittle its buildings by associating them with cosmetic or culinary utensils, since appliances daren't aspire to the self-sufficient condition of beauty. Henry James called the skyline a pincushion or a comb with some teeth missing, Huneker likened it to "a mad medley of pepper-boxes perched on cigar boxes" and said the windows of the office blocks on Wall Street resembled waffles. But Ford Madox Ford, who returned to New York in 1906, sensed another meaning in the Flatiron: it symbolized the staid, genteel city's renovation of itself. He professes to find the Flatiron beautiful because to do so is to offend the pieties of old New York. "Very beautiful it used to look," he comments, "towering up, slim and ivory white when you saw it from the Fifth Avenue stage or from on top of a trolley descending Broadway." Two aspects of this description make the Flatiron beautiful in a new and disconcerting way—its carnality ("slim and ivory white" like a slender human body) and its mobility. Ford was in motion when he saw it; Stieglitz saw it as if in motion toward him, advancing "like the bow of a monster ocean-steamer." Its locomotion freed it from the

Alfred Stieglitz, "The Flatiron Building" (1903). The Metropolitan Museum of Art, New York, The Alfred Stieglitz Collection, 1933.

Edward J. Steichen, "The Flatiron Building." (1909). The Metropolitan Museum of Art. Gift of Alfred Stieglitz, 1933.

anchored being of architecture and embarked it on a process of becoming. It was growing into, moving toward, a symbol. Stieglitz had already photographed the meaning Ford discerned in it. He saw the Flatiron as "a picture of the new America that was still in the making." His father called the building hideous, and when he saw the photograph said, "I do not see how you could have produced such a beautiful thing from such an ugly building." His incredulity compliments the empathy of romantic vision: Stieglitz has made it beautiful by his metaphoric way of seeing it. But that vision is vagrant. The wonder that irradiated the structure during that first winter faded for Stieglitz. Later, he admitted, he found it gloomy, no longer beautiful. This sad, puzzled deconversion is an essential stage in the romantic pursuit of the symbol, on which we're granted only a temporary hold. Wordsworth laments the vanishing of an aureole from the earth, Keats can't prevent the nightingale from fluttering off, and Stieglitz after a few years, almost echoing Wordsworth, can't revive within himself "the glory of those many hours, and those many days, when I stood on Fifth Avenue . . . looking at the Flat Iron Building." Because the numinous halo was Stieglitz's revokable gift to the building, it can't fix itself there. Is the photographic imagination therefore only a capacity, like the picturesque, to deceive yourself about the incorrigible reality of things?

Edward Steichen, who came back to New York from Paris in 1902, had a gadget attached to his camera which worked such a metaphoric mitigation: a soft-focus lens. Paul Strand called this an "Impressionistic and Whistlerian" mediation of sight. Strand himself abandoned it in order to accuse the city of a cruel, immitigable geometry. The hard edges and acute angles of the Morgan Guaranty Trust Building in Strand's Wall Street view of 1915 define a mechanical city which is hostile to human purposes. As used by Steichen, the soft-focus lens dims and smooths objects into images. His Brooklyn Bridge (1903) is a dark wedge inset with jewels against a furry gray sky. Structure is befuddled, and the span is pattern, not engineering. His dusky Flatiron (1909) withdraws into the sky, belying its own solidity and angularity, vanishing as we watch. Stieglitz intuits a meaning beneath objects, which he called "the universal seen." Steichen spurs objects to evanesce into that meaning and photographs them as they evolve from matter to spirit. At the George Washington Bridge in 1931 he looked up at one of the towers from beneath, with the cables raying from it to suspend the span. His photograph shows the structure enclosing the sky, because its ambition is to soar into that sky. His is an anti-terrestrial bridge. It recalls his remark about Isadora Duncan posing on the Acropolis and raising her arms in a gesture—like the one made in fine taut steel by the bridge —which seemed to embrace and enfold the sky. Another photographer of New York, A. L. Coburn, valued the camera's ability to record the trajectory or transit of objects in time and through space. His 1912 New York series includes the smeared passage of lights from vehicles which passed during his exposures. When Steichen photographs objects in motion, it's not to demonstrate the camera's technological celerity, its attunement to the haste of modernity, but to speed the object's take-off into image. The fighter planes hurtling from the deck of the U.S.S. *Lexington* in 1943 in a whirl of propellers and shivering wings are spirits taking flight, successors to Steichen's photograph of Thérèse Duncan gyrating on the Acropolis and spinning into a wind nymph. Steichen has to animate buildings before he can photograph them. The Flatiron's mobility symbolized to Ford and Stieglitz its march into the future. Steichen incites a similar mobility, encouraging buildings to spiral out of their stone bodies and diffuse themselves in the air. The Empire State Building baffled him until in 1932, by multiple exposure, he could represent it as a maypole, the transparent imprints of its own form dancing round one another.

Views of the city are statements of dissociation from it. The city is seen from within the subjective stronghold of a room, whose window interposes itself to hold at bay the clamorous objects outside. In Glenn Coleman's painting "The Mirror" (1927) the view through the window —of sordid back streets—is relayed by a looking glass, which shares a cheap dresser with a gin bottle and an ashtray. The urban artist here is an impoverished Lady of Shalott. He sees the city only at second hand. The camera symbolizes this subjective begrudgement of the city's objects: it's a boxy room which looks out on the world; it's sealed in darkness, yet it allows the light in through a briefly opened aperture. Both Steichen and Stieglitz express their qualms about and hopes for New York by photographing it from their studio windows. Steichen's 1925 series from his window on West 40th Street makes urban objects sympathize with his subjective moods. There are, after all, equivalences between the individual and the city, and between the city and nature. In one of these photographs, streetlights explode into stars, and Sixth Avenue becomes galactic; in "Sunday Night on 40th Street," the sliver of artificial light on Broadway, deep down among the cold, blank, moon-lit buildings, is an electric sunrise, proceeding in the opposite direction from the actual dawn, which first catches the peaks of the buildings and only later—if at all—reaches the gouged crevasses of the streets. In "Drizzle on 40th Street" rain smears the light and washes the long straight lines of the buildings into streaky tears. The lachrymose pane, like the soft-focus lens, is a means of sympathetically correlating the inner with the outer. Looking out of the window, Steichen is looking into himself. Steichen had made an earlier series of views from another window, that of his apartment on West 68th Street. Here too the nondescript city outside is ordered by the camera into consonance with what's inside the room and inside Steichen. "Milk Bottles: Spring, New York" (1915) shows the season encroaching on a brick backyard, with trees budding and the milk bottles on the fire escape dazzling in the sun. Another photograph, taken about 1922, looks at some cartons discarded on the fire escape. Steichen called it "Laughing Boxes," and the title is his metaphor. One of the boxes is tilted on its side: Steichen invites us to see in the haphazard litter a jocund dishevelment, as if the boxes had been surprised in some prank. The metaphor enlivens the city, making it grow and sprout in the spring scene and laugh in the picture of the boxes. But not all of these views are so sure of their power to fuse subject and object. In "Sunday Papers" the camera is aimed only at another parodic version of itself. The box which is the camera looks out from the box which is Steichen's room and into another claustrophobic obscure box, a neighbor's apartment across the yard. Here the tenant is housed in the temporary tent of the Sunday paper, his dwelling for the day. It coaxes him away from the reality outside— the empty air well between his room and Steichen's—and interns him. He reads about the world; Steichen, doubly dissociated, photographs him doing so; neither of them is experiencing the world. The city is comprehensible to both only if boxed, by the dark room of the camera or by the paragraphs and pages of newsprint.

Stieglitz occupied various rooms looking out over the city—from 1905 to 1917 at 291 Fifth Avenue, where he established his Photo-Secession Gallery; then on the twenty-ninth floor of the Shelton at 525 Lexington Avenue; after 1929 on the seventeenth floor of 509 Madison Avenue, which he christened "An American Place"—and he took photographs from them all. Each room is an aerie, a shuttered sanctum like the camera itself. From it, the observer inspects and oversees the mercantile aggregations outside. Georgia O'Keeffe, who married Stieglitz in 1924, conducted the same visual assay of the city in painting, with views across the East River from the Shelton. In her survey of the murk of Queens, the smoky, sullen air interferes with sight and the sun's nimbus is smoggily discolored; but O'Keeffe insists on bearing witness. She and Stieglitz are testing themselves against the city, struggling to balance an equation between its indiscriminate physical energies and their own mental superintendence. Looking from his gallery at the skyscrapers he'd been photographing, Stieglitz warned of the need for this equilibrated truce between the kingdom of Mammon outside and his own preserve of aesthetic conscience within: "If what is happening in here cannot stand up against what is out there, then what is in here has no right to exist." On another occasion, of the same view, he said, "I have seen it growing. Is that beauty? I don't know, I don't care. I don't use the word beauty. It is life." Beneath that disavowal is a boast. Beauty may not belong to the skyscrapers; Stieglitz, however, can award it to them. They are blessed with it when the photographer, in collaboration with nature, chooses the time and place to make images of them. The views from the Shelton or An American Place show the buildings sliced across by shadow and sometimes half eliminated by the disposition of light. This is nature's humbling of them and the photographer's means of understanding them: he encapsulates in his arcane box the luminosity of the air.

Stieglitz's photographs progressively and superbly master the city. "From the Rear Window, Gallery '291,' Snowstorm" (1915) looks out on a dismal prospect of backyards. The choice of the rear window intimates a pining introversion. In another image, the same view, also taken in 1915 and at night, contains evidence of life—washing strung out to dry, lamps in uncurtained windows—but no people. The lights in the building immediately across the yard signify tenancy, the possibility of companionship. The office blocks beyond are ablaze, though their light is cheerlessly remote, unreachable and unconsoling, perhaps intended as advertisement, perhaps merely denoting that they're being cleaned. These views are designed by Stieglitz as abashments of the urban dark. With his light-sensitive eye he seeks an answering light elsewhere, which the city occludes. In "From An American Place, Looking North" (1931) a building is under construction opposite Stieglitz's window. At present he can see through the girders. When it's complete, it will block his view. Even from this height, his visual dominion is threatened. Through the black skeleton he looks at the distant white blocks, tall and thin, on East 57th Street. Mirage-like, they share the gleaming silveriness of the clouds above them. From darkness nearby in the right corner, the photograph advances to far-off whiteness at the left. Out of a hole, Stieglitz has a view of infinity, which he can focus but not grasp. "From the Shelton, Looking Northwest" (about 1932) also marches from an immediate darkness at the right to distant brightness at the left, and as the eye travels into the space of the photograph, it forces the shadows to retreat before it. The buildings make way for the sky, and the frame of a tower under construction, ignited by the sun on its steel, seems to catch fire. Stieglitz's vision is prophetically illumining and inflaming the world. Another image in this sequence, "From the Shelton, Looking West" (about 1933), sees New York even more transcendentally. The time of day is dusk. The foreground again is thickly dark, obfuscated by the looming stump of a building. There are some lights

Alfred Stieglitz, "From the Shelton, Looking West, 1933." The Alfred Stieglitz Collection, Museum of Fine Arts, Boston.

below, like gems in a mine, but they don't help, since you can't tell to what they belong. Beyond, however, is the new pinnacle of Rockefeller Center, lit from below, from within, and from behind by the setting sun, which also gilds the clouds. Reading from right to left, the eye advances from black by way of Rockefeller Center's gray to the white of the sky. Its passage is a triumphant ascent toward the heavenly city, hovering there in midair on the other side of Fifth Avenue. When he acquired his first camera, Stieglitz said he felt himself to be lord of the elements. He could, he believed, "work miracles." In these views he makes good that boast, miraculously cowing New York, as a god (or as nature) might, by the sheer and piercing ferocity of his eye.

In 1926 Georgia O'Keeffe painted a series of exterior views of the Shelton, which are tributes to the perceptual power Stieglitz exercised over the city from inside it. Looking at the place which is his lookout and hers too, she sees a skyscraper with a facade of oblong glass eyes. No longer blind, the building has become an ocular eminence. In "Shelton with Sun" the sun burns behind the building and, peeping around the corner, dazes the viewer in a glare freckled with sun spots. The top of the Shelton is obliterated by this smoldering halation. The sun now seems to shine out of the Shelton, and from there it irradiates and fires the city: the burning upper storeys are a camera eye seared in the stone by Stieglitz's power to see through it. If Coleman's "Mirror" or Steichen's "Sunday Papers" transfers to the city Plato's allegory of the cave, proposing that we perceive it only by means of images and reflections, turned away from the dangerous brilliance of the sun, then Stieglitz—in this painting and in his own photographs—is the man who dares to affront that flaming source. Outstaring it, he gazes steadfastly at the truth and becomes himself an emissary of enlightenment. The sun, newly headquartered in the Shelton, actually shines from within Stieglitz.

5

Realism and Beyond

New York, named as a reincarnation of cities elsewhere—first Amsterdam, later York—begins by imagining itself pictorially in an analogy with pre-existing places. J. Monroe Hewlett in 1921 called it "a Venice in the making"; Pennell sees it as a latter-day Rome, subdued to picturesqueness by an anticipated decay; the painters contemporary with him render it as a transatlantic Paris, an impressionist pleasance. Impressionism is about the hedonism of vision. It finds in visual impressions a delight as intense and as transitory as the gratification of appetite. Paris, its capital, is therefore given over, in the paintings of Renoir, Monet, Pissarro, and Seurat, to eating, drinking, and the body's enjoyment of the open air. Childe Hassam and Maurice Prendergast worked in Paris on and off during the 1880s and '90s; William Glackens traveled there in 1912 to buy impressionist pictures for the millionaire physician Albert C. Barnes. Returning to New York, all interpret it as a would-be Paris. New York encourages them to do so. When Hassam came back from Paris in 1889, he took a studio at 95 Fifth Avenue. Stanford White's homage to the Arc de Triomphe in Washington Square was new, and it provoked Hassam—whose first impressionist canvas, in 1887, had shown the Paris gentry mobilizing in their carriages at the Arc de Triomphe for the journey to the Grand Prix at Longchamp—to see the avenue as New York's Champs-Elysées. He painted the arch in spring, shimmering through a haze of pigment like one of Monet's molten cathedrals.

The impressionist city is a picnic site. These painters concentrate on New York's outdoor amenities. Prendergast favors Central Park, where in a 1916 painting his crowded humanity is a herbaceous border blossoming into dots of dazzling color; Glackens in 1912 shows Washington Square as a circus of amiable riot, with children leaning from the tops of buses or tumbling off park fences or crashing their bicycles or racing away from police or parents, and at Christmas represents Madison Square as a giddy havoc of shoppers engaged in sportive contest with the wind, which confiscates their hats; Hassam paints Union Square in spring 1896, its green and budding yellow freshness shining against the dusty red and burning blue asphalt of the streets. Weather can't dispirit this reveling city. In Glackens's Washington Square during March 1912 the rain leaves the pavement a gleaming sheen across which his characters flounce; when Central Park ices over, his people, impressionist devotees of open-air pleasures, skate or sled there. A blizzard is a bombardment of color. The snow in Hassam's "Late Afternoon, Winter, New York" (1900) glows violet and soft blue.

Impressionist New York is an arboretum because flowers are nature's colored and painterly celebration of itself. The foliage in Hassam's "Washington Arch in Spring" emits light and smolders into color. One of Hassam's etchings pays tribute to Flora who, a bouquet in her hand, is the tutelary goddess of this transformation of city into park; in another, titled "New York, 1931," a couple—apparently under Flora's protection—sit on their penthouse terrace at a meal, looking down at the smoky, discolored city but hedged off from it florally by a balustrade of potted plants and a vase of cut flowers on their table. For a street to be included in this vision of the city, it must be an avenue because an avenue is defined by its having been planted. It's a trail through a landscape, not a mere route for traffic. The recovered Arcady of these painters is Fifth Avenue, an Elysian Fields with flags as its foliage. Hassam began a succession of Fifth Avenue paintings, *The Flag Series*, in 1917. The banners that the avenue flaunts in these works are patriotic (it was briefly renamed Avenue of the Allies in 1918) but also horticultural: they look like a vegetative outgrowth on the dour stone of the buildings. The prototype is once more Paris, where in 1910 Hassam had painted the tricolors bedecking the rue Daunou for Bastille Day. The parades he depicts on Fifth Avenue, on 4 July 1916 or on Allies Day in May 1917, are seasonal rites as much as military drills. On Hassam's flag-hung avenue, political demonstrations are floral pageants: impressionist nature on a conquering march through the city. The tradition persists in the Easter parade on the avenue, where a new bonnet is millinery's imitation of a blossom-festooned nature and where people aim to look,

Childe Hassam, "New York, 1931." Collection of The Corcoran Gallery of Art, Washington, D.C. Museum purchase.

for a day, like elegantly ambling flowering trees. Some of the women Prendergast sketched in the Boston Public Garden between 1895 and 1897 seem to be metamorphosing into shrubbery. Their faces are veiled, and their heads sprout in posies of poppies, so they look as if they're carrying vases or flowerpots on their shoulders. Prendergast's frieze of promenading carriages in Central Park in 1903, George Luks's proces-

Maurice Prendergast, "May Day, Central Park" (ca. 1901). Watercolor on paper. 14½ x 21½ inches. Collection of Whitney Museum of American Art. Purchase (and exchange).

sion of the Blue Devils Regiment in 1917 or his Armistice Night painting of 1918 recruit the city to nature's festivity. Glackens in 1905 even located a maypole, symbol of the phallic rite of spring which is impressionism's pastoral cult, in Central Park, and set a crowd of children to romp round it.

Impressionism is inaugurated when, in 1863, Manet's model takes off her clothes to enjoy her lunch on the grass. Realism in American painting commences with another act of divesting. Thomas Eakins's practice of using naked women as models for his anatomy classes at the Pennsylvania Academy caused a scandal. Before he resigned in 1886 Eakins made a last gesture of defiance. In a class of women, to whom he was explaining pelvic structure, he plucked the breechclout from his male model. The uncovery has consequences for the pictorial understanding of the city. John Sloan, who had been a student at the Academy, shows New York in dishabille, its shop windows bulging with corsets and ample brassieres, its inhabitants disheveled in their furnished rooms or sleeping undressed on rooftops during the summer or baring themselves at their windows or cheerily urinating in the gutter or ogling the legs of girls whose skirts flare in the hot drafts on the subway stairs. Realism in the city means exposure of the city's body. Sloan's initial predecessor is the confessional Whitman. Robert Henri, Sloan's mentor, called Whitman an ideal for the art student, since his work was breast-baring autobiography, and art should aspire to tell such unashamed truths. Sloan's New York is lovingly stripped of the defenses in which it's clad and shown to be a body, warmly comforting and carnally needy. O. Henry too had unwrapped the urban body. It may seem, he says of New York in "Between Rounds," cynical on the surface, but "beneath the hard crust of the lobster is found a delectable and luscious food." It suffers small medical crises and surgical incisions: the characters in "The Elusive Tenderloin" sympathetically visit "the cavity that had been drilled in the city's tooth, soon to be filed with the new gold subway." Its aliveness is certified by the hearty and versatile stench it exudes. In "The Marry Month of May" an olfactory cloud of "hot asphalt, underground caverns, gasoline, patchouli, orange peel, sewer gas, Albany grabs, Egyptian cigarettes, mortar and the undried ink on newspapers" drifts across Gramercy Park: the city's body odor. Congestion is the penalty of its corpulence. The hero of "Mammon and the Archer" sees a superflux of traffic cramming itself into the convergence of Broadway, Fifth Avenue, and 23rd Street "as a twenty-six inch maiden fills her twenty-two inch girdle." In the polymorphous, orgiastic democracy of New York, the proximity and entanglement of bodies defeats social distinction. The tenants of the Beersheba Flats in "The City of Dreadful Night" have to sleep in the park during the torrid weather, and "Mrs. Rafferty, that despises the asphalt that a Dago treads on, wakes up in the mornin' with her feet in the bosom of Antonio Spizzinelli."

Sloan, for whom the female nude was—in spite of its physical flagrancy—a symbol of the lofty Platonic spirituality of art, anatomizes New York as a plumply appetizing woman's body, a body like those belonging to the swimmer Annette Kellerman (whom he saw diving at Hammerstein's roof garden) or the eurythmic Isadora (who represented to him "human animal happiness"). From his studio on West 23rd Street he could spy on such women bathing in rooms across the backyard or sunning themselves on the roof, and he would often walk east to the Flatiron, where the impudent air currents between the buildings caused the skirts of passersby to billow around their knees. In adjacent Madison Square he would "soak up a little sunlight," his own urban body luxuriantly roasting itself. For him, artistic creation was cognate with the body's alimenting of itself. In February 1909 he ate at a Chinese restaurant, where he saw a girl with a red feathered hat playing with the

John Sloan, "Looking Out on Washington Square" (1933). Courtesy Kraushaar Galleries, New York.

resident overfed cat. He painted the scene, then the next month returned "for my dinner to refresh my memory of the place": fueling the body, at the same time he resuscitates the pictorial memory. Sloan jokingly identifies art with appetite in the etching "A Thirst for Art." A gaggle of socialites gossips and drinks martinis at a gallery opening. No one looks at the paintings, which have anyway been obscured by the crush. But though they ignore the art, they're faithful—in their heedless drinking—to the physical craving which created it. Painting can also be an intimate and soothing bodily titillation. In one of Sloan's subway etchings, a girl, baring a solid length of leg, sits reading a book. Behind her an advertisement smirkingly recommends "Rub with Sloan's liniment." Pigment becomes an ointment applied to the body's tenderest and most secretive parts. The lights that rake the urban night sky are engaged, in Sloan's perception, in an adventure of comic sensual excitation. In 1906 he noticed "the searchlight from Madison Square Garden scratching the belly of the sky and tickling the buildings." Like the impressionists, he hunts through the city for anecdotes of physical joy and dalliance: for instance, watching some girls on swings in Stuyvesant Square who are themselves being ogled at by a fat man. The impressionist city renders sex pastoral, absorbing it into the budding fecundity of nature; the streets of Sloan's New York pulse, as he says in his journal, with "warm blood and a feeling of animal love," a frank biological arousal symbolized by the throbbing fountain in Madison Square, which fascinated Sloan with its eruptive, ejaculatory spurts.

He and his colleagues of the Ashcan school make New York an arena for the expending of physical energy. Everett Shinn paints revue girls flirting over the footlights, George Bellows naked boys hurling themselves into the river, Luks wrestlers grappling in sweaty combat, Glackens a boxing match or the dispersal of excess animal spirits at a roller-skating rink. Glackens's "Curb Exchange" (1907–10) monitors the city's financial health by studying the flailing, thrashing exuberance of the urban body. His sketch shows the trading of securities on the street outside the Stock Exchange. Dealers argue, touts cry their wares through loud hailers, a mounted policeman parts the crowd. In this rowdy open-air economy, monetary transactions are as sportive and physically skillful as boxing or roller-skating. Luks's *New York Nights* series chronicles life in the city as a succession of binges. The sequence ends with a soused man-about-town being ejected from Carey's Hole-in-the-Wall onto the pavement of 13th Street. Luks himself was as much an urban bravo as his character here: a brawling, disputatious drunk, he turned up dead on Sixth Avenue in 1933.

If realism in New York means denudation, it also connotes besmirchment. The city's is a grubby, often odorous body. Sloan made a logical copula between the two conditions in his remark about J. B. Yeats at his 29th Street boardinghouse: "his vest is slightly spotted; he is real." Realism enables him to tolerate, even to delight in, the physical soiling of New York. Walking on Ninth Avenue with Jerome Myers in 1909, he admires children playing in the mucky snow. The following year, he goes for a walk with Yeats on the pier from which rubbish is shipped, watching the barges being loaded with the offal the city has evacuated. Among the impressionist pleasures of Washington Square—"shade of trees, heat of sun"—he lists the possibility of smelling the humid city's "odors of human life and sweat." His own bohemian youth is synonymous with dirty linen: "I think of the days when Shinn's underclothes were unspeakable." The city conscientiously launders itself (Shinn painted a laundress in a backyard in 1903), but its aspiration to cleanliness is hindered by those for whom small clothes are confidential physical witnesses. Sloan etched a scene he'd observed in 1921 from his studio on West 4th Street, "a connoisseur of woolen underwear" stealing some choice items from a washing line on the roof. The woman to whom the undies belonged resents the theft, in the imagery of Sloan's corporeal city, as a physical extraction. She sees "these gashes on her line like missing teeth." Sloan himself describes creativity, using the same image, as physical travail. When trying to illustrate Wilkie Collins's *The Moonstone* in 1908, he says it's like pulling teeth.

Sloan's subway etching sees paint as a sensual lubricant. But it's also dirt. The painter is a licensed mess-maker. "I can paint," Luks bragged, "with a shoestring dipped in lard!" Sloan can enjoy the soiled and stained reality of New York because his own profession contributes to that festal grime. When writing his diary, he takes pleasure in his new fountain pen "which is making these marks" and sullying the paper. With the same comically scatological thrill, he records having taken delivery of an expressed box of printing ink. Part of Robert Henri's teaching was a messy and incontinent liberation of pigment. His students were taught to be unashamed of the filth they dabbled in, just as they were unembarrassed by urban ugliness. At the New York School of Art on West 57th Street they flung the leftovers from their palettes at a wall, which soon became impasted with an iridescent murk. When Henri established his own school uptown, his alumnus Stuart Davis remembers the same mudlarking: "paint was all over the place," not least on the smocks of the students. Sloan concedes the alliance between paint and dirt when, on a walk through the East Side slums in 1906, he comments that the "grimy and greasy door frames" of the tenements look "as though huge hogs covered with filth had worn the paint away and replaced it with matted dirt." Here paint and dirt compete, but they're allies all the same. Paint is the accretion of sentiment, the varnishing of age and affection; dirt too testifies to use, wear, long familiarity. Dirt, like the spot on Yeats's vest, vouches for the reality of things, as paint is trying to do. One of Sloan's pictures—his scrubwoman in the Astor Library in 1910—shows the city being scoured and cleaned. Yet the artist undoes the woman's labor by muddying the scene all over again in paint. The previous year he had enjoyed the mishaps of a salesman who was demonstrating a "One Minute Washing Fluid" in the Sloan kitchen. The detergent is supposed to cleanse, but the salesman makes more mess in trying it out than there was to clean up. His wife is irritated, Sloan himself comically gratified. He takes pleasure in the city's dirty weather, its dust storms and its slushy snow, just as he salivates over the viscid food he eats at Coney Island in 1906 ("popcorn and peanuts, frankfurters and roast beef sandwiches") and admires the bleary lights which stain the sky there.

Sloan assumes O. Henry's mission of individuating the crowd and saluting its members as his brothers. Walking up Broadway, he avows that "each face [is] beautiful and individual," and on another promenade with his wife he restores individuality of character to the avenues which have been rendered uniform by their numerical naming, differentiating unscrupulous Sixth ("tenderloin, fast") from demure Eighth ("neat lower class, honest") and piteous Third ("poor, foreign"). Sometimes the fraternal benediction requires an effort of forebearance. Among the mob at Coney Island, where Blinker in "Brickdust Row" achieves his generous epiphany, Sloan notes that "the crowds near kill you in the rushes for the trains. . . . One must strive for good nature." In 1908 he sets out on a hopeful religious quest in the streets, but is disappointed. He has been asked by a newspaper to provide a drawing of the head of Christ. He goes for a walk, scrutinizing "the face of each Jew I met . . . to see some Christlike traits," searching for divinity in the crowd. He finds no one who qualifies for the role. And increasingly his politics persuaded him not to trust in this messianic retrieval of individuals from the crowd but to unionize the disparate crowd into a rallied mass. Sloan, who attended socialist meetings in Union Square or at the Cooper Union, refers to Christ as a fellow party-member. It's no longer the individual who is sought out in order to be blessed, but all men who must, organized into a collectivity, be saved. Sloan marveled at the "power of a large crowd" to command change and to provoke retaliation from police and soldiers. On strike, the holidaying, untamable, boisterous citizenry of his early New York scenes grows more concentrated and more violently determined. "Six O'Clock, Winter" (1912) is somberly toned. An El train flares against a lurid sky, a compressed and perhaps oppressed mob surges beneath its tracks. On the day Sloan began the painting he had twice been involved in the panic of an agitating mass, first at Grand Central, where some socialists from the west had missed their train and blamed a capitalist plot, then at the Labor Temple. The same week, his wife obtained a police permit to lead a parade of the children of striking workers down Fifth Avenue. The procession, for Prendergast or Hassam a token of order and plenty, is now a political mobilization. At the same time the ashcan, which had been the emblematic trophy of the realists who scavenge among and rejoice in the city's refuse, undergoes conscription. Sloan the socialist assails it as a totem of authoritarian restriction and a vehicle of anarchist revolt. He points out that "the waste cans on Fifth Avenue are marked 'It's against the law to throw litter into the streets—use this can,' " and imagines "the Anarchist joy in plunging into the can and scattering the waste over the avenue!" He is predicting the artistic affronts of a later and more desperate period. André Breton in 1930 defined a surrealist act as the commission of gratuitous violence: blindly firing a pistol into a crowd on the street. Dali staged a succession of such comic outrages in New York: for instance, designing a window display for Bonwit Teller that capsized and flooded the pavement, provoking the police to arrest him. Sloan's impish pleasure in the city's uninhibited disorder, which makes him dream of overturning those waste cans, will turn when the surrealists arrive into a calculated assault from beneath on the normality and reality which the official city purports to uphold.

Meanwhile, Sloan's celebration of the physical democracy of New York—its undressing of its inhabitants and of its own lusty, greedy urban body—persists in the work of Reginald Marsh. But a change has already occurred. The city's self-exposure is less flirtatious and skittish than it was when the breezes round the Flatiron helped Sloan to study female discomposure. In the mechanical metropolis, the body is cordoned off from exhibition and discloses itself either tawdrily at burlesque shows or in a wrestling adipose mass on the beach at Coney Island; and when they are unclad, the urban bodies in the work of Marsh are grossly overdeveloped. The modern city so discourages our physical existence that improving on your body becomes a fanatical specialism, and once you have labored to perfect it, you're trapped—like Marsh's plumply gyrating stripteasers or his muscle-bound bathers—inside it. At both the burlesque shows and Coney Island, Marsh had been anticipated by Sloan. In 1908 Sloan went to a "leg show," but considered it a salacious parody of life classes, like those of Eakins which inaugurated realism: "a shocking kind of imitation nude." The girls were still coyly attired in tights, and Sloan thought that "straight naked would be better and more decent." Nakedness, like that of Sloan's unselfconscious New Yorkers stripping in their rooms, has no shame; nudity is a teasing self-advertisement. At Coney Island too the body discloses itself at the cost of a licentious vulgarization. Spectators glimpse underwear on the slippery slides at Luna Park with "a roar of natural 'vulgar' mirth," and on the beach the women look "like soft sandstone sculptures, full of the real 'vulgar' human life." Those inverted commas provoke us to suspect that realism is from now on going to mean a heroically concupiscent vulgarity. So it is with Marsh, who considered Coney Island an alfresco life class and carried anatomy textbooks with him to the beach, "where a million near naked bodies could be seen at once, a phenomenon unparalleled in history." Yet at Coney Island the reverence for the body taught by Eakins, Henri, and Sloan has changed to voyeurism. Coney Island is a problem for interpreters of the city because it can be a lesson in the glad democracy of human fates—as it is for Blinker—or in their individual insignificance. It aggravates the psychological problem of the city: are we akin to our neighbors, or do we dissever ourselves from them in gloating at them? Two photographs of the beach argue the latter. In 1940, Weegee watched a rescue there. A swimmer has been hauled from the water to be given oxygen. The spectators who surround his body may have been attracted by commiseration, or by a ghoulish glee. Their collective emotion remains ambiguous. For one girl among them, though, the scene has already composed itself into a photograph, of which she, rather than the victim, is the center. Spotting Weegee, she stares back at him with a sly grin. There may be, as Marsh asserted, a million bodies on the beach, but none of them is much concerned about any of the others. The scowling crowd photographed by Weegee is not the extended family which Blinker hails. When Margaret Bourke-White was taking photographs from a helicopter for a 1952 *Life* picture-essay, she flew over Coney Island just as another rescue was occurring. From the air, she sees a knot of helpers clustered round the girl they're reviving. Beyond this solicitous or perhaps merely curious core are the concentric rings of onlookers, who gradually thin out across the expanse of the beach. In a bottom corner of the print, bathers are wading out of the water, and for them the meaning of the scene lies not in the small tragedy on the sand but in the exciting presence of a helicopter with a photographer aboard above them. They wave at it delightedly. If you read Bourke-White's photograph centrifugally, all movement and all emotion on the beach converge on the victim in sympathetic unison; if you read it centripetally, everything is rotating away from that point, and the spectators aren't advancing across the beach but being spun back from there into their own indifference until at the fringes the most intense emotion is the pleasure of those bathers in seeing a helicopter and, like Weegee's girl, in having their photograph taken.

Despite its devaluing of the individual and its vulgarizing of the mass, Coney Island was necessary to Marsh because realism continues to demand denudation. He said he'd rather paint an old suit of clothes than a new one because things used and frayed have "character, reality is exposed and not disguised." The wealthy, he thought, "spend money to disguise themselves." These pudic pretences force the realist to go slumming in quest of his subject matter, as Marsh did through the dumps and docks of New York or (when Mayor La Guardia drove the burlesque shows out of town) the cheap theaters of Union City in New Jersey. As reality goes into hiding in the prudish city, realism becomes an illicit art. Sometimes Marsh was denied permission to sketch in the burlesque houses, so he taught himself to scribble on paper concealed in his pocket. Marsh worships the body and trusts, as Sloan did, its humorous contented calm. A watercolor of 1944, looking out from his studio window on Union Square at S. Klein's "Fat Men's Shop," derives a political reassurance from the body's sated placidity. The store's banner depicts a leering gourmand, his naked belly and thighs distending his swimming trunks. Underneath is printed his Falstaffian philosophy of pastoral nonaggression: "If everybody was fat there would be no war." But the only bodies the city can supply Marsh with are, unlike those girls of Sloan who bathe near open windows or lift their skirts to leap over fire hydrants, bulbous and bovine. Or else dead. Sloan understood in advance the miscegenation of the urban body, predicting its mechanization, when in 1908 he paused to watch a crowd on Sixth Avenue admiring a dummy in a shop window. The mannequin sported a sheath gown slit to the knee. Through the slit, however, she extended a wooden leg. For Marsh, the urban body has undergone a further humiliation and presents itself as a cadaver. As part of his anatomical researches, he dissected corpses at the Cornell Medical School in New York.

Marsh's city compounds bodies, packing them together or piling them in orgiastic heaps. On the beach at Coney Island, girls climb on the shoulders of their men to make toppling human pyramids; on the rides at Luna Park, bodies are compounded, glued together in ersatz copulation on the horses for the Steeplechase (a girl mounts one of the wooden horses and a sailor straddles her as if mounted on her) or spilling down a chute, tumbling and entwined, so you can no longer tell whose limbs belong to whom; at dance marathons, those hillocky bodies, fatigued by their remorseless pleasuring, sag in one another's arms. The city's sensual promise is here the loss of self. Merged in these frenzied mobs, you are joined to the palpitating, elephantine body of desire which is the city, plugged into the many-orificed polymorph. The economy of Marsh's New York exists to cater to this exigent, opulent body. His streets are loud with advertisements for tattoos, permanent waves, and cosmetic aids; the wax models in the window of the "Hudson Bay Fur Company" (1932) strut in their capes as lewdly as the burlesque queens; the cinema in "Twenty Cent Movie" (1936) is a carnal circus, vending "Dangerous Curves" and "Joys of the Flesh" or offering "Human Emotions Stripped Bare." Even the subway is a tunnel of love. Traveling on it inducts you into the city's erotic underground. Because the subway is New York's id it's able, in Marsh's "Why Not Use the 'L'?" (1930), to trump the competing elevated railway. The subway carriage in this painting contains an ad for the El: "The subway is fast—Certainly! But the Open Air Elevated gets you there quickly, too—and with more comfort." But Marsh outwits this appeal by implying that the El, being above ground, is less duskily sexy, for on the floor of the carriage lies a discarded paper deciphering the subterranean life of the city, asking if the sex urge explains the strange disappearance of a judge. The judicious superego has capitulated to the id. The same upsurgence from the nether regions, whistling through a vent, sends a screaming girl's skirts ballooning in "Air Hole at Coney Island" (1938), as if the city were lecherously panting under the streets.

In coaxing the city to abandon itself to the pleasure principle, Marsh changes from a realist to a mythologist, for whom New York is a romping bacchanal, a feast of blowsy, corpulent, promiscuous gods. He acknowledged as his predecessors not Sloan but Michelangelo and Rubens, of whose saturnalian compositions he was reminded by the milling, churning bodies at Coney Island. Marsh was ambitious to paint murals, reinterpreting the city's public spaces as idylls of surfeit and athletic sensuality. His Coney Island with its wrestling musclemen is a tribute to Michelangelo's bathing soldiers; his Luna Park with its barrage of indiscriminate bodies is an orgiastic heaven based on the hell of Michelangelo's Last Judgment; his nocturnal Central Park in a painting of 1932, with patrolling sailors and tempting girls trailing off to couple in leafy alcoves, is a scene of unprotesting ravishment that corrects Rubens's "Abduction of the Daughters of Leucippus." The following year, Paul Cadmus located a similar bacchanal in Riverside Park, where he painted sailors on shore leave gamboling, among a litter of emptied bottles and circumcised, consumed bananas, with a gaggle of floozies. A girl strains playfully away from the two men who grip her, adopting the posture of one of the Rubens daughters—except that she's not resisting ravishment, only pretending to.

The developed body is for Marsh a prodigy which can no longer realistically belong to an ordinary citizen. It must be the prerogative of

Reginald Marsh, "Coney Island Beach" (1934). Yale University Art Gallery. Gift of Mrs. Reginald Marsh.

a pagan god. The sideshows at Luna Park advertise such gods, who perform mythic marvels. "Smoko the Human Volcano" in Marsh's 1933 painting guzzles flaming torches, his heroism a matter of redoubtable digestion. Cadmus homosexually reinterprets this mythology of pumped muscle and bulging thews. Instead of the burlesque show, he frequented the locker room at the West Side YMCA on 63rd Street and the changing sheds at Jones Beach where, in 1933 and 1935, he watched the boisterous divinities of his agora at play. Those at the Y soap and deodorize their toned-up bodies, erotically fraternizing, as the conventions of that room allow them to do, without suspicion; those at Jones Beach, with the grins of proletarian satyrs, flick each other with wet towels. Many of Marsh's pictures show these rude divinities descending onto New York, falling from the sky. The trapezists in the

1936 etching "Flying Concellos" are brawny Michelangelesque deities
somersaulting from their aerial swings. Cadmus in 1935 painted one
such acrobatic god being prepared for flight. The interest of his work,
"Gilding the Acrobats," is that the qualification for aerial majesty is
pictorial: the naked flier is being smeared with golden paint before he
begins his act. Cadmus, like the black boy toiling at the acrobat's taut
leg with his brush, applies paint as a mystic sheen which turns a man
into an idol. In Marsh's "Naked over New York" (1938) a skein of
torsos unravels into the Hudson, with a liner passing and the skyscrapers on parade. The bodies might be boys diving; they might just
as well be gods thunderously alighting. Another god arrives precipi-
tately in the 1940 watercolor "Prometheus in Rockefeller Center," and
is greeted by an idolatrous crowd: the gilded bringer of fire, having
leaped perhaps from the top of the skyscraper above (which is as
hubristic as he), lands in the ice rink, and the pirouetting skaters dance
for joy on their blades or abase themselves in adoring, humbled heaps.
Marsh was commissioned in 1937 to paint a set of murals in the rotunda
of the Custom House at the Battery. The panels narrate the arrival of
a liner in the port of New York. Their concern, however, is not the
delivery of freight but the unloading or unveiling of some semi-divine
and also concupiscent cargo. As the liner docks, Garbo poses on deck
for the flashbulbs of the newsmen, who acclaim a celebrity as a latter-
day divinity, while a publicist behind a funnel attends to the sacra-
mental trappings of the occasion by releasing a pair of doves.

One line of influence connects Sloan with Marsh, as painters of New
York's corporeal flagrancy. Between them, the city's body has grown
coarser and more florid, its physique fitter for Marsh's welterweight
Olympians than for Sloan's averagely sensual humans. Sloan titled a
1915 etching of a soused harridan arraigned by the police "Mars and
Bacchante." The caption is for him a joke; for Marsh—whose Bowery
belles are maenads with pendulous breasts and crimson mouths and
whose navvies are gods of war—it would have been a hyperbolic truth.
Sloan's realism evolves into socialism. The row of laughing girls, linked
arm in arm, of his etching "Return from Toil" (1915) was adapted into
a cover design for the radical magazine *The Masses*. The entwining of
bodies which constitutes a mass for Sloan also, in Marsh, leads beyond
realism toward mythology. His crowds are bacchic herds, conglomerated
not by politics but by a maddening and heaven-sent ecstasy. Another
line of influence, which also traces the gradual renouncing of realism
in the depiction of New York, runs from Sloan to a very different
descendant, Edward Hopper. Again, between them, a change has over-

taken New York. Much as Hopper admired Sloan, his city can't be won over by Sloan's solicitude. Alienated from the city, convinced of its unknowability, Hopper abstracts it.

The painter's surest way of knowing his fellow citizens is to spy on them. Marsh does so without compunction, watching the city's over-ripe nymphs bare themselves to sunbathe on smutty rooftops. His subjects don't resent his prurience and, on the BMT platform at 14th Street or under the marquee in "Twenty Cent Movie," they return his gaze with an equal frankness. But Sloan worries about the ethics of the spying in which his profession requires him to engage. In 1911 he and some tittering guests watched as his neighbors, knowing they were being observed and exhibitionistically consenting, stripped in the heat. Sloan had qualms. When the spying is done so blatantly, it encourages those you're looking at to perform for you, rather than behaving as if bereft—along with their clothes—of self-consciousness. Hence his disapproval of the burlesque. He was offended as well when, in his new studio on West 4th Street, some Italians salaciously bored holes through the wall to peek at the artist closeted with his models. Sloan's looking is a speculative sympathy, a guessing fascination with the lives of others, like the couple he observes across the backyards on West 24th Street. The woman has bleached hair, the man lacks a hand. "I have rather fancied," Sloan records, "the notion that he is something of an outlaw." Across the gap of those backyards he extends an anguished commiseration. In June 1906 he watches a baby die in a neighboring room and is as helplessly concerned as the men who can only clumsily force a drink on the distraught mother. Often his glances, like those of Marsh, are reciprocated. On West 26th Street he sees "eyes between the slats of shutters" and hears soft voices inviting him. Hopper too looks in through windows, and what he sees are people, enclosed in suffocating rooms, looking piningly out at the city; but his gaze and theirs never interconnect. He commented that his "East Side Interior" (1922) derives from "memories of glimpses of rooms seen from the streets in the eastside in my walks." The woman he has painted, sewing in her room, is as much a victim of isolation as the voyeuristic artist, who in overseeing the lives of others no longer fancifully participates in those lives as Sloan did but makes do with an urban substitute for human relationship. Hopper denies any affinity between himself and the subject, either sensual or political (which were Sloan's two modes of empathizing with his fellows). "No implication," he says, "was intended with any ideology concerning the poor and oppressed." He is as little interested in the woman as she would be in him, a casual

John Sloan, "Night Windows" (1910). Etching: 100 proofs. 5⅛ x 6 13/16 inches (composition). Collection of Whitney Museum of American Art.

passerby in the street. It's this austere denial that gives Hopper's New York its desolate formal beauty. Because he is abstracted from it, he must represent it abstractly.

Abstraction is the failure of empathy. Hopper looks at the city and sees only a pattern of planes and startling angles. People disconsolately accept their placement in the composition because, sweltering in their rooms or moping behind the counter of an all-night diner, they have nothing else to do. Though the people Sloan watches may be alone, they're never solitary. Out of his back window he sees a boy making faces at himself in a mirror and notes it down as a possible subject for a picture. If you're left alone, as the boy is, you cheer up yourself by becoming an amusing stranger to yourself in the mirror, relying on it to supply you with company. A boy who poses for Sloan tries to paint down an unruly sprig of hair which Sloan has made to stand up: he plays with his own image as if it were a companion. Hopper's listless creatures have no such recourse. Sloan suffered occasionally from the disconnection—interpreting the city and its human contents as mere flat appearance—that begets abstraction. During the Easter parade on Fifth Avenue in 1907 he feels himself to be wryly disengaged from these "very funny humans. I didn't feel at all one of them, just then." But he's shamed by his detachment, and repents when he doesn't give to a bum who begs from him.

The view out the window is, for the romantics, a visionary expectancy. Keats's magic casements open onto fairy lands. Stieglitz commanded New York by looking at its mercantile skyscrapers from the Shelton, subjugating them both to nature and to his own imperious perception. The romantic windows also open inward. Through them we look at what lies behind, not before, the eye. André Breton said that a surrealist painting is a window onto an inner landscape. This is true even if the view is of other windows. Paul Outerbridge's New York photograph "Night Windows" (1923) watches the lighted rectangles which announce the presence of his neighbors across the way. In the apparently empty city, they're heartening beacons to the photographer, whose contact with the outside is usually mediated by his window and by the camera's supplementary pane. Windows are the eyes of buildings, the outlets of consciousness. If you can see in through them, you live in a city of commonality. The consolation of the young Wallace Stevens in New York was the companionship—as he wrote to his future wife—of "strange yet friendly windows burning over the roofs." Perhaps because of this conviction that the city is a confraternity of minds, each of which illuminates a window with a sign of its sentience, he was outraged to read in 1906 an assertion by a fatuous Englishman that there were "300,000 inhabited, windowless rooms" in New York. A room without a window is a life denied consciousness of itself and contact with others. Or a life which has abstractly declared itself to be inscrutable. Thus in June 1900 Stevens describes "tall office buildings closed up for the night" with drawn curtains, so that "the faces of the buildings looked hard and cruel and lifeless." The windows of abstract New York are blinded eyes, like those of Paul Strand's Morgan Guaranty, which he felt to be "rather sinister" in their lidded blankness, or the black holes of windows, chimneys, and of a plunging air well in his 1924 New York photograph "The Court," where instead of having its gaze returned the eye is impeded by a succession of lightless, unseeable chasms. Hopper's city also blocks off the exterior space of fantasy and freedom. "From My Window" (1915–18) shows only mean rooftops, fire escapes, and untenanted windows. The most that can be hoped for from outside is a cooling breeze to make one's imprisonment more bearable, as in "Evening Wind" (1921). A traveling view is equally unavail-

Edward Hopper, "Night Windows" (1928). Oil on canvas. 29 x 34 inches. Collection, The Museum of Modern Art, New York. Gift of John Hay Whitney.

ing. The girl on the El in "House Tops" (1921) gazes at a procession of chimney pots, but her motive is boredom, not curiosity or yearning. Sloan's subway, like Marsh's, is a place of cozy libidinal intimacy. Hopper's El is ungregarious. The couple in "Night on the El Train" (1918) have turned away, twisting awkwardly together in their desire to guard themselves from observation. Hopper likes the El stations because they abstractly dislocate the city: the couple in "The El Station" (1919–23) stand in midair on an empty platform against a row of featureless windows. New Yorkers carry their solitude around with them and employ it as their protection, which is why it's improper—tantamount almost to trespassing—to read the newspaper over your neighbor's shoulder in the subway. Hopper's people make the park too a replica of the solitary confinement of their rooms. The man in "Night in the Park" (1921) has gone there to read his paper, his back turned to us, under a lamp.

Abstraction, entering the city, evacuates and disassembles it. Its people are sent into retreat, its buildings are flattened or else sliced in half. It becomes beautiful by being rendered humanly unintelligible and uninhabitable. In Paul Outerbridge's photograph "Stores for Rent" (1923) the city has emptied itself in deference to abstraction. The shop fronts are identical, colleagues in empty-headed vacancy, windows which resemble moronic faces harboring a nullity behind their eyes. Hopper's work depicts urban alienation, and also creates it. For us, as for the people in his paintings, the city is a disorienting visual puzzle. Aerial perspectives cantilever bare rooms in a bleak sky, as in "Office in a Small City" (1953); or elide architecture, propping up unanchored arrays of water tanks, chimney pots, and cornices with no buildings to belong to, as in "Skyline, Near Washington Square" (1926); or see things from such a steep height, as in "Night Shadows" (1921), that faces are obscured and objects supplanted by the shadows they cast. Hopper's compositions contrive to diminish or efface human beings, as the city does. Either they're seen walking out of the picture, aware that it has no place for them—as is the man at the end of the platform in "Manhattan Bridge Loop" (1928)—or else they're painted out by Hopper. He at first positioned a figure in one of the store-front windows in "Early Sunday Morning" (1930) but then canceled the intruder, leaving only a depopulated façade, as flimsily provisional as a stage set. Hopper's fondness for painting street corners also steals from his architecture its bodily third dimension. The "House with Bay Window" (1925) exists only as a jutting bay which seems to have overlapped into a painting where it has no right to be, for Hopper's concern is the expanse of pavement, an inhospitable prairie across which two bent pioneers are trekking, psychologically miles away from the house. The pavement is white, the figures black. On this tonal desert the house's sliver of red imprints itself as an intrusion, not a reassurance. The saloon in "New York Corner" (1913) is also depleted by its situation. None of the black-coated, slouching passersby enter (unlike Sloan's roisterers, lured into a Greenwich Village cellar called "Bandit's Cave," which served alcoholic teas during prohibition). How could they? The funeral black gaps of the door and the windows announce that there's nothing behind the comfortless surface. A Hopper interior is never a shelter. Seeing into his rooms, you see through them, as with that glass box which contains, as if in a cage or an aquarium, his "Nighthawks." No blinds mask the scenes of depression or sexual discontent he looks in on because the emotional lives of his people are as unfurnished as their rooms or the streets they frequent in the small hours.

Hopper abstractly resists the anecdotal temptation, which would house these characters—even if only temporarily—in a narrative. "Office at Night" (1940), suggested by a ride on the El, has a physically lavish secretary working late with her preoccupied boss. Hopper called the woman Shirley and nicknamed the painting "Confidentially Yours," but he excited the suspicion of a plot only to censor it. Just as he had denied an ideological purpose in "East Side Interior," so here he hoped that "the picture . . . will not tell any obvious anecdote, for none was intended." The painter, shuttled past on the El, can't wait for a narrative to ensue. Nor do his people have stories to tell about themselves. They're seen waiting for something to happen—like the pasty nude keeping vigil at the window in "Eleven A.M." (1926) or the theater patrons in "Two on the Aisle" (1927), settling themselves into the otherwise empty stalls and studying the program of a nonexistent, putative show—though they know it never will. The moment of time in which the painting detains them is for them an eternity of inertia. This is why Hopper likes Sunday in the city: it's a term of compulsory inoccupation. The man in "Sunday" (1926) spends it on the sidewalk, sullenly gripping a cigar between his lips. Rather than anecdotally pursuing the people who stroll across his canvases, Hopper snubs or strands them. The nurse with the baby carriage in "New York Pavements" (1924) has her bottom half amputated and is further rebuffed by the title, which declares that the subject is the pavement, not the stray passage of a human across it. The wind lifts her cape and ruffles a curtain in the house; this evidence of motion and anecdotal happening is contradicted by the imperturbability and indifference of stone (the house front) and cement (the pavement), which will outlast the advening of both the nurse and the breeze. Sloan's interest would have been in the sudden improvised encounter between character and building. When the new cathedral opened on Fifth Avenue, he was fascinated to see a nurse superstitiously hold a parasol over her charge's pram as they passed the central door. She thus enabled the infant, which couldn't doff its hat, to make obeisance to the building.

In opposition to anecdote and to the novelistic extrapolation of lives, Hopper espouses the theater with its frail unrealities. Robert Henri urged Hopper to go to plays, hoping he would find in the performances that raw, passionate liveliness which, in Henri's view, thrilled through the city. Instead, the theater is for Hopper another venue of wistful absence. His people are characters in search of a play, either to watch or to act in. No such transforming fiction is vouchsafed them. He paints the auditorium either before the play begins or during intermission, when the salving illusion is in abeyance, or—as in "The Circle Theatre"

(1936)—he paints the theater from outside and behind, the drab industrial package for a mass-produced magic, a dark imprisoning box inside which people imagine they're escaping. Marsh's hoydens use the cinema as a model for their own sensual self-projection. The woman positioned beneath the poster of Claudette Colbert as De Mille's Cleopatra in "Paramount Pictures" (1934) has based herself on the serpentine queen and is practicing her wiles on passersby. In Hopper's "New York Movie" (1939) the illusion isn't a preparation for sexual combat but a sad refuge from it. Hopper segregates the cinema vertically, cordoning off to the left a solitary couple divided from each other by their individual concentration on the flickering blue screen (which has been shifted out of the corner of the picture), and to the right, pensively stationed by the stairs which lead back up to the daylight world, a bored usherette, for whom the shadowy half-life of fantasy is no longer enticing, since it's so drearily familiar. The theater is a metaphor for Hopper's city because it renders experience unreal, abstracts you from yourself. Dreading the vulnerability of self-exposure, we all devise protective false fronts (like those apparently paper-thin Hopper buildings) and wear them on the street as a defense against the crowd's assault. The woman in the window of "New York Office" (1962) poses for the sidewalk as if the plate glass were a proscenium. But no one appreciates her performance, and the utilitarian cavern which is her theater remains a notional and merely conceptual cube, not a personal habitat. Encroaching unreality eventually unmoors and abstracts Hopper's rooms, which become illusory cartons containing nothing but sunlight and opening—as do the astonishing "Rooms by the Sea" (1951)—onto an improbable watery nothing.

The motive of Hopper's abstraction is fear of and withdrawal from the city, a solemn refusal to represent it. Because his New York is less a place than an idea or perhaps a neurosis, his most alarming image of it is one in which the city doesn't need to appear. This is "Approaching a City" (1946). A railway tunnel drags the viewer (there is no train) into an underground obliteration beyond the edge of the picture. The unseen destination of the line is the most ominous of all Hopper's absences. Above the wall of the embankment, a dull-visaged row of factories and apartment houses witnesses the extinction. No city is specified, though Hopper may have been recalling another fearful tunnel, an underpass in Central Park. In his "Bridle Path" (1939), the park's granite escarpments divide it from the street and maroon three fashionable equestrians in a crevasse. Ahead of them a tunnel dips under the roadway. The arch is black, and one of the horses rears away from it in

Edward Hopper, "Approaching a City" (1946). The Phillips Collection, Washington.

panic. Hopper said that he meant the railway aperture to suggest the "interest, curiosity, fear" of arrival in an unknown city. More than this, the cavity, like the one on the bridle path, evokes the urban terror of reduction to nonentity. The tunnel to an invisible city depicts that city as an area of self-extermination, a subway to nowhere or to the ultimate estrangement and abstraction of death.

Over this change from a realistic, abundant, and fleshly New York to a sinisterly unnamed and unrepresented place, Whitman still presides. He first of all links Sloan with Marsh. In his journal during May 1909 Sloan noted, "Read some of Whitman's 'Song of Myself.' Then out for a walk into the sunshine," and the juxtaposition makes it seem that Whitman, the sponsor of urban intrepidity, prompted the walk. The following May Sloan walked over the Brooklyn Bridge for the first time, thinking as he did so of "Crossing Brooklyn Ferry," then wandered in Brooklyn, "which was the town Whitman knew so well." Sloan adopted Whitman as a traveling companion on the open urban road;

Edward Hopper, "Bridle Path" (1939). Oil on canvas. 28⅜ x 42⅛ inches (72.1 x 107.0 cm.). San Francisco Museum of Modern Art. Anonymous gift.

Marsh made him a tutelary deity of his carnally democratic New York. In "Coney Island Beach" (1951) he sat Whitman among the mob on the sand. Whitman described Coney Island as "a long, bare, unfrequented shore," a romantic solitude owned by him, into which his oratorical ego could dilate: he delighted to "declaim Homer or Shakespeare to the surf and sea gulls." In Marsh's painting he is no longer alone. He sits naked, bearded, wearing a sun hat, and watches the gymnastic revels of a crowd he might have invented. A female bather—his muse perhaps— studies him from her deck chair.

Yet Whitman is so-opted as well by the abstractors of New York. In 1920 Charles Sheeler and Paul Strand made a six-minute film about the architecture of lower Manhattan, which they called *Manahatta* and interspersed with title cards from Whitman. They invoke him, however, only to contradict his vision of the city. Theirs is a geometer's New York of sharpened edges and extreme angles, a city which, in the process of rebuilding, can be seen recomposing itself abstractly, purged now of Whitman's organic ferment. Even the city's mobility is belied. *Manahatta* is a motion picture that emerges from and returns to immobility. One of its images was developed from the leadenly arrested Wall Street of

Strand's 1915 photograph, where the blank oblongs of the Morgan Guaranty windows threaten the workers (like Hopper's railway tunnel) with a deathly servitude to mechanism; others were adapted by Sheeler into Precisionist paintings. Strand was exercised by the problem of expressing the city's dynamism within the stalled moment of a photograph. While A. L. Coburn's longer exposures in the New York streets allowed vehicles, shedding trails of light, to complete their temporal journeys through his plates, Strand's technique was to capture moving bodies and suspend their animation. The people in his "Fifth Avenue" (1915) are stilled in midair, arms seesawing and feet raised, as they cross 42nd Street. To convey movement, he halts it. This is the ironic meaning of his Morgan Guaranty photograph. He wanted, he said, to show "the rushing to work." But the people in the photograph—frozen in their tracks by the camera, their volition overruled by it as by that building, whose windows like a maw (as Strand says) consume them— aren't rushing to work at all: they're being magnetized there, whether they like it or not. The photograph's stillness implies the involuntariness of their haste. Contrariwise, Sheeler's "Church St. El" (1921) is a single frame removed from the film and fixed on canvas. *Manahatta* begins from and issues in an eerie calming of the life Whitman animated in the exclamations of "City of Ships." By exaggerating perspective, it levels and empties buildings. The city is a planar surface where light and shadow do battle. Sheeler prided himself on starkly abstracting things from context, rendering them unrecognizable to inhibit "emotional response." When he returned to photographing New York in 1950–51, he studied buildings as Precisionist theorems, sundered from urban setting and human use. What interests him in the RCA Building is the sheer number of its windows, its system of multiplication; the United Nations Secretariat is perfect for him, a decapitated pyramid with its edges chiseled against a darker sky, depthless and unornamented.

The city of realism is congested. Abstracted New York is empty. Human life has been expelled from it (in Sheeler's photographs the streets are glimpsed, if at all, only in a bottom corner between the contending cubes of the buildings) and its perimeters are blank walls, the screens for invisible vistas. Ben Shahn painted several such white and featureless expanses, counterparts to the black engulfing tunnel of Hopper or the blind eyes of Strand's Morgan Guaranty—the vacant lot in a 1939 painting, based on photographs Shahn had taken in 1932 of the playground on Houston Street; the whitewashed wall against which, in another 1939 painting, some boys play handball. Walls like

Ben Shahn, "Handball" (1939). Tempera on paper over composition board. 22¾ x 31¼ inches (57.8 x 79.4 cm.). Collection, The Museum of Modern Art, New York. Abby Aldrich Rockefeller Fund.

these, in their very lack of signification, have a symbolic provenance in American art. They're the infinitudes of a negative sublimity, a pallor that appalls, like the incomprehensible whiteness of Moby Dick or the uncharted extent of American geography, which weary human beings have to trudge across and fill up. The first task of the American painter is repletion of this emptiness; but his way of colonizing it is simply to color it white. Tom Sawyer has been sentenced to whitewash "thirty yards of board-fence nine feet high." He pauses, dismayed, to compare the few streaks he has accomplished with "the far-reaching continent of unwhitewashed fence" yet to be conquered. Tom's canvas, like the unsettled continent or the white paintings (fleetingly colored and inhabited by the shadows of viewers, travelers through this vacant infinity) made by Robert Rauschenberg in 1951, is a void. So too is the city once it has been abstracted: a clean, well-lighted place, its walls are as wide and as depressingly open as the continent they're meant to occlude. In O. Louis Guglielmi's "The Church of St. Vincent de Paul" (1930) the Gothic quirks of the spire on West 23rd Street are partly obliterated by the bare rectangle of an office block. The shrine is stamped out by an empty box. And in Guglielmi's "Nocturne" (1931) the navigator on his column in Columbus Circle plaintively confronts the featureless pile of the General Motors Headquarters. Absences begin to ventilate urban narrative. Hopper admired Hemingway's "The Killers," and the menacing elisions of the writer correspond to the baleful emptinesses of the painter. In both, the descriptive or depictive exigousness derives from the first and most crucial of omissions, that of motive. Hemingway's killers have no reason for murdering Andreson. He, helplessly awaiting them, has no reason to defend himself. In him, absence of motive and motion is a deathly nullity. Hopper's people too have no cause to be where they are when they are. No plot offers to take them in or to supply them with reasons for being. The pictorial blankness is itself a killing, an elimination. Against the exterminating darkness, which thickens outside the diner in "The Killers," the only defense is an exposing whiteness: Nick Adams negotiates the nocturnal streets by moving from one arc light to the next. His decision at the end of the story is a self-whitening. He retreats from responsibility and advances into the nullity where Andreson already reposes. He decides to leave town, and when he says he can't stand to think about Andreson waiting to die, George offers him the counsel of abstracted despair, which is indifference: "you better not think about it."

Shahn both collaborates in and protests against abstraction's whitening erasure or demolition of the human city. His source for "Vacant Lot" was a photograph he made in New York in 1934, which showed three boys playing baseball on the lot. Two of the boys were omitted from the painting, as if the city itself had painted them out. The lot is now a place of pictorial memory, a chimerical souvenir of the city before abstraction: on its blank wall is the imprint of a demolished house. Perhaps, on the other side of the blankness, there's still a realistically populous picture. The fence in Shahn's "Sunday Football" (1938) has slits through which the characters can peep at a presumed but to us unseen game. Shahn always associates these urban vacancies with children's games. His 1947 painting of East 12th Street is based on a photograph he took in 1933. But in the transition from one medium to the other he has both blanked out the street, which now ends in a terminal emptiness, not (like the photograph) in a gasworks, and replaced the trudging workers with some girls he had photographed roller-skating up the steps of the Post Office on Eighth Avenue in 1933. While he abstracts the street, he makes it a scene of children's play, which inventively counters that abstraction. Even in the photograph, the girls skating up those perilous steps represent an infantile victory over the inimical, regular, hard-edged city. Similarly, in a 1943 painting a girl jumps rope before a half-demolished house, a brick shell with an arbor of floral wallpaper inside. Bequeathed an empty wall by the city, Shahn's handball players whitewash it as Tom Sawyer was made to do, then rule and number it as a goal area. They're completing its abstraction by smoothing it into a diagrammatic field, but they're also repopulating it, reclaiming it for realism, dedicating the void anew to a human and ludic use.

6

New York Abstracted

Realistic art seeks accommodation in and with New York. Realism's project is realization: the reconciliatory making real of a world from which abstraction retreats. The realism of the American painters and photographers who wished to feel at home in New York is their discovery of beauty in it, their beatification of its skyscrapers and tenements and saloons. Coburn photographed industrial New York at the same time as the sublime nature of Yosemite, and for him the city and the landscape were equivalent in their demonstration that "nothing is really 'ordinary,' for every fragment of the world is crowned with wonder and mystery." As his verb proposes, realism is a coronation of the real. Stieglitz's Flatiron or O'Keeffe's Shelton have aureoles encircling them; Sloan's girls tittering in a nickelodeon are, as he says in a note to his *New York City Life* series, a "bouquet," an untended growth garnered by him in the arboreal paradise which was the impressionist city; Marsh's body-builders at Coney Island are pagan gods. Yet the artists who give a local habitation and a name to the beauty that is the city's indwelling reality were not to remain for long the owners of New York. The city almost at once became the headquarters of international modernism, and the Europeans arriving there between the post-impressionist Francis Picabia in 1913 and Mondrian in 1940 dispense with or deform its realistically venerated actuality.

Internationalizing New York, they of course abstract it, for abstraction—as in Hopper's case—is the pictorial resort of those who do not feel at home in the city and who do not want to feel at home anywhere. Thus Marcel Duchamp could praise New York for a deracination which was the condition of the migratory modernist, who must be a world citizen: "the artist," he said, "should be able to work in one place quite as well as another." The invaders hail New York as a synonym for and an injunction to the permanent revolution of artistic modernity. Picabia called it a cubist city in 1913, and on his return in 1915 credited it with his conversion to the mechanomorphic style, for America shows that "the genius of the modern world" resides in machinery. The cubist Albert Gleizes told a reporter, "New York inspires me tremendously." Duchamp declared, "I adore New York." In Duchamp's America, art had been supplanted by engineering. The country's creativity, he thought, went into its plumbing and its bridges; all art had to do was make selections from its utilitarian stock, as he did when he tagged the Woolworth Building as a ready-made. Because New York was already "a complete work of art," it absolved Duchamp from the necessity of creating new works of art. Its gift to him was that it silenced him. "I have not painted a single picture since coming over," he boasted. For the Mexican muralist J. C. Orozco in 1929, New York constituted a challenge to the modernizing artist. Its architecture stood as a rebuke to the inequity and fatuity of ancestral Europe, and where the buildings had boldly led, Orozco proclaimed, "painting and sculpture must certainly follow." Mondrian too saluted the city's overthrow of a tyrannical past, a liberation symbolized by its engineering, its electricity, its jazz, and the displays in its shop windows.

Picabia's first act of abstract defiance was his refusal to paint what his eye saw in New York. He roamed the city from the Battery to Central Park, and enjoyed in it the same vital hubbub that elated Sloan, "the crowded streets . . . , their surging, their unrest, their commercialism, their atmospheric charm." But in the transcription to paint, his city forfeits this anecdotal abundance. Picabia absorbed impressions only to overcome them. He had passed, he explained, "entirely beyond the material, therefore there is nothing materialistic in my studies of New York nor anything sensual." He painted what his brain saw, a conceptual, not an actual, New York, a huddle of jostling oblongs and aspiring triangles plastically corresponding to the élan he felt in the buildings,

Francis Picabia, "New York" (1913). Beinecke Library, Yale University.

bridges, and hurrying avenues. As he says in the title of a 1913 water-color, his is a "New York seen through the body." Perception, as the caption suggests, is a mode of mediation. We don't simply see a thing, we visualize it, submitting it to a retinal discipline. Our notion of it is composed inside ourselves, prejudged by the disposition of the eye. Such seeing is a dislocation of the object. The camera, where objects appear upside down in the viewfinder, mechanizes such a reorientation, and it has been argued that Picabia designed and signed this watercolor upside down. It reads better if rotated, in which case its restless shapes seem to be thrusting themselves into the sky, rather than tumbling out of it. This experimental inversion is the image's ocular fate. It's also subject to a kind of alimentary decomposition. In its transit through the body the city has been ingested impressionistically and regurgitated abstractly, consumed as material or sensual food but transformed within Picabia into an unnutritious idea, a conceit, or what Duchamp called a "cervellité." Picabia is seeing through New York's body as well as through his own. The city feeds on people to fuel its mechanism: he has shown the organism to be a contraption of fleshly engineering. This is why, in his pictorial studies of them, Americans emerge from this process of meditative digestion abstracted into machines. Picabia's nude American girl is a spark plug, his "Américaine" is a light bulb, and his Stieglitz is a camera.

New York invites such a re-formation because it's a world city. Abstraction is the universal regime of structure beneath the variety of local appearance; it confounds and then rationally rearranges the visible world just as New York draws from and then resynthesizes the old political world of quarrelsome nationalities. Picabia thrills to the internationalism of New York because he finds in it a license for his own abstraction. "Your harbor in the daylight," he told the *New York American*, "shows the shipping of a world, the flags of all countries add their color to that given by your sky, your waters, and your painted craft." Gathering into itself all ships and all flags, New York makes a summary of and a distillation from the world, equalizing all nations and all creatures, as cubism does in showing them all to be recombinations of a few unitary and universal forms. Abstraction, like New York, is a melting pot.

Socially, politically, and ethnically, New York performs a benign reduction resembling that of the cubists, who see within all objects those ideal, ideational forms—the sphere, the cone, and the cylinder. It takes immigrants from every country and recomposes them as Americans. At the same time, New York devises an international language to accompany the visual universality of abstraction. In its streets, Picabia eavesdropped on a gibbering Babel. "I hear every language in the world spoken," he said, "the staccato of the New Yorker, the soft cadences of the Latin people, the heavy rumble of the Teuton." Auditorily as well as visually, he absorbed the composite. "The ensemble remains in my soul as the ensemble of some great opera." The words in an operatic ensemble are, of course, unintelligible, and are meant to be. Picabia, in choosing this analogy, suggests that he is listening in on the abstract structure beneath visible appearance; he is thinking back from this argumentative ensemble to the time when, before the toppling of Babel tower, all men spoke as one. Pictorial abstraction is conceived linguistically, as the generative grammar of form which reunites all languages and is their common matrix. Myth is the matrix of all stories, the genetic code that begets an infinite offspring of divergent narratives. Abstraction, likewise, is an Esperanto, a world language of forms. Picabia is delighted by the conflict of tongues in New York because his art wants to reach the plastic or grammatic universals that those clashing tribal dialects have in common. Audited correctly, New York can be heard speaking the Esperanto of abstraction.

Since Babel, the only language that remains globally (but abstractly) intelligible is music, and this too can be heard in New York, in the mechanical bruit of the streets. Kurt Weill, writing music for Elmer Rice's play *Street Scene* in 1946, thought New York innately operatic because polyglot. The city's streets, he said, "embrace the music of many lands and many people." Picabia's friend the composer Edgard Varèse, who lived in New York after 1915, heard the din of the city as improvised modern music, spurning the assuagement of tone and harmony. Like Duchamp, Varèse marveled at the engineering of America, particularly the Brooklyn and George Washington bridges, and identified its technological future with the sonic future predicted in his music. Varèse sought the liberation of sound: music as exultant, untempered noise. Helmholtz's experiments with sirens had transcribed what Varèse called "beautiful parabolas and hyperbolas of sound." In New York the sirens changed from scientific hypothesis to urban commonplace when fire engines—which can be heard in Varèse's "Déserts" (1954) and in his "Amériques" (1926)—shrilled by. "Music is made of sound," Varèse insisted, and New York's foghorns, piercing police whistles, rattling hammers, percussive El, ground bass of automobiles, and stuttering radios are an organization of sound, mechanically emitted and (in the orchestra) mechanically imitated. The music Varèse learned from New York does not melodiously happen through time. Rather it accumulates in and deafeningly congests space as the city does, tiered vertically in layers of battering sound. It is cubism in music, a piling-up, like those New York buildings that Picabia interpreted cubistically, of solid masses. "Amériques" refers both to the country and to its symbolic benison as a projector of the future. The sounds are American because Varèse heard them from his room on West 14th Street, but also because they're intimations of the sonic new world discovered eventually by electronics. The Orphic placidity of music fails to subdue the savage New York outside Varèse's window. "Amériques" begins with a trusting Orphic spell—a pacific melody on the flute—which is progressively beaten down and brutalized by a cacophonous arsenal. The orchestra thuds, thwacks, and flails, until the sirens screech in despair. Melody is a peacemaker, but Varèse's city, like his orchestra with its coarse eructations and violent rampages, is made for war. Using percussion as ordnance, Varèse builds ramparts of sound, the city's unyielding garrison.

In Anatole Litvak's 1940 film *City for Conquest* the music which begins in the hubbub of the streets returns there to rejoin and compete with the uproar. Arthur Kennedy conducts at Carnegie Hall a jazzy symphony based on the sounds of New York and on the career of his boxing brother James Cagney, whose pugilism is cacophony by other means: "he made music with his fists," says Kennedy. Now blinded and the proprietor of a newsstand on Broadway, he listens to a relay of the concert on his radio while selling papers. He has kept faith with the music, which in any case derives from him, by transferring its auditorium onto the sidewalk. The affinity between the clangor of New York and a music that rejects the equivocations of harmony persists. John Cage, interviewed in 1982 in his loft on West 18th Street, might have been speaking for Varèse: "I'm just crazy about the noise [of New York]. I consider it musical."

New York abstracts bodies as gadgets (in Picabia's diagrams of its citizens) and music as noise; words it also analytically abstracts, breaking them down into arbitrary conjunctions of syllables, signs signifying only to a single tribe, which must be translated before they qualify for inclusion in the new dictionary of universal form. Words, in many cases signs, occur talismanically in the American paintings of the abstractionists, and the point of their presence is that they're meant to be *not* read, at least not as dully meaningful English tags for things, but to be understood as shapes, the visible vocables of abstraction's Esperanto. This happens to the name of the city in a drawing by Jan Matulka, the Czech cubist whose parents had migrated to New York in 1907. His "Cityscape" (1924) includes, among the chimneys, El tracks, and searchlights of an abstractedly jumbled New York, the lettering on a marquee announcing "NEW YORK." The words, however, are deliberately rendered unreadable by lopping off the first two letters, and the drawing is subtitled "W YORK." A Walker Evans photograph of the advertising logos at Coney Island in 1928 performs the same abstract abbreviation. Luna Park is reduced to a patterned LUN, and the Nedick's concession forfeits its initial capital. When Paul Outerbridge photographed the 42nd Street El in 1923, he positioned the camera so that a post eliminated part of the station's nameplate on the platform, thus warning that his image—of the hut on stilts, its mansard roof blearily alight with ads: an electric mirage propped improbably above the streets—should be read as pattern, not information. Albert Gleizes was fond of the advertising signs painted across New York office windows, but chose to see them from inside the building where the words are unintelligibly reversed, as in his back-to-front "Kelly Springfield" (1915). This device abstracts the sign. Ceasing to signify, it can become a formal symbol.

G. K. Chesterton remarked in 1922, of the neon hieroglyphs which bemused Gleizes, that Times Square would be "a glorious garden of wonders . . . to anyone who was lucky enough to be unable to read." From the Catholic Chesterton, the comment is damning. His America is guilty of a nominalist heresy. It impiously reveres names and hopes to make them flesh. Things in America bestir themselves to live up to their names, which proclaim their messianic ambitions. Chesterton reports that "there really has been an effort to keep the White House white." These encomiastic namings offend Chesterton, who considers it blasphemous to call a city San Francisco and finds St. Louis to be much less beautiful than its irrelevant name. New York so worships names that it recites them as free-standing—and thus inane—spells, which no longer need refer to things. As a result, Chesterton says, " '271 West 52nd Street' is the easiest of all addresses to find, but the hardest of all addresses to remember." The sky signs would like to think that they're abstractly illegible. Chesterton, however, knows how to decipher them, and he sees them as encoded divine premonitions. Above Broadway flare portentous "words written with a fiery finger, like that huge unhuman finger that wrote on Belshazzar's wall."

A version of Chesterton's remark about Times Square was attributed to Mondrian in 1940. "How beautiful!" he is alleged to have exclaimed, "if only I couldn't read English." By now, the perception has lost its Chestertonian theological reproof. Abstraction's benefit to Mondrian is to make the city unreadable, at least in English, and to validate it as the paradise which in Chesterton's view it gaudily, even infernally, parodied. Mondrian referred to abstract vision as a gift, because it enabled the artist to perfect the visible world by restoring it to the immaculate idea from which it messily emanates. The grid of the New York street plan was to Mondrian an abstract heaven, a metaphysical surety, "a plastic representation of pure equilibrium." He defined the city as "concrete space-determination." It directs and orders the random life of phenomena, as do the Place de la Concorde and Trafalgar Square —of which Mondrian had painted planar representations while living in Paris and London—compelling existence into circulatory patterns.

"New York—New York City" (1941–42), a cage of intersecting colored tapes, perceives the same celestial harmony in Mondrian's new home. The strips of adhesive tape applied directly to the canvas are lines of determination, disposing space and directing traffic, as town planning does. But they are neither stringent nor restrictive: they promulgate laws for growth and enable Mondrian to celebrate what he calls "the splendor of dynamic movement." New York dynamizes the ideated grid. In "Broadway Boogie-Woogie" (1942–43) the polychrome squares begin to dance and flash, shuttling along the routes prescribed by the composition like traffic interweaving in the cross streets and on the avenues of midtown Manhattan. Jazz dancing, which the monkish Mondrian took up in New York in tribute to the spirit of the place, was to him geometry in motion: he boogied angularly, in straight lines and squares. New York animated the plastic universals which his art sought to define. It's jittering, nervous, in constant motion, yet it stays always the same. "Broadway Boogie-Woogie" is as hectic and restless as the fleet of yellow cabs it seems to allude to; it's also as serenely static as the night sky with its patterned stars (which Mondrian in 1919 had declared to be an image of the abstract discernment of primordial relations). It catches New York in entropic exertion at the rush hour and from that chaos makes a Utopia, rescued from the disintegrativeness of time and happening. Art, Mondrian said, "establishes life in its unchangeable aspect: as pure vitality." The paradox—that life is eternal in its very mutability, that its discharges of energy are programmed and delimited, not wastefully impromptu—is essential to New York, whose existence paraphrases this law of Mondrian. Its feverish vitality *is* "its unchangeable aspect," for the only constant thing about it is that it's always changing. Beneath the thermodynamic panic, Mondrian is able to see a theosophical calm. Perhaps those aren't pushful cabs jockeying and tooting in the streets beneath us on the earth but angels silently going about their salvific business above us in the sky, logically revolving within the orbits fixed for them by the celestial grid.

Chesterton's remark about Times Square is a Catholic anathema. Only by not knowing English could you mistake this accursed place for a garden of wonders. Mondrian's comment (if indeed he made it) is a theosophical dream, devoutly wishing for the sublimation of matter into spirit. If you didn't know English, you'd be able to see this place aright, as the dawn of an abstract enlightenment. Times Square supplied Fernand Léger with a comparable abstract epiphany. He noticed that you could be talking to someone on Broadway when suddenly that person's face would turn blue in the reflected glare of the neon, and then with equal arbitrariness would blush red or yellow. These patches of gratuitous radiance were free-floating color, palpably existing in space and exploiting their dissociation from form and function. Léger set about transferring these unattached, itinerant colors to his painting.

Language impedes these abstractors of New York. Charles Demuth's "I Saw the Figure 5 in Gold" (1928) conjures up visually a poetic image from William Carlos Williams, but in doing so opens a gap between the provincialism of words and the abstract internationalism of number. Williams had seen a fire engine in a Manhattan street, its numbered insignia hurtling into the distance. Demuth, in compliment to his friend, disperses Williams's name throughout the canvas. But it's always abbreviated (as initials) or fractured (as "Bill" or "Carlo," which glints in light bulbs against a skyscraper, its final letter burnt out). This dispersal or dismemberment of words contrasts with the confident duplication of number: three gold fives reverberate from the red side of the engine. Linguistically, New York's nearest approach to the world language of abstraction's Esperanto is in its bastardizing of tongues. Picabia heard all the languages of the world being spoken there. Sometimes more than one language is spoken in a single word. The pidgin English which results comically gestures toward monoglot Babel. Vladimir Mayakofsky, visiting New York in 1925, hears the émigrés on Broadway conversing in mispronounced English catchphrases which he transcribes as Russian neologisms—"chuingam" for chewing gum, "Mek monei" for the admonition to get rich. Still, this multiplicity of tongues can't reconvene Babel. Instead, it absurdly frustrates communication. Mayakofsky sees a model demonstrating shaving gear in a Woolworth window. Through the plate glass he tells her in Russian that she's being a fool. She lip-reads him and imagines he's asking her in English to open the door. You've been made an idiot, he rails; she translates his fulmination into a declaration of love.

Henry Roth's novel of immigrant life on the Lower East Side, *Call It Sleep* (1934), is about the difficulty of reading a city that has made itself abstractly illegible. Survival in New York requires linguistic assimilation. The immigrant is branded as an alien by his inability to master English. David's mother mispronounces because she is wonderingly disconnected from the city. If the store window with the scribble on it were washed, she'd be unable to find her way home. She says she knows that she lives at 126 "Boddeh Stritt." Even this isn't correct, since her husband demands that she call it "Bahday Street," which she reconverts to German where it means, meaninglessly, "bath street." When David gets lost, he claims to live on "Boddeh Stritt." A passerby chucklingly translates this into Potter Street, and an Irish policeman into "Body Street—sounds like the morgue" or "Barhdee Street." David's additionally vulnerable because he can't, to save himself, spell the street's name. After his accident on the electric rail, he gives his address with more certainty, but by noting down the slangy mispronunciations and by having the address immediately translated from a street number into the different idiom of the avenues Roth continues to imply that language cannot orient you in the city: David says he lives at "S-sebm fawdynine N-nint' Street," which someone in the crowd alternately locates as "on de cunner Evenyuh D."

The abstract indifference of uptown New York in *Call It Sleep* is its muteness. It speaks no language at all. When David's aunt takes him to the museum, they walk along 86th Street toward Fifth Avenue and, remembering the "avalanche of sound" on Avenue D, he notices that "the further they got from Third Avenue, the more aloof grew the houses, the more silent the streets." The Jewish parents in Waldo Frank's *City Block* (1922), taking their retarded child for a consultation uptown on 59th Street, also experience the city as an unintelligible language. Even the noun that names it is intimidatingly and abstractly capitalized: "The City rose in high hard words. Each building was a word. . . . The City was a sentence, harsh, staccato, in an alien tongue." The city is a language, its people entries in a vocabulary. They know their own names, but those words mean nothing to them because they can't learn the rest of the language. Thus Godfrey Carber in *City Block* contrasts the integer of his own frail being with the multitudinous lexicon of the city and reflects that "it's all but one name . . . New York . . . shorter than mine which is Godfrey Dunnimore Carber. Names do not count, it seems. I am a bit of a man with a seven-syllabled name in the vastness New York." Roth himself has to write *Call It Sleep* in a repertory of languages to match the noise of the city—ceremonious Yiddish and the demotic English of the streets, together with the maimed English used by Polish or Irish learners of it. The malapropisms of David's aunt—"kockin" as cocaine or as Yiddish for sitting on the lavatory; "molleh" as the Jewish pronunciation of molar and as a Yiddish reference to circumcision—dangerously flourish across the borders between these languages. A member of two linguistic communities, she can make puns, and her verbal dexterity is an abstraction of language from single meanings. The pun is a cubist whimsy, made from the overlapping or interbreeding of words, just as objects in cubist pictures abut or merge with one another. David escapes from this confused colloquy when he learns to read. Now, graduating from Yiddish to Hebrew, he can talk to God, understanding the language in which the world was, at the beginning, uttered.

According to Mondrian, that language would have been as ascetically abstract as the skeletal New York grid. There is one artist, though, who evolved from realism to abstraction in New York without denying the idiom and idiosyncrasy of the place's pictorial language; who inflects it with a local accent rather than reforming it into Esperanto. He is Stuart Davis. As a student of Henri, Davis toured New York in quest of rude vivid life to draw, frequenting Chinatown and Bowery pool-rooms, McSorley's Saloon, burlesque shows, and jazz dives in Harlem. Gradually he began to see New York cubistically, as a system of "impersonal dynamics": not a convocation of people but a continuum of objects, activated by the impatience of the urban eye, as are the fire escapes, cast-iron pillars, barbers' poles, and light fixtures which bounce through the visual field of his "Sixth Avenue El" (1932). Ezra Pound in 1921 interpreted the city as a cubist sentence, a collision of substantives: its impressions succeed each other nonsequentially, in "a flood of nouns without verbal relations." Davis's "Sixth Avenue El" logically pictures such a sentence.

He too describes the city's pictorial contents linguistically. Its vernacular architecture of store fronts and gas stations, its billboards and awnings, were its "visual dialect," an idiolect whose vocables are shape and sign. Abstraction had purified that dialect out of existence. Mondrian, Davis said, expunged "all the paraphernalia of pictural usage." In its subversion of pictorial shape and material appearance, abstraction naturally assaults language, which names the things abstraction has pledged to abolish. Sloan, like Davis, objected to the linguistic extremism of the abstractionists. They had exhumed a deep structure which reunited all languages, but its subliminal grammar could generate no sentences: "cubism," Sloan said, "is not art in itself. It is the grammar and composition of art." Davis heard the same threatening reduction of visual particularity in the verbal habits of his friend Arshile Gorky, whose stubbornly eccentric speaking of English was "no mere matter of foreign accent . . . but an earthquake-like effect on sentence structure." Mastery of a plastic language entails renunciation of any single spoken language, which won't be comprehended beyond the confines of a single tribe. Hence Gorky's abstract massacre of English, for his purpose in coming to New York was, as Julien Levy explained, "to become more than American—to become international."

The sponsor Davis chooses for his restoration of visual nationality and his repopulation of the urban void is Whitman. In 1921 he claimed

Stuart Davis, "New York—Paris, No. 1" (1931). Oil on canvas. University of Iowa Museum of Art, Iowa City.

to "feel the thing Whitman felt—and I too will express it in pictures—America the wonderful place we live in." His is therefore, as he put it in the title of a 1954 painting, a colonial cubism, marrying the "historical elegances" of Europe to the American vulgate, rejoicing in a linguistic impurity. Davis's *New York—Paris* paintings of 1931 are a pictorial equivalent of franglais. The tribal fetishes of the two cities float into propinquity. El stations and sidewalk cafés are ranked as interchangeable amenities, and the lean needle of the Chrysler Building, tilted on its side, aims itself in the direction of a shapely Parisian leg. Rather than insisting on internationalism, abstraction here permits two different nationalisms to cohabit within the picture, which is cheerfully bilingual. Davis called New York a "frenetic commercial engine." As such, it resembles the utensil he progressively abstracted in a series of paintings made between 1927 and 1930: an eggbeater. The beater pleases Davis because it's an instrument for abstracting. It mashes, melds, and recomposes substances, as a percolator (the subject of a 1927 painting) circulates fluids in its hiccups. New York operates similarly, contriving from the collision of forms a mélange or melee which

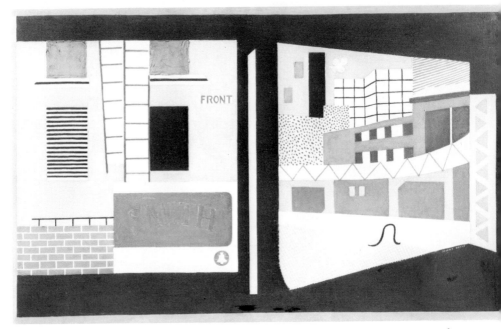

Stuart Davis, "House and Street" (1931). Oil on canvas. 26 x 42 inches. Collection of Whitney Museum of American Art. Purchase.

is an abstraction. Davis assists its mess-making. He resembles Whitman in the permission he extends to the perceptual democracy of the New York streets, which gate-crashes his paintings. He said in 1936 that the painter should not be content to look through the window and must "step into the street." He meant the comment metaphorically: he was talking about the political affiliations of the artist. But his own painting literally accomplishes the transition, for instance in "The Mellow Pad" (1945–51). This work is based on Davis's "House and Street" (1931), a view beneath the El on Front Street at the corner of Coenties Slip, but it advances beyond realistic representation because the antic, jiving life out there won't consent to the disciplinary framing of the window and gyres through space in a riot of what Davis called "Hot Events"—a jazz dance of the city's spare parts, with boogying scrap metal and lithe, pulsating iron. The painting is the mellow pad on which these accidents are allowed to happen. Davis's tolerance of this syncopated mayhem demonstrates that abstraction needn't fear the incursions of the real and can befriend the chaos and contingency of New York.

7

Invading Isms

Invading New York, the modernists put it through a succession of iconographic torments. It's demolished by the cubists, electrified by the futurists, sterilized by the purists. Cubism piles up New York's architectural building blocks only to capsize them. Surrealism carnivorously interprets its stone and steel as flesh, of which it makes a meal. Inside the body, the surrealist city rots; purism arrests that fate by setting its temperature at a sanitary degree zero. But the radical muralists, unrelenting, inscribe on the city's walls a prophecy of doom.

John Marin's first watercolors of New York, made in 1910, are impressionistic. Their bleary wash of color suits the city's maritime nature. He represents the harbor as an inky indigo pool, with the buildings deliquescing into air above and water beneath. The grainy paper absorbs this elemental fluidity: a dry ground consumes the stains and blots of color, so Marin's early New York looks, as does Huneker's, like a thirsting Venice. Marin's conversion to cubism occurred at the same time as the city's. A zoning law imposed a compulsory cubism on New York. A new regulation in 1916 prohibited buildings from rising in solid blocks. To aerate the streets, setbacks were required. Building from now on was a vertical arrangement of cubes, accumulated in stepped masses. The Shelton on Lexington Avenue, the site of Stieglitz's aerie, was one of the first buildings to solve the problem of articulating these tiered boxes. Georgia O'Keeffe's paintings of it, illuminated fiercely from within or freckled with sun spots, are futurist accounts of a cubist object. The cubes glow or melt in the electric or solar glare that futurism trains on them. Marin reported to Stieglitz in 1911 that he had "started some downtown stuff, and to pile these great houses one upon another with paint as they do pile themselves up here." This emphasis on the piling of architectural forms bespeaks cubism. In landscape, cubism tilts the horizon vertically toward you and, instead of making space recede into distance, has it climb the paper or canvas, stacked like cubic building blocks up the flat surface. For Marin, the masses of New York architecture are not distributed inwardly and regimented by perspective. They mount atop each other, crowding the paper and jostling for precedence. Instead of retiring into the picture's point of disappearance, forms jut out from it at angles. Cubism's third dimension extends outside the picture. Marin's buildings seem always about to spill off the page or to collapse into one another. Rather than conveying the exhilaration of altitude, Marin's aerial perspective from the Woolworth Building levels the city beneath him and layers the buildings horizontally. Within this jammed, competitive domain, objects tussle for occupation of the available room. Marin's new style enables him to be true to both the city's congestion and its ambitious pushfulness. The buildings dispute the space they share in a combat of what Marin in 1913 called "warring, pushing, pulling forces," each mass bullying its neighbors.

Reasoning that "if these buildings move me they too must have life," Marin animates architectural forms, charging them—by the seismic impatience of his brushwork—with a shuddering energy. The mobility of his objects is that of things on the rebound, violently ricocheting. The zoning ordinance had sought to make peace between the contentious cubes. Marin reawakens their aggressiveness. He called his later works "Movements in Paint," and the New York watercolors impulsively mobilize hitherto stable and inert architecture. The tower of St. Paul's in lower Manhattan looks (to Marin) as if its vertebral column had snapped, leaving its separate levels knocking about independently of each other; the arches of his Brooklyn Bridge tilt giddily to one side; the Municipal Building seems about to teeter forward into the crevasse of a street; and the structures flanking the Telephone Building dash themselves insensible on its sides. A 1921 pencil sketch of the Woolworth Building traces the course of the apparently foundering skyscraper as it crumples through the air. The building's architect, Cass Gilbert, was allegedly outraged that Marin had made it look so unstable.

Cubism usually studies a stilled life. The energy which jerks and

John Marin, "Lower Manhattan (Composing Derived from Top of Woolworth)" (1922). Watercolor and charcoal with paper cutout attached with thread. 21⅝ x 26⅞ inches (54.9 x 68.3 cm.). Collection, The Museum of Modern Art, New York. Acquired through the Lillie P. Bliss Bequest.

jumbles Marin's New York belongs to futurism rather than to cubism, for whereas cubism analyzes objects in repose, futurism watches them ignite, explode, and gutter. Cubism attends to the spatial form of things, futurism to their accelerated and elated temporal careers. For the Italian futurists, the most exemplary modern artwork was a sports car. Marin exists between the two styles and advances from cubism to futurism when he makes buildings shiver, tumble, and collide. Because he applied a futuristic propulsion to cubistically static objects, he could liken his art to games such as billiards and golf, which lance projectiles careening across space and through time. During his European period between 1905 and 1909 he remembers, as if the two activities were allied, that he "played some billiards, and incidentally knocked out some batches of etchings," and for the Maine watercolors he adopts a golfing meta- phor, saying that "the fewer strokes I can take, the better the picture."

Economically, Marin's cubism sees New York as a rampant and expansive free market. In his 1924 watercolor the Stock Exchange, a glimmering white temple in a gray murk, distributes shock waves through the composition, conducting the city's business by rumor, impulse and alarm, all of which are futuristically represented by lightning bolts cleaving the overcast fringes of the design. As the affronted Cass Gilbert recognized, Marin's New York is a place of ebullient anarchy. Cubism was adjusted to a different interpretation of New York by Louis Lozowick, who imigrated to America from the Ukraine in 1906. Lozowick saw in the city, as he said in an interview in 1970, an "icon of the socialist future," and his cubism imitates the social engineering which, by the enforcement of "order and organization," will bring that future to pass. His masses are not precariously piled or ambitiously strenuous like Marin's. They have been subjected to a logical standardization, and their structure—as he wrote in the catalogue of the Machine Age Exposition in 1927—precisely fits their intended function. In Lozowick's "Urban Geometry" (1925–27) Marin's building blocks, vertically stacked, do seem likely to tumble forward in a pell-mell chaos. They're held in equipoise, however, by the diagonal bands of shade that slice across them, like beams of surveillance, from the skyscrapers in the depth of the picture. Geometry in this city maintains an inflexible civic discipline. Lozowick called the lithograph he made in 1927–28 of the streets under the El tracks "Checkerboard." The rails imprint a strict, ruled field of shadow on the thoroughfare, where, as in checkers, only certain strategic moves are permitted. In "Allen Street (Under the El)" people proceed in straight lines, at right angles to cars, on this checkerboard, obedient to the rules of the city's orderly game. The lithograph Lozowick made in 1927 of the Whitehall Building at the Battery sees the state as a container of the city, and the cube as a social capsule. The Whitehall Building was remarkable because it comprised an entire block. Lozowick shows it monolithically presiding over a hunched plain of smaller office blocks and over the scurrying dots of the people farther below and farther off. With a thousand eyes, it oversees the indoor workings of the city's economy. It doesn't proclaim an egotistic triumph, as do the later hubristic skyscrapers of New York; it exemplifies, with dour impersonality, the collectivist power of the state. And that state is to be run like a cubist painting. In his 1927 catalogue essay, Lozowick describes the artist planning a composition as a benevolent socialist dictator, who must treat his plastic subjects as if they were laboring citizens, demanding from each according to his capacity, allotting to each according to his need: the artist will "note with exactitude the articulation, solidarity and weight of the advancing and receding masses, will define with precision the space around objects, and between them he will organize line, plane and volume into a well-knit design." Cubist solidity—in Marin's New York a source of friction between proximate objects—is here a matter of cooperative solidarity. The abstract painting will be a model of distributive justice. The masses Lozowick refers to could, just as well as the spatial constituents of his art, be the coalitions of citizenry which Marxism activates.

Futurism was cubism dynamized or electrified. It agitates the objects cubism stills and describes their trajectories through space (as in the cases of Giacomo Balla's speeding car and trotting dachshund) or their stuttering emission of energy (like that from Jacob Epstein's rock drill). The futurists conceive of the city as a panic of forms and forces, interlocking or clashing like the maddened mob in George Grosz's "The City" (1916–17). Calling his New York street scenes movements, Marin is already making a futurist declaration, for he applies the theory of sequential motion—exemplified by Balla's dog, Duchamp's splintering nude seen in the act of descending a staircase, or Umberto Boccioni's sculpture of "Continuity in Space"—to those most properly immobile of objects, buildings. Marin said he had tried to express, in these New York scenes, "this 'moving of me' " by the city. He means that it has emotionally roused him, yet he also intends the word literally. The buildings provoke movement from him: the spasmodic rapidity of his handiwork, a signature of the nervily vital city dweller, who must, like the buildings, be a doughty shock absorber. Marin's skyscrapers are the expression of "great movements"—the social and economic tug-of-war of those "pull forces"—and they in turn discharge movement to their jagged or jittery surroundings. Their surfaces are warped or rippling. The Brooklyn Bridge is seen swaying. This bridge, for the painter Joseph Stella as for Hart Crane, sums up the aspiration of the futurist city because its life is in tense suspension, not safe earthly foundation. A bridge doesn't extend a level platform across the void. Rather, it makes a dynamic assault on space, its cables strained nerves, its buttresses a distraught torso.

Electrification is a symptom of this violent mobility. The lighting-up of cities boldly advertised their advance into the future. In Gustave Charpentier's opera Louise (1900) his lovers, whose illumining physical delight has driven them beyond the mean morality of their society, look down from Montmartre on the city electrically and erotically glowing beneath them; fireworks detonate and subside above Paris as they go in to bed. Kurt Weill's song "Berlin im Licht" ribaldly greets the electrification of that city in 1928 and senses in it the promise of sexual titillation. John Sloan was startled in 1908–9 by the "special electric light" which was altering New York and watched a snowfall spark sudden crackling flashes from the third rail of the El tracks. The electric carnival of Times Square dismayed him at first because of its commercialism, but by the 1920s its brazen effulgence had come to signify, as in Paris or Berlin, the future's emancipation from the craven past. In Janet Flanner's novel *The Cubical City* (1926) electricity is "New York's protest against the demoded restrictions of night," and against the dim-out of prohibition. The lights express the spirit of "lawless, liberty-loving New York," as does the orchestra of whistles, gongs, sirens, and bells with which the city utters a "hearty, semi-Christian, pro-hibition-drunken" welcome to the New Year. The electric currents have been harnessed by eager human bodies too. Janet Flanner's heroine feverishly expects a cable or telegram from her lover: she lives "in an age when electricity . . . had come to be the passionate medium for lovers too impatient to wait and whisper what they had to say"; an age when consummation is entrusted to the twangling, tingling wires. Paul Morand, astounded in 1929 by the tropically sensual summer solstice which blazes all night in Times Square, also sees light as New York's. rejection of the puritanism which cows the rest of America; and in the cinemas of the area electricity has invented an alluring opiate, "a machine for fascinating, a machine for obliterating."

The electric light bulb is a self-image for the futurists. Balla painted one in 1909. It doesn't just suffuse the atmosphere around it but explodes into it, expending its radiance in a quiver of arrows. Marinetti declared that we are all born from electricity, and one of the futurist manifestos saw the history of an electric lamp as a tragic agon, a coital anguish of expiring intensity like Charpentier's fireworks. As it dies, the lamp suffers and screams its pain in hallucinatory bursts of color. Futurism could be defined as cubism wired to the mains. The planes that cubism piles or makes overlap now strike sparks from each other, every filament bristling in an orgy of electrocution. The painter who imports this futurist vision to New York is Joseph Stella, who arrived there from Italy in 1906. To see a city galvanized into being by the divinity of electricity, he traveled to Coney Island. The Electric Tower at Luna Park was a conflagration of bulbs, studded with a hundred thousand ardent lamps. In Stella's "Battle of Lights, Coney Island" (1913) gyrating, ejaculating lights advertise the city as a deranging carnal carnival. The machines at Coney Island, revolving in orbits of acid light, are turbines generating pleasure. On Broadway too, in Stella's

"The White Way" (1920–22), light whirls and zags out of control. Coney Island and Broadway represent electricity at play; another of the canvases from Stella's *The Voice of the City of New York Interpreted,* showing the port, is about electricity at work. Here the lines that lace the surface are Whitman's masts and at the same time telegraph poles. Their business is more than the transmission of messages: conductors of an etheric spirituality, ministers as well as media, they knit distances—as Stella wrote in a prose poem explaining his design—"in a harmonic whole of vibrating love."

The structural principle of the *New York Interpreted* paintings is fission: a symmetrical cleaving which, as if splitting an atom, unleashes the city's explosive energy. The Broadway pictures spin outward from that shattered center in a centrifuge of errant light. Down the center of "Skyscrapers," Stella aligns the bisected Flatiron. Halved, it is set in motion, mounted on wings in readiness for flight, or sharpened into a prow which slices its way nautically out of the space where it has been tethered. At the midpoint of "The Bridge," the central arch of the Brooklyn Bridge is cloven. The operation leaves (at least in the 1939 Whitney Museum version) a blue wound, a vertical sliver of flame which glows as if the bridge's stone, like its steel, remembered its initiation by fire. The vent allows the energy the structure stores to escape outward. From that central line, the cables that support the platform are strung. Stella sunders these objects to release their voltage. He saw New York by flashes of lightning, as a maelstrom or an astral catastrophe. The lights on the bridge at night resembled, he said, galaxies of falling stars, and the tops of the skyscrapers, stranded in the air by fog beneath, were "like flaming meteorites held momentarily motionless in their tracks." A "new DIVINITY" made itself immanent to him on the bridge, and he devised a form of worship for it: a cult of fire and of the dynamo which is a demiurge, a tireless manufacturer of life. Stella believed that "steel and electricity are the creative factors of modern Art." They are also the components of modern New York, and there's an interior alliance between them. The steel that enables the city to attain such arrogant heights is a hero (like the futurist light bulb) of heat's agony, having withstood the sufferings of the forge. In Stella's New York paintings, the genius of electricity expresses itself as color, that of steel as taut and supple line. Stella sought to electrify his palette, wanting his colors to glare as blindingly as the lights to which they paid homage. Hence the frenetic vermilion or vitriolic yellow of his Coney Island, the "silvery alarm" (as he called it) of electricity shining from the bridge, or the sulphurous effulgence which burns inside the

Joseph Stella, "The White Way II," from *The Voice of the City of New York Interpreted* (1922). Collection of the Newark Museum.

Joseph Stella, "Battle of Lights, Coney Island" (1913). Yale University Art Gallery. Gift of Collection Société Anonyme.

skyscrapers. Electricity is anarchic. Its god, Prometheus, is a heaven-storming rebel. It needs the stricture of steel, just as uninhibited color needs the restraint of line. So the precarious balance of Stella's compositions records the way light is controlled by structure, as the city's giddy radiance is chastened by its steely rectilinear geometry. Interlocking diagonals or barred verticals steady the exuberance of light in the Broadway paintings; the "infinite latitude" of the wires in the port scene channel color into an orderly circuitry; the cables of the bridge metallically segment the clustered asymmetrical view seen through them. As much as Lozowick's Whitehall Building, Stella's New York is a theorem about the city and about art. Lozowick treats of the precise equation between social form and economic function, Stella of the uneasier equilibrium between insurgent light and coercive linear structure, which are manifest in the city as the opposed motives of pleasure (at reveling Coney) and work (typified by what Stella called "the iron fists and steel nerves" of industrial Brooklyn).

Like all modernist ideologies, futurism is a prescription for society. It therefore announces itself in tracts as well as in works of art. Marinetti's initial salvos supplied the machine age with an epic diction by animating industry. The ancient epic poet invests the implements of warfare with human energy; Marinetti does the same for railway engines, which to him are dragons breathing smoke, or bridges, which he acclaims as gymnasts bestriding empty air. A metaphor lies dormant in our calculation of locomotive horsepower. Marinetti reactivates it by describing trains pawing "the tracks like the hooves of enormous steel horses bridled by tubing." Stella's prose poems about New York are the manifestos of his futurism. Their excited exclamations kindle metaphoric aspiration within mechanical objects. Instead of merely connecting two boroughs, the Brooklyn Bridge conjoins two worlds, fusing earth and heaven; the skyscrapers are a collective cathedral; New York is an angry cyclops, gesticulating with steel girders in defiance of the gods. This epic intuition of an angry will in machines means that when, on Brooklyn Bridge, Stella's predecessor Whitman appears to him, the poet pilots an engine which is a futurist icon of velocity and volatility. Exerting himself to equal the challenge of the city, Stella remembers that he "appealed for help to the soaring verse of Walt Whitman." As he does so, his metaphoric invocation itself takes off, and he sees Whitman's poetry "soaring above as a white airplane," extraterrestrially guiding Stella's own lowlier, fluvial craft, "leading the sails of my Art through the blue vastity of Phantasy."

Futurism makes an inferno of New York. Stella's Brooklyn is a seething cauldron which fuels the war machine, and beneath the bridge he hears the purgatorial moaning of the tugboats. Purism cools this incendiary hell into a chaste mechanical heaven. The purist refrigerators of New York were the painter Léger and the architect Le Corbusier, who coincided there in 1935, when the Museum of Modern Art mounted exhibitions of their work. Futurism exults in a thermodynamic despair—the perdition of heat loss, experienced by Stella's multitudinous guttering bulbs and by the crowds in his Coney Island bacchanal. Purism preserves New York from this fate by a cautionary lowering of its temperature. Purists envision society as a concord of grooved and adjusted parts, an engineered idyll like the "Grand Déjeuner" (1921) of Léger's serene female mechanomorphs. While futurism thrills to New York's combustibility, purism—to ensure the hibernating peace of mechanism—

puts it on ice. George Grosz, who came to New York in 1932, felt himself to have been morally laved by it. He admired the cleanliness of its ice-cream parlors, the coolness of its shaded lobbies in the summer, its chilling nasal sprays, and its compulsive washing and ironing of one's garments. Soon he no longer needed to produce graphic satire: the porcine monsters of his Berlin days had been banned from this laundered city. Léger, in his recollections of New York in 1931 (the year of his first visit), describes the postal tubes in skyscrapers as ducts traveling through the city's frigid, nonvisceral body. Letters posted on the fiftieth floor would catch fire from static irritation, he says, before they reached the ground; to guard against this, the conduits are iced. Le Corbusier also celebrates—like Grosz rhapsodizing over the ice-cream parlors—the intense visual coldness of his view over the city. Sunrise in New York is for him "an Alpine spectacle." The concomitant of this mountainous chill is a snowy and surgical pallor. To purify New York, Léger and Le Corbusier blanch it. Le Corbusier titled his account of his American tour *When the Cathedrals Were White,* and in it he invidiously contrasts the crystalline White World of his ideal, therapeutic New York with the befouled Brown World of the past. The whiteness of New York's mercantile cathedrals signifies their clinical disinfection, free from the soiling patina of age. Glass, with which New York walled its buildings, is a medium of moral superiority, hiding nothing, not straggling back into mud and murk like brick and stone.

Appropriately, Le Corbusier's first view of New York was from his liner while it was anchored in quarantine. He sees it from within a sanitary cordon and admires its gelid beauty. Disembarking, he finds it to be carnally real and repellent. Before he can approve of it, it must be pristinely repackaged, insulated from the bacterial atmosphere. He commends the cellophane casing of sandwiches, the polished bar tops, and the trains in Grand Central, which are kept spick and span by legions of black janitors. But the apogee of his cleansed and hermetically sealed New York is Radio City, where he goes with Léger to make a broadcast. As its name proclaims, it's a city within—and immunized against—the city. It's installed "in one of the skyscrapers of Rockefeller Center," safe from the savage, infested outdoors. He likes the claustral hush of its elevators and corridors and gratefully breathes its filtered and tempered air. Radio City is one of his bloodless cathedrals. Inside the studio he sees another room made by muting and insulation: a glass aquarium for spectators, who can chatter at will without being heard because their booth is soundproofed. Léger experiences the serenity of mechanism, reverenced by Le Corbusier inside Radio City, when New

York is stilled after midnight. He makes pilgrimages to the sites of peaceful, dozing machinery—a bus garage on Avenue A or B at two in the morning, where in a silence of metal only a solitary horse breathes and declares itself alive, though sleeping; Wall Street at the same hour. So purified is Léger's New York of biological urgency, so laid asleep and preservatively frozen, that it appears to him as a necropolis, a posthumous city. Wall Street is a pyramidal burial ground, exhibiting the monuments which the millionaires have erected as their cenotaphs. He fancies that a ghost is stirring in the machine. On his nocturnal rambles, the street seems to be murmurously snoring, like the horse in the dormitory of buses; but it's only a drill at work early—the travail of a mechanical and therefore enviably immortal body. The city relaxes into what Léger calls "la vie méchanique," freed from the importunings of the perishable human organism. He notes that in New York everyone smokes, even the streets. He couples the human habit with the mechanical exhalation of subterranean steam because smoking, properly understood, chastens the body's cravings. It subdues greedy organism to disciplined machine: a girl tells Léger that it's good to smoke during a meal because it distracts your appetite and saves you from getting fat.

The heroism of puristic New York is no longer a reflex of overweening human will but a matter of automatic mechanical intellection, like the foresight of those doors that open in advance of Le Corbusier's step. Such sleek obsequious engineering prompts him to exclaim, "They are gods." He's praising a race of cybernauts. The divinity of engineering is summed up by the doors of safes, "so extremely well made," in a bank he visits. Léger too was impressed by the steel vaults of the Irving Bank. In this impregnable tabernacle resides, perhaps, the posthuman genius of the city. Le Corbusier selects jazz as the music of New York's robotized future, declaring that "Manhattan is hot jazz in stone and steel." As interpreted by him, jazz gives up its syncopated liberty— the mellowness that enables it to absorb the visual accidents of Stuart Davis's street—and becomes a mechanistic discipline. He describes the trumpet in a Harlem band as a turbine, a tireless self-repetitive dynamo, and admires tap-dancing for similar reasons, because it's the choreography of the factory, "as mechanical as a sewing machine." The human energy that raised New York and made it an erectile, aspiring image of man is slighted by Le Corbusier. He snubs New Yorkers as "timid people." Their city still has too skulkingly human a scale. Though its buildings are fabled to be awesomely tall, for Le Corbusier they're not tall enough, and he quotes demeaning statistics about the average height of structures in the city. Because it's an unplanned city, the skyscrapers flaunt themselves as brainless exhibitions of physical prowess, mere "acrobatic feats." The machine age can do without their effortful fortitude because it accomplishes miracles by precise calculation instead of sweaty exertion. The city's eminences are a sorry collection of antediluvian weightlifters or warriors made obsolete by technology. Le Corbusier dismisses the Brooklyn Bridge with faint praise, calling it "strong and rugged as a gladiator." He prefers the unornamented, severely exact George Washington Bridge, which is "a young athlete"—beautiful but regressive, still trusting in the athletic training of the body. Whenever Le Corbusier employs anatomical imagery for the city, it's mocking or defamatory, characterizing New York as a messy overfed organism. The division of the island by Fifth Avenue reminds him of the spine of a sole (which, in any case, you prize out and discard in order to get at the soft and yielding flesh), and the traffic-clogged avenues are costive digestive tracts, their excretory exits blocked. The city ought to learn the appetite-suppressing wisdom of Léger's girl with her cigarettes between courses.

Le Corbusier plans the reconstruction of porous, stony, old-fashioned New York in rigid steel and cool glass. Its remade whiteness is fantasticated by Léger, who reports that scientists have found a way of making glass from curdled milk and imagines the cows of America laboring for the reification of the city and its conversion to transparency. The joke indicates the difference between the pair. For Léger, such a perfecting of the real can occur only in fantasy or art; but Le Corbusier has power over the real, power to demolish it and to build the future in its place. Léger favors imagery of games—cyclindrical soldiers, their bodies supplanted by steely prostheses, play cards in a 1917 painting; "La Belle Equipe" (1944–45) has a team of cyclists—because only people who have banded together to play a game and temporarily agreed to its rules possess the interdependent, mechanized harmony which purism longs to impose on society. His recollection of New York is beautiful because playful. It's a society made a family by mechanical interdependence. The indispensable personage in New York, Léger says, is the telephone. Its flex is an electronic umbilical cord, knitting people together and reconvening the family of man. He compares it to the lifeline mountaineers loop and link around themselves, ensuring the safety of each by the interreliance of all. It's a machine you rely on and reward with your love. Infants learn how to master it and to love it by playing with it as if it were a toy. When Léger proposes a puristic enforcement of order in the city, he does so only as a dictatorial whimsy. He wishes, for instance, that some aesthetic tyrant would make amends for the grayness of New York by decreeing that all the avenues be painted in contrasting colors. Le Corbusier actually craves such autocracy and envies a statue for possessing it. On the steps of the Subtreasury, confronting the skyscrapers of Wall Street, the statue of George Washington achieves a regimentation of refractory space, an absolutism of visual power deriving—as the dictator's should—from the intimidating direction of his gaze, which is itself a command and a threat. The implacable visage of the statue focuses the massive landscape "on the right angle formed by the arch of the eyebrow and the nose, where the eye is placed." Washington presages the omnipotence of the purist architect: he can abash Wall Street by merely looking at it.

In the bleakly radiant, renovated New York foreseen by Le Corbusier, the ideal citizens would be the effigies of femininity he admires in the window displays on Fifth Avenue. He sees them as colleagues of Washington, posed before a Doric temple on Wall Street: they're classical statuary in wax, and he inscribes in his notebook the wondering exclamation "Aeschylus!" The malleability of wax appeals to the dictator in him. With it he can make human bodies, as well as buildings to house them. The faces of the dummies sport a "conquering smile," a winsome female version of Washington's forbidding grimace. Like him, they're creatures of austere angularity, with "square shoulders, incisive features, sharp coiffure." Their perms resemble Doric or Ionic decoration, and their heads are those of Delphic goddesses. They would make apt caryatids for the Wall Street temple. Their pallor, sympathizing with the whiteness of Le Corbusier's future New York, pleases him because it's deathly. "When polychromy appears," he says of statuary, "it means that life is breaking out," which is by no means to be encouraged, for the purist city is a death chamber, and the people in it, like these models, must possess a statuesque rigor mortis. Next door to that shop window is the Empire State Building, in whose polished stones and mournful black lobby Le Corbusier finds a tragic gloom and grandeur: it too, like the wax museum, is a mortuary. In these comments on Washington and his harem of mannequins, the French alliance between neoclassicism and a coldly wrathful revolutionary fanaticism—imaged in David's oath-taking Horatii or his Marat in that chilly bath—has been transplanted to New York.

Léger too had a theory of the shop window, more benign than Le Corbusier's (for whom it's a laboratory where the cybernetic future is exhibited and a funeral parlor proclaiming the necessary extermination of the human present), less violent than Dali's (who in 1939, as will be seen, chose a New York window as the theater for a surrealist event). Léger's friend Frederick Kiesler had in 1930 in *Contemporary*

Fernand Léger, "Adieu New York" (1946). Musée National d'Art Moderne, Centre Georges Pompidou, Paris.

Art Applied to the Store and Its Display seen window-dressing as an abstract Esperanto, an international (and conveniently mute) language of form: "a store window is a silent loudspeaker. . . . Its language appeals to everybody and has proved to be the most successful Esperanto for promoting merchandise." When leaving America in 1946, after spending the war years there, Léger paid a similar grateful tribute to the country's receptive internationality. It wasn't a nation, he said, but a world. And the painting that was his valediction, "Adieu New York" (1946), sees the city as the genial container of an international flotsam, like one of its own shop windows and like larger and limitless America. In "Adieu New York" the shop window frames a city of Emma Lazarus's "wretched refuse," a scrap heap of commodities which have found refuge there—junked metal, tailors' dummies, a flapping row of neckties, a banner labeling the display and naming the picture—while over the emporium play those contentless bands of red, blue, green, and yellow which excited Léger in Times Square. The objects float across the canvas as they please, and the color that stripes and striates them is as free as they are, abstracted from function. Purism, almost despite itself, manages a last act of thanksgiving to the liberality and generous chaos of New York.

Abstraction seeks to order the city, wishing on it either system (in Lozowick's case) or rationality (in Le Corbusier's). Surrealism emphasizes its disorder and disintegrativeness. The two motives quarrel in Nathanael West's *Miss Lonelyhearts* (1933). West's hero, convinced of the ancient enmity between man the regulator and lawless nature, sees the New York skyscrapers as symbols of man's revenge on nature, hewing its stones into geometry. As therapy, Miss Lonelyhearts orders the view from his window. He sorts the skyline into a pattern and flinches when a bird flies across and disrupts it. But though the character's reason keeps an abstract watch on the city, emotionally he capitulates to its disorder. The agony columnist's is a surreal profession. He is the custodian of the city's dreams and desires, which manifest themselves as deformities. Driving back into New York through the slums of the Bronx, Miss Lonelyhearts looks at the "broken hands and torn mouths" of his correspondents, and longs to alleviate their misery. His column traffics in the surreal horrors on which the city's uneasy order is founded. West himself, even more perilously, dared that order to combat. He delighted to outsmart it by driving across town at speed in defiance of red lights. His joy in disordering the city is surreal because it accelerates the process of self-destruction, as surrealism hastens the decay of organisms by exposing them to ruthless heat: West was killed in a car crash in 1940.

The New York projected by abstraction is a Utopia—socialist for Lozowick, Cartesian for Le Corbusier. Surreal New York is a pornotopia, a jungle of regression or (as Miss Lonelyhearts experiences it) an infirmary of the psychologically maimed. The surrealist vision arrives in the city with the poet Federico Garcia Lorca in 1929, five years before the invasion by his friend Dali. Lorca came to study at Columbia, and in *Poet in New York* (1940) he situates the surreal underworld of the city to the north of the university, in Harlem. In this suppressed sureal region, the physical delight and native lyricism of the blacks has been enslaved to the service of the city's machines. The blacks are the victims of the abstractly ordered metropolis. Le Corbusier applauds their helotry: his jazzy trumpeters and tap dancers are piston-operated rhythmic gadgets. Lorca's poems lament this same servility, for which his surrealism is an enraged restitution. His blacks fear relapse into their prerational past, terrified of forgetting the menial skills New York has taught them—lighting stoves, fastening collars, driving automobiles. The city has perversely robotized them, tortured flesh into an automaton. Surrealism proposes the opposite transformation: machinery's morbid decomposition, its reclamation by a nature which rots because it has been abused. Louis Aragon called sureralism an art for an era of metamorphosis. But the surrealist metamorphosis—through which Lorca's New York suffers—is putrefaction, not evolution toward an ideal future like that posited for the city by Lozowick or Le Corbusier. Léger's dream of human relations as Meccano is Lorca's nightmare. Discussing the imagery of Góngora, Lorca says that "epic poems can be written about the struggle of the leukocyte in the confining network of veins." His city is a body in diseased extremism, and his images are its lesions, because the surrealist image records the agonizing dissolution of form. Dali's flayed and quartered corpses, the scattered innards of his spectral cow, his lachrymose telephones, or his eyeball (in Buñuel's *Un chien andalou*) sliced by a razor are all cases of objects becoming images by dismemberment or mortal anguish. In a lecture delivered in Havana on his way home from New York, Lorca defined the mysterious potency of images, which he called "duende," by saying that the "duende" loves wounds and inhabits "areas where form dissolves in a passion transcending any of its visible expressions." Surrealism is the morphological crisis of this traumatized form. The surreal poet's subjects are the same people who supply Miss Lonelyhearts with his constituency: those whom the city has wounded, whose physical integrity it has sundered, breaking their hands and tearing their mouths. The first of the poems in Lorca's cycle proposes as alternatives the mechanistic mutation of objects sponsored by abstraction and the different mutation of surrealism, which encourages the degeneration of objects and records their pathological histories. Lorca is surrounded, he says, by shapes seeking to become crystalline and shapes turning serpentine. Confronted by a choice between contrary metamorphoses, he makes the surrealist decision to let his hair grow, surrendering his own body to the logic of its decay, since hair is the body's excrement.

Lorca's black hero, "El Rey de Harlem," is a surreal gourmand who punishes the mechanical city by cannibalizing it. As the surrealist must be, he's an assassin of forms. Dali, in words recalling Lorca's account of the "duende" as a dweller within wounds and of the image as a vivisector of the body, describes form as "the product of an inquisitorial process of matter." Living matter is screwed and analytically racked into new shapes and meanings. Eating is for Dali a surrealist inquisition of his victuals. Hence his appetite for crushing the skulls of tiny birds and sucking out their squashy brains or for enticing a snail's entrails from its shell on a pronged fork. Crustaceans are a gastronomic challenge to the surrealist because their armor-plating is a defense against what he perceives as the horror of the organic. They think they've outwitted nature by wearing their skeletons on the outside. Dali outwits them by consuming them, and Lorca's exultant king in Harlem likewise gouges out the eyes of crocodiles, smashes little squirrels, murders brandy merchants, and pounds Jewesses into a blubbering lather. Indiscriminate violence is his inquisition of the city's matter. He revives the savage joy abstract mechanism censures. He acts, Lorca says, from a negroid fury in the blood. The skin tries to contain and conceal that frenzy, but it erupts through its integument and flows over rooftops, inundating New York. The king's interior becomes the city's lurid ulterior. The fat lady at Coney Island in another of the *Poet in New York* sequence, "Landscape of the Vomiting Multitude," prosecutes the same war against matter by turning cuttlefish upside down and leaving their exposed, anguished pulp to perish. Like Dali discarding those eviscerated mollusks, she proceeds through the streets leaving a trail of pigeon skulls in her wake.

The making of a surrealist image is a monstrous birth because it's a miscegenation. Dali disassembles Mae West's face to furnish a room: her tumescent lips become a sofa, her nasal cavities the fireplace, her hair is hung as drapes, and her eyes are framed on the wall as paintings. The mother in Lorca's "Abandoned Church" realizes she has a fish for a daughter. Such hybrids are the offspring of a New York that has surreally mated mechanism and organism. Everything in the city dreams of reincarnation. The horse in "Death" wants to be a dog, the dog a swallow, the swallow a wasp, the wasp a horse. Machines breed within themselves the same putrid longings as organisms. The fruit in the bell tower of the abandoned church is wormy, and the iron on the bridge in "Dance of Death" is corroding. Natural growth can express itself only in vile and cancerous excess, as it does within the condemned boy of "In a Farmer's Cabin." In "New York (Office and Denunciation)" Lorca listens to the blood coursing under the city's rational routine of adding and subtracting and diagnoses the fatal malady of the machine, which in its sickness feeds on its own flesh. The city to him is an abattoir where matter can be put through its dissolution or inquisition in efficiently herded wholesale consignments:

> Every day they kill in New York
> four million ducks,
> five million hogs,
> two thousand doves as delicacies for the dying,
> a million cows,
> and two million cocks.

144

Surrealist poetry is the elegiac "song of the worm," an anthem for slaughtered creatures, whether they're the brutalized blacks of Harlem or the shipments of animals sacrificed to keep dying humans temporarily alive; it's an agony column like that of Miss Lonelyhearts, tabulating the city's griefs and exorcistically assuming its sins, extending compassion—as Lorca does in his equation of "oxidation, fermentation, earth eruptions" (comparing the debilities of iron with those of yeasty nature and interpreting both as symptoms of a surreal and subterranean disturbance)—not solely to people but to machines, which must abide diseases of their own.

For Lorca as for Miss Lonelyhearts, surrealism is a ministry to the city, a commiseration with its ravaged body. They assuage its wounds; Dali, when he arrives in New York, in 1934, gleefully inflames them. His surrealism is a means of conquest, not, like Lorca's, of confession, and he demands the surrender of New York because he has after all invented it. Surrealism desires a newfound land, a "treasure island" of delirium and irrationality, as Dali says in a 1941 article which boasts "New York Salutes Me": he found this mental province in Manhattan. His first imaginative act there is to symbolically revise its color. Le Corbusier whitened it; Dali proclaims it to be a sanguinary, intestinal red. He dismisses the asepsis of modernism, which portrays the city as a germless and stainless machine. Le Corbusier had wanted to cleanse New York. Abstraction is the application of a laved and featureless new skin. Paul Strand's photographs render New York abstract by laundering it of realistic grime—"Geometric Backyards, New York" (1917) is geometric because of the fresh, drying domestic linen strung on the line, with a sheet seen from above stretched out like a trampoline; a new coat of white paint performs the same sanitary, abstract service for a building in "Apartment, Repainted, New York" (1925) that snow does for Central Park in the series of photographs Strand took there in 1915. Abstraction bleaches a surface which realism characterfully stains. But for surrealism the addition of paint is a psychic sullying. It was a surreal fancy of Apollinaire's to imagine that the New York Public Library was made of white marble and owed its present soiled hue to being washed each day with brown soap. The building's excremental tint is the suffusion of its shame, a blush (originating, like the King of Harlem's rage, in the blood that boils beneath the skin) cosmetically affixed, a cleansing which paradoxically dirties. As Dali sees it, the surreal nature of New York is evinced by its maggoty carnality. The talismans he at once attaches to it testify to its ripe fleshliness—uncooked meat and cheese. The reporters asked him, when he landed in 1934, whether it was true that he had painted his wife "with a pair of fried chops balanced on her shoulder." He corrected them by pointing out that the chops were raw because his wife was too. The story is the first scandalous tidbit he tosses to America, and it circulates with such speed that Dali imagines he has turned New York into a jungle of ravening carnivores. By the end of his first day there, the entire city, he says in his *My Secret Life* (1942), was chewing on those bleeding chops. When he wakes the next morning in the Hotel St. Moritz, the city confirms the bloodthirstiness he has excited in it by the temptation of meat, for the first thing he hears is the roar of hungry lions in the Central Park zoo. Cheese, like raw meat, is a surreal appetizer for Dali because it becomes tasty by the excavations of worms. The molten watches in his "Persistence of Memory" (1931) derived their formlessness from runny Camembert. Thus he compliments New York by associating it with a favored cheese. When he sees the skyline from his boat, he likens it to "an immense Gothic Roquefort cheese," adding, with the imperious gustatory intent of Lorca's King of Harlem, "I love Roquefort." Since the city's architecture is grisly biology, not celibate mechanism, Dali also interprets the skyline priapically. From the ship, he sees Manhattan as the rearing multiple erection of some couchant, many-phallused monster. After sunset, lights burst on in the skyscrapers as if in response to a libidinal massage, which caresses the prongs until, Dali says, they void themselves in the sky's vagina. Traveling on the subway also inserts you, through the door of a gash (the wound which houses Lorca's elvish "duende"), into that body. Dali declares that the cars run "not on iron rails" but "on rails of calves' lungs!"

Surreal metaphor disinters an id within objects and invites them to act out the fantasies they cherish beneath their steel and concrete casing. The city's electrification is explained by the pornography and pathology of metaphor: lust, Dali exclaims, keeps the buildings alight and warm. They're on heat, and their febrility aids the advance of those maladies with which surrealism infects them, speeding their ripening and their decadent decomposition. Like the deserts that concentrate a deranging, reforming heat on those timepieces or that turn flesh in his "Sleep" to dripping wax, Dali's New York is a laboratory of intensified entropy, where things become surreal in a thermodynamic malaise. What he called "the hurly burly of New York life" works like a furnace to change "solid things . . . into soft ones." His art records the agony of their metamorphosis. In a 1935 cartoon titled "Gangsterism and goofy visions of New York" the surreal forfeiture of identity demands the demolition of architecture. Fists clasping guns and knives smash through a sequence of walls: irrationality levels the defensive partitions we raise

Salvador Dali, "Gangsterism and Goofy Visions of New York" (1935). Menil
Collection, Houston, Texas.

around our lives and call reality. Dali sees the stylish streamlining of New York in the 1930s as a premonition of the exhausted, dissolute state toward which the city surreally hastens. In some impressions drawn for the *American Weekly* he sketched a stone he had picked up in Central Park. It already had the shape of a skull; he augmented this with aviational sleekness because the object to him symbolized the speed of death. For the same paper he drew a New York socialite with airplane wings added to her costume: she had transformed herself into a surreal suicidal angel, anxious to propel herself toward her inevitable disintegration. She was wearing the deathly longing of her id. Like the guests at the Bal Onirique given for Dali on the eve of his departure for Europe in January 1935, she was dressed in a metaphor. He called this occasion a "dream betrayal" of New York. His visit had begun with a carnivorous betrayal; it ended with this incitement of an oneiric treason. At first the city had been lured, by those chops, into loosing its prurient and greedy instincts. Now it was encouraged to liberate its even more ashamed and secretive life of imagination. The guests were expected to let ideas—those bacilli of mad, sick desires—literally germinate. Associatively, these morbid ideas closeted within would manifest themselves on the outside as sores, rashes, carbuncles. The guests arrived at Le Coq Rouge on East 56th Street attired surreally in their symptoms. Some painted mutilations or tumors on themselves, one wore a supernumerary mouth on her stomach, another paraded in a blood-spattered nightshirt. Like Lorca's gluttonous king, Dali had effected an evisceration of the city.

The uprising unconsciousness of objects punches its way through walls (in Dali's "goofy visions") and gores an aperture in flesh (when the partygoers pierce themselves with painted safety pins); on one of Dali's later visits to New York, this surreal impetus shattered protective glass. In 1939 Dali was commissioned to design a shop window for Bonwit Teller on Fifth Avenue. He began from a detestation of those mannequins by whose arrogant imperturbability Le Corbusier was so impressed. Dali dislikes them because they're immune to decay and refuse to be consumed: "so hard, so inedible," as he calls them, they have defeated surrealism. He revenges himself by surreally aging them. In the window he placed some musty, cobwebbed models exhumed from an attic. They extruded—as corpses continue to do, and as Lorca surreally chooses to do when deciding, on arrival in New York, to let his hair grow—"long natural dead women's hair." For Kiesler and the purists the shop window had been a laboratory exhibiting the abstract future; Dali makes it a charnel house of surreal memory. At Bonwit

Teller his elderly mannequins bathed in a tub with a hirsute lining of astrakhan and slept on charred sheets under a canopy from which trickled the blood of a pigeon. The management of the store, aghast, dismantled the display. Dali insisted on its restoration and, when the management refused, clambered into the window to upset the furry bathtub. His intention was only to embarrass Bonwit Teller by spilling the water, but as he dislodged the tub it slid across the floor, smashed the plate glass, and deluged the sidewalk. Dali followed it through the gaping pane (another of Lorca's wounds) to join the crowd on Fifth Avenue. In doing so, he was acting out the forced entry into consciousness which he wanted his irrational images to make. They too crave to splinter the glass that flattens and suppresses them, to rebel into a third dimension. They are the interior which vomitously—as Lorca says of the multitudes at Coney Island—insists on exteriorizing itself. Dali was arrested for his pains and remarked that the affair did more for his glory than if he'd devoured Fifth Avenue entire. This constitutes his triumph: a parabolic digestion of the city; a surreal conquest by cannibalism.

Creating art is for Dali synonymous with scandal-mongering. Irrationality attains power by causing offense and—even better—damage. A comparable onslaught on New York, serving a different modernist cause, had been mounted by Diego Rivera in 1931. Though their tactics are incompatible—Dali trusts in an antic effrontery, in licentious self-publicizing, while Rivera organizes and trains a cadre of infiltrators—their ambitions converge. Both want to make New York betray itself, Dali by interpreting its dreams, Rivera by inscribing on the headquarters of capitalism a prediction of the Marxist reckoning to come. Dali foments a psychological and Rivera a political revolution. Dali perverts New York, dressing one of its skyscrapers in kinky furs and setting a gargantuan lamb chop on its (or, as Dali insists, her) pinnacle, catering to the depraved wishes of the place; Rivera subversively mines the citadel from within.

The muralist arrives in the city as both prophet and guerrilla. His task is to write denunciations of the city on its walls—to invoke a retributive future, and then (as happened with the painting Rivera was commissioned to make in the lobby of Rockefeller Center) to do battle on behalf of that pictured millennium. Rivera nominated the mural as the form in which capitalism would read of its own demise because the mural remembers the social conditions predating capitalism and prefigures the new dispensation made possible by capitalism's overthrow. Craftsman-like and collaborative in execution, it repudiates the bourgeois fallacy of art as personal property. Its existence portends the confiscation of all personal property: Rivera said he was painting not for the magnates who had commissioned him but for the day when Rockefeller Center, liberated and renamed, would belong to the common man. He learned the techniques of mural from masons and house-painters in Mexico, but he exercised them in the United States, decorating a lunchroom for the San Francisco stockbrokers, a courtyard for the Detroit Institute of Arts, and finally an elevator shaft at Rockefeller Center. The mural originates in the naive collectivity of a rural economy; once transferred across the border it becomes an augury—in its distribution of labor—of the juster, socialized collectivity ahead. Rivera planned to "show the Workers arriving at a true understanding of their rights regarding the means of production" and then achieving "the liquidation of Tyranny." A statue of Caesar crumbles; so, accused by the mural, will Rockefeller Center. A mural's ambition is to topple the walls on which it's painted, or at least to see through them. It's a denial or denunciation of architecture. Contemporary Californian muralists like to depict on the sides of buildings the eroding coast and the untrustworthiness of an earth which will no longer sustain architecture; their counterparts on the Lower East Side of New York reconvert the industrial city to a tropical isle dreamed of by deracinated wage-slaves, abolishing the buildings that are their canvases. Ever since that fiery exhortation at Belshazzar's feast, the mural has been a view through or instead of a wall, not on one. This is true even of a nonmural painting like Rivera's "Frozen Assets," shown at his Museum of Modern Art exhibition in 1931. It X-rays the previously opaque pictorial surface. In his Detroit mural he painted the internal anatomy of the machine, representing the pipes and belts of the Ford automotive works looped and coiled like the sinewy coordinated innards of a human body; in "Frozen Assets" he more morbidly diagnoses the fatality of the commercial city, cross-sectioning it for purposes of autopsy. The city of "Frozen Assets" is a dead but avariciously retentive body. At the top of the composition rear the skyscrapers of the financial district. They are its superstructure, cramping beneath them the dormitories of exhausted toilers and, on a lower level, the subterranean bank vaults hoarding those assets. Rivera penetrates the walls and can see that the lodgings of the workers and the strong rooms of the bank are alike prisons. In rendering those rooms transparent, he has uncaged them, proleptically liberating their inhabitants and their pecuniary contents.

Everything in the painting is frozen, petrified in an acquisitive death. The skyscrapers are gravestones planted above the earth, the workers

Diego Rivera, "Frozen Assets: A Cross-Section Through the City" (1931). "Mobile" fresco.

the dead sleepers beneath it, and the assets are coffined money. "Frozen Assets" depicts New York as a mortuary; the Rockefeller mural was to show its uprisen afterlife. The painting plumbs downward, excavating the city's cemeteries and its iniquitous secrets; the mural streams upward to a socialist heaven, greeting the unchained sky. As Rivera saw it, "the main plastic function of the central panel" of his work was "to express the central axis of the building, its loftiness, and the ascending echelon of its lateral masses." The elevator shaft charged his mural with a task of dialectical graduation. Placed between the designs of Frank Brangwyn (whose subject was ethical evolution) and José Maria Sert (who recorded the evolution of technical power), Rivera's scheme was to overtop theirs, urging a development beyond and above the stages at which they had rested content. As Rivera's mural grew up the walls of Rockefeller Center, it would enable man—shown in his design stealing fire and harnessing electricity, commanding the stars through telescopes, using the equipment of Radio City to beam missives throughout the universe—to reach into the sky and unseat the dynasty of rentier gods. It was a dream of the millennium, and an agenda for revolution. Once man had reattained divinity, he would seize and reconsecrate the temple of the capitalists. But the usurers were not so easily routed. The bosses objected to Rivera's inclusion of Lenin as the instructor of workers and soldiers, and when he wouldn't repaint the face, they discharged him and destroyed the work. He repainted it in Mexico; Sert blandly filled in the offending space.

From the debacle, Rivera salvaged a rhetorical victory. He intended, he said, to portray "Man . . . in his triple aspect," in a successive promotion from the Peasant (who garners from the earth the raw material of all earthly riches) to the Worker (who, having migrated to the city, transforms those agricultural raw materials into manufactures) and ultimately to the Soldier (whose ethical enlightenment, once he has been radicalized, defends the economy owned and managed by his two emblematic colleagues). But this triad is subsumed, as politics retreats into art, in a fourth figure: the Muralist, whose heroic mission reunites Peasant, Worker, and Soldier. The alliance between the first pair was cemented when Rivera introduced the rural artisan's murals to the industrial cities of America. The muralist is defined as a worker, not an artist—the Mexican practitioners of the medium were paid the wages of a laborer—and his painting must have a toughness and resilience like the proletarian's physical sturdiness. In the 1930s Edward Laning was commissioned to paint an account of the activities of a settlement house in Hell's Kitchen. The institution's founder took him on a tour of the place and pointed out "wallboard partitions in the corridors through which the neighborhood boys, to demonstrate their strength, had poked holes with their fists." In self-defense Laning decided on fresco, which the local ruffians couldn't injure.

The next dialectical transition, which makes of the muralist a soldier as well as a peasant and a worker, comes with Rivera's declension from painting to text. After his sacking, he wrote up the incident in his *Portrait of America* (1934). Here he treats his dismissal as a battle. From the midst of the fray, he issued a "military dispatch," as he called it, concerning the assault. The lobby becomes a besieged fort, with the bosses manning a blockade at the entry onto Fifth Avenue. Rivera's defeat is engineered by subterfuge: he's lured away from his post to negotiate a truce, while "a platoon of sappers, who had been hidden in ambush," charge and occupy his defenseless scaffold. The capitalist contractors enroll in a gentlemen's army; the painter and his assistants are a contingent of nimble guerrillas. Their assailants pompously inflate the odds, doubling their numbers and calling in airplanes to buzz the imperiled building; Rivera's force is gallant because paltry, consisting of himself and six helpers. The rhetoric of Rivera's memoir works in two ways at once, ridiculing his opponents by exaggerating their cowardly violence but flattering his own small band of loyalists. The affair, as completed by the text, is a mock-epic, as absurd as the armed avenging of a raped lock. The mounted police in the streets outside evince "their heroic and incomparable prowess" by clubbing an insurrectionary seven-year-old girl. However, in another sense it is authentically an epic. The capitalists seem to have believed, Rivera concludes in amazement, that the city could be "destroyed utterly by the mere presence of an image of Vladimir Ilyich." If so, they were right: the image existed to upbraid and undermine the actuality. And consequently, the text is no anticlimax but a continuation of the painting by other means, since when the porters and detectives and plenipotentiaries in the lobby take up arms, they are obeying the dictates of the mural, which, as an allegory, militarizes life by rendering it militant, conscripting its characters and requiring them to adopt postures of moralistic aggression and defense.

Modernism, in all these assaults on New York, is programmatic and ideologically zealous, using art to effect a change in society. But Rivera's coup is accomplished only in a painting and, once that is impounded, in a tendentious, hyperbolic literary text. Rather than being the model for revolution, the mural itself becomes the revolution. New York meanwhile remains its unregenerate self.

8

The Photographer
as Citizen

Because their art is pledged to the analytic rearrangement of appearance, the modernist painters are roused to demonstrate their power over
the resistant substance of New York. They hope to demolish it, as
proof of reality's submission to them. Picabia reroutes it through the
body, Marin makes it tremble volcanically, Dali on his first visit admonishes it with an attenuated and crusty phallic breadstick, Rivera plots
its political capitulation. The photographers, whose discovery of the
city advances in parallel with theirs, treat it more tactfully. To them it's
not a challenge to establish a visual dictatorship, declaring that things
exist only as they're perceived. Instead, the city instructs them in visual
modesty, even in visual shame. The camera seemed made to record the
velocity of urban existence. In 1922 Paul Strand experimentally tracked
cars past Grant's Tomb with a movie camera: one machine competitively raced another. But as soon as the machine solicits people it encounters an impediment. The necessary diplomacy of photography
consists in convincing people to pose for you. If they're willing subjects, however, your record of them will probably be cheesily unreal.
The truth about them can be revealed only if they're caught off guard.
How do you justify this sneaking and spying?

154

The aesthetics of photography at once get entangled with the ethics of citizenship. The camera's presence in the city offends against that urban pact whereby we abide the congestion which has denied us privacy by politely ignoring one another. To be photographed is to be stared at, which urban etiquette forbids (except to out-of-towners, who have come to gape). The photographic image knows that it's accosting and perhaps defrauding its subject because its purpose in the city is to create visibility, to coerce reality out of hiding. Thus the photographic act becomes that rudest and (in a city) most perilous of denotations, a pointing of the finger. It's a visual citation: an image is compelled, maybe against its will, to bear witness. The accusing stigmatism of photography literally intrudes into one of Jacob Riis's photographs. Dated about 1890, it shows an "ancient lodger" arraigned at the Eldridge Street police station. She has been backed up against a filthy wall next to a blunt post, to which she is—at least metaphorically—tethered. Her eyes are shut, presumably against the glare of the flash, but also in self-defense. By not looking, she is disputing the camera's right to make her testify against herself. The image's overbearing indexation of her happens in the right corner, where a hand, holding between thumb and forefinger the cord for the flash, juts into the photograph. One finger of this bodiless hand points at the woman, aiming slightly above her head. It's a finger of indicativeness, signifying Riis's achievement in having brought the abused woman to light. Riis's combustible flashes created a scandalous visibility, as did, in the 1940s, the snooping "invisible light" used by Weegee to see what the eye couldn't and shouldn't discern—couples amorously wrestling on the beach at Coney Island after midnight or in the balconies of Times Square movie houses. Weegee also used a flash when his aim was to startle his victims, not to spy on them. For Riis it had been both a means and a symbol of indictment; for Weegee it's a weapon. The photographic act is the equivalent of a holdup—the robbery by violence of a person's image or aura. The analogy is implied by Weegee's 1943 photograph of a gun shop opposite police headquarters on Centre Street. The flash explodes in the dark street, and its flare lights up a huge revolver suspended over the pavement to advertise the gunsmith's wares. The camera shoots on behalf of the gun, which will also emit light along with its missile when the trigger is pressed. Photographic denotation alarmingly approaches detonation. The same equation between the camera and the pistol occurs in one of William Klein's photographs, taken on the streets of Little Italy in 1954. Three ragamuffins giggle for the camera. A fourth figure, older and taller, her head chopped

Jacob A. Riis, "Police Station Lodgers—An Ancient Lodger, Eldridge Street" (ca. 1890). (With the bed on which she slept.) Jacob A. Riis Collection, Museum of the City of New York.

out of the frame, grips the little boy's fist with apparent affection while with her other hand she aims a toy gun at his head. She's the photographer's surrogate: reassuring with one hand, threatening with the other; a good-humored mugger. To compound the ambiguity, Klein has identified her as the little boy's mother.

The photographer's trade is visual trespass. He can only practice it on the streets of the city—where one's gaze is entitled to be free on condition that it doesn't linger—by camouflage and subterfuge. The city imposes the unique creative condition of forcing him to make art while pretending to be doing something else. Strand, working in New York in 1915 and 1916, worried that he might be found out and denounced by his quarry (as he was by an old woman with a cage of parakeets or on another occasion by a gang of rowdies). In his "Lower Broadway" a pair of women turn back to smirk knowingly at him. Their complicity demeans him: to them, the photographer is just a peeping tom. His docile, unsuspecting subjects are those who can't defend themselves with pretense or (like those shoppers on Broadway) with flirta-

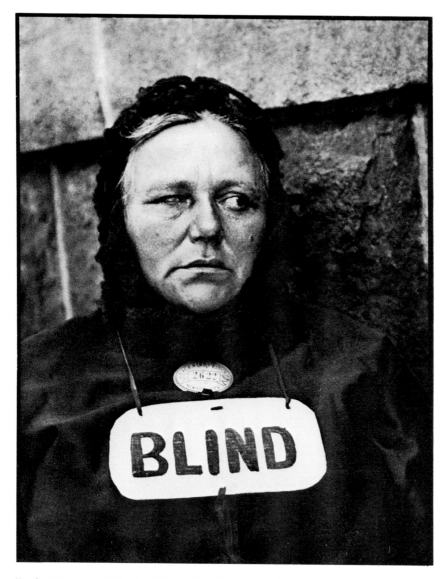

Paul Strand, "Blind Woman" (New York, 1916). Lunn Gallery, Washington, D.C.

tious acquiescence—the down-and-out on park benches like the lined, bitter woman is "Washington Square Portrait"; the "Man" wearing the derby in Five Points Square, whose gaze meets the camera but looks through it, too dejected to care; most disquieting of all, the "Blind Woman" selling newspapers on Lexington Avenue at 34th Street. One of her eyes is pursed shut, the other is glaucously averted. A hand-lettered sign around her neck announces that she's blind, and thus invites the photographer to take advantage; another tin badge, classifying her as the photographic image does, or bureaucratically indexing her as the disembodied hand does to Riis's "ancient lodger," certifies that she has been licensed as a peddler by the city of New York. Like Klein's scene of the gun-wielding woman, it's a case of photography's self-inculpation. Strand claimed that he never doubted the probity of what he was doing, but his concealment and self-counterfeiting argue otherwise. For work in New York he fixed a dummy lens to his camera and pretended to aim it while the real lens jutted out from under his arm. At least he has the sensitivity to apologize or prevaricate. Later on, Weegee deals out a rough justice to the city's malefactors, who are sentenced by the camera before they're brought to trial. His characters in *Naked City* (1945), hustled into the police wagon, hide their faces behind handkerchiefs or hats and vainly beg Weegee not to publicize their shame. He expects resistance and delights in it as an admission of guilt. Whereas Strand has qualms about his blind woman, Weegee, in a comparable instance, feels compelled to explain why a character so meekly accepts the obloquy of the photograph. A quiet and genteel old man, who has just knifed a blonde in a hotel room, paces by into custody on his cane. Weegee's caption points out that he didn't cover his face "as he couldn't see my camera because he was blind."

The movie camera also affected a self-protective anonymity. King Vidor, making *The Crowd* in New York in 1928, hid the camera inside a barricade of packing crates on a corner or mounted it on the back of a truck from where it peered out through a hole in the flap. Vidor loitered alongside, posing as an idler on the street, and muttered his instructions to the cameraman under cover. This absconding of the camera is its relegation to the crowd. At the end of the film the hero, having survived economic calamity and personal tragedy, disappears into the urban collectivity of comedy. Enjoying himself in a theater, he dwindles—as the camera withdraws from him—into the immense audience and into the city, rolled around in earth's diurnal and reliable course. He is not singular enough to qualify for tragedy. Averageness and anonymity are his comic salvation. The camera, by effacing itself, keeps the same low profile, aspiring to a safe, comic characterlessness. When Weegee's *Naked City* was adapted into a film in 1948, the camera's reticence acquired a different, slier meaning. The director Jules Dassin called *The Naked City* "my answer to Rossellini's *Open City*." *Roma, Città Aperta* (1945) began as a documentary about a priest executed for fomenting dissidence in Nazi-occupied Rome. Filming was at first illicit, though the

Allies arrived before it was completed. So, for Dassin, the denudation of New York by Weegee's scandalous camera is equated with the liberation of Rome by Rossellini's underground camera. Even though in New York he was not opening up a captive city, Dassin's documentary camera remains a spy, versatilely taking refuge during the filming in phone booths, dummy ambulances, or a superannuated moving van with a two-way mirror on the tailgate. The filming was organized with a devious skill worthy of the criminals whose activity it investigated. To allay the suspicions of passersby, diversions were staged: a juggler performed and a man propped on a thirty-foot ladder waved the American flag. Street-smart imps relished the way the camera was picking the pockets of the citizens by cheating them of their fees as extras. A shoeshine body remarked to the producer, Mark Hellinger, that the crowd distracted by the juggler "should be getting twenty-five a day for being in the movies and they don't know it." Sometimes, while conducting surveillance, the camera unintentionally saw things it shouldn't have—not breaches of the law but incriminating social details which Dassin was forced to cut from the release print, such as Bowery bums selling off their last possessions outside the Diamond Exchange.

Weegee boasted that neither he nor his camera had any inhibitions. He conducted his sex life with the same importunate publicity that characterized his photography. His initiation came while he was sleeping out on an East Side rooftop during a heat wave. "Poor people," he claimed, "are not fussy about privacy; they have other problems." The inhibiting conscience of the urban camera is Walker Evans. The beauty of his work is its ethical scrupulousness: he accuses himself in advance of prying. His great volume *American Photographs* (1938) begins by acknowledging the cheapness and mendacity of the photographic image. Its first two plates are the medium's self-castigation. One shows a shanty on Baxter Street in lower Manhattan which at a charge of five cents takes photos for driving-license tests; the other is a penny picture gallery of affable nobodies from Savannah. Together, these images state the paradox to which Evans's unposed portraits of New Yorkers recur. We use photographs as a means of identifying ourselves—to qualify for a license or to commemorate our kinship—but also of concealing ourselves, since we hide from the camera behind our mistrustfully guarded or feature-lessly bland expressions. Photography abets our evasion by equalizing us. All posed against the same studio sky, all wearing the same smiles, the people in the gallery of 225 images merge into a single extended family, just as, in the den dealing in licenses, photography serves as a means of classifying and indexing people, not of individualizing them.

All the photos taken on Baxter Street will be filed away in the offices of the traffic police. On Baxter Street the medium is too brutally indifferent, in Savannah too cozily sentimental. In either case, its subjects don't reveal themselves, only their opinion of the camera—gloweringly hostile or innocently fond.

In Evans's "Posed Portraits, New York, 1933" a short-order cook and a dungaree-clad colleague consent to be photographed on the steps of a diner. Their wariness of the camera encourages them to overdo the appearance of relaxation. The cook has one hand jauntily on his hip, the other around the neck of his friend: it's the kind of draped and sinuous posture you adopt for a holiday snapshot, where you must show that you're having a good time, and it's oddly wrong for the grubby setting with its menu of inexpensive sandwiches. The black woman in Evans's "42nd St., 1929" looks mildly affronted by the camera's presence but determines to outstare it, confident because—behind her hedge of fur, with a garniture of jewels—affluent. The truck drivers Evans photographed in 1933 lounge against the cab of their vehicle but aren't appeased. In their stance there's sullenness, even menace. And though Evans's friend Ben Shahn believed that his right-angled viewfinder enabled him to observe New Yorkers with impunity, they scowl back at him, scenting a trick—a man on a bench in Seward Park in 1933 grips his chin pensively and frowns at the camera; another on the Willis Avenue Bridge steadies himself and gazes levelly at it, wondering why it can be interested in him, unshaven and indigent as he is; a barber on the stoop of his shop glares from behind the ambuscade of a walrus moustache. Two of Evans's street scenes are unposed. The girl with the sensual pout on Fulton Street in 1929 and the grimacing middle-aged couples dressed in their Sunday finery to sit on a bench in the Bronx in 1933 don't adopt expressions to keep the camera at bay. On the contrary, they're looking elsewhere, and doing so with the predatory intentness of the photographer. The girl crossly turns back against the crowd to eye someone, a woman on the Bronx bench cranes her neck for gossipy inspection of some neighbor's behavior. Other Evans characters are the camera's uncomplaining victims either because—like the couple arm in arm at Luna Park in 1928 or the girl leaning over the boardwalk at Coney Island in 1929—their backs are turned or because they're in a stupor, like the bum stretched out asleep on a doorstep in "South Street, New York, 1933." But not even the prostrate, who seem to be beyond caring, can be observed without misgiving. Another of the South Street scenes is a triptych of contrasting reactions to the photographer. In the middle doorway is the same bum, abjectly asleep. To his left a man reads a newspaper, glumly preoccupied. Right of center another grizzled wayfarer sits. He looks at the camera with suspicion but resignation. One man can't see it, the other prefers not to, the third does notice it yet—professionally accustomed to having things done to him—passively accepts its insult. Though these men surrender to the camera, Evans can't purge himself of the feeling that he's exploiting them. Perhaps this is why he resorts to making portraits of people in their absence, by photographing rooms which house their ghosts along with their discarded clothes—the cave of a lodging-house bedroom on Hudson Street in 1931, the brassy chic of Cary Ross's bedroom in New York in 1932, the austerely tidy impoverishment of the sharecroppers' cabins in Alabama in 1936.

Some of these qualms he overcomes in the series of photographs he made on West 61st Street between First and Third avenues in the summer of 1938. Here he's licensed by the season, which breaks down the barrier between domesticity and the street, where the photographer —who deals in the publicizing of the private—plies his trade. In the heat, the residents take their lives outdoors. Washing is strung on fire escapes or across the courtyard between buildings. A fat woman uses her windowsill as a patio. The window is equipped with a sagging grate, into which one of her pudgy arms just fits. Its purpose is to repel intruders, but she's pressing against it from inside, employing it as an alfresco room for socializing, as she's seen doing with a neighbor who pauses on the stoop. She's an adipose overspill from inside the house, as are the plants in window boxes in another of these photographs. The room within seems to be a summer garden, a seething hothouse where things grow so riotously that they spread across the sill and send roots trailing into the street to tease the pavement. The people clustered round the stoop have annexed the street as a gregarious sitting room. The children playing with dolls and comic books domesticate the pavement, erecting there a fantasy house which, to accommodate the camera, is transparent. One of the girls wears a toy stethoscope and is supplying medical services to the dolls.

At the same time, Evans began a series of unposed portraits on the subway, which he continued until 1941. Underground, he's at once recalled to the guilty reservations he could afford to dismiss when working on 61st Street. Summer coaxes the people of that street to air their private concerns outdoors, which is why they tolerate the camera. But subway travel has a different and defensive code of manners and presents the photographer with an acute problem. On the subway we behave as if a raucous, unrespectful public space were a private sanctum.

Walker Evans, "New York, N.Y. 61st Street between 1st and 3rd Avenues. Children playing in the Street" (Summer, 1938). Documentation scene for Farm Security Administration. Library of Congress, Washington, D.C.

We construct chimerical rooms around ourselves with newspapers. Cowering behind them, we resemble the children playing house on 61st Street, except that we're doing in grim psychological earnest what they do in jest. This is why the camera's violation of those frail, pretending walls is permissible above ground but reprehensible beneath it. The photographer's avocation of looking has its own strict rules on the subway. Gazes must be neutral, so that they never intersect. Everyone's eyes cruise in search of an area of space to look into which hasn't been occupied by someone else. In this region of visual obliquity or avoidance, the camera commits the outrage of focusing its eye. Because it looks at people who don't know they're being looked at, their expressions are painfully intimate. One woman in Evans's sequence has a hurt, lined face and keeps her hands resignedly clasped. A girl stares straight ahead, achieving the undercover evacuation of our faces we practice on the subway, in the hope·of appearing so blank we'll seem not to be there. A man yawns, his mouth a black gap. The camera is immune to embarrassment and doesn't politely avert its gaze, as we do if someone to whom we're talking yawns. Evans here snaps a footnote to Strand, who in 1916 photographed a "Yawning Women, New York."

Walker Evans, "Subway Portrait (Male)" (1938–41). Gelatin-silver print. 5 x 5 1/16 inches (12.8 x 12.9 cm.). Collection, The Museum of Modern Art, New York. Purchase.

Fat, frumpish, and stubble-chinned, Strand's woman looks away from the impertinent camera. Others among Evans's riders sleep or perhaps play possum, because in doing so they're guaranteed a certain privacy. As with that yawn, the camera here disregards a taboo. It's improper to look at someone who's asleep unless you do so lovingly—watching over your child or your bed partner—and with no wish to take advantage of their vulnerability. Evans had already flouted a similar taboo when, in "Quick Lunch, New York City" (1933), he photographed three men masticating in a cafeteria window. One has his mouth open, the others have angrily shut theirs. Two of then grip bitten sandwiches. The unmannerly photographer, who respects the ruminative privacy of eating as little as he does the profounder self-surrender of sleep, is lucky to be outside on the street. The men behind the glass look as if, were he within reach, they would retaliate. In homage to Strand, whose blind newspaper vendor was the only image Evans admired in Stieglitz's periodical *Camera Work*, he concludes the subway sequence with a shot of a blind begging accordionist who gropes his way down a crowded carriage, unheeded by the newspaper readers. They might make a donation but pretend not to see him. The camera at least takes cognizance of him. Yet is its attention compassionate?

His fear that he may have been victimizing these people kept Evans from publishing the photographs for twenty years, and when he released the first of them to *Harper's Bazaar* in 1962, he implied that he had, in penitence, chosen to be looked back at by these unsuspecting sitters for two decades. He's spent that time in the dock, while they sat in judgment on his motives for having photographed them. "These," Evans said in introducing the selection, "are the ladies and gentlemen of the jury." He had submitted himself to trial by his peers and believed that he had at length earned their pardon. Still, a doubt persists. James Agee claimed that the photographs cherished an individuality that posed portraiture could not convey: each face is "as matchless as a thumbprint or a snowflake." The reference to the thumbprint, however, suggests the use of photography for keeping an official and uncaring tally of people; so do the plaques identifying subway lines above the heads of some subjects (7TH AVE. LOCAL or LEX. AVE. LOCAL), which deputize for the name and number tags in mug shots, locating the culprit at the place where he or she was captured. When the complete sequence was published in 1966, Evans titled it *Many Are Called*. Does he mean that photography is a spiritual election? Many are called to the subway; the choosing of the few who will qualify for the lens's gift of grace is the photographer's godly prerogative.

To compensate for this arrogation of power, Evans impeded himself technically. The difficulties of making the shots were so great that he embraced them as a test. With the lens poking at the opposite bench through the buttons of his coat, he couldn't control what he saw or how it was lit, and every choice of a moment to shoot—which he did by pressing a cable in his sleeve—was arbitrary. By this self-abnegating trust in luck he recognizes the accidental nature of urban encounters. Reaching for the shutter and hoping for the best, he bravely chances it, as he would if he approached one of these people and began a conversation. In that case he'd risk rebuff, as the pictures risk failure. His weighting of the odds against himself vouches for the generosity of his impulse. These images of yearning, unconsummated urban relationships have the same baffled compassion as those of the poor Alabama farmers, for Evans recognizes that, however it may long to ameliorate what it sees, the camera is a means of mediation, not communication, mechanically interposing itself between the operator's body and that of his subject.

Exoneration was eventually granted to the camera by Steichen's *Family of Man* exhibition at the Museum of Modern Art in 1955. In contrast with Evans's admission of the cheap reproducibility of photography in that Baxter Street lean-to, Steichen makes the camera an instrument of electoral franchise, a universal census-taker. The jubilant masses in his display accept that sooner or later everyone in the world will be photographed. The camera can reproduce us as we reproduce ourselves, and its global inventory of the human family corresponds to the models of democratic participation which the exhibition salutes: ballotting at free elections and a debate at the General Assembly of the United Nations. *The Family of Man* is a photo album of birth, copulation, and death, not for a single family but for the entire race. Though to Evans the camera's subjects are reluctant, knowing they have been deprived by it, the people in Steichen's show greet it as an ally, employed inside the copious family with the special liberty allowed to love.

Photography's initial tense is the present. It prizes the moment—those serendipitous instants after which Cartier-Bresson capered. But in the act of catching such moments it alters their tense, by consigning them to the safekeeping of eternity. The art is about the sad custody of the present moment, which in the photo album has value because it is, by now, all that remains of our past. Photography offers this same emotional service to the city. Evans trusted that time would mitigate his subway photographs by withdrawing them into the past. By 1966, when they were published, many of the characters would have been the dear dead faces of the family album. Dating palliated the images by making them funereal. Because of this duty to preserve the past and tend its graves, photography assumes a special responsibility for the city, which lives by change and by the obliteration of its past. Coburn thought the camera's qualification in New York was its instantaneousness, its openness to a changeful perpetual present. Cars speed through his plates, leaving streaky wakes of light, tugboats let off plumes of smoke. Their mechanical consumption of fuel is equalled by the photographer's swift energy in pursuing them. But there is always another tense, from which these excited moments emerge and into which they are absorbed. As Stieglitz realized, the instant must be pondered, because it derives from a meditative eternity. On 22 February 1893 he stood for hours in a blizzard on Fifth Avenue, awaiting "the proper moment" for photography. As soon as that moment arrived, he made it into ancient history. His snow scene doesn't look like an anecdotal instant: it seems to represent an arctic world, prior to human society.

During the 1930s, Berenice Abbott documented New York's reckless reconstruction of itself. Because her subject was impatiently hastening into the future, her technical equipment had to mimic the city's speed. The moments she sought to catch were even more unrepeatable and fraught than those in Coburn's photographs. In an article contributed to *The Complete Photographer* in 1943 she discusses the almost frenetic spontaneity she required of her implements—lenses with shorter focal lengths and quicker shutters, Rolleiflex cameras with "still faster movement"—in order to provide for such urban exigencies as a frantic "dash into the street surrounded by traffic." Yet, as with Stieglitz's long watch in the snow, the hectic present dies at once into the past. The purpose of this technical urgency was to arrest the traffic which Coburn had allowed to stream through his long exposures. With a reducing back, Abbott says, "action may be stopped." The technology of rapidity exists so that the photographer can prohibit motion. Abbott advises that "where more traffic must be stopped, a smaller camera is necessary." The faster the act of photographing becomes, the more placidly still the ensuing image seems. Abbott is haunted by impermanence. In our own lives we rely on photography as a defense against imminent death; she sees the same mortality—which makes the photo album so necessary—in the city. The skyscrapers have a life expectancy even shorter than that of human beings, with an "average time of usefulness" of twenty years. When Berenice Abbott wrote this in 1943, they were only a decade old, but their value had already been halved and their demise had begun. The sociological data that her photographs record—the change from corner groceries to the mass-marketing of the chain stores, for instance —are significant to her because of the generational remembrance made possible, inside the family, by the treasured album: "Certainly a Super A & P store is something our grandmothers would have marveled at; and our grandchildren may well feel the same wonder."

In Berenice Abbott's New York series, photography becomes a visual elegy. One of photography's original purposes is to criticize time, to dispute death's power over us. Family photographers are narrators— "America's storytellers," as Kodak calls its cameras—who protest against the development of narrative, adhering to rhythms of recurrence, telling the same tale over and over to a child who loves it because it's known by heart. Abbott documents those changes which were casualties of New York's self-modernizing in order to mourn them. Her photography is the city's memory and thus (because the unprincipled and heedless city, having forgotten its past, can go on to destroy it) its restraining conscience. Writing about realism, she says that although Drieser and Sloan have sometimes been called desecrators, their purpose is affirmative, and what she calls "living photography" also "builds up, does not tear down." There's a poignancy to the verbal image she chooses, for some of her finest photographic images are of tearing down. Against this demolition, photography proposes a re-erection in memory, like rites for the commemoration (and wishful denial) of a death. Her New York destroys its own architectural past and dynamites the very earth on which it's founded. The photographs she took in 1932 of Rockefeller Center under construction make this point: the aged and weathered, almost fleshly formations of rock are gouged out and carted away, to be supplanted by the riveted skeletal steel of the rising buildings. Her images overlay or juxtapose two ages in the history of New York, which are also the two tenses of photography—its agitated contemporariness and its lamenting stewardship of our past. On East 48th Street she photographs the cohabitation of these twin times. An elderly brownstone has as its neighbor a new residence fronted in glass brick, vitreously and metallically immaculate, all right angles and streamlined curves. Like different generations, they sit together amiably enough to be photographed, but they're biologically at war. Even so, the victory of the present is temporary. It too will soon enough be the past. Indeed, it already is, for the glass-faced newcomer is the identical twin of its senescent companion and has simply had cosmetic surgery. Both were built about 1860; one was remodeled in 1934. Elsewhere the present is glimpsed through the transparency of the past, as in a view of the Wall Street skyscrapers through the masts and rigging of a schooner moored at Pier 11; or the past is visually canceled by the efficient present as it is by the refrigerated containers for bananas parked in front of the arches of the Brooklyn Bridge. One of Abbott's most wryly beautiful images sets the two eras into competition in the air. Next to the steeple of St. Mark's Church a skywriting plane traces an arabesque of smoke. Of course, the plane is far above and beyond the church, but on the photographic plate they share the same two-dimensional space, and contest it. The elegant tapering spire is contradicted by the writhing coil of smoke. The tower is mottled and spotted by age; in contrast with its endurance, the smoke wraps itself into the shape of a spring, a device for storing energy ("250,000 cubic feet of smoke a second," we're in-

Berenice Abbott, "St. Mark's Church with Skywriting. East 10th Street and Second Avenue, Manhattan" (March 23, 1937). Federal Art Project "Changing New York." Museum of the City of New York.

formed), which is doomed to exhaustion and will, when emitted, soon evaporate. Both building and machine have proclamations to make: the age of faith here meets the age of advertising. The painter Ralston Crawford also pointed his camera upward in 1940 or thereabouts and photographed a skywriting plane above New York. His smoke—as befits

Crawford's Precisionism—is exhaled at right angles and aligns itself with the rectilinear rooftops of the skyscrapers. In contrast with Abbott's vaporizing coil, the first of Crawford's three shots observes the intersection of two perfectly straight lines. Smoke is apparently proving a geometric proposition up there. But as the sequence proceeds, the angle grows another crossbar and forms into an F. By the third snap, it has emblazoned the name of the product it's advertising across the blank sky: FOX FUR. Abbott's image is a poem, lyrically elegiac; Crawford's, austerer and unemotional, spells out a theorem.

Abbott's images are obituaries. "These houses no longer exist," she noted in 1943 of a Cherry Street row she had photographed in 1931. For her *Changing New York* volume in 1939, Elizabeth McClausland provided captions that are sepulchral prognoses, and sometimes far too optimistic in their estimate of the patient's chances. In her note to Abbott's photograph of the El, McClausland allows the railway to look forward to a Methusalean future. Its lease won't expire "till 2878; and no doubt by then all the 'Els' will be torn down." In fact, they didn't last much more than a decade, let alone the anticipated thousand years.

Looking down—in one of her finest prints—from the superb heights to the graveyard of Trinity Church, an underground album where the past is interred, Abbott sees the architectural history of New York as the disintegration and dispersal of a family. The statues she photographs are the grandparents who defy change, the forbidding elders who survive into the present but won't compromise with it: the bewigged Abraham de Peyster, imperturbably ensconced among the office buildings on Bowling Green, refusing to believe that the place is no longer the pleasant estate its name declares it to be; the statue of John Watts in Trinity churchyard, seen from behind as he looks up at the skyscraper which has made him redundant; a matronly backview of the Statue of Liberty, deallegorized by the angle so as to become another venerable ancestor; then, with wistful comedy, the statue of Father Duffy in Times Square, mummified on his pedestal by a shroud of plastic sheeting. Bundled in his sacking against his cross, against a sky of streaming neon and balletic peanuts, he is one of the city's ignored wiseacres or failed deities. On Water Street in 1930 Abbott photographed a shop specializing in such futile divinities. In its window a community of insipidly pious madonnas do obeisance to one another. Sumner Healey's antique shop on Third Avenue, which she photographed in 1936, is a retirement home for discredited gods, refugees from all world religions—a turbaned Oriental potentate, the figurehead of Mars from a warship, an Indian chieftain. In her view of Columbus Circle, the navigator's statue has been dwarfed by the commercial dignitaries around him. Apart from his single, insignificant figure, it's a scene populated by signs, not persons. Columbus has been upstaged by a hotel, the Mayflower, which hoists its plaque into the sky in celebration of another voyage. The new gods the city has installed in its heaven are the theatrical stars named on its billboards: Beatrice Lillie, Ethel Waters, and Eleanor Powell are appearing in *At Home Abroad* just off Columbus Circle. But even in a city of signs, Abbott finds an effort at sociability. Her view is a conversation picture, with a billboard for a brand of wedding rye bread (from behind which she takes the photograph) engaged in dialogue with a neighbor extolling Coca-Cola on the other side of the Circle.

The desacralization that attends the breakup of the family reorganizes the city's commerce. The cluttered stores of the Lower East Side photographed by Abbott, with tools and appliances lined up on the pavement, are models of the family's do-it-yourself economy. In kosher markets gastronomic rules are tribal customs that have acquired the force of religious edict. Mass production and distribution abolish this familial nurture. At the new A & P on Third Avenue, vacuum-packed and glossily uniform wares are sponsored by performers, those new deities of consumerism who replace parents as homemakers and providers: one endorsement pretends that "Kate Smith invites you to try Red Circle coffee." The newsstand on Third Avenue at 32nd Street, "typical of what the public reads," as McClausland's note asserts, is an open-air cathedral for the new city of consumerism. A solitary stargazer lingers among the ranks of movie magazines. In contrast with those calcified grandparents unregarded on their pedestals, a goddess is now an etheric pinup. The votive images—photographs used for erotic reverie and spiritual entrancement—at this shrine are Greta Garbo on the cover of *Picture Post*, Claudette Colbert on *Modern Screen*, Eleanor Powell on *Movie*. The next stage in the city's disruption of the family economy comes with the automat on Eighth Avenue, which Abbott photographed in 1936. Here the mechanically confected pies and cakes repose pristinely in their cubicles on the wall. A client is observed inserting his coin and making his selection. The maternal responsibility of provisioning and victualing is accomplished, somewhere behind that wall of deposit boxes for sweets, by an unseen task force. It's as if machines were feeding you. Squalor yearningly redomesticates this cleansed and regimented city of automata, as in Abbott's view of the courtyard of the early model tenements in the East 70s, with washing-lines strung across it. The kin groups of linen hung in midair—fraternal gatherings of pendulous long johns, sororities of stockings, nurseries of diapers—decorate the grim brick square and testify to the presence of families in it.

As our means of shoring up memory and reckoning our loss, photography recurs necessarily to our childhoods, of which it is ultimately our only souvenir; and, even in the city, infancy is pastoral—a garden of perfection from which we're tearfully ejected. The point is touchingly made by one of the photographs Berenice Abbott took for *Greenwich Village Today and Yesterday* in 1949. It shows a courtyard behind Washington Square South. Inside a barred, open window, with potted plants on the sill, a nurse holds a squalling—or perhaps merely yawning?—baby. Outside the window, fallen through the bars into a flower box, is a floppy rag doll. The mews is a small urban effort at a garden. The doll lies in it dejected and abandoned, while wailing infancy is penned in a room whose grille defines it as a prison. The bohemian Greenwich Village depicted by Abbott may prolong adolescence, but it can't restore childhood. Instead, it vends a falsified version of the lost and longed-for past: on the facing page of the book is the signboard of a shop on West 11th Street where Dinty Moore, Inc., tautologously protesting too much, offers for sale "ANTIQUATED Antiques."

Beneath the changes Abbott documents, her city nourishes an idyllic rural recollection of another time and place. This surfaces toward the end of *Changing New York*, in images of bucolic idleness ignoring the commandments of change. A mother sits in a vacant lot on Tallman Street in Brooklyn with her children; tramps laze on a waterfront shelter at Coenties Slip, with the industrious towers chiding them from a distance; a drunk snoozes against a pillar of the El, insulated from its clatter. Ben Shahn makes the same point in a sad and beautiful photograph taken in Cherry Street in 1934. One of the city's economic casualties stretches out asleep against a brick wall beside some oil drums. No longer working, he has regressed to infancy: he's fetally curled up on top of a baby carriage. Abbott's idlers take their ease in the city, though now such countrified shiftlessness is the deportment of the economically defeated. New York is pastoral only to those who are out of work. Or else it is pastoral in genteel dereliction, as is the cloister of St. Mark's Church, with creepers entangling its decayed pilasters. Otherwise it rules out the otiose timelessness of childhood. Hence that compulsory acceleration which, as Abbott's technical prescriptions specify, is one of the camera's two contradictory rhythms. Many of the photographs Walker Evans took in 1963 before and during the demolition of Pennsylvania Station reflect on this affinity between his art and the city. He places at the center of his composition the great clock over the concourse, with a label beneath certifying its accuracy ("TIMED BY BENRUS"). Thus the photographs elegiacally measure the gaps between three temporal layers. The reliability of that clock stands midway between the instantaneousness of the camera and the eternity of the classical building, and presides over a changing of places between these time zones—for though the camera can capture for only a moment the changing life of a station, it will soon supersede that station, which when it's pulled down, will exist always in the moments detained by Evans's camera. The moment—3:15 or 3:17 by that Benrus timepiece—is now eternal, thanks to the camera's stopping of the clock. Abbott called her image of the clock on Fifth Avenue at 44th Street "Tempo of the City." In obedience to this clock, pedestrians step smartly. They're monitored and hustled by the city, in contrast with the infantile and rural indolence of the older, outgrown New York where (in another of her prints) children sun themselves in deck chairs in an Astoria garden.

The new city is a machine for speeding people—like those on Fifth Avenue or those who will travel on the Greyhound buses she photographs lined up expectantly at their terminal—to their destinations. It copes with the millions who teem through it by mechanical classification and containment. Whereas the spaces of the elderly, childish New York are gardens, even if they're rubble-strewn vacant lots or tenement courtyards bedecked with dripping laundry, those of the new New York are jails. The shadows cast by the El in the streets beneath construct a caging lattice of light; the steel tiers of Rockefeller Center as it rises are a penitentiary. The girders trap the steelworkers inside a system of endless repetition, allotting to each a see-through cell in which to labor. The El projects an illusory prison of barred shadows; Rockefeller Center rearing in the air is a diagrammatic, conceptual prison. Lewis Hine's workers, photographed during construction of the Empire State Building, are heroes of technological epic, altitudinously daring. The few workers glimpsed in Abbott's Rockefeller Center series are serfs of the machine, which here masters and enchains nature. Abbott uses one machine to portray the encroachments of another; but she employs her apparatus anti-mechanically. The photograph, she said, should be detached, like "a sensible human being," not an unfeelingly objective machine. The plate's sensitivity to light exemplifies this sensible appraisal, observing changes so as to criticize and resist them. The shuttered eye, like a curtained window, opens to light reluctantly. And behind that eye, the camera's sealed and darkened chamber is a strong room of memory, reproaching the amnesiac and ungrateful city it oversees.

At first the photographer camouflages himself on the street, apologizing to the city for his impudence in observing it. As he acquires power, he dispenses with such equivocation. He has learned that the camera can modify what it claims to be merely documenting. Berenice Abbott's

Berenice Abbott, "Tempo of the City, Fifth Avenue and 44th Street" (May 13, 1938). Federal Art Project "Changing New York." Museum of the City of New York.

camera isn't an investigative note-taker but a revenant consciousness, and it discloses what the city *was*, rather than how it currently is. In succession to Abbott, the camera becomes a fabulist, able to show how the city might be, how it could—with the requisite technical trickery— be made to look. This is how it's subjunctively (but at last unavailingly) used by André Kertész who, born in Budapest, came to New York in 1936 after spending eleven years in Paris. His camera tells lies that we wish were truths. New York to him is a pulchritudinous grove, home to a convocation of airborne Venuses. A sensuous vision about to alight, a ballerina in 1937 practices a bend—her body boneless elastic—on a ledge of Rockefeller Center. A shopkeeper in 1957 arranges a street display of frilly crinoline petticoats which, hung above his doorway, seem to be floating through the air to the pavement like angels with parachutes. In 1969 Kertész took a photograph at the circus in New York, looking up toward the ceiling of the tent where a company of spangled female fliers are suspended: this is his galaxy of goddesses, enskied above the city. Four ballerinas in another image leap in concert from the dingy sidewalk against a discolored wall, watched by amazed children. They are visions in orbit through the city. Sometimes these visitants are captured and put on display as mannequins, immaculately outfitted and attitudinizing in a shop window at night or nude and virginally sheeted in cellophane. Their robust sensuality defeats the city's attempts to douse or chill it. In a 1967 photograph, a thick-hipped and swollen-breasted nude (a sculpture by Lachaise) ignores the snow on the Museum of Modern Art courtyard, tilting her pelvis at the muffled landscape. She even sports a snowball as a hat. Cloud-descended, these Venuses in transit between the sky and the streets land on the city's rooftops. Kertész adores these make-believe terraces and lives in Washington Square because the rooftops there remind him of Paris. In midair, an amiable or sensual or relaxed life can be enjoyed, which the streets forbid: pleasure has defensively levitated. Kertész's high angles, from his twelfth-floor balcony or from his own roof, and his telephoto lenses, enable him to intrude on a life which is unbuttoned because it doesn't know it's being observed. Rooftops deputize as beaches (a girl wearing only the bottom half of a bikini arranges a bed on which she'll sun herself) or as patios for conversation (two men sit above West 8th Street). On an upper East Side rooftop in 1956 Kertész finds a Greek nymph, clutching her lyre as she surveys the city: her terrace is a chapel, sacred to a Mediterranean cult of physical delectation. Washington Square is the Latin piazza where pleasure becomes performance. Kertész photographs concerts and a play after dark, lovers romping on the grass, children hosing themselves in the heat, a Hare Krishna troupe, or Bella Abzug messianically campaigning. Around the square, these amusements also take to the heights, and in 1962 he photographs a jam session among the sooty chimneys. Kertész's voyeurism is too candid and too joyful to be embarrassed. When in 1970 he takes his camera onto the subway, he chooses as his subject—undeterred by Evans's scruples—a girl who has fallen asleep, her head lolling, her mouth slightly agape. His other characters have designated their smutty roofs as beaches; she has declared the carriage to be a boudoir.

During snow or spring, nature collaborates in Kertész's costuming and affoliation of New York. Snow blankets and soothes his city, bleaching its downtrodden pavements. The patterning of tracks in Washington Square after a blizzard is decorative rondure, and the Lachaise lady sculpts herself a fur hat out of snow. Spring buds—through which he also looks down on Washington Square, the branches gently screening it from him—make the city bloom. In 1938 he photographed plants sprouting from a brick cliff beneath Tudor City, and in 1962 the television aerials on his own building look like pruned and spiky saplings, sunning themselves in the hope that they too may grow. But such beauty can be sustained only by keeping a distance. The rooftop, after all, is a retreat. The nymphs who in his early New York scenes flutter down onto the city from the sky have returned to midair and live there in celibate claustration. One of Kertész's Washington Square scenes is of a nunnery roof garden, with two votaresses at their orisons in the sun. Other plates in the Washington Square series, collected in 1975, suggest that the beauty of the area is a frail and self-flattering pretense. Greenwich Village supports its claims to be a transatlantic Left Bank by a narcissistic trade in images. A camera team is making a movie of some actors impersonating lovers; street artists sketch passersby or sell canvases arranged on the walls.

Accepting that it can visually rearrange the city but not—as those alighting ballerinas or trapezists had promised to do—transfigure it, the vision retires indoors. Kertész defensively relies on reflection or refraction, the indirect stratagems of Plato's cowering cave dweller. A puddle, like a camera, makes the reality stand on its head and so achieves its capture as an image: in 1967 Kertész sees the spire of the Empire State Building reflected in a pool on the sidewalk. Steichen could only photograph the Empire State once it had, by the overlaying of exposures, made a metaphor of itself and impersonated a gyring maypole. Kertész needs to see it at two removes—upside down and beneath him in the gutter, not towering aloft. Among Kertész's recent series of Polaroids is a case of window-ledge refraction, where the curved surface of a brandy glass (doubling as a vase but also performing the function of a camera lens) capsizes the skyline of Washington Square South, holding it afloat and inverted. Here the image, like a photographic print in development, seems to be made by saturation: the city acquiescently melts in the transparent chambre claire of the glass. Kertész's disenchanted withdrawal can be followed in a long succession of photographs of New York taken, like this Polaroid, from inside his apartment at 2 Fifth Avenue. In 1952 he places a metallic cock against a rain-bleared window, with the stormy sky and the smudged downtown towers outside. The view doesn't, like those of Stieglitz, assert supremacy; it counsels re-

André Kertész, "Puddle, Empire State Building, New York" (September 17, 1967). Courtesy Susan Harder Gallery and © 1983 by André Kertész.

clusion in the company of one's private idols. By 1972, the same view is terminated by the brutal stumps of the World Trade Center, against which is outlined the cross of the Judson Memorial Church on West 4th Street. The cross once had the sky to itself; now all it can do is feebly imprint itself on those mercantile pinnacles by which it has been superseded. In Kertész's most recent photographs, the birds that fly through his earlier New York images, enjoying, like his dancers and acrobats, a spirit's freedom of the air, have been remolded as glass toys and immobilized on his window ledge. He focuses now on that altar of sentimental totems (honoring his dead wife) and leaves the city outside a lachrymose blur, the windowpane often spotted with raindrops. The subject is a person along in a room with his memories. As for Abbott, with her studied recollection of the city's past, the camera's symbolic service is its exclusion—not its admission—of light. The aerial perspective, which assured Stieglitz of dominion, becomes a nervous last resort. During the war, a voluntary internment was forced on Kertész who, as an enemy alien, was advised not to brandish his camera in public places. Then a few years ago at Christmas, he was mugged at the corner of 8th Street and Sixth Avenue and had his camera stolen.

9

In the Streets

At first, the symbolic gesture of the novel in New York is its closure of a door. The house of fiction, for Howells's couple in *A Hazard of New Fortunes* or for Catherine Sloper, is a fort of privacy. The new literary ethic of naturalism censures such a retreat. The city irresistibly summons us to vital combat. Naturalism restores the city to membership of a relentlessly selective, biologically competitive nature. Upton Sinclair calls Chicago a jungle in his novel about the stockyards. Theodore Dreiser's hero in *The "Genius"* (1915), having traveled from Chicago to "do battle" with New York—to subdue it and mentally mate with it in celebration of his conquest—visits the Museum of Natural History to estimate his adversary. He sees there the stranded, lumbering skeletons of prehistoric beasts and wonders "at the forces which produced them, the indifference, apparently, with which they had been allowed to die." Nature's atavistic unconcern about its creatures corresponds to the modern city's carelessness of its harried inhabitants. Dreiser's Eugene learns from these redundant hulks a willful determination to be among those whose fitness will ensure their survival.

The naturalist, not the realist, inherits Whitman's urban heroism. The only heroism available to the characters of the Jamesian novel is a meditative forbearance, a studied detachment from the city; the characters of naturalism welcome the city as what Dreiser, referring to New York in *A Book About Myself* (1922), calls "a field of endeavor"—a field in the bellicose epic sense of a place for feats of arms, and also in the biological naturalist sense of a habitat where's one primal endeavor is to provision oneself to stay alive and to reproduce oneself before inevitable extinction. Dreiser himself, advancing on New York by way of sojourns as a provincial newspaperman in St. Louis, Toledo, Cleveland, and Pittsburgh, calls it the goal of "all really ambitious people," the place which defies them to vanquish it, which most dauntingly challenges their conviction of their right to survive. Dreiser denies that the city is a place of cultural amenity or social ease—as James or Edith Wharton had hoped. American cities, he says, are "busy with but one thing: commerce." He sees this commerce as a natural travail, a vengeful rending of the earth by financiers who have overcome evolutionary necessity and can now order the ground to rumble and belch flame, as it does in Pittsburgh, in obedience to them. Dreiser models himself on these omnipotent industrialists, the Fricks, the Vanderbilts, or the Rockefellers. Friendless in Cleveland, he assesses his own meager quantity of power— "my sole resource was my little skill as a newspaperman"—and capitalizes on it, invests therein his entire energy. He puts himself into training, in Pittsburgh before the assault on New York, by studying the accounts by Huxley and Herbert Spencer of the "struggle for existence" and by reading Balzac, whose Rastignac vows to beat Paris as Dreiser swore to do with inimical New York. Eugene in *The "Genius,"* arriving at Jersey City and crossing to Manhattan on the Desbrosses Street ferry, is the callow trainee for heroism who beards the city. It roars at him to scare him off, but he resolves to presevere and to slay the monster. Dreiser likewise dreams of heroic exploits to be accomplished there: piratical triumphs of will, libidinal victories of instinct. He intends, he says, to "bag an heiress or capture a fortune." Even seeing the city is for Dreiser an acquisition of power over it, a visual annexation of terrain. Eugene, when rich, moves to an apartment on Riverside Drive, purchasing the sunsets which can be seen from there. Mrs. Dale in the same novel has a home on Grimes Hill in Staten Island, which from its "commanding position . . . controlled a magnificent view of the bay and harbor," as if the scenic lookout were a means of military prevenience. The heroine of *Sister Carrie* (1900) graduates from being in the view to looking down on it. She begins as a lone, dispirited walker on Broadway; later she can afford to patronize the street from her hotel room and enjoy the misadventures of pedestrians slithering and tumbling on the snow. The window is her ecological niche, where she's safe from the depradations of nature.

Dreiser's own first response to New York is to frame his view of it in an act of visual will. He arrives, like Eugene, at Jersey City. Across the river he sees foggy New York "as through the proscenium arch of a stage," fitting into the open-ended pier. The image is his assumption of control: the city's a theater in which he will perform. In City Hall Park he subjects the newspaper offices to the same ocular defiance. He outstares them, or glares at the financial piles of Wall Street "with the eyes of one who hopes to extract something by mere observation." His ambitious eagerness resembles, as he describes it, the recklessness of the epic hero spoiling for a fight; it's also evolution at an increased speed, as plucky vitality vaults over the obstacles to its growth. Dreiser bursts through the barricaded lobbies of editorial offices, past a rabble of jeering youths, into the presence of the men from whom he can demand a job.

His desire to work as a journalist conforms with his theory of the city, for the newspaper is the school of naturalism. Zola, distinguishing between realism and naturalism in 1880, contrasts them as modes of perception. The one is mere observation, the other an inquisition of phenomena, an inductive investigation of life under laboratory conditions. Naturalist observation is coercive (Dreiser's eyes, scrutinizing Wall Street, extract or exact a reckoning from it), a judicial examination followed by an arraignment. The professional character who perfects this accusatory style is the journalist. His beat comprises those venues that Zola's mentor Claude Bernard had nominated as the laboratories of naturalism, scenes of life at its most fetid and palpitant: the hospital ward, the indigent hostel, the factory. The same journalistic curriculum was proposed for his pupils by Robert Henri. Many of those he sponsored—Luks, Shinn, Glackens, and Sloan—began work as illustrators for newspapers. Henri rallied them with the same evolutionism that goads Dreiser: "the battle of human evolution is going on. There must be investigations in all directions." The investigative mission means quitting the studio (Henri told his students to "go out into the streets and look at life") and has as its goal the speeding-up of evolution. "The future," Henri declared, "is in your hands." Illustrations Henri classified as "life documents," scientific reports on the strivings of the vital will.

It is journalism that instructs the naturalist Dreiser in the relativity of realisms. The magazines depicting the racy nightlife of New York which he reads in Pittsburgh have already, in their meretricious untruth, disclaimed realism because they exclude "the hard contentions and realities such as everywhere hold and characterize life." Dreiser consumes their fictions uncritically and "refused to allow myself to cut through to the reality." Genteel or glamorous journalism persuades him that realism can't be trusted because its authority is merely the reporter's decision about what constitutes reality. Howells, while working for a paper in Ohio, was censured by his editor when he turned in a story about a crime of passion: "Never, *never* write anything you would be ashamed to read to a woman," he was told. The reality on which realism is grounded is a code of polite prevarication. The truth can be told only by nature, by the "grinding and almost disgusting forces of life" which pullulate through the "gross and cruel city." Dreiser's New York journalism exposes a world "realer," as he puts it, than that of evasive factitious realism. His assignments take him to the city's proscribed areas, the East Side ghetto or the Brooklyn waterfront, whose existence enables him naturalistically to indict Fifth Avenue. The places he describes are the city's sanitary outlets, its moral sluices—the East 27th Street police station, Bellevue, the Charities Department which runs the morgue, the insane asylums, and the poorhouses. His zealous victory as a naturalist is his uncladding of the city's orifices, its excretory "back door" which shunts off the rejected to "the river, the asylums, the potter's field," and the wastage of anonymous death. Since his subject is the city's corporeal guilt, the reporter must turn into a detective, who (like the naturalistic scientist of Zola and Bernard) is trained in espionage: observation as the subtlest of extortions. The journalistic pieces about New York collected by Dreiser in *The Color of a Great City* (1923) show him learning the skills of the urban intelligencer. He eavesdrops on coal-heavers as they lurch into a saloon on Eleventh Avenue, interrogates witnesses after a brawl in Hell's Kitchen or slyly bribes them, as he does the sandwich men, to test their responses. Sometimes he trails them, following a pushcart man or a butcher home; he even adopts aliases to work incognito and boards at a hostel for the down-and-out or lodges in Hell's Kitchen so he can study its squalid criminal society. These undercover episodes recall Stephen Crane on the Bowery, and Crane was one of the influences acknowledged by Dreiser during this period in New York; but whereas Crane's experiments were conducted on himself, in an epic proving of his own fortitude, Dreiser's are the scientific assays recommended by Zola, and their subject is the city's nature, not his own. The flophouse and the tenement are his clinics where, under the controlled conditions of financial extremity, social life can be studied.

Zola proposed the extension of the scientific method from inert to living bodies, from physical substances to sentient creatures. It's Dreiser's achievement to see New York as such a being, an instinctual character as blindly willful and potently energetic as Zola's Thérèse Raquin. The hungering organism of New York adapts itself to a regime of natural selection. The actions of realism—social climbing, the vertical ascent of Broadway undertaken by Arthur Townsend in *Washington Square*— exemplify, to naturalism, a remorseless biological law. Thus the social classes can be differentiated by their attitude to the cycle of the seasons. In October, the poor begin to dread the onset of a winter which to them means "cold and storm and suffering," while the affluent, who can afford to protect themselves from it, anticipate with "renewed vitality" the resumption of social activity after their "idle summer." The city chal- lenges people by making them battle against the elements. Dreiser writes about those engaged in this campaign—men in the dark who loiter out- side a newspaper office to grab the early editions advertising employ- ment; men in the snow who profit from nature's inclemency by signing on to clear the streets; men in the storm, lining up for admission to a Bowery hostel. Most afflicted of all are the swart toilers at an oil refinery on the Bayonne peninsula. Charred by smoke, choked by fumes, they're subjected—as are the experimentalist's laboratory specimens—to ele- mental torture, but they labor on "in extreme heat or cold, under rain or snow." Nature is a feud of elements, to which human purposes are irrelevant. Dreiser interprets a tenement fire on the East Side as a skirmish between fire and the antagonistic demon of water. The people killed are merely "chance occupants of the field upon which [the ele- ments] chose to battle." Consumption by one of these oblivious elements can seem a mercy: the purpose of the city's rivers is to wash away the biologically unequal despairers who drown themselves there. Neighbor- hoods suffer the same genetic deterioration that hinders human beings and that strands those mastodons in the museum for Eugene to wonder at. The Bowery, Dreiser notes, has degenerated from its "tawdry spright- liness" as a vaudeville center and is now derelict, the beached hulk of a superseded creature. The writers of popular songs make poetry from this urban calamity of natural selection. Their art is itself a product and a victim of nature's ruthlessness. Dreiser's brother composed such short- lived trifles in New York. These tunes, with their abbreviated season of success, are allegories of joy retrieved from misery and are extermi- nated by the same hazards which they temporarily assuage. In a com- petitive market, they perish because of its cruel selectivity. Their human begetters share that fate: once his song is forgotten, the composer returns to the penury from which he'd accidentally been reprieved.

Dreiser saw his own career in New York as a "grueling contest" with a city pledged to defeat him, as it had driven a former St. Louis colleague to suicide. Citizenship means a permit to work, because the vigorous use of the body is our only means of attaining evolutionary fitness. Even the mad in Dreiser's city possess an obsessive, unproductive industry. A tramp tirelessly but futilely scribbles notes in the Astor Library. Dreiser admires petty criminals, like an Italian he watches on Sixth Avenue maneuvering his pushcart away from the police, because they have nimbly adapted themselves to their social milieu; he despises the bums for adhering to an industry they don't serve but from which they derive life. In the winter he sees them sleeping over "some grating covering a shaft leading to an engine room . . . from which warm air pours." Like small animals snuggling up to a parent who feeds, warms, and guards them, the bums bask in a vital heat not of their own making. Dreiser's city is ruled over by a Darwinian matriarch, an indiscriminately fecund "Mother Nature," who spawns (as Eugene in The "Genius" marvels) "such seething masses of people; such whirlpools of life!" In the congestion of urban kinship, Eugene has his loneliness crushed out of him, and as he merges with the crowd, he recognizes that "mere humanity in massed numbers makes a kind of greatness."

Though many of Eugene's paintings are based on Stieglitz's photographs, Dreiser's evolutionism alters the source. Eugene paints Greeley Square in a drizzle and Fifth Avenue in a snowstorm. But whereas to Stieglitz such scenes were the pathetic fallacy's entreaty to the city—a plea that the external world should sympathize with human feeling— to Dreiser they betoken the city's mettlesome resistance to the elements, "wet or white." The individual, invisible behind the lens yet anxious to project himself by equivalence in front of it, is the solitary hero of Stieglitz's New York nocturnes; he has been inundated in Dreiser by the tidal life of the crowd. In Eugene's street scenes faces are indicated by a spot, an inspecific speck which numbers the single being as a statistic, significant only in the aggregate. One of his first efforts depicts "a mass of East Side working girls flooding the streets after six o'clock." Among dark buildings and flaring gas lamps, he daubs in "many shaded, half-seen faces—bare suggestions of souls and pulsing life." Dreiser's reading of the picture advances from flood to pulse, obscuring and consuming individuals as it goes. The torrent is shown to be a life-force, beating in systolic regularity. Eugene's painterly vision, like the investment policy of the financier Cowperwood in The Titan (1914), effects a mobilization of masses. Eugene embroils the factory girls in a flood; Cowperwood's business, mass transit, is the circulation of that flood through the urban body, and he admires the El as an exact solution to the problem of traffic in New York.

Is the individual's urban reunion with the mass an enlargement or a diminution? Because Dreiser's city is a state of nature, he reestablishes there a regime of romantic sublimity. Eugene in the crowd is sublimely reminded of his own paltriness and finitude, as against the annihilating infinitude of nature. The sublime requires a death—the body's cowering admission of its weakness when confronted by the landscape—before it will glorify the self-transcendent spirit. And so it is in Dreiser's New York. In *Sister Carrie* the heroine is granted a sublime urban resurrection, while her shamed and ruined lover Hurstwood suffers only deduction and demise, the lesson, when he flees with Carrie from Chicago to New York, of his own nonentity. Her fate is celebrated, and his enforced, by the urban agency of the newspaper, which pulps individual histories into a mass. Hurstwood, scanning the papers, sees his own plight compounded and aggregated in them. He reads stories of particular distresses, but their individuality is effaced by the anonymity of the reporting: "a firm failing, a family starving, or a man dying on the streets." Then a *World* banner agglomerates the jobless into a nameless, numbered multitude: "80,000 people out of employment in New York this winter." Among this quotient Hurstwood has to recognize himself. His personal identity and tragic uniqueness have been canceled. When he's spurned in the streets by those he begs from, he knows they consider him "a chronic type of bum." At last he's freighted off into unremembered and unconsecrated oblivion like a deleted statistic, shipped from the 27th Street pier to the potter's field. The less the newspaper cares about what it reports, the more hyperbolic is its affectation of caring. It can only express emotion typographically. During a blizzard, the papers "played up the distress of the poor in large type." The papers conceive of the poor as a species; having erased individual cases, they then offer the factitious, collective consolation of a more strident typeface. It's a mechanized parody of that sublime sense Eugene has of disappearing into the crowd to emerge from it magnified and generalized. While they're eliminating Hurstwood, the same New York papers are contriving the salvation of Carrie. But they don't value her because she's a human individual; they bestow on her the halo of celebrity, outfitting her with a new identity. Perhaps because lives are so cheap and expendable to the papers and the city, both institutions invest in the manufacture of new lives, selectively reinventing a few enchanted characters for the delectation of the mass. This happens to Carrie when she goes onto the stage, for she owes her success there to the compliments of the papers. Two of her reviews are quoted, as if to balance those banner headlines which are an obsequy for Hurstwood.

The individual's expunging in the mass (which is Hurstwood's fate) and rebirth from that mass as its fantasy (which is Carrie's) propose problems for the novel. The city seems to prophesy the obsolescence of both character and narrative. Lives in it are atomic particles or jostling electrons, as Dreiser declares in the prose poem *My City* (1929), and you can't tell stories about such molecular existences, whose vicissitudes are like events in physics or alterations in mechanical state. In accomplishing Zola's project to make the novel scientifically experimental, Dreiser finds himself disabled. If people are chance items of matter, what happens between them is not relationship but collision. Once it has disallowed character, New York must rule out any narrative that grows from voluntary affinities. Its dwellings are constructed to enforce this denial. Carrie's apartment building on West 78th Street has unhoused fiction because it collectivizes people without relating them, piling up families while ensuring that they remain "strange and indifferent to each other." Their only means of communication is the service shaft. The flats are united by the mute mediation of the dumbwaiter: doors open into this empty column from every apartment on each floor, so commingling is confined to the chute reserved for the delivery of groceries or the disposal of garbage. The same combination of proximity and estrangement unpacks narrative in Waldo Frank's *City Block*. At the beginning of his novel, Frank does two contradictory things. He lists the inhabitants of the block like a register of tenants; then, having randomly counted them, he insists that there's a necessary sequence to the monologues—each corresponding to the solitary, unsocial rooms these people occupy—which follow: "the author assures the reader that CITY BLOCK is a single organism and that its parts should be read in order." The novel's problem is this assignment of contiguous characters to narrative, since they're all shut in their separate flats, walled off from sympathy with each other by barriers made of newspaper. Whitman thought the paper an urban forum, a common ground of citizenship. Waldo Frank's hero Rudd, perusing the tragedies of near neighbors in the press, reflects that their calamities are served up to him for a fee, like plots in the movies. Since he's entertained by them, he can't be genuinely concerned. Relationships between these people, each allotted to the incommunicability of a chamber, must be laboriously constructed. Love becomes a matter of engineering, sponsored by Whitman, whose mechanical intercession welds New Yorkers into amity. Two neighbors on the block toil to decide on some linking experience between them, which the man, a civil engineer, sees as a verbal bridge-building: he tells the girl, "I'm building a Bridge between us. . . . Words . . . bridge-building words have power against men. . . . I am building a Bridge into you."

If Whitman, whose ferry predicts the marrying bridge, here empowers union, he's invoked by another novelist of the metropolis, John Dos Passos, to effect a decomposition of character and of narrative. Dos Passos claimed that his trilogy U.S.A. (1938) derived from Whitman, not Marx. Whitman's average, democratic epic hero is represented in Dos Passos by that "body of an American" who's the unknown soldier: a postmortem return of Whitman's archetype. The eugenic ideality of Whitman produces in Dos Passos people whose lack of individuality isn't a boon of democracy, where, as in Whitman's New York, all men are comradely look-alikes, but a function of economic determinism. Some of them, like the man walking alone through the unheeding crowd as The 42nd Parallel begins, aren't characters because they're helpless, economically manipulated wage-slaves; others—the entrepreneurial geniuses whose histories are recited throughout U.S.A., Hearst or Frank Lloyd Wright or Edison—aren't characters either because they're projections of implausible financial hope. New York itself, in Dos Passos's Manhattan Transfer (1925), ritualizes this unmaking of character. People don't belong there, but arrive, like Dreiser, to wrest their fortunes from it—Thatcher from Onteora, Bud from Nyack, Zucher from Frankfurt, Emile the cabin boy from France—and New York will admit them only after they have submitted to a self-alteration. Bud gets a haircut; the bearded man on Allen Street shaves in order to resemble the sleek figure in the Gillette ad; Emile is instructed by the headwaiter to acquire "soing"; James Merivale abandons his cane because "the younger men down there don't carry them." These anxious adjustments, by which the characters render themselves unreal, are matched by the city, which is remaking itself as a metropolis. At the start of the novel the New York Bill is signed, pronouncing the city the "world's second metropolis." The boast has to be made good by aesthetic renovation, and as the new recruits cut their hair or change their manners to qualify as New Yorkers, so Speaker the architect, experimenting with vitreous tile, promises to refabricate a New York of brick in steel and glass.

These new materials will etherealize New York. No longer needing to found itself in the earth, it will be held up by the gravity-disdaining ingredients of its construction. It ascends beyond the reach or comprehension of Dos Passos's trudging pedestrians, who traipse through the city or disconsolately sit in it but are disjoined from it. No mass, as in Dreiser, welcomes their individual existences. The bearded man walks up Allen Street "without hearing the yells of the children or the annihilating clatter of the L trains overhead or smelling the rancid sweet huddled smell of packed tenements." Survival in the city isn't biological engagement with it but a blissful capacity not to hear, see, or smell it. Sometimes it's seen without being described, as if it existed only in the individual's bewildered dream of it. When the boy returns from Europe, the sights of the harbor are pointed out to him as the liner docks. He's enjoined to see things—"That's the Elevated . . . and look this is Twenty-third Street . . . and the Flatiron Building"—but the things themselves are unseen by, inaccessible to, the narrative. People experience the city as a madly involuted system that excludes them. Bud limps down Broadway looking for work. His journey is a search, parodying a chivalric quest, for the center of the mazy city. If he could locate that, he's sure he'd find work. Eventually, he gives up the effort and takes to sitting down instead. As he explains to another bum on the Bowery, this is his occupation: "I used to set in Union Square most of the time, then I set in Madison Square." From their sedentary depression, characters gape up at the unattainable city. Others own and man its heights: the novel takes place during a real estate boom. These altitudes are coveted by characters who will never scale them, so the skyscrapers become enchanted fictions and the city a mirage made from the lies its inhabitants tell themselves. Jimmy imagines himself roller-skating down the streets into the sky, using the buildings as a launching pad, "up the Flatiron Building, scooting across the cables of the Brooklyn Bridge." Stan, who when drunk wishes he were a skyscraper, sweet-talks Ellie by saying she should live on top of the Woolworth Building. Compliments work on her like an elevator, dizzily lifting her to an orchidaceous roof garden in a heaven of gold and scarlet electric signs. But these characters can rise to their phantasmagoric aeries only by wishful thinking; in truth, the most practical use they can make of vertical New York is as an aid to suicide, as Bud employs it when he slips over the edge of the Brooklyn Bridge.

Seeing the city was for Dreiser a means of commandeering it. The characters of Dos Passos are tourists who can never master New York, only look at it—like Joe in *U.S.A.*, surveying the shipping from the promenade of the Brooklyn Bridge, or Charley Anderson and Nat Benton, gazing down from the visitors' gallery of the Stock Exchange—and they must also suffer it to scrutinize them. Eveline Hutchins, arriving at Grand Central in *U.S.A.*, sees it as "full of blank faces staring at her." The narrative imagination falters. People in *Manhattan Transfer* look at one another but daren't—because the city is a device for disjunction—interconnect. Thatcher observes but can't relieve the misery of the

Italian during the tenement fire, Emile ogles the showgirl in the restaurant, the lawyer Baldwin sees the story of the milkman's accident in the newspaper. Relationship is a friction of bodies in passing, as when the messenger boy is squeezed against an odorous blonde in the subway.

Space in the novel is cellulated. The voice of the city isn't choral but a simultaneity of monologues. In *Manhattan Transfer*, Dos Passos's image for this urban and novelistic partitioning is the revolving door. One of the chapters is named after this invention, which belies itself by being an instrument of exclusion, not admission, insulation, not ventilation. Those who use it are subjected to the city's segregation: each whirls inside his own glassy cell. The revolving doors of Vicki Baum's *Grand Hotel* (1929) speed up novelistic narrative while breaking it down. A revolution of those doors doesn't constitute an event because they're in perpetual motion. What happens to a guest between arrival at the hotel and departure from it is therefore, she says, "nothing complete in itself." Describing their own fickle roulette, the doors are a wheel of fortune, and the porters preside over the mutability of fates. Since the doors are continually circling, their rhythm is not tragically terminal but comically giddy; in the novel's final sentence, the hotel door "turns and turns—and swings . . . and swings . . . and swings . . . ," its repetitions drifting off into dashes and dots which semaphore the postponement of an end. Such continuousness frustrates narrative, which insists on arrival at a reckoning and an end. It was therefore enthusiastically embraced by Scott and Zelda Fitzgerald. They used the doors hedonistically, as a vortical carousel of pleasure. When ejected from the Biltmore Hotel in 1920 for rowdiness, they moved down 42nd Street to the Commodore, where they staged a symbolic take-over by spinning themselves to distraction inside its revolving doors. Dos Passos treats the image more dourly. The desideratum of novelistic character, given over to introversion, is a room of one's own. Rudd in *City Block* meditates in and on his fourth-floor flat, "hidden among close halls, in layers of life . . . a place among others in a house among others." Carber the teacher in the same novel works obscurely in "a room propped stiff in a pile of bricks with other stiff rooms like it." The revolving door renders such urban, novelistic structures—compartments of privacy and privation—transparent. In *U.S.A.*, Dos Passos's image for the novel's ordination of space is the honeycomb. The buildings of Frank Lloyd Wright, he says, "determine civilization as the cells in the honeycomb the functions of bees." His own novels are sites of functional congregation and reallocation where characters, relegated to different areas and uses, cooperate but don't intermix. Ben Compton, the agitator in *U.S.A.*, sees

New York as an assembly of cells or cadres which he must syndicalize, a hive of separate neighborhoods, each with its own economic specialism. He speaks to "garment workers on the East Side, waterfront workers in Brooklyn, workers in chemical and metal-product plants in Newark, parlor socialists and pinks at the Rand School or on lower Fifth Avenue." His organizational victory is to summon these autonomous groups into concurrence, as the novelist does by making all his monologuists overlap: Compton at last addresses "the vast anonymous mass of all classes, races, trades in Madison Square Garden."

Drama's spatial norm is different, and it therefore articulates the city differently. The recurrent situation of the novel is solitary confinement, while that of the drama is overcrowding. The peace of novelistic character is the relief of Richard Savage in *U.S.A.*, who leaves Grand Central and is absorbed into "the crowded New York streets where nobody knew him, where he knew nobody," or the comforted reflection of the Texan girl in the same novel that in New York "nobody paid any attention to you except now and then a man tried to pick you up in the street or brushed against you in the subway, which was disgusting." People in novels walk around inside padded cells. But drama's perpetual subject, in contrast with this novelistic defense of mental dominion, is the territorial imperative and the human dispute—nowhere fiercer than in a city—over our shared living space. Hence the triumph of Hamlet's monologues, which narrow the stage to a nutshell and then declare that space a limitless kingdom because he inhabits it alone; hence too his sense of rivalry with Fortinbras, for whom the same stage space is land to be colonized. In the attic of Harold Pinter's *The Caretaker*, another dramatic war for Lebensraum occurs, with characters jockeying for possession of the bed away from the drafty window or using a vacuum cleaner as a means of eviction. Elmer Rice's plays find in this spatial contraction—symbolically necessary to drama—a parable of life in New York. His characters are psychological victims of congestion. *The Subway* (1929) begins in a windowless office walled with steel filing cabinets, where "not an inch of space is wasted." The theatrical vice progressively tightens: the heroine, released from the bureaucratic confinement of the filing room, is filed away in the steel box of a subway car, where she's so jammed in by the circumambient gropers that she can only move her head; her home too has vertically striped wallpaper like bars, and her bedroom is an even more exiguous cubicle.

The oppressive dramatic unification of time and place in Rice's *Street Scene* (1929) means that the inhabitants of the tenement own one another's lives. Mrs. Maurrant's adultery is observed by her neighbors,

since Mrs. Olsen is dusting the halls when Sankey sneaks into the Maurrant apartment; as soon as Mrs. Maurrant quits the scene, her fellow
tenants—driven out of their rooms by a scorching June day—assemble
to pass gossipy judgment on her, in the sort of impromptu parliament
which the novel's houses, like Carrie's apartment on West 78th Street,
make no allowance for. In Rice's drama, too many lives overlap in the
same unitary arena. Kaplan the revolutionary intervenes in a spat between Miss Simpson and Mrs. Hildebrand and is warned to mind his
own business. With Italians cursing Germans and Swedes reviling
Jews, Rice's street is the stage as a small and refractory world, where
races and nations quarrel for priority. Privacy in drama can be had only
in the crowded anonymity of the streets. Mrs. Jones's daughters come
home to sleep, Maurrant (who even eats out) to have a wash. When
he returns inconveniently early to find his wife with Sankey, he shoots
them both behind the lowered shades of the apartment. Because Rice's
scene is the street, the deed happens offstage and exists merely to become the possession of the spectators. By midafternoon, nursemaids in
the play's third act are wheeling their prams past the building and chat-
tering about the story in the evening paper. Rose Maurrant concludes
that congestion is to blame: "if my mother had really belonged to herself,
and . . . if my father had really belonged to himself, it would never have
happened." They depended on others "for what they ought to have had
inside themselves." The drama and the city concur in denying them that
interior mental freedom which is the novel's gift.

The house of fiction shuts out the street. But the dramatic façade is
a street that shuts out the house's interior: action has an inescapable
publicity. Rice claimed that his set—a mean, rotting brownstone, modeled after 25 West 65th Street—"derived from the Greek drama." The
Greek settings, outside the doors of palaces or temples or outside the
city gates, impose a compulsory unification. The stage's entrenching
architecture closes off alternatives of action. In re-creating this dead-end
condition of drama on West 65th Street, Rice encountered a problem,
for a street must allow for transit. Drama requires him artificially to
prohibit passage through it and to isolate the house he'd selected from
those abutting on it. He prided himself on having managed both exclu-
sions in ways which were wittily characteristic of New York. To justify
"the absence of vehicular traffic," he placed a tar barrel at the curb announcing "Street Closed." New York itself is forever decreeing such
gratuitous embargos, impeding the sidewalk with barriers announcing
"Police Line—Do Not Cross." Rice reasoned that "anyone who knew
New York" would accept his artifice as natural. The separation of his

brownstone from those adjoining it he accomplished by placing "on one side a building in process of demolition, on the other the blank wall of a storage warehouse." Once more the aesthetic proviso had a local plausibility: the flanking structures were "two typical bits of New York topography."

The novel's beatitude, since it's concerned with what Terence in Virginia Woolf's *The Voyage Out* calls "the things people don't say," is silence—the spectral quiet of the house Charlotte dreads to enter in "Pomegranate Seed," the graced quiet enjoyed by Paula and Broaddus who in *City Block* "were in their room, with silence." Drama can't permit such introverted calm. Noise is as necessary to it as are its constricting unities. Mrs. Maurrant longs for people "to live together in peace and quiet without making each other miserable," but in a walk-up apartment house that will never happen. Rice prescribes for *Street Scene* an unremitting urban sound track, mingling sirens, the whistles of steamships, the metallic clatter of the El, the crackle of the radio, human voices, and barking dogs. Recorded from an open window in Times Square, this sound track eavesdropped on the city. Walking across the stage had to produce its own correct noise. The wooden platform representing the sidewalk sounded too hollow when trodden on, and Rice demanded its replacement by an expensive layer of cement. The cessation of voices is the freeing of noise. The first act ends with a scream from a woman in labor, snoring, and a clock chiming midnight; the second begins with a reveille of jangling alarms and chirping canaries. Rice attempted to make plays about the metropolis which would consist of noise, not words. The episodes of his *Sidewalks of New York* (1925), one of the sources for *Street Scene*, have been muted by the city's uncaring taciturnity. In "Landscape with Figures," a boy waiting for his date outside a drugstore wanders off frustrated; she then turns up, too late. In "Exterior," set in front of a brownstone lodging house, a girl moves out, and the landlady advertises a room for rent. Silence suits these transactions: the terse city can't be bothered wasting words on people. Gail Levin has suggested that Hopper was recalling the set for *Street Scene* in his "Early Sunday Morning"; if so, he has restored Rice's noisy play to the silence of *Sidewalks of New York*, for in abstracting the city, Hopper depopulates and forcibly quietens it. Rice considered his wordless plays to be symphonies, and adjusted the sound track of *Street Scene* in accordance with the urban mood, sometimes deafening, sometimes a murmur. Yet the play's medium is noise rather than music. Noise is the unsparing assertion of an environment the characters can't escape. Music, added by Kurt Weill in his operatic version of Rice's play in 1947, grants them an interiority, a mental and therefore lyrical liberty, begrudged by the drama, which makes their lives pitilessly public. As soon as Rice's people begin to sing Weill's music, they have wished themselves out of their predicament. In the play, Mrs. Maurrant vainly dreams of going to a concert in Central Park. In the opera she can give voice to her dreams and make them true, casting off her domestic drabness and turning as we listen into a grandiloquent dramatic soprano. Rose and her boyfriend join in a duet about their plans to leave New York. To sing is to have fled already into a lyrical obliviousness. Music affords Rice's people the gratifications which Brecht, Weill's former collaborator, despised as culinary: one of the opera's early ensembles is a hymn of praise to ice cream. As if acknowledging that its province is beguiling fantasies and temporary, melting pleasures, music refuses the challenge of dramatic calamity. The murder of Sankey and Mrs. Maurrant and the subsequent panic are conducted in dialogue alone.

10

The Decadent Decade

Whitman the housebuilder and (as a newspaperman) manufacturer of literature works to construct an epic city. After him, no one seems to work there. At best they have careers. Margie in *U.S.A.*, reflecting that "a career was something everybody in New York had," sets herself up as a dancer. A career is the careening pursuit of a self-image, the enactment of a fantasy more than a job, and New York is the theater where such histrionic fictions can be played out. Since work has been censored, the meditative New York of James and Edith Wharton—consuming, not producing—issues at last in the 1920s in a city of orgies. Now it's New York itself which is being consumed—worn, drunk, eaten by a populace of partygoers. F. Scott Fitzgerald's Gatsby, lavishing wealth on clothes, entertainment, and the purchase of a dream, is a latter-day version of the Jamesian New Yorker, except that the superstitious Jamesian reticence about wealth has changed to the alternative policy of apologetic splurging. Gatsby's extravagant consumerism uses wealth for the satiation of appetites and the requisitioning of visions. He desolidifies possessions. He'll never wear all the shirts he owns; he seldom attends his own parties. He spends to expend, disperse, dissipate himself. The orgy is an experiment in controlled self-destruction, and New York is the emporium catering to such exorbitant and drastic whims as these.

Fitzgerald dated the beginning of this "most expensive orgy in history" from the May Day riots in 1919, when the police charged demonstrators in Madison Square; its end was the stock-market crash of October 1929. Fitzgerald devoted a story to the inaugural episode, "May Day" (1920). Like all his narratives, it's about a party that sours into a destructive frenzy, a spree that lurches into a binge. It's classifiable, like his own life, as a festive tragedy. "May Day" begins by disestablishing New York as a place of work and consecrating the city to pleasure. Provincial capitalists gather there "to buy for their women furs . . . and bags of golden mesh and varicolored slippers." Those who can't afford such trinkets dream of them: working girls spend their lunch hours window-shopping on Fifth Avenue, fancying themselves the purchasers of jewelry, feather fans, silk gowns, and strings of pearls. A floral triumph greets the troops returning from the war. Merchants and clerks forget "their bickerings and figurings" to watch the parade. As well as this welcome to the carousing troops, the city houses other festivities—a fraternity dance at Delmonico's or the sordid revels at which Gordon Sterrett meets Jewel Hudson (who'd made a career for herself out of showing a good time to the soldiers back from France). Political outrage, when the mob besieges the offices of a left-wing paper, is, like pleasure, fueled by drink.

What begins as an orderly procession develops gradually into a bacchanal. The party ends in the accidental death of a marauding soldier and the suicide of Sterrett. Initially, the battalions parade ceremoniously down Fifth Avenue. But then those ranked and regimented columns are loosened into the indiscriminate crowd, which detests soldiers when they're no longer lined up to entertain it: "the great city [was] thoroughly fed up with soldiers unless they were nicely massed into pretty formations." That "fed up" resounds sinisterly, for while the soldiers imagine they're hedonistically battening on the city, it's consuming them and is surfeited by them. Having lapsed from a march-past into a mere thronging crowd, people are next maddened into a mob. The motley rabble of soldiers, marines, and hangers-on which hunts the Bolsheviks down Sixth Avenue is ironically called a "procession." The debutante's radical brother explains the degeneration to her: the soldiers "are used to acting in large bodies, and they seem to have to make demonstrations." The demo for them is a political version of the party. All Fitzgerald's characters take their cue from these riotous troops, since they use the city's thoroughfares processionally—as parade grounds for the strutting sartorial ego, or as racetracks for games of lordly misrule. In "The Rich Boy" (1926) there's an echo of that May Day celebration, for Fifth Avenue is here itself a deserted, dithyrambic procession. Anson

Hunter the millionaire walks up it at 4 a.m. from a nightclub on 53rd Street to his home on 71st and ponders as he goes his ancestral ownership of New York, marking "the mounting numbers, significant as names, of the marching streets." He receives the salutation of the reeling avenue. Fitzgerald ended an alcoholic rampage of his own on Fifth Avenue early one Sunday morning in 1919, and instigated a giddy parade by rolling empty champagne bottles down the roadway.

For James, Howells, and Edith Wharton, the grid is a map of social esteem. Its divisions are the perimeters of polite acceptance. Stephen Crane with his epic hardihood and O. Henry with chivalric wistfulness take that map and use it, as the social cartographers never intended, to assist their exploration of areas it has deemed to be off limits. Dos Passos interprets the grid industrially, as a production line like the assembly system and conveyor belts of the Ford plant in Detroit. In a taxi on Lafayette Street, Charley Anderson in *U.S.A.* travels on a "stream of metal, glass, upholstery, overcoats, haberdashery, flesh and blood . . . moving uptown." Itself a machine, the grid organizes the traffic as its cooperative component parts: "cars stopped, started, shifted gears in unison as if they were run by one set of bells." The street is an unpausing factory. When Fitzgerald's characters embark on the grid, they expect it to move them along without their needing to bestir themselves. The streets do the imperious Anson Hunter's walking for him, and Anthony Patch in *The Beautiful and the Damned* (1921) sees New York's longitudes as a provision for automatic social ascent. Fifth and Sixth avenues are "the uprights of a gigantic ladder stretching from Washington Square to Central Park." The source of Anthony's wealth is lodged downtown in banks and trust companies; he ventures to Wall Street once a week to see his broker. He lives, however, on West 52nd Street, and uses the grid as a horizontal elevator to speed him toward the satisfactions he has promised himself. Fitzgerald's characters treat the lift as a hydraulic pander. It thrusts them to the height of their overweening fantasies. Two drunks in "May Day" stagger into the Biltmore and are sped skyward by the elevator. When they arrive at the top floor, they instruct the operator to have another story built on. One urges him "Higher," the other calls out "Heaven." The elevator serves Gloria in *The Beautiful and the Damned* as a vertical boudoir. Traveling up to the tenth floor of the Plaza, she adjusts her hair in its mirror. But the elevator's course can't go on forever in the same direction. Its rise portends a fall. Within its buildings, New York harbors an invention that summarizes the careers of its people: giddy aspiration, doleful hungover relapse. Anthony Patch, reduced in circumstances, feels an affinity with the lift operator in his new building on 57th Street and remembers "a hoary jest about the elevator man's career being a matter of ups and downs." Employed as a salesman to peddle stocks, he now uses the elevator to facilitate his own descent. He selects a tall office block, rides to the top story, and works down from there, touting his wares as he goes.

Before his decline, Anthony expects the streets to be mobile on his behalf. They shunt him along, and from his privileged platform he reviews the city as a performance staged to divert him. As he rides into Grand Central on the train, he can't believe that the leaping and laughing in the Harlem streets won't cease as soon as he has passed, leaving the gallant actors to skulk back to their tenements. The moving road of the railway grants him detachment from and amused superiority to the city. He can't accept the grid's efficient conveyancing of crated people as its merchandise, which pleases the Dos Passos character on Lafayette Street. Since the street is ambling along at your bidding, you are free to sidle off it at any point. There's a neat spatial logic to Fitzgerald's city of pleasure. The avenues may be ladders of ascent, but the cross streets at right angles to them are exits to daliance, resorts of indolence. On a mild October day in *The Beautiful and the Damned*, sunshine is said to be "loitering in the cross-streets." The avenues won't even permit the light to dawdle. If it wants to be idle, it must do so around the corner. But the avenues can be won over if you stroll on them at leisure, rather than hurrying like the preoccupied men of business. Anthony plans, after his bath, to wander down Fifth Avenue to the Ritz, where he'll meet friends for dinner.

Above all, if the grid is to be converted to the purposes of the epicurean, its numerical regularity must be confounded, because its plan presumes a linear rectitude in one's conduct. The faddishly dissonant composer Titus Hogg in Carl Van Vechten's *The Blind Bow-Boy* (1923) snubs it by composing his "Manhattan Suite" unsequentially. He plays his musical transcription of 14th Street, a cacophony of harsh seconds; when 15th Street is requested as an encore, he demurs: "I haven't written all the streets, only twenty-five of them, and not consecutively." A character in Dos Passos finds a resourcefully modern use for the grid as a depressant of jangled nerves. Ellen in *Manhattan Transfer*, traveling down Fifth Avenue to the hotel where she's to meet Baldwin, counts the blocks as she goes and reflects on the sedative, steadying rite of enumeration: "Perhaps that's what old Peter Stuyvesant thought, or whoever laid the city out in numbers." To Fitzgerald's people the rigorous necessity of numbers is an accusation. The wayward Amory in

This Side of Paradise (1920), too distracted to read the street numbers from the northbound bus he's caught on Fifth Avenue, mistakes 127th Street for 137th. He tells himself that "two and three look alike," then admits that they don't really. He alights on Riverside Drive and rambles down the sidewalk "with no distinct destination" toward a yachting pier. The grid reproaches the flaneur. Amory considers alternative places that might accommodate his degeneracy, among them Shanghai and Port Said. Anthony Patch and Gloria complain, during tea at the Plaza, that an American should have the right to be gracefully lazy. New York resents the divagations of characters within it, and they must seek out its recessive palaces of pleasure—cabarets in Harlem, cellars in Greenwich Village—or wait to inherit its streets just before dawn (like Anson, or Fitzgerald with his team of champagne empties) or during summer. On humid evenings, Nick in *The Great Gatsby* (1925) roves through its garden of tantalizing delights, singling out women from the crowd and following them home; Jordan Baker finds it alluring on summer Sunday afternoons, "over-ripe, as if all sorts of funny fruits were going to fall into your hands."

In this delicious sweltering fatigue, New York seems to Nick "almost pastoral." He expects a flock of sheep to turn the corner. To Fitzgerald's partygoers, who hire a Plaza suite to drink in or go to movies (as Jordan proposes) to keep cool, the city is a lush Eden. You can regain there, if you're rich enough, the paradise we all lost when we were ejected from infancy—a world where your smallest squalling whim is an order; a feast of sensory fulfillments. Yet that trustful quest for an original perfection is as futile as Gatsby's quest for an ideal Daisy and an unsullied America. The reality is our perdition. Fitzgerald writes about this forfeiture of paradise in an essay and a story about New York, "My Lost City" (1932) and "The Lost Decade" (1939). Recalling the city of May 1919, he describes it as the innocent prelude to history: "New York had all the iridescence of the beginning of the world." He is banished from the luminous white citadel because, shuttling between cabarets or brawling with policemen, he has profaned it. His loss of its equals his loss of himself. Hence the anguished retrospection of the 1939 story, written during his recuperation from his worst drinking bout. It's about an architect who has been drunk since 1928; he recovers his health and shakily surveys the city where he has spent a decade in delirium. When a journalist points out the new skyscrapers to him, the architect remarks that he designed one of them, though he's never properly seen it. Gatsby's hope is exemption from history and its mean, diminishing succession. This the architect Trimble has, as the cruelest of jokes, been granted. Since 1928 the city has upended itself, sprouting the Empire State and Chrysler buildings, Rockefeller Center and Trimble's own Armistead Building; but for Trimble himself this epoch has been effaced. In Fitzgerald's memoir, he loses the city. Trimble builds the city yet loses himself. His tower at least attests to reality and permanence. The journalist Orrison at the story's end superstitiously touches its granite, wanting from it a reassurance that he—for the time being—exists. "My Lost City" concludes with Fitzgerald's first ascent of the Empire State in 1931. It's a moment of visionary premonition, like that foresight of a future history through which he'll have to trudge permitted to Adam on a mountain top in Milton's paradise, shortly before he is sent down into the fallen world. New York has built for itself a pinnacle from which its own insignificance can, for the first time, be contemplated. Fitzgerald perceives that the city *"had limits*— . . . that it faded out into . . . an expanse of green and blue that alone was limitless,"* just as Adam on his specular eminence is made to study the short and sorry limitedness of postlapsarian life. Such knowledge attends a fall: the toppling of that "shining edifice" which was Fitzgerald's now irrecoverable New York. The city, seen from the Jersey ferries or (in *Gatsby*) from the Queensboro Bridge, once promised him "eternal youth," such as the imparadised Adam enjoyed. Now, far from being proof against death, its buildings— like Trimble's skyscraper, or the Empire State which exposes the city's illusions—mime the mortality on the other side of paradise.

Still, the writers of the 1920s persist in seeing New York millennially. Ronald Firbank was writing a novel set there at the time of his death in 1926, though he had never visited the city. His ignorance of it seemed to him a positive qualification, and he assured his publisher that New York would "be the New Jerusalem before I have done with it!" So, in the fragmentary *New Rythum*, it is: a paradise planted with exotic blossoms, caressed and incited into bud by the promiscuous goddesses Flora and Zephyr. Its nature, rankly flourishing under hot-house conditions (Bertie Waldorf cultivates strawberries indoors) supplies Firbank's New Yorkers—who lash each other using twigs of birch and premature chrysanthemums—with the means of sensual arousal and of chastisement. This is a paradise impatient to effect its own fall, and to do so it imports a profane phallic totem. The central episode of Firbank's work is the arrival in New York of the Praxiteles Hercules, "the very apple of Pagan art" and "the World's Greatest Nude." This priapic deity, swung ashore from the liner while a group of sybaritic socialites extols his fearsome buttocks and an insurance officer computes the dimensions of his prodigious phallus, inaugurates a new and heathen cult of fleshliness and luxurious glut.

Carl Van Vechten, whose first novel was placed by Edmund Wilson midway between Fitzgerald and Firbank, proposed two alternative locations for the epicure's paradise he establishes in New York. In *The Blind Bow-Boy* its headquarters are at Coney Island; in *Nigger Heaven* (1926) it has migrated to Harlem. The voluptuary Campaspe inducts Harold Prewitt into the city's erudite vices and recondite sensations by taking him to Coney, which she calls "the pagan idea of heaven, and the Christian conception of hell." It's simultaneously heavenly and hellish because it's a reserve of proscribed, angelic abnormality. The jaded socialites go there to gape at creatures even more perverse than themselves. The malformations of the freaks in its amusement arcade shame the residual physical normality of Campaspe and her friends, who don't have bodies to match their distorted spirits: "You have only two legs, the three-legged man seemed to assert sneeringly." The monsters are supreme dandies, who have accomplished the conversion of nature into artifice. The same small miracle is managed by the place's greasy air with its "confusion of artificial and natural odors: the fishy, salty smell of the sea; the aroma of cooking-oil, steaming clams, sausages, frying pork." There's synaesthesia even in Coney's stench. As Coney Island is a carnival of the damned which his characters declare sacred, so Van Vechten's nigger heaven isn't a jazzy Elysium but a segregated limbo. His title refers to an area of a theater. Harlem is the cheap, vertically distant "gallery of this New York theater" from where the blacks "watch the white world sitting down below in the good seats in the orchestra." The heroine Mary has found that, in theaters downtown, it's prudent to stay in the balcony. She can pass for white and sit in the orchestra uncontested, but when she's accompanied by darker escorts they are chased upstairs. The nigger heaven doesn't redress but institutionalizes an earthly injustice.

Such heavens are all maps of hell, for the dandy is a condemned soul, defiantly sainted by his vocation of sensual excess. The 1920s in New York are a belated version of the aesthetic European 1890s. The city is a lurid electric inferno, the site for an itinerant orgy. Fitzgerald's Amory lurches from the Knickerbocker Bar to the Biltmore and thence to the Cocoanut Grove, a pilgrim in quest of satiation. New York purveys a franchised decadence to the pious midwest. Whirling in their affluent otiose limbo, New Yorkers "do nothing," as Campaspe says: she admits that there are people in Chicago who work, but they slink furtively to New York "to be naughty, like American sophomores in Paris," before returning to respectable cohabitation. New York's new identity is as the American Paris. It becomes cultured by its importation of vice. This is why it purchases the Prax Herc, and why in *The Blind Bow-Boy* it

makes a bid to bring over Firbank himself. When the ephebic Duke of
Middlebottom wants to produce an opera during the New York summer
(the unseasonal timing is his obligatory offense against nature), he
proposes as a text Firbank's admirably indecent *Princess Zoubaroff*,
and intends to invite Firbank to take bows.

All experience must be eroticized. This is what will make New York,
as Campaspe puts it, a pagan heaven which is to abstinent Christianity
a hell. The skyscrapers, for instance, are places of business. Their height
is strictly utilitarian, a device for maximizing space and increasing reve-
nues. It's therefore necessary to deny their dour usefulness and make
them a sensual amenity, as Beverly Nichols does in *The Star-Spangled
Manner* (1926). He treats the towers as inducements to sexual delight:
"a skyscraper is the most exquisite setting for a passionate love-affair
which has yet been devised by man." For Van Vechten things as innocuous as the interior remodeling of houses or traffic jams become
polymorphously sexy. The Duke outfits a floor of his house on West
12th Street as a theater. "Old New York houses," Van Vechten comments, "are as capable of countless metamorphoses as Ovidian gods."
The gods changed shape to forward their careers of sexual conquest;
so, it would appear, do the houses, since their function is to cradle their
tenants inside a fantasy, like Anthony Patch with his canopied bed and
his bathtub with its book-holder. A traffic jam in *The Blind Bow-Boy*
catches the vehicles in the act of coupling. On Broadway near 28th
Street "a heavy truck had become entangled with a taxi-cab in so intimate a manner as to completely obstruct the pavement." Alice, with the
aesthete's reverent trust in appearances, blames the crash on her error
in having taken a pistache- rather than a cherry-colored cab.

For the first time in its literary history, the city exists to be enjoyed.
The new skyscrapers, aloof from the earth, determine on chimerical
careers of their own. The Cunard Building (1921) at 25 Broadway raises
the ocean to roof level, setting atop itself a Nereid frisking on sea horse
among a ruffled bed of waves. It announces in this way its own anti-
architectural ambition to set sail. At this period it became so conven-
tional to see buildings as shipping—the angled point of the Flatiron
parts the traffic as if cleaving the ocean—that Dos Passos can reverse
the simile's direction in *Manhattan Transfer* and describe a liner as a
navigating skyscraper: "the *Mauretania* stalked like a skyscraper through
the harbor." The buildings ape the ornamental vainglory of Fitzgerald's
or Van Vechten's libertines, and sport nattily useless hats as triumphal
declarations of stylishness. The Royal Insurance Company Building at
150 William Street (1931) balances a Greek temple on its head, while the

Bank of New York at 48 Wall (1929) has for its headdress a copper eagle with upraised wings. And if skyscrapers can afford frippery for headgear, then the simile can be switched backward, as it is by Dos Passos when he describes the *Mauretania*. A coiffure can imitate architecture: one of Van Vechten's merrymakers in *Parties: Scenes from Contemporary New York Life* (1930) pomades "his hair with bear's grease until it shone like the silver tip of the Chrysler Tower." The skyscraper also erogenizes its height by likening itself to a spindly heeled shoe. Raymond Loewy designed an advertisement in 1927 for a new shoe called Metropolis. An athletic female nude holds a sample in the air on top of a pyramidal pile of skyscrapers, the sky behind her raked with searchlights. The shoe's a metonym for the buildings, and the comparison associates architectural vertigo with the stratagems of sexual enticement, since the high heel is the female's signal to the male that she won't be able to outrun him.

The city no longer needs to be constructed, which was Whitman's self-appointed task. On the contrary it flirts, as Saks's naming of the Metropolis shoe indicates, with its own teetering imbalance. Nor do you need to do battle with the city, like Dreiser's characters wresting from it the means of survival. It offers itself as a succulent banquet of sense. Fitzgerald describes it comestibly. Exiled to Claremont Avenue by economic distraint, Gloria consoles herself by feeding on the spiced tidbits of 125th Street, which to her is "rich and racy and savory," like a dish made from dubious leftovers by a cunning French chef. Recooking is a brilliantly apt image for degustation as a preying on pleasures, which you insist on repeating even though the second time around they require the addition of extra condiments and stimulants. The characters in *The Great Gatsby* taste New York as candy or confectionery. They're romantic eaters, addicted only to the substances that are useless, unnutritious. Therefore the building on West 158th Street used by Tom for his adulteries is "one slice in a long white cake of apartment-houses," and New York seen from the Queensboro Bridge rises "in white heaps and sugar lumps all built with a wish out of non-olfactory money." This association of lucre and sugar is one of Fitzgerald's best and subtlest jokes. Money is smelly, guilty refuse. Amassing it not in cloacal hoards but in an arrangement of sugar lumps sanitizes it, for sugar symbolizes a romantic inutility. The anti-saccharine campaigner in Thomas Love Peacock's *Melincourt* decries it as "economically superfluous" and "physically pernicious"; as well, it's garnered by slave labor. Its being both unnecessary and deleterious commends it at once to the decadent palate, and the slavery on the plantations where it's grown simply demonstrates that your idle pleasure is—as it should be—made possible by the sweated labor of others. The New York skyline first deodorizes wealth, then makes it sweetly edible. But all the while, the city which Fitzgerald's gormandizers feed on is itself consuming them. The lobby of the Biltmore in *The Beautiful and the Damned* ingests debs: "down at its low, gleaming entrance, [it] sucked in the many-colored opera-cloaks of gorgeously dressed girls." Interestingly, their clothes and hair styles, not their bodies, constitute its nutriment. It's victualed by style. Fitzgerald notes that the hotel's "transitory dome of pleasure" gobbles the girls up, "coiffure, cloak and all." By 1929 New York had choked. Fitzgerald found it then "bloated, glutted, stupid with cake and circuses"—sickened by surfeit.

As well as volunteering to be eaten, New York in the 1920s serves itself up as a potable city. Hart Crane remarked in the summer of 1923 that the lemon-yellow shades of the lamps on Fifth Avenue give "the street and everybody the color of champagne in the evening." Van Vechten bragged that he'd spent the entire decade drunk on gin and sidecars. What he'd been drinking—as his own novel *Parties* and Benjamin de Casseres's *Mirrors of New York* (1925) make clear—was the fluid toxin of the city itself. De Casseres, a newspaperman who ran unsuccessfully for mayor, contributed a polemic encouraging decadence to *Camera Work* in 1912. Here he argued for the overturning of all life-hating prohibitions and all venerable truths and invoked in opposition a region of moral uncertainty which he called "the scarlet paradise of intellectual intoxication." That bibulous heaven is located in New York. For the Nietzschean de Casseres, drunkenness was the gay science. Huneker's heroine imagined New York as a stony Venice, from which the seas have despairingly receded. De Casseres liquefies it again and believes it to be afloat on an ocean of alcohol. He nicknames it a Booze Venice and dubs its main thoroughfare the Great Tight Way. The journalistic pieces collected in *Mirrors of New York* describe the city as a Dionysian playground. The eyes of the lions in front of the library on Fifth Avenue are heavy-lidded, de Casseres says, with the load of sensual experience granaried inside the building; architectural altitudes supply you with vicarious pleasures, since from the Woolworth Building "you can take your vacation mentally" in the circumambient states; dinner parties are frequented by a tippling horde of "nymphs, satyrs, fauns and dancing dervishes"; and jaywalkers are the city's homegrown breed of Nietzschean supermen, who dodge between the streetcars and dice with death because they believe life's sublimest joy lies in risk. De Casseres has his own tactics for confounding the grid, which to him stands for the "monorail, unilateral, prohibition type of mind." The grid reproves the roistering, fluid, unstable motion of the city; New Yorkers who resent its marital prescriptions defy it by lounging at corners. These angles are de Casseres's favorite bits of New York because they're "elbows of the mind." A corner is a place around which you can disappear: a non sequitur enabling you to beg a moral question. Or it's a place where progress forward is interrupted, allowing you loungingly to abandon the effort of thought. In de Casseres's New York, corners are the locations for saloons and grog shops, sacred both to drinking and to voyeurism. They foment gusts of air, and de Casseres recommends—as Sloan's painting had done—the licentious junction at the Flatiron, "where skirts never cease from troubling and the Old Adam is never at rest."

As de Casseres's volume ends, this Corybantic mayhem is officially forbidden. His last mournful episode describes the Gin millennium of 17 January 1920, the night before prohibition. In it he has a vision—or a fit of delirium tremens—which anticipates that enlargement of view, like Adam's on the mountain, experienced eleven years later by Fitzgerald up the Empire State. Dozing on Riverside Drive, de Casseres imagines he sees the buildings of lower Manhattan trudging uptown. They are the city's ghoulish spirits, departing from the gargantuanly lustful body which has been snuffed out that night. The Statue of Liberty has doused her torch, and the Brooklyn Bridge crawls along, rattling skeletally, "its cables making a most unearthly racket." Like Nietzschean divinities of physical delight, the buildings decamp from a world too chastely Christian to house them. The Woolworth tower tells de Casseres that it's retreating to "the deep earth-quarries whence I came." The Saint-Gaudens Diana, quitting her perch above Madison Square Garden, intends an astral, not a geological, exile. Announcing "I am Paganism, the ancient glory that is no more," she departs for the moon. The library lions refuse any longer to guard people who believe that wisdom lies in books and vow that they'll repatriate themselves to Africa, "where there is still some freedom." These absconding gods are replaced by a new breed of psychiatric magi. The gods infused New York with ecstasy, obtainable in bottled form; now in the morose city after prohibition the nearest thing to this vital joy is the prescriptions against depression marketed by those whom de Casseres calls the "bootleggers of happiness"—a band of "cheero yogis, hopesmiths, smile brokers and psychic joy doctors." After the carnival of the 1920s, the next New York is an invalid city stricken by the existential ailment of anxiety.

Parties is Van Vechten's autopsy on the decade and Scott and Zelda

Fitzgerald, the prototypes for his David and Rilda Westlake. Less downcast than de Casseres, Van Vechten welcomes prohibition as an incentive to boozing. Other nations tax drink; by banning it altogether, the American government denied itself the revenue from sales, so "one could drink wherever and whenever one pleased," as if drunkenness were a charter of liberty. The characters of *Parties* drink vocationally. The bar is the center of their apartments, and in its shuttered and black-mirrored laboratory they toil over the invention of new cocktails. Several of their concoctions are listed—the Woojums, consisting of five parts gin to one of Bacardi, with bitters, absinthe, lemon juice, and grenadine; the Hard Daddy, which mixes whiskey with lemon juice and maple syrup; the kinkajou (a name for the honey bear), a blend of grapefruit juice, gin, and honey. There ought to be a theory of the cocktail. If one existed, it would serve as a description of the New York of the 1920s, for two of the city's boroughs—Manhattan and the Bronx—gave their names to these drinks. The cocktail is the product of a period when drinking is equated with style and art. The purpose remains the brain's annihilation; but the means to that obtuse end must be fantasticated and ritualized. Nature and its thirsty cravings must succumb, as at Van Vechten's Coney Island, to artifice. The same mutation occurs when Fitzgerald says the New York skyline is fabricated not from money, which is ordure, but from sugar. The cocktail is a liquid symbol of decadence in its contradiction between function (getting drunk) and form (doing so by tippling grenadine or honey or maple syrup). It corresponds to the sexual habits of Firbank's New Yorkers, who administer sadistic slaps with bouquets or with checkbooks. The instinctual urge, complicated by optional extras and fetishistic detours, turns toward perversity.

Decadence always entails a controversion of function. Firbank calls a skyscraper under construction on Fifth Avenue "a fifty-five story clouds' rest." A building has to be stalwart, to stand up straight. Its erectness can't be impugned, so Firbank modifies its purpose: it stands up only so that the listless clouds can settle on it and lie down. Because the cocktail is a chemical formula for decadence, there's a necessary opposition between the virulence of the spirit which is its base and the candied effeminacy of the additives—juices, syrups, or in the case of an old-fashioned, which someone in *Parties* asks for, a sugar frosting round the rim of the glass. As when Roy Fern viscously verticalizes his hair to make it resemble the Chrysler spire, or when Firbank's skyscraper serves as a bed for clouds, the cocktail forces the hard and the soft, the potent and the insipid, into a union. The mixing of unlike ingredients, accomplished with gestural aplomb by those flourishes of the wrist, is essential: drinking can thus become performance. The professional drinkers of fashionable New York in John O'Hara's *Butterfield 8* (1935) practice cocktail-mixing as a process of chemical refinement. Farley recommends to Mrs. Liggett that she should shake her martinis, not stir them, "so that the gin and vermouth would be cracked into a proper *foamy* mixture." Agitation creates a solution of the components, and products a cocktail to be sipped rather than swilled. Talking about the cracking of liquids, Farley uses a term from industrial science. Cracking —the breaking of molecules—is a stage of the process of refining that makes gasoline from crude oil. The preparation of a martini must be undertaken with the same inductive rigor, and Mrs. Liggett, convinced of the fallacy of stirring, goes off to fetch her shaker.

When not drinking, Van Vechten's people are dancing. Their cocktails are chemical experiments, promoting alcoholism to a scientific profession; the new dance steps they pioneer are stumbling improvisations which first get encoded in a drill and are next universalized as a craze or a cult. Van Vechten tabulates the dance routines as he does the cocktail recipes, and each is an elaborately perverse digression from a norm—the cakewalk, the bunny hug, the turkey trot, and the novelty which the characters go to Harlem to see, the lindy hop. Like the cocktails, the dances combine an uncontrolled frenzy with the pedantic precision of technique. They are dissipation as virtuosity. Van Vechten likens the dancers both to nineteenth-century coloraturas, extemporizing decorations in a cool, formal demonstration of skill, and to flailing epileptics, whose bodies have jerked out of control. "The Lindy Hop," he explains, "consists in a certain dislocation of the rhythm of the foxtrot, followed by leaps and quivers, hops and jumps, eccentric flinging about of arms and legs, and contortions of the torso only fittingly to be described by the word epileptic." The sentence begins with an accident (the dislocation) and ends with a seizure. The dancer's pleasure is the onset of a disease. Since decadence enjoins a graduation from sensual delight to religious fervor and encourages Firbank's New Yorkers to enjoy asceticism by relishing castigation, the lindy hop extends beyond sexual arousal to devotional observance. It's perverse precisely because it's so chaste. It doesn't "incline its hierophants towards pleasures of the flesh." Instead it's "the celebration of a rite," danced by couples who never touch.

The rubbery elasticity of the jazz-dancing body, liquidizing its limbs and curvaceously grooving, corresponds to the fluctuant nature of de Casseres's city. To him New York is a sensorium of fickly migrating pleasures. The centers of nervous or erogenous sensitivity aren't fixed;

they float about in quest of new intensities, like Baudelaire's drunken boat. This mobility of pleasure zones suggests to de Casseres a New York whose body is rendered fluid by desire, its internal organs spurning allocation to a single place and function but circulating in a hedonistic flux. The gambling centers are constantly on the move, the outlets for whiskey change once a month, the fashionable social precinct moves steadily north. Van Vechten likewise believes that the architectural mutability of New York contradicts the solid stony permanence most cities aim to possess. New York commits itself to a more promiscuous, truant element—"if a city may conceivably be compared to a liquid, it may be reasonably said that New York is a fluid: it flows." Pleasures well and gush there in streamy succession, catering to the insatiability of urban appetites. Among the most liquidly unstable sites mentioned by Van Vechten are those which trade in the watery elements, speakeasies and the business places of the bootleggers. The stream flows too fast for those navigating on it. By the time the characters in *Parties* get the phone number of the newest place, an even newer place will have emerged elsewhere. At the end of *The Great Gatsby*, that hurtling tide is stilled by seekers whose concern is now the past, not the eddying, elapsing present of sensation. Like boats against the current, Nick and Gatsby strive upstream, instead of surrendering to the flow. Theirs is an elegiac quest for the source. But in *Parties* the imperative remains a fickle fluency. Though the city's monuments endure, sight refuses to acknowledge their perpetuity because like all the senses it is vagrant: "The Brooklyn Bridge is still to be observed, but the Hudson Tube is a more modern wonder."

In this dissolute New York, the purpose of party-giving, like that of cocktail-mixing, is to acquaint unlike ingredients and shake up the compound. Van Vechten achieved such a spiritous heterodoxy by his innovatory introduction of Harlem to his guest lists; the parties given in his novel stir together dashes of European nobility and dapper gangsters with bootleggers and blacks. When the exhausted Rilda proposes that she and David should change their lives by transferring to a new social set, he laughs that "there's no such thing as a set any more and you know it. Everybody goes everywhere." A set assumes limits: its delineations founder in this new buoyant continuum, through which everyone opportunistically swims. During Van Vechten's "splendid Drunken Twenties," New York undergoes an imaginative liquidation.

11

Two Mechanomorphs

The city is a built dream, a vision incarnated. What makes it grow is its image of itself. Fitzgerald in *The Beautiful and the Damned* describes New York "struggling to approach the tremendous and impressive urbanity ascribed to it," in competition with its own publicity. Having already grandly imagined itself, it confronts the artistic imagination with a rebuff. The city promulgates values of its own: how can it then be made to speak for the different values of the artist? New York's monuments—the Empire State Building, the Statue of Liberty, the Brooklyn Bridge—defy the symbolizing faculty because they are already symbols, prepackaged and self-expounding. They therefore provoke in the artist a mischievous revisionism. If he is to capture the city, he must reinterpret them. Whitman's primary act of naming is followed by a series of impudent or insurgent renamings which announce a take-over. His biologically continuous Brooklyn ferry becomes the tense, distraught Brooklyn Bridge of Hart Crane; the Statue of Liberty, when Mae West slinks into her garments in 1934, is redefined as a statue of ignited libido; and the Empire State Building, which to the photographer Lewis Hine in 1931 is a trapeze for supermen, finds itself within two years assailed by King Kong, who from its spire briefly rules the city as a debased and tyrannized jungle.

The image solemnizes a fusion between subject and object. The romantics called it the marriage of the mind to nature. In the city, such coition has to be engineered because the object the subject seeks to marry is a machine. Artists persist in describing their infatuation with New York as a courtship or a wedding. On his early trips into the city to attend Broadway shows, Fitzgerald identified New York with the sirens of the stage: the city took the form of a composite girl, offering him romance, and in 1932 he remembered it as tall, white, and glittering —a slender sequinned female torso. Joseph Stella connubially declared, "New York is my wife." His paintings of it were their offspring. Ezra Pound, in his poem "N.Y." (1912), sees the image-maker's duty as insemination of the city. But he knows himself to be broaching a reluctant bride, and his sexual possession of her is the baffled impregnation of a machine. Picabia in "Fille Née Sans Mère" (1916–17) and Duchamp in his "Large Glass" (1915–23) both represent mechanism as an immaculate conception. Duchamp's bride teases her revved-up bachelors, without ever permitting them to conquer her. Pound too—after giving the poem New York's initials for its title, as if celebrating it in the intimate shorthand lovers use—discovers the city to be "a maid with no breasts." His erotic address is rejected; the merger of subject and object which gives birth to the image is aborted. The city is not a maid, nor will it respond to the tuning of his instrument. It is just a chaos comprising *"a million people surly with traffic."* They won't submit to the poet's authority, so the coercive invocation which enables Whitman to regiment New York turns plaintive, a futilely lyric adoration: "Listen! Listen to me," or the even more abject "Listen to me, attend me!" The courtly mistress's elusiveness is now a mechanical recalcitrance. The automaton declines to accept the implant of a soul which the poet longs to breathe into her.

The image must be an idea made flesh, the mind's progeny. But an image of the city means the embodying of a machine. Pound's N.Y. is an unsubmissive androgyne. His mistake perhaps is the misattribution of gender. The city resists his characterization of it as a maid. Its body can, however, be described as male, its skyline as a map of priapic rivalry. Even in this case, it's not the city which has been subdued to the image but men who are glorified by association with the city's proud heights. Failing to make an image of the city, you can at least make an imposing image of yourself by likening yourself to it, as does the cop in a Ring Lardner story who, when a lady motorist he's upbraided flirts with him, feels he has grown into a human Woolworth Building. This is how imagery works in the city. Instead of anthropomorphizing the Woolworth Building, it mechanomorphizes the cop. The men who ordained the construction of the skyscrapers strove to keep up with them, fancying they'd become taller if they could reach the same altitudes as their buildings. Every tycoon was a nascent skyscraper. Frank Woolworth and Frank Taft clambered to the tower of the Woolworth Building, shinning up ladders to scrawl their names on the rafters. Pound sends his initialed New York a love letter; Woolworth and Taft with boyish roguery inscribe themselves on the city. Pound offers the city immortality. If it will consent to receive a soul from him, it will live forever. Woolworth and Taft hope to derive immortality from their association with it. The Empire State and Chrysler buildings did battle on their owners' behalf. At first the Empire State was to be only four feet taller than the Chrysler, and John Jacob Raskob worried that Walter Chrysler might cheat by hiding a mast in his spire and suddenly raise it to win the race. For these men the buildings symbolize a power over mortality and over the human body which, for all their wealth, they themselves don't possess. The skyscraper is a device for automatic transcendence; it rises to superhuman heights simply by wishing to do so. Al Smith, the former governor of New York who became a mascot for the Empire State, demonstrated that the building was a prodigy by having himself photographed on the observation deck looking up through a telescope at an 8'7" giant, reputed to be the world's tallest man.

With the skyscrapers, image literally outdistances actuality. They won't defer to our imagery; the best we can hope for is that we might be allowed to become images of them. The skyscraper betokens the rearising of prostrated man. Its upper tiers reclaim the sky from which he has been hurled. Whereas the image tentatively reaches out toward the infinite, the skyscraper boldly reaches up to it. Its architecture is a ladder of evolutionary elevation. Ayn Rand's megalomaniacs in *The Fountainhead* (1943) build or reside in skyscrapers because their heretical aim is to restorm heaven. Gail Wynand the newspaper magnate, who when a Hell's Kitchen waif vowed he would vanquish intransigent New York, dominates it from a glass penthouse in midair. The Zarathustrian architect Howard Roark designs buildings that express his own vertiginous self-conceit. At the end of the novel, he is erecting the world's tallest tower, to be named after Wynand. Commissioning Roark after he has dynamited a democratic housing project, Wynand demands a structure that will be terminal and apocalyptic, a launching pad for the superman's vertical departure from an earth profaned by mob rule: "The age of the skyscraper is gone. This is the age of the housing project. Which is always a prelude to the age of the cave. This will be the last skyscraper built in New York. . . . The last achievement of man on earth before mankind destroys itself." Contempt for gravity gives the skyscraper a hydraulic sublimity. It enables Rand's characters to levitate. In the last chapter, Roark's consort Dominique is swung aloft on an outside hoist to join him on the top platform of his tower, and her passage into the air is a mechanically assisted Assumption. Roark himself stalks such existential heights. As a superman, it's his destiny to vault over abysses. He burns steel with an acetylene torch five hundred feet above Central Park and even on the ground behaves as if enskied: he quivers like "a man walking a tightwire" as he explains an architectural scheme to a critic. He likes to prowl his own uncompleted buildings at night, treading "on shivering planks hung over emptiness . . . to the open edges where girders stuck out like bones through broken skin." Rand's image suggests that the skyscraper is a body which has dispensed with the soft cladding of flesh—a transparent skeleton of steel, naked but armed. To such a mechanomorphic physique Roark himself aspires, and it was accorded to him in 1949 when, in King Vidor's film of the novel, Gary Cooper was chosen to play him. The phlegmatic Cooper has none of the character's fanaticism, but he does have a lean, spindly, elongated body: as much as the giant whom Al Smith scrutinizes through the telescope, he looks like a skyscraper on legs.

Because the skyscraper asserts a mechanical immanence, it's an inevitable location for the photographer, whose art entrusts seeing to a machine. Stieglitz moves to the Shelton; Margaret Bourke-White establishes herself in the Chrysler Building; Lewis Hine, suspended in a derrick lift a quarter of a mile above the streets, records the construction of the Empire State. The skyscraper permits the photographer to claim a share in its altitudinous vision and confers on the camera a headily supervisory power. Bourke-White photographed the Chrysler under construction during the winter of 1929–30. As the handmaiden of the machine, she had to learn its hardihood. She worked on a tower eight hundred feet in the air, which swayed eight feet in gales. Often the temperature was below freezing. Descending from open scaffolds, she had to negotiate flights of unfinished stairs. Photography became an existential balancing act, as architecture is for Ayn Rand's hero: the welders and riveters instructed her in equilibrium. After the building's completion, she decided she must have a studio on its sixty-first floor, level with the stainless-steel gargoyles. She often crawled out onto those gargoyles to photograph the city and was herself photographed on this perch by her assistant Oscar Graubner; Walker Evans too had been photographed by his helper Paul Grotz kneeling underneath his tripod on a parapet of the building next to the Chrysler during its construction in 1929, peering perilously into the gulf of the street. Bourke-White declared her new premises to be "the world's highest studio." The aerial perspective here—as in her later studies of parachutists, of airplanes overflying Manhattan, and her 1943 mission on a U.S. bomber attacking Tunis—makes the photographer's a winged vision. Like the skyscraper and the airplane, the camera grants us a new view of the world, which we see for the first time from far above. Bourke-White identified her art with aeronautic daredevilry. She was delighted by the whirlibirds that she rode during 1951 and 1952 for a *Life* photo-essay, staring the Statue of Liberty in the face, hovering above the traffic of midtown Manhattan, or surmounting the Coney Island parachute jump, because they didn't seal her inside a machine but seemed to suspend her "from a skyhook, which is what," she added, "a helicopter really is."

The magnificent studies of the sky boys conjuring the Empire State out of thin air collected by Lewis Hine in *Men at Work* (1932) constitute an essay on the affinities between the building and the camera, and between the technological skill of the hoisting gangs, derrick men, and riveters and that of the photographer. Hine's caption to his shot of workers on the Empire State's mooring mast for dirigibles places them at "the highest point yet reached on a man-made structure." Yet the higher the building reaches, the higher it spurs the camera to go. Both building and camera are instruments for elevation, making possible an overview of society, such as Hine had already attained in his studies of Ellis Island immigrants and of East Side sweatshops. The heroes of his volume are the connectors, whose job is to hang aloft and bolt beams into place. Once they have completed work at one stage, they're hoisted farther up, where they wait for the building to catch up with them. They are instructive models for the photographer, who as society's conscience must be the overseer even of the sky boys. They are as corporeally joined to the machine on which they work as he is to the one through which he sees; they have achieved the marriage of organism and mechanism frustrated in Pound's poem, for from their straining muscles they produce this skeleton of steel. Hine compares the connectors to "spiders spinning a fabric of steel against the sky." The spider's web is, like the incomplete Empire State, a see-through house which hangs suspended, having been extrapolated from inside the builder's body. Hine's captions fondly claim that the steel is forged by a bodily change within the workers, who "fuse the iron of their nerves with the steel of the girders": nervous iron strengthens itself, as by the addition of carbon, and results in indefatigable steel. The male body begets a girder. Ancient epic heroes wanted to become as sturdy as their weapons or their armor. The modern technological heroes photo-

Lewis Hine, "Building the Empire State" (1931). George Eastman House, Rochester, New York.

graphed by Hine don't need the augmentation of chain mail or bullet-proof vests, for they secrete their own steel. Yet their bravery and toughness are, as Hine makes clear, efforts of imagination. They depend on a metaphorical talent, a capacity to see what's not there. In his foreword he calls his workers "men of courage, skill, daring and imagination." Their imaginativeness consists in their agreement to treat midair as if it were a room, to behave as if the notional building already existed and they were securely housed inside it, to proceed as if there were a floor beneath them. At first this sounds, in their self-deprecating language, like a banal lack of imagination. "It isn't really as dangerous as it looks," they assure Hine, and when he's launched in a box from the hundredth floor, the gang boss argues that it's "safer than a ride on a Pullman or a walk in the city streets." But this pretense that they're on the earth, not in the air, is, Hine's photographs reveal, the triumph of a native

gift for making and then inhabiting an invisible image. His workers—
kneeling on or bestriding girders and flimsy planks, posing on top of
pulleys in the stratosphere, domesticating the unbuilt building by toast-
ing their sandwiches on the rivet forge—have taken up residence in a
metaphor. The danger and excitement they refuse to feel as they concentrate on their jobs is felt on their behalf by the photographer, whose
steep angles disclose the vacancy—ignored by them—yawning beneath.
For us, the photographs are sublime because they allow us to enjoy and
overcome a vicarious fear. For Hine in his box eight hundred feet up,
coping with a real, not a spurious and secondhand, terror, they're an
exhibition of fortitude and also of technical craft. For the subjects, there's
nothing remarkable or especially heroic about what they're doing; but
this literalness is the highest imaginative faculty of all. They no more
suffer from vertigo than the skyscraper does.

Soon this citadel is seized by King Kong, whose presence on it changes
the Empire State's meaning. Hine acclaims it as a summit of human
evolution, the point at which man lifts himself again into the clouds.
It doesn't stand on earth: rather it's an anchor for the sky. The spire
was for tying up airships. Kong reverses that confident evolution. He
keeps a vigil there over the city, from whose dream life—as in the scene
where he peers through a window at the sleeping woman he takes to
be Fay Wray—he has emerged. If the city is his kingdom, then it must
be an atavistic jungle. The film anarchically argues that the ape belongs
in and to New York, that the Empire State is the proper ecological
niche for him. Ernest B. Schoedsack, who had made *King Kong's* predecessor *Rango* in Sumatra, was asked by the *New York Times* about the
hazards of the location. He replied that these had been no worse than
"your poison liquor and your automobiles here in New York." Tigers
had slaughtered some livestock; New York taxi drivers, Schoedsack insisted, did the same. He is paraphrased in *King Kong* (1933) by the
producer Denham who, when trying to recruit a starlet for his voyage
into the unknown, maintains that any girl would be safer with him than
among the dangers of the city. A sailor sneers that the girls are prepared for "that kind of danger." New York is a zoo of lubricity. When
the captured Kong makes his Broadway debut, a brassy girl asks her
escort, "Say, what is it anyway?" He says he understands it's "some
kind of gorilla." At that moment an oafish man thrusts her aside to get
to his seat: "Ain't we got enough of them in New York already?" she
demands.

If for Schoedsack Kong looms out of the swampy, matted under-
growth of sexual fantasy in the city, then for his co-producer, Merian C.

Cooper, the beast is charged with conducting a personal vendetta against that city. He's an image of urban paranoia on the rampage. He wrecks the Third Avenue El to appease a private grudge of Cooper who, when living in the city, had been tormented by its night-long din. He used to dream of tearing it down, and when he found he needed an extra reel showing Kong amok in Manhattan, he decided it would be "a helluva scene" if he set the monster to rip a train from its tracks. Denham remarks that Ann (Fay Wray) has, after her abduction by Kong, "lived through an experience no other woman ever dreamed of." But the film intimates that everyone has dreamed of it and has desired it. That's the suggestion when Kong glowers through that bedroom window, and it's the meaning of Cooper's testimony: Kong does what Cooper could only helplessly dream of doing. Because he is the puppet of violent human purposes, it's right that the ape in the film should be a gadget, an engineered incubus. He is, after all, devised and activated by human desire. Because he's a wishful projection, his most terrifying appearances—on the ledge outside the bedroom or at the El train window— are themselves back-projected. Kong's brief reign on the spire is the fulfillment of a surreal prophecy about New York. He effects the reversion of culture to barbarity, of immutable metal and concrete to clammy, hirsute flesh. Surrealism is about the repellence of softening, the runny loss of strict form which makes Dali's watches melt and leaves his telephone receivers disgustingly moist. *King Kong* interprets this degeneration as the tragedy of the machine. Denham tells Ann that the beast in his film is a tough guy who goes soft when licked by beauty. So it is with Denham, the "hard-boiled egg" rendered weak, humidly made molten, by loving Ann, and with Kong, who first turns the city from an inflexible unfeeling machine into a traumatized body and then himself undergoes the same disgusting declension. The technocratic toy ape— who on the Pacific island can dismantle a dinosaur because inside its armory of scales it's a lumbering, inefficient machine—becomes an infatuated, solicitous man, and when this happens, the airplanes, still invincibly mechanical, can mow him down. Evolution, tending toward humanity, is the death of him.

The image in Pound's poem is a trustful wooing of the city. In Kong's case though, the image is the city's bad dream of itself. New York imagines Kong and is driven mad by him. As its ruler, he derives his authority from the city's fear of him, and like all dictators he can dominate it because he's a night worker, manipulating its unconsciousness. Kong is a symptom of the incommensurability and uncontrollability of urban metaphor because—like the factory in Fritz Lang's *Metropolis*

(1926), which dissolves into a greedy monster swallowing its workers—
he's a machine run wild, an engine metamorphosed into a beast. To his
male rapacity, the Statue of Liberty is a belligerent female counterpart.
She too is an image alarmingly disproportionate to the idea she's meant
to serve. Why is she so menacingly gigantic, and if she's Liberty, why
does she frown so illiberally? Instead of a mother, is she another mechanized bogey? Those who are made uncomfortable by her rewrite the
allegory and reassign the image. Her torch, for instance, is meant to en-
lighten the world. Yet she seems to be raising it as a weapon, in hostility
or at least admonishment. The aesthete Alfred Stone in Huneker's
Painted Veils reviles the statue because it's offensively industrious and
uncouth and sees the torch as "in reality a threatening club: 'Get to
work,' it commanded," while the demoralized immigrants arriving in
Roth's *Call It Sleep* watch the torch belie its function in the late afternoon shadows, when it appears as "the blackened hilt of a broken
sword." Liberty has not kept her promise to relieve them. Christopher
Isherwood, fleeing to America from home and family, found established
in New York the parental totems he had hoped to escape. He described
the skyscrapers, in a letter to John Lehmann in May 1939, as "Father-
fixations," and he remembers the Statue as "the Giantess," an overbearing and unnurturing mother. Isherwood's images are the demons of
paranoia: objects invested by him with a subjective life that enables
them, though he has created them, to conspire against him.

Because the Statue is a woman, she's more the victim of interpretative
impertinences than her male architectural colleagues. The interpreters,
themselves men, feel challenged to broach her undefended femininity,
and she proves more malleable than Pound's flat-chested N.Y. She
licenses their misuse of her, since she stands for a welcoming promiscuity. In O. Henry's story "The Lady Higher Up," she chats with Miss
Diana of the Madison Square Garden roof and justifies her shift in
ethnic sympathy. Her nationality is French, but she speaks now in an
Irish brogue. Her excuse is a cheery permissiveness. Because she's a
woman, she's fickle. " 'Tis with statues," she reasons, "the same as with
people—'tis not their makers nor the purposes for which they were
created that influence the operations of their tongues at all—it's the
associations with which they become associated." She's altered by the
company she keeps, and to G. K. Chesterton this change of allegiance
expresses itself in a new political coloration. O. Henry makes a verbal
pun about her "cast-ironical welcome to the oppressed of other lands."
Chesterton's pun is visual. By association with the Irish, for whom
America has been an asylum, her verdigris-tainted bronze has, he claims,

taken on "a semblance of the wearing of the green." Walter Winchell called her "America's Lady Luck," both terms of his phrase begging the question of her symbolic meaning—for liberty and luck are different values, one a guaranteed birthright, the other a slim statistical chance; and Sky Masterson, the gambling hero of Winchell's friend Damon Runyon, wonders as he throws his dice in homage to Lady Luck in *Guys and Dolls* whether she has ever been a lady, since she has so often treated him like an unprincipled floozie.

The image ought to be the embodying of an idea. But with the Statue there's a constant interpretative temporizing between the principle and the physique. Her presence in the harbor as a character is so dramatic that you forget the emblematic job she's doing there or venture to confer on her a meaning more appropriate to her appearance. Her female policy of liberality excites the libertinism of male interpreters, who insult her with their allegorical retitlings. Max Beerbohm, for instance, renamed her the Statue of Vulgarity. Her indiscriminateness is to him not a political boon but a social gaffe. In 1903 he advised the Englishman arriving in New York to dispense with letters of introduction and carry instead "letters of preservation" entreating that he won't be killed by the kindness of his hosts. The Statue herself "seems to be passionately striving to express through her lips of stone the hope that he will have a 'lovely time.' " For Cecil Beaton in 1938 she appeared as a frumpish matron in last year's ball gown; for Beerbohm she is an overeager hostess. By reading her character, they have rewritten her allegory. Liberty seems to them not a universal, millennial reunion of all races but a prescription for throwing an overcrowded and ill-conceived party. Beerbohm told Robert Ross that the Statue must come down. Shaw once said that his reason for not going to the United States was that he couldn't bear to see the Statue, and when he did go, he denounced her as a Statue of Anarchy. In a lecture delivered in New York in 1932, he criticizes the American habit of frustrating government by invoking a liberty or privacy which is averse to legal restriction. This leads, he says, to gangsterism and petty tyranny. To symbolize this resistance to rule, he accuses the New Yorkers of having set up in their harbor "a monstrous idol which you call Liberty," and he recommends as a more suitable inscription for its pedestal, Dante's warning from above the gate of hell. Shaw's objection is as much to the image as to the idea, since imagery is idolatry—a worship of sham gods, both a political error and a disease of language, traducing an idea by making a verbal or corporeal effigy of it.

This mistranslation of the spirit by the letter or the body amuses the

Czech Dadaist Jindrich Styrsky, who in 1939 drew the Statue in construction. For a torso she has girders and pulleys, but she flaunts a swollen human mammary. Her mission is the suckling, not the enlightening, of the world. Yet we're gaining this sustenance from a rickety contraption. It's another case, as in Pound's urban courtship, of intercourse with an engine. Paul Morand, visiting the Statue in 1929, conducts an inquiry into the nature of symbolism which is also an interrogation and an erotic penetration of the symbolized object. To Morand, her costume is that of an unkempt and deranged woman rather than an allegorical uniform. She resembles a disturbed sleepwalker, wearing a bronze dressing gown and carrying a huge candlestick. It's easy to interpret her as a noctambulant neurotic because the logic of the symbolic statement she's supposed to be making hasn't been thought out. Why, Morand asks, is she turning her torch in the direction of Europe? Does she want to light her homeland first? Why has she been stranded on that islet? "Are they afraid of her setting fire to things with her torch in the wind?" He both comically tests the symbol by taking it literally (since its flame is immaterial and noncombustible) and ironically questions the symbol's propriety: does liberty have to be encircled by water because it's too incendiary a notion and may need a cautionary quenching? Morand achieves with her the hermeneutic seduction Pound's virginal N.Y. resists. She's a symbol you can enter. But this erotic decipherment—reading the allegory by trespassing inside the body—ends in fear and frustration, as Liberty traps him within her. "From near by, the towering, green, abstract figure terrified me," he reports. He valiantly thrusts himself into the abstraction: "I penetrated her skirts by fortress casements." Once inside, he discovers a disquieting truth about her. Though she professes to be Liberty, her interior resembles a prison, and though she claims to be the impersonation of an idea he finds, when he climbs to the top of her, that her head is empty. It remains for Mae West to justify Liberty's possession of a body, as she does in dressing up as the Statue; for rather than deriding the political idealism of the image, she is vindicating it. Mae West was a liberator, not enlightening the world but inflaming America, summoning it to cast off its enslavement to puritanism. She earns the right to pose as the Statue because she's a superwoman contemptuous of the official morality. Kong on the Empire State characterized the city's mechanical monstrosity; if Mae West, mounting the Statue's pedestal, is a monster, she's at least a sacred one. Kong is the city's nightmare of itself, Mae West its lubricious daydreaming.

These are all heroic images: the ego erect on its spire, like Ring

Mae West as the Statue of Liberty (1934). The Museum of Modern Art/Film Stills Archive, New York.

Lardner's cop or Hine's sky boys or Ayn Rand's architect; the id on its plinth, an ardent torch in its hand. Allied with the city's vertical rulers, these people transcend themselves. The contemporary artistic vision, however, resents such hierarchical presumption. In 1950 Weegee photographed the Statue through one of his distorting lenses and warped her

Weegee, "Statue of Liberty Distortion" (ca. 1950). Courtesy of the Weegee Collection, Wilma Wilcox, Curator.

strict uprightness. She bends lewdly at the waist, vampily redistributing her weight and acquiring a disheveled femaleness. The spikes of her crown, elongated and blurred by the lens, fly out of control like unraveled braids of hair. Though she's no longer an allegorical mentor, the new litheness of her body bestows a more up-to-date iconic status on her. She's as sinuous in her wreathings as a Coca-Cola bottle, and her torch, also squeezed out of shape by the lens, resembles a hot dog. Weegee has made her a deity for the age of advertising, the logo of a product, not the emblem of an idea. And her visual association with fast food—with Coke and frankfurters—revises her monumental meaning. Her virtue is her infinite reproducibility, like the commodities of junk food. She forfeits heroic singularity but gains in recompense repeatability and ubiquity, which augment her power: Coke and hot dogs are themselves symbols of the consumer economy, that great boon of American liberty.

While Weegee buckles her, Robert Rauschenberg levels her. He too by mishandling her is inquiring into the nature of symbolism and of the city. In his "Die Hard" (1963) she floats sideways, bobbing in the ocean with splashed-down space capsules, or lumbers like a dirigible across the sky above the water towers on the New York rooftops. Horizontality at once changes her meaning. It's a more democratic posture than standing up straight, though it also allies her with the cruising weaponry—submarines and planes—which supposedly exists to defend her. Tilted sideways, she's both an odalisque and a missile. Rauschenberg, like Weegee, is amused by the fact that we now manufacture images rather than invoking or envisaging them, and he reduces Liberty (who is herself a symbol) to the symbolic miniatures of her that are mass-produced as souvenirs of New York. In the poster he designed for the exhibition of his work in 1977 at the Museum of Modern Art, she stands next to the Flatiron and is dwarfed by it—a crude figurine, one of the clichés the city merchandizes as a remembrance. Set up as a universal remonstrance, she has become a parochial sight. Her symbolic reference now is to the place where she happens to stand, not to the idea she was pledged to uphold. She's a symbol of New York, whereas New York should be a symbol of her. Rauschenberg sees in this redeployment an analogy to his own artistic procedure. Inherited symbols we consign to the junk heap; the only objects which are authentically symbolic for us are the tacky castoffs of the city's gutters or its dime stores. A cheap replica of Liberty is to him more truly iconic than the Statue itself. He knows also that the idea she represents can be most acutely analyzed by retranslating her into a woman. He does so in a jokey version of a *Time* magazine cover, where she's ranked among the paraphernalia of patriotism, like the American flag and other symbols of a putative reference as cosmic as her own: the see-through globe from the 1964 New York World's Fair and an aerial map of the fair grounds. Again adverting to her mechanical replication, Rauschenberg has her appear on this cover twice, once as herself, the second time as a harassed lady sheltering her torch from the inclemencies of the harbor weather under an umbrella. Has she wearied of the allegorical charade and changed back into a human being? Or is liberty itself in danger of being drenched? Rauschenberg is fascinated by the chore of symbolism —by that dreary labor of lugging meanings about which we impose on objects. She is a case of this conscription, as are the trucks with advertising banners on their sides, which he sees choking the streets around his studio in lower Manhattan. "With sound scale and insistency," he says, "trucks mobilize words broadside our culture." The trucks are in the business of transporting words, freighting symbols. The Statue's job is also an onerous, indentured portage. By supplying her with that umbrella, he's offering her relief and wondering about her restiveness at this enforced work of being a sign.

Our sign language is a random matchmaking between ideas and objects. Rauschenberg dreams of liberating Liberty from the arbitrary task of having to represent liberty, inviting her to step down from her pedestal. He delights in the city's free-for-all. Iconography shackles its helter-skelter, blown-about things to a system and chains each one to a meaning. Rauschenberg protests that art should consist, as do the streets of New York, of happenings with no particular order or significance. Deposed as a statue, Liberty is reclaimed as litter. The same critique of the urban image is advanced by Andy Warhol, except that while Rauschenberg seeks to release the image from its enslavement, Warhol's different strategy, tried out in 1964 on the Empire State, is to kill it. His paintings are death notices for the image, which he despoils of aura and individuality—which he metaphorically slays as nature and resurrects as mechanism. The face of Marilyn Monroe is to him as potentially plural as a box of soap flakes or a Campbell's soup can. No single life matters, since humanity can be mechanically reproduced and mechanically exterminated. Warhol's series of disaster prints began from a newspaper headline announcing such a collective end: "129 DIE IN JET." These are pop deaths, superficial with a vengeance, seen not felt; and Warhol practices the same mortification on the Empire State, which has the temerity to imagine itself singular, unrepeatable, worth looking at. In 1964 he made an eight-hour silent film of it from the forty-fourth floor of the Time-Life Building. The exercise is intended to humble the image, to demonstrate that anything if looked at long enough will be boring. Though Warhol has said that he likes boring things—and envies in them the insentience of the machine—he doesn't pretend to be other than bored by them. He couldn't even bear to make one of his films, a six-hour study of someone sleeping, and faked it by looping footage. At the first screening, a member of the audience complained of the work's excruciating dullness and was tied to his chair and compelled to go on watching; Warhol himself walked out after a few minutes. In *Empire*, he leaves the moronically bland camera eye to do his looking for him. Only a machine could keep up such a vigil, and only a machine would want to. The film is one gadget's homily to another, a correspondence or courtship between lifeless partners. The circulation of film in the camera's innards is its metabolism, and the only life the Empire State can be seen to contain is electrical, not human, the flicking on and switching off of lights. Instead of the fertilization of object by subject which Pound wants to attain with his N.Y., Warhol contemplates a sterile parthenogenesis. The art of the city isn't subject's merger with object but object's sanitary cloning of itself.

12

Looking Through Brooklyn Bridge

The object in New York which most keenly attunes itself to the subject is a bridge. If you anthropomorphize the skyscrapers, you get either an overweening ego or an ape; if you ponder the inner life of the Statue of Liberty, you discover a head empty of thought; but the Brooklyn Bridge seems to take on naturally the attributes of a human body. It's as vibrant as a body, receiving from and transmitting to your body as you walk across it the hum and clatter of the traffic using it, and it's a lucid mental apparatus as well. Being transparent, it segments the city with its cables and instructs you—if you look at New York through it—in a way of seeing it. The bridge's engineering is the effortful but gracious enforcement of synthesis, holding contraries together with the violence of spun steel. And its bravest feat of this kind is visual, not architectonic. It analyzes the city, proposing itself to the artist as a mediator between his subjective retreat and the throng of clamoring objects which is downtown Manhattan.

This is how Vladimir Mayakovsky, who visited New York during his world tour in 1925, experienced the bridge—as a structure exemplifying his own rectified physical life; as a theorem for the understanding of the modern city; and as a paradigm for his poem about it. He reads the bridge as capitalism's unwitting self-controversion. It prophesies the advent of dialectical materialism, for its own constructive means, advancing beyond the stolidity of stone and suspending masses in the air by the agency of tense steel, take matter and raise it to spirit, as poetic imagery does. It's not a weighted, completed, obstructive thing, but a field of forces distributed through space. Not planted in earth, it unfolds in air, and the logic of its design suggests a similar engineering of society and history: man would be released from his servitude to material forces if only those forces could be operated on, directed, articulated. The bridge is built in time as much as in space. It's a passage into the future as well as a conduit across a river.

Earlier, Mayakovsky had attempted to arouse upsurgence in the Eiffel Tower, whispering sedition into its radio ear and inviting it to head a revolt. His poem about Paris summons the city's engineering to cast off its human burden. The Métro will vomit the crowds from its tunnels, the Seine bridges will batter foot passengers to death with their buttressed piers, and the Eiffel Tower will (he hopes) migrate to Moscow, marching on steel legs and broadcasting jubilation as it goes. The Brooklyn Bridge also has, potentially, the power to organize and reintegrate society. Mayakovsky sees it as a prehensile predator, standing with one steel leg in Manhattan while extending a paw to grip Brooklyn. The revolutionary man of action models himself on its riveted or bolted stringency. Mayakovsky praises Lenin for possessing "the relentless / temper of steel." The bridge with its coercive bolts is a realization of Mayakovsky's own physical presence and a poetic manifesto, since it disdains the clothings and concealments of arty style in favor of harsh structural membrification. Mayakovsky dreads metal fatigue—relapse from this gleamingly steely, electrically crackling rigor to the limpness of the human form. If the Eiffel Tower stays too long in wanton Paris, it will, he fears, get flabby and sell out to the frivolous values of Montmartre. Traveling home across the Atlantic in 1925, he worries about the same mechanical disfunction in himself. He has been estranged from his activist purpose while abroad and feels himself to be tarnished, corroded:

> steel words rust,
> > blacken copper brass.
> why is it,
> > under foreign rain,
> I get wet,
> > and rot
> > > and rust?

The capitalist, in Mayakovsky's obituary poem on Lenin, is credited with the invention of machines but accused of failing to live up to them. Like the sagging Eiffel Tower or like Mayakovsky oxidizing abroad, the capitalist remains a creature of obdurate, massive, acquisitive stone, refusing to learn from the lean transparency of steel. His muscles fatten, and he grows as overweight as his bulky ledgers. He should have heeded the parable of the Brooklyn Bridge and its juncture between two architectural modes, which to Mayakovsky are two historical epochs—the rooted conservatism of stone, in its arches; the radical uplift of steel, in its strung cables.

Mayakovsky does not look at Brooklyn Bridge. Instead he announces:

> I look at New York
>
> through Brooklyn Bridge.

The structure regulates and thus analytically directs the scene. With its bifurcating cables it serves up the city to him as a construct, not a view, enabling him to comprehend it step by step, rather than succumbing at once to the importunate general impression. He adopts the bridge's own method of segmenting in his poetic punctuation. Mayakovsky experimented with a punctuation that would array sentences in space, rather than hastening them through time toward a dying fall, with every comma an expression of reserve or hesitancy, every full stop an obsequy; and this new punctuation, stepped or tiered or zigzagging, works like the bridge, whose cables divide New York in order to rule it. Each image is allotted its own isolated space, and you vault across emptiness from one line to the next. The words send out a trajectory— as the bridge does through vacant air—over the blank page. Mayakovsky sees himself on the bridge, making a poem about it by an architectonic assemblage of words. He isn't descriptively coveting and accumulating them, like the capitalist with his accounts. Learning from the architect who builds strength into steel, he has compressed words. The complex man today, Mayakovsky argued, compacts fraught emotions in poetry, which is why he needs a new kind of punctuating to grip those taut fibers together. Thus he declares of himself on the bridge:

> here he stood
>
> putting
>
> syllable to syllable.

Writing is a discipline of construction. Words are to be aligned like girders or wrapped like stranded steel into cables. Mayakovsky's poem about the making of the bridge takes the bridge to pieces—unraveling its muscular wires, capsizing its building blocks—in order to refabricate it as a poem. The operation is a formula for revolution, demolishing a system so it can be recomposed, but also an account of the way we all experience the bridge when walking across it, since it seems to be dynamically, dialectically alive, happening around us and in response to us, quivering with the impress of traffic (to which we contribute), its cables rethreading and rearranging the view as we proceed. The bridge is voyaging with us.

This volatility makes it, for Mayakovsky, a constructivist contraption. For Hart Crane, its benison is less metamorphic, more stabilizing. Crane uses the bridge to hold New York and himself together. His friend Waldo Frank in *Our America* (1919) commented of New York's nervous stress that the city "was too high-pitched, its throb too shattering fast. Nerves and spiritual fiber tear in such a strain." The bridge's secret is to tauten without tearing. Its steel offers Crane a means of psychological resistance to, its stone a mode of anchorage in New York.

The city, when Crane came there in 1916 (aged 17) from Cleveland, permitted him immersion, inundation, the watery death of self-loss. He loved the shapelessness of its society and would take bus rides out into the Bronx to experience its oceanic unmappability. Awash among its multitudes, you might, he thought, "find somewhere in this sea of humanity, your lost identity." That recovery can only happen if you commit yourself to New York's liquid element and consent to go wherever it takes you, as he recognizes in a letter written after his return to Cleveland in 1920. He longs for New York, wanting "to lose myself" in its "chill vastness," then adds, "I should better have said 'find myself.'" The anonymity is Crane's induction into the city's erotic opportunism, which left him—after a series of casual encounters—in 1924 with a case of urethritis. He vowed to withdraw from "beckonings and all that draws you into doorways, subways, sympathies, rapports and the City's complicated devastations." The bridge symbolizes this stern determination of restraint. It arrests the deliquescent sexual expenditure of the self, opposing to the fluidity of the river and of urban society its solid piers of stone. The city also thrills Crane with its nervous tension, its excess of emotional voltage. Back in New York in 1923 he visited the burlesque shows on the Lower East Side where "they do everything but the ACT itself right on the stage," and praised the street life of the area because congestion engendered excitement: "life is possible here at greater intensity than probably any other place in the world today." He admires the children dancing on the pavements in spring, exerting themselves to discharge an energy they can't contain, and recommends—

as adult tactics for achieving the same relief—using the tummies of policemen as tom-toms or rowdily hallooing at dawn from your windows. But how much of this intensity can the human body absorb or exude? Crane begins to complain of a dejected exhaustion. The manic city depresses him. "The N.Y. life is too taxing," he admits in 1923, and has left him insomniac and irritable. The summer heat sucks away his vitality and brings him near collapse. "New York takes such a lot from you that you have to save all you can of yourself or you simply give out." For this depletion, as for the watery dissipation of self, the bridge prescribes a remedy. Its steel has been readied for such tension, which it converts into a fortifying intensification.

In 1924 Crane removed himself to Columbia Heights, where he could be at a meditative distance from the city. Now, instead of living in it and being spent by it, he could look at it and understand it from afar. Across the river, it has receded into an image; between himself and it he has placed the Brooklyn Bridge, "the most superb piece of construction in the modern world," as he called it, which engenders or engineers that image. The bridge suggests a reconstruction of himself. The valor of structural steel is its resilient preparedness for stress and tension, the inner ailments (as Crane discovered when abraded by New York) of modernity. In its combination of stone piers and steel cables, the bridge dramatizes a change in architectural physiology. There's a difference in building materials between strength and stress, between plastic and elastic deformation. Iron is strong but breaks easily and can't be pulled about. It has to be cast or molded, fixed into a solid shape. But if you add carbon, you change the properties of iron and make steel, which is tensile and abides stress. Engineering is the calculated application of stress to a material. Steel is manipulable, and if you know it must withstand a certain stress, you can ensure that it will do so. It copes by flexing, by giving slightly, like the upper tiers of the Empire State swaying in a gale. The cables on the bridge are examples of those contrary "pull forces" that John Marin saw as the dynamics of cubism. Under pressure from both ends at once, they're stressed to maintain form despite that tug-of-war. Rather than snapping, they bend, because the big cords are woven of smaller ones which cooperate in the chore. When in 1930 Crane was commissioned by *Fortune* magazine to write about the construction of the George Washington Bridge, it was the plaiting of these cables which most impressed him.

Crane himself in New York internalizes this structural tension. It becomes an in-tensity, contrived by the city to test his psychic resilience. "N.Y." is, he says in June 1919, "a series of exposures intense and rather

savage"; it "handles one roughly but presents also . . . remedial recess."
As heat is applied to iron to melt it to make steel, so New York subjects
Crane to the trial of its summer fire. "New York has been like a blazing
furnace for the last two days," he reports in June 1923. Yet the temperature vouchsafes him "the intense and interesting spectacle of the
streets." He analyzes his own plight in the city structurally, as if he
were the bridge, its resistance overtaxed: summer there "takes all the
vitality you have to give and gives you back nothing to build with or
repair." Writing about the despair of the city's unemployed in 1930, he
treats their mood as a distress of metal. Neurosis is rust. "I'm pretty
well convinced," he says, "that unmitigated anxiety has a highly corro-
sive effect on the resilience of the imagination." Whereas steel is architecture as an existential trapezism, suspended and managing to sustain
stress by distributing it in midair, thriving on punishment as Crane wants
to do, stone—as in the bridge's traditional and rooted bays—is an
architecture of anchorage, which is what he recommends to his mother as
a solution to her psychological problem. Persuading her to settle down, he
says, "you've got to have anchorage somewhere if you are ever to have
peace of mind."

Sex for Crane is a similacrum of the steel mill's furnace, where twin
selves are smelted and the Word (as he says in a letter to Waldo Frank
in 1924) is made Flesh, or where flesh in the onslaught of heat hardens
to steel: "I know now that there is such a thing as indestructibility. In
the deepest sense, where flesh becomes transformed through intensity
of response to counter-response, where sex was beaten out. . . ." That
beating out is the hammering of metal, to purify and fortify it. And the
celebration of this new-forged union between himself and a lover is
transferred at once to the bridge, whose hymeneal arcs are made by the
same fierce process as this bodily juncture. Embracing, the men are
mutual reinforcers, like the bound cables. Crane writes of "the ecstasy
of walking hand in hand across the most beautiful bridge of the world,
the cables enclosing us and pulling us upward in such a dance. . . ."
Inside his poem *The Bridge* (1930), the fraternal colleague with whom
he travels hand in hand is Whitman, his predecessor who prophetically
exhales the bridge by setting breath in steel. Engineering is the transmutation of substances; the joy Crane experiences here is a transfiguration of self. "I believe I am a little changed," he told Frank, ". . . tran-
substantiated as anyone is who has asked a question and been answered."

He builds *The Bridge* as the bridge itself is built: by a structural
preparation of materials which is, as in steel-making, transfigurative. He
achieves admixture by intensification, as the foundry does. The project

of the poem was a synthesizing of America. Crane had tried, he said, to raise fact, location, and history to myth. The bridge is "of the fury fused"; *The Bridge* also wants to attain, in a white heat which melts down words until they punningly run into others, "a fusion of our own time with the past." The fusing derives from an increase in pressure, an overheating which, instead of disordering words, compacts and compounds them, readying them to discharge several functions simultaneously. When, for instance, Crane addresses the bridge's "curveship," his coinage envisages the bridge nautically, its cables as sails, its piers a prow; animates it, by describing the curve it traces through the air as, like the whirling seagull, it dips down from eternity into time, from the sky to the sea; ceremonially beseeches it, as if calling it "your lordship" or "your worship," since he's asking of it an act of noblesse oblige—the charitable lending of a myth to a depleted God; and at the same time adverts to a courtship of the bridge which, like Pound's overtures to the city as a mistress or Joseph Stella's nomination of it as a wife, is necessarily frustrated. The word gathers into itself and binds together this multiplicity of references, all straining, as the strands of the cables do, in different directions. The gull's curve at the beginning of the poem was called "inviolate." The bridge's curve makes good a violation. Myth originates in a theft, the Promethean expropriation of a divine secret; now man, no longer needing to purloin myths, can manufacture them and return them to the robbed gods, for the bridge's curving ship, breathing the Atlantic air or galactic with traffic lights, will sail vertically—into the sky, not across oceans. What Mayakovsky describes as compression Crane refers to as an "intentional condensation and 'density' of structure." For both, words are matter which becomes spirit (or symbol) by an engineered deforming or elasticizing. Crane empowers the bridge to "condense eternity": to fix the invisible in a shape, attaching to it a specific gravity. His own poetic idiom does the same, accumulating within words an infinity of implication, holding meanings in suspense. The increase in heat (which is the intensifying) begets an increase in fortitude (which is the polyvalent density of the words, their con-densing). From the fire, where words seem about to disintegrate by the loss of singularity, is forged resolute steel.

Still the poem is guiltily aware that it's engaged in an experimental destruction of language and constantly questions whether the pull forces to which it subjects words will disentangle and diffuse them. Crane's poetry is the enforcement of semblances—between the bridge and a harp, an altar and a world mind—which can't exist anywhere but in those portmanteau words of his. In interpreting the words, we undo the compounding he has plaited into them, untwining the bridge's cables. Hence Crane's reference, at the beginning of *The Bridge*, to the chimerae of the cinema: it too, like his poetry, is an engineered, illusory idealism. His purpose is to mobilize the bridge, which can be done only by rhetorical pretense. It seems to be marching across the harbor, but that seeming is a visual error, induced by the glint of sun on its girders, and Crane has to conclude that it only looks "As though the sun took step of thee." The poem's imagery, unable to effect physical alterations, must content itself with being what it calls "apparitional," foreshadowing metamorphoses possible only in the linguistic interim between unlike objects which is metaphor. The images, like Pound's compliments to N.Y., are the spurned tributes the pathetic fallacy pays an indifferent machine. The bridge has, after all, decided on a symbolic meaning for itself and has no need of Crane's encouragements. It prefers convenience to transcendence and, as Crane remarked to Waldo Frank, is satisfied with being the symbol of "an economical approach to shorter hours, quicker lunches, behaviorism and toothpicks."

Crane saw the poem's symbolism as a coercion of correspondence, a deed of structural daring that bestrides an abyss of dissimilarity. Thus he promised his patron Otto Kahn that Cathay would be worked upon until it underwent transmutation "into a symbol of consciousness, knowledge, spiritual unity." Metaphor mimics the architecture of steel, vaulting over empty air. Sometimes, more cautiously, Crane adheres to the founded architecture of stone, as when he hopes that the transcendentalism of the poem's concluding anthem will be supported by "the pediments of the other sections." Either way, the poem is an act of conceptual or mystic engineering, the construction of a bridge with words. Crane said he'd be happy "if *The Bridge* can fullfil simply the inferences of its title." Its initial transmuting is to raise the bridge into a metaphor; it then proceeds to make a metaphor of itself, offering its own poetic arc as a parable of the "transition" which Crane said was the predicament of the age. The activity is not only one of assemblage, like Mayakovsky's on the bridge, putting syllable to syllable. For Crane the bridge isn't riveted but woven or knitted together. Mayakovsky sees it, and his own poetic homage to it, as Meccano, a pyramid of segments notched and slotted into place. With Crane, the adjustment of parts isn't automatic. He has to plait the resistant cables that hold up the structure: "thousands of strands have to be searched for, sorted and interwoven" prior to "a final welding into their natural form." He disparaged *The Waste Land* because it wasn't welded in this way. Eliot had nihilistically allowed it to sunder into fragments. In contrast with

Crane's use of the bridge as a structural admonition and a lyrical imperative (for a bridge also means a modulation between subjects in sonata form), one of Eliot's refrains is the nursery lament that London Bridge is falling down. Myth engineers analogy, welds historical epochs into solidarity, as Crane proposes when he comments that "N.Y. is getting to be a really stupendous place. It is the center of the world today, as Alexandria became the nucleus of another older civilization." Because the myth-maker is a primordial engineer, centering the world on himself and rigging up structures to be believed in and thence inhabited, he naturally allies himself with American industry, like Melville analyzing the technology of whaling in *Moby Dick* or Whitman extolling the bardic agency of the printing press; and when Whitman appears in *The Bridge,* it's as the prophet of a mechanical resurrection. He makes possible the bridge's construction by launching across the river and the continent an avenue of consciousness. Crane salutes him as "Our Meistersinger": the poet as artisan and member of an urban guild, the practitioner of a craft.

A bridge exists to permit transit, to pave water. The purpose of Crane's bridge, though, is ascension. He seeks—in a reconsecration which is also a re-engineering—to upend it. The alteration announces myth's entry into and protest against history (in contrast with the fracture of myth and its diaspora into history which, in Crane's opinion, *The Waste Land* countenances). The poem's epigraph from Job opposes the two motives that vie throughout it: the quotation summarizes the devil's itinerary, "going to and fro in the earth, and . . . walking up and down in it." Toing and froing is the historical flux, the randomness of happening, the motion of time and the river. Up and down is the different axis of eternity, along which spirit descends into or arises from matter and myth interrupts or arrests history. The poem argumentatively shifts the bridge from one use to the other. Its redefined destiny is to stay the river and (as the first stanza suggests) to chain its waters. Imposed prohibitively on the river, it fixes the streaminess of phenomena, as for the painters and photographers it framed and contained the chaos of New York which they looked at through it. By the end of Crane's poem it achieves the elemental miracle of drawing the waters and the city into itself. Here its technological and musical meanings concur. Like a dynamo, it's a machine through which matter passes to be energetically emitted as spirit; like a lyre, it's a device for producing from wayward air a spherical harmony. It stands upright as a reproof to the horizontality of history, imaged by the river and by the road across the continent on which Rip van Winkle sets out in one of the poems of Crane's sequence. The highway unfurls in time, the medium of van Winkle's shuttling travels. Hurrying to the subway, Rip is reminded to pick up his copy of the daily *Times*. He's an imp who flourishes in the remissness of time. Like the river in the following poem, his fate is to be discarded by the time which freights him. He's as disposable as the daily paper. From his entrapment in time, music supplies release. The ancient mariner Crane encounters in South Street beats time with bony hands. Marking it at rhythmic intervals, he is musically organizing it, making it recur, and thus beating it by evading it; and his conducting gestures toward the successive mythic rebirths, which also defeat time, of the seasonally reincarnated Pocahontas, who "rose with maize—to die." The river's obsession, like the road's, is the torture of history: "its one will—flow!"

Two of the poem's New York landscapes express this amnesiac fluency, rendering everything liquid so as to carry it into oblivion, which the bridge resists. The nocturnal harbor is a drowsing reservoir of memory, where things float in limbo. The subway likewise serves as an underwater ferry, disposing of people in its sluice. Both harbor and subway are watery graves. A congress of shifting vapors—water uprisen as ghosts—prowl, wander, and lapse into blankness. When the dawn comes, it brings a pallor of mortality to the window and exterminates the stars. Water for Crane is, like history, an element of dissolution. "The Tunnel" sees Broadway as a river with no bridge to detain it. Instead, beneath its hectic dismissive conduit, it has another current of perpetual motion, even more uncaring and forgetful than the river—the subway trains, "rivered under streets / and rivers," a reckless flood in which you involuntarily drown and are endlessly circulated, like the newspapers revolving and winging in corners of carriages. The trains lurch in "a monotone / of motion," a time which, like the glass doors at the subway entrance, goes around in circles without ever arriving at the ordered recurrences of music. Ejected from the tunnel beside the river, Crane reflects on his salvation from a death by trickling, temporal, fickle water:

> Here at the water's edge the hands drop memory;
> Shadowless in that abyss they unaccounting lie.

The bridge has been his protection against the negligent stream, and in the final section, "Atlantis," it enables him to claim for himself the poet's vatic elevation: he employs its cables as a musical instrument. Previously, he had been able only to bless and guard the accord between two people in the harbor aubade. Now, armed with the bridge as his Orphic lyre, he can compel nature and compliant machinery (the ships at sea which respond in amity) to choir in harmony. Lyric song is entreaty; the ode (which is what Crane, who wanted to be the Pindar of the machine age, writes in "Atlantis") is the proclamation of order, regulating nature, a song which "devoutly binds." Hence the choral sound of the ending: Crane is directing elements and machines in a coordinated hymn of jubilation. From the frail and short-lived love between strangers berthed for a night together in the harbor poem, he advances to a kingdom of love made vibrant by the bridge; from the subway mined through a neurotic individual brain, its forking tunnels "interborough fissures of the mind," he emerges onto the "steeled Cognizance" of the bridge, which is a cosmic cranium, dazzlingly transparent, not, like the subway, a devious chasm. The bridge now synopsizes the city and the entire world. Its span is a lariat sweeping through air to round up and encincture the riot of phenomena. Instead of meagerly traversing the harbor, it aspires to put a girdle around the earth. And at the same time as enmeshing the city, it draws up through itself and imbibes the river, where the poet was cast away by the diving subway but from which he's now rescued:

> O River-throated—iridescently upborne
> Through the bright drench and fabric of our veins.

The first poem glimpses the bridge obliquely and addresses it tentatively. Its purpose is invocation, and it has a superstitious reluctance to profane the god whose patronage it seeks by direct confrontation. Thus Crane looks at the bridge out of the corner of his eye, seeing it across the harbor from the sliver of an office window or from the streets, only daring to approach under cover of night when, like Milton's God dark with excessive bright, its shadow is clear. It tantalizes him like a millennial mirage on the horizon, "obscure as that heaven of the Jews." He can ask himself questions about it ("how could mere toil align thy choiring strings!"—which, thanks to his choice of punctuation mark, turns the impious interrogation of God into an exclamatory tribute to God's unknowability) but mustn't expect it to respond. Hence this poem's humble tendering of itself in its title, "To Brooklyn Bridge." Within the poem, it won't name the bridge; instead, it reverently paraphrases. The subject—that unquiet urban "I" who drops from his office in an elevator or lingers on the piers after dark—desires but flinches from the numinous object. The final poem conquers this intimidation and can jettison the personal pronoun. There's no separate, inadequate "I" in "Atlantis," only the bridge's triumphant "Thou," which has absorbed the poet. In praising it, he's assuming its power, since his breath and his plucking have attuned its cables and he, the prophetic singer, is the god who issues from its strings. Crane achieves what Pound's N.Y. denied him, the wedding (or welding) of subject to object which generates the symbol.

Because his poem's ambition is the metamorphosis of fact into symbol, Crane is concerned with the range of iconographic options he has in his view of the harbor. Every time he looks at it, he says, it's different. The revisions are tests of his symbolizing faculty, experiments in engineering the transmutation of fact. In May 1924 he arranges a landscape of impressionist imprecision inside the frame of his window. "At twilight on a foggy evening . . . it is beyond description," he says of the harbor—beyond description because beyond perception, atmospherically smudged, the top of the Woolworth Building swallowed by a cloud. Indistinctness encourages misty reverie, but the bridge summons him to think of the view as agitated structure. On this evening its span is an electric grid alight with El trains and cars, and their small trails—the transpirings of energy—provoke Crane to see the whole harbor as industriously ignited. Every object carries a beacon to announce that it's at work. The tugs have lights on their masts and decks, the Statue of Liberty brandishes her torch. The impressionist temptation to drown in that all-absorbing pool where things lose shape is checked by the busy vigilance of light. The El trains shine with a vital incandescence which won't be put out by the watery dark: Crane calls them glow-worms. By October 1924 cold has sharpened and purged the scene. "On such days one gets an even better edge to the glorious light here by the harbor." The brightness is aggressive, "the water so very blue, the foam and steam from the tugs so dazzlingly white," but the harsh, bladed brilliance purifies. The view is a mortification of the flesh, "a cold bath." Though this clarity is laving, like the degree-zero purism of Le Corbusier's New York, fog in February 1925 embroils the harbor again in sick and guilty fantasy. It blots out the view (nothing can be seen more than "six feet from the window") and makes of it a phantasmagoria. Crane is kept awake by an assembling orchestra of tormentors, a bedlam of "bells, grunts, whistles, screams and groans of all the river and harbor buoys," which persuade him that he's at "the mouth of hell."

The harbor can be a radiant heaven—as it was for the critic Paul Rosenfeld, who in 1924 called his volume of essays on American modernists *Port of New York* because he saw the port as a tolerant open space for the exchange of ideas, a clear sky beneath which a new America accedes to its spiritual destiny; it can also, for the insomniac

Crane, be a hell where you're plagued by the city's exotic devastations. As a fact, it is immutable, but as a symbol it has an indefinite relativity. To open up this spectrum of possibility, diffracting the object into an array of subjective apparitions, Crane organized an elaborate iconography for the edition of *The Bridge* published in Paris by Harry Crosby in 1930. Photographs were commissioned from Walker Evans, and Crane asked Joseph Stella's permission to reprint his essay on New York, together with three of the *New York Interpreted* sequence and (as frontispiece, to be reproduced in color) the version of the bridge now in the Brooklyn Museum. As fact and as machine, the bridge is best documented by another machine, the camera. As symbol, however, it requires the illumining of itself achieved by Stella. The photographer makes a diagram of its structure in black and white, while the painting conveys its inflammation into meaning in a glare of color. The photograph's therapeutic task is to fix and tranquilize the moment. Writing to Stieglitz in 1923, Crane praised him for having used his camera to heal the city's "brokenness" and soothe its febrile intensity by meditating through the lens on instants in time or fragments in space. Photography studies the thing for what it is and seals it in its chamber of safekeeping; painting encourages the object's unfolding into luminous illusion. The camera investigates the bridge with the patient attention of science or the calming concentration Crane admired in Stieglitz. The painter meanwhile contrives disintegration: the bridge's efflorescence into what it's not. Between them, Evans and Stella with their different media graphically reprise the ambition of Crane's poem.

Because the photographer has to scale down the world in order to recompose it in his shuttered box, the choice of angle is important to him. He must decide on the best way to capture it, and in planning his approach he's dramatizing his relation with the thing he snaps. In anticipation of the photographic strategy, Crane changes angles and attitudes throughout his poem. "To Brooklyn Bridge" places the bridge in the distance, glimpsing it indirectly, or else, drawing closer after dark and knowing it (as the photographer does) by tracing the shadow it casts, gazes up at it. In the dawn poem, Crane has protectively placed a window—which in Stieglitz's work stands for the mediating camera—between himself and the harbor. Light's penetration of that space is like its entry into the sealed camera and its exposure of the dark plate: "The window goes blond slowly." At the end of "The Tunnel" he is standing again, presumably, beneath the bridge; in "Atlantis" he has surmounted it, climbed "onward and up" through it into transcendence on its "loft of vision."

Walker Evans in two of his 1929 photographs chooses to look up at the bridge. What Crane in a letter to Stieglitz called the "mechanical perfectibility" of the camera does obeisance to the grander mechanical perfection of the bridge. One of the photographs sees the bridge indeed as a cosmic camera: an obliterating darkness vanquished by the invasion of light. The bridge at which Evans is looking up with his camera's eye looks back down at him through an ocular aperture of its own, as if he, who is entrapping it in his small cell, were himself held prisoner within its vaster room. In this photograph, Evans tilts the roadway so that it runs diagonally across the print and places at the corner one of the bridge's buttresses, which also inclines at a dangerous angle. The print is ominously dark. Roadway and buttress occlude light and press on Evans like a lowering ceiling. Yet the buttress has a window in it, the arch we pass under when crossing the bridge, and this is the structure's eye: the orifice, like the camera's optic, through which light squeezes to expel the dark. Evans has photographed a metaphor, making real the omniscience Crane attributes to the bridge and relating that to the modest, studious seeing of his own art. Another photograph, taken from directly under the span on the Brooklyn shore, magnificently communicates the bridge's change in the poem from traversal to ascent. The photograph includes the river traffic and the skyscrapers beyond, yet Evans denies its recession into depth so as to confer on the image an indefinite height. Though the bridge is seen in extreme perspective, we don't—when reading it—follow that perspective downward to its vanishing point, which Evans has left dark; as Crane urges, our eye travels "onward and up." The parallel lines of the bridge will in nature never meet. The vanishing point, creating an illusion of their convergence, would leave the bridge finite and diminished. Evans prevents this by flattening the bridge in the photograph's depthless space and forcing it to rise, growing as it goes like a branching tree. The lines of its span shoot off in different vertical directions and will meet only in returning home after they have encircled the earth. Nor is the ascent insubstantializing: the bridge is an expanding volume. If the previous photograph sees the bridge as a pantheistic mind whose thoughts express themselves by pressing through a camera eye, here it's a ladder extending both outward and upward to infinity. Light leaking down through the slats of the roadway characterizes them as that ladder's rungs, and beneath it are propped—by inspired fortuitousness—a succession of smaller ladders, for a boat is passing under the bridge and two of its masts have pairs of ladders running up them. The advent of the boat is one of those photographic accidents which, as Crane said of Stieglitz, eternalize the instant. It's passing through and will soon be gone, but Evans has made

Walker Evans, "Brooklyn Bridge" (1929). Gelatin-silver print. 8¾ x 5½ inches (22.2 x 14.0 cm.). Collection, The Museum of Modern Art, New York. Mr. and Mrs. John Spencer.

it belong there, allying it with the bridge's permanence. Boat and bridge are both verticalized. One of the masts has just drawn level with the span, and the overlapping declares their coincidence of aim. Whitman connected the masts of New York's shipping with the aspiring towers of its architecture; Evans makes the same analogy, lining up on either side of the bridge two of the altitudes of lower Manhattan, the Woolworth Building to the left, the Municipal Building to the right. The mast next to the Woolworth actually overtops it. The rungs of those ladders could be measuring the tower and inciting it to grow. Both the buildings and the masts terminate in spires. The bridge alone is safe from ever having to conclude its career of ascent by attaining a vanishing point. It dilates as it rises. Perhaps after all the terrestrial point where it vanishes into its foundations is its true apex, since Evans— associating it with the masts and the skyscrapers, which are also parabolic ladders, while exempting it from the limits restricting them— makes it look as though it might have been built from the sky downward, ending on earth, not commencing there. His photograph, in an apt tribute to the poem, describes the bridge as metaphysical engineering, like the passage let down from the stars in *Paradise Lost* which the angels descend when visiting mankind. All our myths, from Babel (New York's prototype) onward, are our human attempts to re-erect that ladder from the ground up: our bridgings of the sky.

The camera is a structure prized open by light. This is how Evans photographs the bridge. Light questions the stolidity of structure, making the arch an eye and the roadway—as it defines the gaps between the slats—a ladder. A photograph draws with light, and Evans shows light discovering the imagistic meaning of the bridge. In his medium, structure is black, light white. But in the feverishly colored art of Stella, light, rather than serenely white, is a polychrome havoc, which structure must hold at bay. For Evans the bridge is matter through which spirit shines, as light begins to make a transparency of it; for Stella it is violent spirit constrained by matter. Robert Hughes says that "the fundamental image of modernity" in painting is "light seen through structure." The painter, systematizing seeing, relies on structure to analyze the light he looks at. It's this that Stella's bridge accomplishes. The maelstrom of battling light that is the city is fended or fenced off by the bridge's cables. You look at the city through the bridge and are thereby saved from its enchanting, deranging luminescence. In Stella's Coney Island painting there is no structure to resist this carnival of light, so the composition is a distraught whirligig, spinning you into distraction. The city in the fifth panel of *New York Interpreted* is an alluring siren, its glowing purple ridge beckoning us to pleasure. Between himself and it Stella places the bridge, which with its lacy vertical webs and thick, muscly diagonals structurally steels him against the importunings of light. The stringent lines of the cables, as Stella explained in a letter in 1944, contend against "the fluctuating swirling curves of sounds and lights." Color is exhortation, imprecation, seductive beseeching, which is why Stella synesthetically makes it correspond with noise and calls his polyptych a symphony. His Coney Island is carnal vermilion and acidulous neon lemon: colors are the siren's blandishments. On Brooklyn Bridge, color glowers from an inferno. The "green and red glare" of the traffic lights signaled to Stella the seething of the pit. Colors are vocally shrill, wailing or screeching as they suffer. He hears the electric light as the ringing of a "silvery alarm"; the trolley wires sibillate with a "sulphurous voice"; from under the bridge tugboats moan in pain. His Broadway clamors "with sounds and lights." Color is the scream emitted by expiring light. If to the futurists a single dying light bulb is tragic, then the skyline Stella observed from the bridge at night was a rain of meteors, a planetary holocaust. The lights resembled "suspended falls of astral bodies or fantastic splendors of remote rites." The bridge's structural responsibility is to cage light, to imprison an explosion. Standing on it, Stella felt it trembling with the effort. It shuddered at the vibration of passing trains, and his body shivered with it. But its cables withstand the visual strain that color places on them. The bridge, he said, "emerges victorious," subjugating the hellish "fluvial abyss" of the torrent beneath; it defends him against his own vision. Returning to it in 1939, in "The Brooklyn Bridge: Variation on an Old Theme," he again uses its mesh of cables to keep out the fulgent city, and in the predella added a meta-bridge which registers the conquest of light by structure. He paints a silhouette of the bridge and the city, its towers blinking, a setting sun raying out behind it, and then draws over them both a vaulting arch, bejewelled with dots of light. It might be a compliment to the end of Crane's poem, since it shows the idea of the bridge spanning the bridge itself and the city and continuing beyond New York to unify the world.

The bridge's beneficence to the painter is its dissection of the view. Like the steel-framed, glass-walled skyscrapers of New York, it is structure not as an impenetrable fortress (which the Jamesian house of fiction aims to be) but as an apparatus you can look through and think with. The scene behind it is a nineteenth-century one—a burgeoning city, symbolizing the plenitude of the real. Yet ruled by the straight lines of the cables and intersected with their necessary stresses, it's a view studied with a twentieth-century self-consciousness. As a lattice,

Joseph Stella, "The Bridge," from *The Voice of the City of New York Interpreted* (1922). Collection of the Newark Museum.

the cables allow matter to be ordered as in a scientific diagram, for the lattice (which the bridge imprints on New York) is the geometric idealization employed by crystallographers to represent the solid state. A solid is designed as a regulated array of points in space, connected by networks of lines which stand for its unit cells. The bridge literally crystallizes the city, since the crystal is matter in a state of maximum order, the whole deducible from the part. The lithographs of the bridge made by Louis Lozowick in 1938 show how this ordering is enforced. He entrusts the task to some workers who, on a high platform, are repairing the cables. They are the artist's surrogates, helping him, as the bridge does, to construct the view, aligning the city and commandeering its objects into place. In another 1938 print Lozowick sets the view of lower Manhattan midway between the tugs and barges on the river and the team of workers on their aerial hoist above the bridge's span. The city and the bridge hang between and are dually sustained by a substructure of economic labor (the river traffic) and a superstructure of artistic labor, dedicated, like the workers on their platform, to refurbishment.

John Marin's early watercolors permit the city to drain into an inky pool because they can rely on the bridge to bisect and diagonally correct, with those taut lines of rectitude, the shaplessness of color. In "New York Skyline, Lower Manhattan from the Bridge" (1912) two parallel lines are traced across the mess of watery pigment; in "Figure Leaning on Railing" (1910) Marin situates an observer, as his deputy, on the span. That figure is the modern artist, seen in the act of seeing, who submits light to the analytic discipline of structure. Albert Gleizes, who compared the bridge with the noblest achievements of European architecture, used it to sieve the city in three paintings made during his first visit to New York in 1915. Always its structure—a black web in one version, more lacily filamented and checkered in another—acts as a grating or a diffractor, stamped on the colored jumble of New York. Eventually, the city can be harnessed within the bridge. In a composition of looping circles, like Crane's lariats, Gleizes makes the span a funnel, with the buildings of Manhattan at one of its openings and those of Brooklyn at the other, while the river, also contained within it, courses through its center.

For the photographer, the bridge serves a related purpose. Instead of delineation—resolving the city into its component parts—which is its boon to the painter, it conducts experiments in optics. It officiates, in fact, as a camera obscura. E. O. Hoppé, who photographed a view of the city through the bridge in 1921, referred in his autobiography in 1946

Albert Gleizes, "On Brooklyn Bridge" (1917). Collection, The Solomon R. Guggenheim Museum, New York. Photo: Robert E. Mates.

to the habit of "seeing everything through something else" as a mere mannerism: "scenes were shot through the legs of a camel or a man, through motor tyres, through anything that provided an opening. . . . I must confess to a strong propensity for making use of steel bridges." The photographer's art is the seeing of things through something else; any object he chooses to look through necessarily does duty as a camera.

Karl Struss, who photographed in New York between 1910 and 1913, adopted the bridge as his technical talisman. On a late afternoon in 1912 he photographed the Singer Building through its cables. The parallelograms of wire exactly apportion the muffled murky sky and the serrated outcrops of the buildings. Like the camera, the cables frame and compose the city. The photographer's arcane box simultaneously denies and admits light. In demonstration of this duality, Struss in 1912 photographed Brooklyn Bridge twice from the same position, once in late afternoon, then again in the evening. Here he is not only seeing through the bridge but seeing it through the framing arches of Ferry Slip. His camera looks out at a pair of architectural cameras. And, to illustrate the opposed values of light and dark, one view is a photographic negative of the other. Objects that are dark by day incandesce at night. In the afternoon the Singer tower is a gray smudge; in the evening it wears a cap of electricity. The bridge's roadway is gloomy too in the afternoon, but in the evening aglow with aureoles. Photography mysteriously traps the emanations from objects, the beams of light they transmit, and closets them in its darkness. Struss associates this spectral activity with the Brooklyn Bridge. Another of his 1912 sequence, " 'The Ghost Ship'—Waterfront, East Side," makes play with the photographic image as phantom, the shadow of substance. On what might be a cinema screen in front of the bridge, a nonexistent ship has materialized. Because its mast and riggings are lined up with the bridge's tower, it suggestively dematerializes the bridge: might that be an illusion too? The ship does exist, but outside the photograph, from where it casts its shadow on the side of a warehouse. By passing it off as a ghost, Struss jests with the undead nature of the photographed thing. The object has a sinister second coming in the image.

Less spookily, he depicts the bridge as a kind of camera by treating it as a perspective box. Two of his 1912 photographs are called "The Vanishing Point." One studies the receding trolley-car rails along Second Avenue and the corresponding recession of the El trestles above; the other watches the El tracks on the Brooklyn Bridge disappear through the vanishing point of the central arch. At the camera's eye, light rays converge, enter, and in steep perspective print the object they derive from upside down on the photographic plate. The shutter is the hole through which objects vanish to reappear, inverted, as images. Struss places in these photographs mechanical agencies that travel on the eye's behalf toward and away from that juncture where all lines run into each other and all objects are obliterated. Under the El on Second Avenue, one trolley is advancing from that point while another retreats toward it,

Karl Struss, "Singer Building and the New York Skyline through the Brooklyn Bridge at Dusk" (1912). Courtesy of Mrs. Ethel Struss.

and on the bridge the eye's ambassadors are a train and two groups of pedestrians, those to the right heading off in the direction of disappearance, those to the left coming toward us, survivors on their way back from the point of no return. The bridge posed a series of technical challenges to Berenice Abbott, who in 1943 lamented that "we cannot yet take a satisfactory photograph from Brooklyn Bridge" because no film was fast enough to catch detail from the requisite distance, and the bridge's lateral swaying disrupted the exposure. All the same, Abbott had used the bridge in 1930 to measure the camera's deepening definition of its field. She classified the photograph as a technical experiment, not a view, calling it "Extreme Contrasts of Light and Shade." It's about a series of mediations, boxing within each other three layers of architectural engineering and three planes of light. Through the crisscrossed girders of the Manhattan Bridge are seen the cables of the Brooklyn Bridge, through which are seen the towers of the financial district. The venture into space is an exploratory progress from dark (the thick black of the Manhattan Bridge) through shade (the finer, filtered gray of the Brooklyn Bridge) to light (the hazy mirage of the distant buildings, the unobstructed sky beyond them). The photographer is positioned at the extreme of blackness. Two stages of mediation away, through two bridges, is the brightness of the air. Berenice Abbott sums up within the bridge the paradox of the camera, that dark room designed for the enclosure of light.

The bridge enables the artist to construct the city. It supplies the form in which New York can be contained. Yet what if that structure and its ordering power fails? The calamity occurs in the paintings of the surrealist O. Louis Guglielmi. Crane heard the bridge harmonically singing, Stella transcribed its outcry as the high-pitched complaint of color. Both had oracularly implanted a voice in mechanism. Guglielmi revokes their gift. He, whose father was a violinist, finds the bridge catatonic, and its muteness is a sonic symptom of the death abstraction brings to the city. Guglielmi's New York scenes are morbidly quiet because life has departed from them. In "South Street Stoop" (1935) the bridge's cables wire the air above a desolate corner. The house with the stoop advertises rooms to let but will have no takers: the abstract city has been evacuated. The bridge's roadway is effaced by a row of featureless warehouses. No one travels across it, for like Hopper's exterminating railway tunnel it's a route to nowhere. Abstraction silences Guglielmi's city by prohibiting those people who remain from communicating. The characters in his most famous image, "Terror in Brooklyn" (1941), mourn soundlessly in the vacuum of a suburban street, trapped inside a glass bell. Their transparent prison forbids the expression of their grief and thus renders it unintelligible. The same silencing muffles the once lyrically eloquent bridge. In 1942 Guglielmi painted it closing off a blank vista which he called "A Muted Street," and the same year in "The Bridge" he affixed to its central tower a damaged, dampening violin mute. A man beneath the span metamorphoses trustingly into a violin and reaches up to grasp the bridge, but it won't consent to be his instrument. Instead of Crane's choiring or Stella's upper register of vocal stress, Guglielmi's bridge plays baffled, silent

O. Louis Guglielmi, "The Bridge" (1942). Collection of the Museum of Contemporary Art, Chicago. Gift of the Mary and Earle Ludgin Collection.

music. In his premonition of war, "Mental Geography" (1938), it has been disabled further. Derelict after an air raid, its roadway still serves as a concert platform for an unheeding harpist. While the strings he plays on are taut and tuned, the bridge's cables (to which in Crane's metaphor they correspond) have buckled, drooped, and twisted out of shape. The bricks crumble, the girders sag sickly. Surrealism with its nauseous dream of decomposition—the punishing and warping of things by combustion or, in this case, bombardment—has pronounced the steely monument to be as perishable as flesh. The bridge now suffers the desuetude and rot which Mayakovsky fears. Its career of iconic ministration ends in ruin.

13

Cosmopolis

The decade lost to Scott Fitzgerald's hero—that period of architectural reconstruction between 1929 and 1939—is the one when New York most irrevocably transforms itself. The raising of the Chrysler Building (1930), the Empire State (1931), and Rockefeller Center (completed in 1940) demanded that the city conceive of itself anew. Its heights are the lookouts of scientific prediction, from where it can espy a future designed in its own image. The decade ended with the provisional building of that future, at the New York World's Fair of 1939–40. Going there was time-travel. The Pennsylvania Railroad undertook to speed you "From the World of Today to the World of Tomorrow in ten minutes for ten cents." The route stretched from actual to envisioned New York: the fair was the city's perfected dream of itself.

Anticipating things to come, the city mobilizes itself. The very buildings seem anxious to take flight, aiming their spires into the air like the nose cones of rockets. New York is more now than the sum of its people and buildings. It makes sense only as a mechanical intelligence, a transport system for the daily absorbing and nightly redeploying of the human multitudes whose services it requires. The perpetual motion of this system is put on show in a compilation by Agnes Rogers, with commentary by Frederick L. Allen, called *Metropolis: An American City in Photographs* (1934). The city's people are processed through it on a succession of conveyor belts, obedient to the whims of the engine that drives them, ambitious to be as infallible and efficient as it is. *Metropolis* photographs a Scarsdale commuter station where the passengers, reading newspapers to use the time in waiting, line up at the spots on the platform where they know the doors of their train will open; once aboard, they return to their papers, and "each car becomes an informal study-group in current events." Another sequence examines a subway car at Times Square in the rush hour, with a crowd milling into it, then exiting. Here is the city's daily regime in little: the absorption and eventual dispersal of its human staff. People are permitted to attach themselves to its outsize mechanical body, like one of the book's anonymous characters, "Mr. Smith, the Man from Middletown," who in his hotel room plugs himself into the city's systems of water, light, power, and communications; for entertainment they can watch its robotized organism undergo surgery—in a street which is being excavated to lay telephone cables, they gather to gape at the city's tangled nervous ganglia. In this futuristic New York, humans are the machine's meek adepts. The girls in the telephone exchange, wired to the city, enable its various sectors to converse with each other; the stenographer in another illustration, fitted with earphones and typing from a tape, is insulated all day from everything but the cybernaut's commands.

Allen's captions abound in recondite statistics. To illustrate the husbandry whereby the city—mostly an importer of the substances it needs —can grow its own provisions, he lists the numbers engaged in agriculture, forestry, and fishing in New York and even calculates that 690 men and 7 women are employed in the "extraction of minerals." His statistics serve less as information than as a technocratic epic diction, enjoying the power of computation and celebrating the machine's prodigal self-reproduction. His numbering extends into a gigantism like the boasting of the epic hero, as when he brags that the water used every day by New York weighs ten times as much as the city's entire population. Such figuring rehearses the capabilities of the Leviathan-like metropolitan robot. Sometimes it enters a realm of impossibility where the machine goes on exponentiating itself until it colonizes the world. Thus, in his caption to a photograph of a street cleaner, Allen vauntingly remarks that if you laid all New York's paved streets end to end they'd bridge the Atlantic; elsewhere he estimates that if all the wires in all the cables wrapped into the George Washington Bridge were stretched out lengthwise, they'd circumnavigate the world four times over. More bizarre still is his contention that "there are so many stenographers and typists in the city that if they joined in copying *Anthony Adverse* they would finish the job in ten seconds each." Those absurd ifs, performing operations which no one would ever undertake, are the wishfulfillments of science fiction: the machine's fantasizing contemplation of its latent power. They express the subjunctive restlessness which makes the New York of this period so eager to arrive at the future. Because the city is a transport system—a traveler in time as well as through space—a motif in *Metropolis* is the vicissitudes of our homegrown mode of transport, our feet. Or rather of the shoes that are our technological adjuncts, doing our walking for us. The book is a folio of metonymic feet. A pair of sleek shoes with buttoned spats is photographed on the subway: the caption guesses that these "are not proletarian feet." There's a series of shots of women buying shoes. A middle-class suburbanite tries on an $18.00 pair of midtown, while a less extravagant spender on Park Avenue at 112th Street worries over a pair costing $1.65. Mr. Smith the out-of-towner, in another ankle shot, sees a bank runner on Nassau Street rewarding his means of livelihood by getting a shine. And urban play is of course fleet-footed locomotion, a blissfully purposeless traveling, as *Metropolis* implies in its photograph of roller-skaters in Central Park.

The photographer most elated by New York's virtuosity in transport is Andreas Feininger, who arrived there in 1937 and worked for *Life* throughout the 1940s. In advance of migrating to New York, Feininger prepared his photographic conquest of it by studying diagrams of its workings. He pored over maps and statistics and memorized "the names and locations of all the major avenues, streets, bridges and buildings." He photographs technical operations, not pictorial appearances. The city's monumentality doesn't interest him because it's locked in a deathly historical rigidity. The camera is pledged to study the motion of objects, and Feininger in 1945 declared that the Hall of Fame and Grant's Tomb were "less indispensable" to his documentation of New York and "less photogenic" than the West Side Highway. Like that highway, the camera is an experiment in velocity. The photographer, loading it with ever faster film, has set it to outrace time. Traveling at speed is Feininger's training for the act of photography. In 1941 he drove to Chicago to work on a picture-essay, and he remembers the car in which he made the journey—a Pontiac coupe with bulbous headlights announcing its secret desire to be a locomotive, able to do 90 m.p.h. on the turnpike— as if it were an item in his equipment. All he knew of Chicago was its systems of transport: the Loop and the railroad and trucking networks that rayed across the continent from there. In exploring it, he finds a society of complementary kinds of motion: the drawbridges on the river saluting and dipping, according right of way now to road and now to water traffic; the roundhouses for revolving trains; the truck alleys for deliveries between the major avenues in the commercial district. Even the marquee for a burlesque show on State Street merchandizes sex, in Feininger's photograph, as the reckless revving of a carnal engine, with a promise of "SPEED! ACTION! SWING!"

New York too functions economically by circulation, moving people and commodities through itself. Feininger's 1945 volume on the city is planned to follow this rotating mechanical vitality. It begins with a distant view of the skyline from the New Jersey marshes. Feininger made a specialty of such perspectives—Manhattan from the horizontal rural greenery of Paterson or seen across a stretch of intervening water from an elevated highway in Brooklyn or looming behind fishermen in Sheepshead Bay. The telephoto lens he used for these shots tells a double truth about the city. It drastically foreshortens distance, emphasizing it in the very act of overcoming it. In the initial plate of Feininger's volume, the spire of the Empire State improbably announces itself in the middle of the lowly suburbs. The lens brings it near in illusion only to measure how remote it is in fact. Seen from afar across water, Manhattan's narrowness and insularity are rendered the more extreme. But the city vanquishes this physical handicap by its regimentation of transport, drawing to itself the tribute it needs. Feininger's photographs show people thronging into it on ferries or across the Brooklyn Bridge or on seaplanes at the downtown skyport, while produce arrives on barges across the Hudson or at the Fulton Street fish market or is unloaded by longshoremen on the Brooklyn docks. The city imperially impels the world to make the journey to it. Feininger photographs the marine terminal for clippers, La Guardia airport, the Brooklyn Navy Yard, the liners nudging the West Side piers. His own lenses recapitulate New York's problem and effortlessly solve it. They traverse the impeding distance by contracting it. Viewing New York from four and a half miles away in Bayonne, eight miles off on a highway in Bendix, or over a ten-mile stretch of the upper bay, he shares the city's luxurious power by waiting for it to come to him. In one of his 1940 photographs, the Empire State visits Weehawken, incongruously burying itself almost to the hilt in a suburban hillside. The lens has closed the gap between expectation and arrival. Like farseeing prophecy, it manifests the future in the instant.

This is the longitudinal reach of the telephoto lens, which by its foreshortening makes the city travel toward us out of anterior time. Laterally, the lens compresses objects, squeezing the space between them. The crowds in "Lunch hour on Fifth Avenue" (1949) don't recede into depth but pile up the height of the photograph, and because the lens has narrowed the space occupied by the cross streets, the cars seem to be plowing across the sidewalk through the pedestrians. Feininger doesn't recoil from this trampling and massing: the lens is a lesson in the summarizing of space and in the superimposition of traffic strata. The cars and the pedestrians don't collide because the city sees to it that they proceed at right angles to each other. The melee is to Feininger, in words he used of New York, a "symbol of human order." The pleasure of photography is for him "the solving of a mathematical equation," an exact disposition of space. The city instructs him in such a solution because it's a triumph of "spatial organization." The more his lens, in its condensing of Fifth Avenue, creates muddle, the more surely does the city sort out the mess. In his 1942 view of "Midtown Manhattan seen from Weehawken" the streets, tilted as crazily as ski slopes by the foreshortening lens, run precipitously down into the river. But the city has already provided for the problem which the lens creates. The streets end in ferry terminals, so the river continues their traffic by other means.

The photographer in the city deals, Feininger said, with a constructional problem. He must devise a balance between its straight lines, and he can learn from New York's ranking and filing of life in its scanty area. When Weegee photographed the beach of Coney Island on 28 July 1940 at 4 p.m., it was as a sweaty compendium of overlapping limbs. Standing or sitting on one another's shoulders to wave at the camera, Weegee's people have been embroiled in an undiscriminating family of flesh. To the photographer, they're all just meat. Feininger, photographing the same scene on a Sunday in 1949, withdraws to a distance and discovers ordering of space where Weegee saw only the compressed elimination of it. Feininger's Coney, which shows strollers on the boardwalk as well as 'the mob on the beach, is an ant colony, with its own elaborate rules of right-of-way to prevent chaos. Weegee's beach with its Sunday "crowd of over a MILLION . . . (I wonder who counts them)" has no order except the carnal common denominator. We all have bodies ("undressing is permitted on the beach"), and we're all therefore voyeurs. Some people, Weegee notes, come to watch the girls, not to bathe. He comes to watch them all, and he makes them acknowledge his power over them by lining them up in their thousands to pose. His beach is a fecund and rampant democracy, Feininger's an enlightened bureaucracy, managing life by spatial segregation. A similar principle orders the urban dead in a Jewish cemetery in Queens, which Feininger photographed in 1952. The only irregularity in this silent city

Weegee, "Coney Island, 4:00 in the Afternoon, July 28, 1940." Courtesy of International Center of Photography, David Schwartz Foundation, Inc. Purchase Fund, and the Weegee Collection, Wilma Wilcox, Curator.

of tombstones must be ascribed to wayward nature: the wintry trees branch at random, in contrast with the mapped placement of the graves. Weegee wonders who counts the visitors to Coney, meaning that he wonders who'd think it worth their while, but Feininger's graveyard is a system for the storage and retrieval of past lives. Each oblong commemorates an individual; there's even a difference between the identical Levys whose tablets are just off center. Here, as at Coney, crowding is relieved by the demonstration that these are no arbitrary swarms. Photographs like "Sunday at Coney Island" required a double-page spread in *Life*, and his colleagues, in a good transport joke, nicknamed him "Double-truck Feininger." His images expand as imperially as the city to fill up whatever space is available to them.

Andreas Feininger, "Sunday at Coney Island Beach" (1949). Courtesy of *Life* Magazine, © 1949 by Time, Inc.

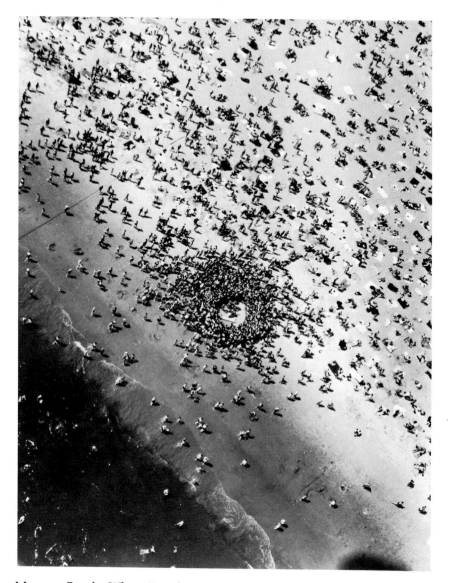

Margaret Bourke-White, "Beach Accident at Coney Island" (1951). Courtesy of *Life* Magazine, © 1951 by Time, Inc.

Feininger believed that curves were a rarity in cities. Where they occur, he photographs them as lines of acceleration—the El's S curve at Coenties Slip, the loop of the tracks at Chatham Square, or their swing around 111th Street. Ever since Eadweard Muybridge's studies of athletes and galloping horses, it has been photography's ambition to trap action in a still medium. Feininger's obsession with transit extends the enterprise to the city. Coney Island delights him because the excursion boats, the boardwalk buggies, the ferris wheel, and the Gyro which spins as it turns are all adventures in ecstatic locomotion. Urban people spend their lives traveling purposefully in straight lines. They come to Coney to enjoy the inane exhilaration of going around in circles. Elsewhere they trudge and plod; here they can whirl and rotate. In 1949 Feininger photographed some of these amusements at night when electricity traces their giddy orbits in the air. The ferris wheel is a series of concentric circles, the Gyro a radiant molecule zooming through the sky, the Hurricane an exploded galaxy of lunging comets. People stand on the sidelines watching these machines, as if assisting at some supernatural advent. The photographs were technical experiments for Feininger: by time exposure, the camera can keep up with an object in motion. But so were the rides technical experiments for Feininger's New Yorkers: rotary thrills, the violent circuitry of pleasure as opposed to the utilitarian drill of those lines, "vertical and horizontal, diagonal and perpendicular," from which he believed the workaday city was constructed.

Though photographing a moment, Feininger doesn't see his art as the meditative stilling of life. The moment chosen belongs in an existence of perpetual change, so its photographic appropriation has to be exactly scheduled. The mutability of atmosphere—"the continuously changing influence of the sun on the subjects I wished to photograph"—was assessed as one in a series of variables, including "rush hours on ferries and streets, sailing times of ships and airplanes, and the arrival of the fishing fleet." His decisive moment is the one when all these coordinates intersect. For a double-truck picture of Manhattan from Governors Island he had to wait from April until December because "two conditions had to converge: I wanted the sky dark and all the windows lighted, and I found that this occurred only within a period of ten minutes before five o'clock in December." For Stieglitz, the wait would have been an eternity of invigilation, the mind's readying of itself for a symbolic wedding with nature, like the hours he spent in the blizzard on Fifth Avenue; for Feininger, it is the precise prescription of a time-and-motion study. The city instructs him in the ordering of space and the occupation of time. He's duty-bound not to represent it scenically. He prides himself in his 1945 volume on having "avoided purely pictorial motifs," which tell a lie about the city because they check its motion. Central Park interests Feininger not as a landscape but—with its model yacht basin and its boating lake—as a surrogate landlocked sea, mimicking the maritime commerce of New York. The Brooklyn Bridge, likewise, is a transport artery. He photographs the barges through its cables, or lines it up above Oliver Street to show traffic advancing on two levels. The elements, reclaiming New York for nature and thus pictorializing it, appear to him as hazards. The Brooklyn Bridge vanishes in a fog in 1948, and the blizzard of 1947 immobilizes the city, icing up the riggings of the fishing boats and obstructing Fifth Avenue with the mounds of buried cars. To Stieglitz this would have signified New York's humbled capitulation to nature. Feininger sees it as the cancellation of function, like the 1943 brownout which, in another photograph, leaves the Empire State girdled with two thin belts of light. New York is scenic only in an emergency.

Once the city is geared for and goaded to transport itself into the future, its buildings begin to resent their anchorage to the earth. The architecture of the 1930s affects to free them from gravity by making them aerodynamic. Streamlining is the sleek mobilization of architectural mass. Its initial purpose was to speed people through buildings, to ease internal traffic by replacing corners with curvilinear shortcuts. Applied to the exterior of buildings, it promises to make the edifice airborne. The brick friezes of cars along the sides of the Chrysler Building employ it as a runway and take to the air at the corners. With hubcaps, fenders, and radiator covers around its shaft and murals of airplanes and automobiles in its lobby, the Chrysler seems straining to lift off. The Empire State's dirigible mast announced its new upside-down ambition. Rather than being founded on earth, it was tethered to the clouds. Buildings that couldn't fly transmitted themselves to the air by broadcasting themselves. The elemental divinities of wind and wave that romp along Radio City are its messengers, through whom it will radiate into the air; the old RCA Victor Building (1930–31) on Lexington Avenue at 51st Street—now the General Electric headquarters—was crowned with spiky lightning bolts, discharging an angry energy; Raymond Hood's American Radiator Building (1924) overlooking Bryant Park also beamed signals to the sky from a torchy tower. Its body is of black brick, capped by flames of gold-tinted stone which make it catch fire as it races upward. A golden mural in the lobby of the Empire State characterizes it as a lighthouse, sending out a consolatory flare across the map of the northeast. The Waldorf-Astoria (1931) had a web of radio antennae strung between its towers as a means of universalizing itself. Inside, it seemed to be constructed anti-terrestrially. Its cellar had levitated and was suspended in a steel cage on the fifth floor; instead of a rooted basement, the building propped itself on stilts inserted between the Grand Central railway tracks. Its disdain for the ground was matched by its infatuation with the sky. The electrically retractable Starlight Roof rejected a building's need to be and to have a sheltering canopy. Since the Waldorf was conceived to be in motion, its roof became a disposable hood, like that of a convertible car, rolled back to allow union with the element through which the building fancied itself to be speeding. If a building couldn't take to the air, it could pretend, thanks to the fluidity of Art Deco design, to be oceangoing. The National Cash Register Company in Rockefeller Center displayed its machines in steel portholes on either side of its entrance door. The World's Fair outfitted its pavilions for both aerial and nautical travel. The Budd Manufacturing Company exhibited sections of an airplane wing's framework, while Swift and Company even streamlined the frankfurter by showing its wares in a mock-up of "a gleaming super-airliner"; the Marine Transportation pavilion sported a finny pair of prows and was entered by a gangplank across a moat.

The flight into the future proceeds upward rather than ahead. Tennyson in the nineteenth century believed that time would progress, as along an infinite railway, down the ringing grooves of change; the modern imagination ascends aeronautically into the world to come. The perfecting of New York demanded its detachment from the earth, where it was mired in social problems. Architectural prediction contemplates the unmooring of the city, its lift-off into the sky. The business of architects is now the suspension of structures. Harvey Wiley Corbett in 1923 proposed for the New York of the future a segregation of vehicular from pedestrian traffic, which would consign cars to ground level and raise people onto elevated walkways. Raymond Hood in 1929 conjectured that apartment houses for three million people could be built on the East River bridges. These would be doubly abstracted from earth, placed over water and hung from the air by cables. Hugh Ferriss, who after 1915 renounced architectural practice and contented himself with the graphic rendering of unbuildable fantasies, saw buildings as landing stages for futuristic visitors from the upper air and planned airport terminals on the upper shelves of skyscrapers. He was sure that the New Yorkers of the future would live in the sky, and his imaginary dwellings are terraced with aerial golf courses, hanging gardens, and swimming pools. Rather than traveling horizontally to the country, New Yorkers find it upstairs. Those heights are dizzy pleasances: Ferriss drew masked balls and carnivals atop his skyscrapers. What he called in 1936 "the air age" had reoriented architecture. Buildings, dangling from the sky into an abyss, should be designed to be seen from above. Following

Hugh Ferriss, "Skyscraper Hangar in a Metropolis" (ca. 1931). From *Architectural Visions: The Drawings of Hugh Ferriss*, by Jean Ferriss Leach (Whitney Library of Design, N. Y., 1980).

his own advice, Ferriss drew the United Nations Headquarters from a helicopter. At the World's Fair in 1939, Norman Bel Geddes laid out a city while hovering in midair. For the Futurama metropolis of 1960 in the General Motors pavilion, which was to be seen from sound-chairs traveling above it, Geddes relied on the drastic aerial perspectives he'd become accustomed to when looking down from theater catwalks during his period as a stage designer. Geddes places you in the future, patronizing the present from a steep vertical distance of foresight. The Futurama passengers disembarked at a street intersection in Tomorrow. As they stepped into "the wonder world of 1960," they were reminded that "1940 is twenty years ago!" and admonished "ALL EYES TO THE FUTURE."

The speculative architect, with his telescopic eye on the future, naturally situates himself in midair. Ferriss in *The Metropolis of Tomorrow* (1929) is loftily incurious about the populated depths "away down there." From his vantage, New York looks sublime. To plunge into the streets is "like Dante's descent into Hades." The terrestrial city is a sunless underworld, impounding the condemned; the aerial city celestially abandons earth and the curse of materiality. For Ferriss, the architectural motive of New York must be a denial of mass. The setbacks imposed by zoning regulations taught him to think of building as the liberation of a spirit penned within the mass, just as Michelangelo is sculpturally freeing with his chisel the slaves who have been imprisoned in the blocks of stone. Zoning made the architect a carver. He must, Ferris said, "cut into the mass to admit light into the interior." Architecture is thus the ventilation of a geological solid, the erosion of a granite lump. When Ferriss declared that the skyscrapers were a "Grand Canyon," he meant the tribute quite specifically: both have been made by reduction, emptying, a sculptural discarding of matter. This process accords with the aesthetics of flight, when objects escape the solidity which persecutes them. An airplane propellor is dematerialized by motion. Ferriss's imagined city has so transcended matter that it can be glassily seen through, having been built with translucent bricks.

This anti-gravitational New York, whirling off into regions of scientific surmise, is no longer a mere city. It's an alternative world, a small planet. *Fortune* magazine in its World's Fair issue of July 1939 treated the citizens of New York as a futuristic race, synthesized from the earth's disparate tribes. The melting pot is an apparatus for effecting chemical change and brewing cosmopolites. "It takes fifty nations to make a New Yorker," says one of *Fortune*'s captions. These encyclopedic beings are more than city dwellers. They're metropolitanites, by which *Fortune* means people who metropolitanize, gathering to themselves the bounty of the world. Their marketing habits are global: the East Side housewife can within a few blocks "shop at will in Italy, Germany, Hungary, Bohemia, or Palestine." Their buildings claim a cosmological status. Each one is ambitious to be a world, to carry worlds—like the Paramount Building of 1927 in Times Square with its glowing globe, or the Atlas sculpted by Lee Lawrie for Rockefeller Center, who bears a see-through earth on his back—or else to contain them. In the lobby of his Daily News Building (1930), Raymond Hood sunk an illuminated, turning earth. The Waldorf had its own hedonistically revolving cosmic totem, a rug by Louis Rigal inside the Park Avenue foyer representing "The Wheel of Life." You climbed aboard its dizzy circle, metaphorically at least, when you checked into the hotel. Such items of decor cast the buildings as autonomous worlds voyaging through space. Veined with pneumatic tubes, internally wired by 2700 telephones and a switchboard which was said in 1939 to be "large enough for a good-sized city," transmitting messages through itself by electrical impulse, receiving dictation on its clattering teletype machines or dispatching radio signals to the air, the Waldorf seemed to have encompassed first New York and then the planet. Hood suspected that the city would follow its example and turn into a geodesic dome encapsulating infinite space. He suggested in 1931 that urban exteriors were no longer of interest and that architecture should attend to a world newly insulated indoors: "possibly we may come (in time) to treating all city outsides like a tent —the Big Top, for example, under which all subways run and the railways arrive—and having all the shows inside." As his own Daily News lobby proclaimed, a single building might qualify as a microcosm of the future city by enclosing the earth. In the gloom, you could look down on the globe in its pit and watch it turn on its axis. The inner space of the building had roofed over outer space.

Rockefeller Center allegorized its height as a metaphysical quest. The philosopher H. B. Alexander devised a thematic scheme for the buildings that interpreted the setback tiers as the stages by which man remounts to godliness. The steps induct the eye through the successive phases which Alexander called "experience, understanding, magnanimity, prophecy." Every ascent in Rockefeller Center had to dramatize itself as a spiritual promotion. Hence the cosmological aspiration of the elevator shaft, where murals narrate man's vertical strife to free himself from want (in the panels by José Maria Sert), from subjugation to material necessity (which was Rivera's commission), and from ethical ignorance (in Frank Brangwyn's contribution). Climbing the staircase in Radio City Music Hall also re-enacts an ascent to paradise, which the movies have made electrically recoverable. Ezra Winter's mural, based on an Oregon Indian legend, describes the search for happiness and perpetual youth. These are located on a pinnacle near the ceiling, across a gulf which deters the old man at the head of the stairs. He won't get there. We will, however, for at the top of the stairs is the auditorium, where we're issued into the etheric Eden of the movies and can gaze in wonderment at the agelessness of those unblemished faces on the screen. If the Daily News lobby is a capsule for the planet, as the newspaper purports to be, then the Music Hall claimed to be an indoor landscape. Its ceiling was a horizon. Roxy alleged that the idea had come to him while watching the sun rise over the ocean during an Atlantic crossing. When the Music Hall opened in 1932, the contoured curtain, with a kaleidoscope of light playing over it, parted to Rimsky-Korsakov's hymn to the sun from *Le Coq d'Or*. Frank Lloyd Wright had dreamed of a wall-less tower so tall that the clouds, artificial if necessary, could wander through it at whim. Roxy's showmanship supplied such man-made weather to match the electrical aubade projected onto the cyclorama. Rain could fall onto the stage through perforated pipes and would then be siphoned into a trough and disposed of; steam, fog, and clouds could be exhaled from nozzles in the floor. Ferriss's project to lift the city into the sky was accomplished hydraulically in the Music Hall. The stage was mounted on elevators, so a peaked or pitted landscape could be manufactured instantly by raising or lowering the platforms.

The metropolis of tomorrow that Ferriss had envisioned in 1929 was built a decade later at the World's Fair, where Ferriss was a design consultant. As its emblems, the fair had a pair of complementary monoliths—the tapering index finger of the Trylon, the ovular globe of the Perisphere. Between them, they sum up a choice of architectural modes. Grover Whalen, the fair's president, thought the Perisphere symbolized the "Greek idea of beauty of form and harmony," while the Trylon represented the "Gothic conception of reaching ever upwards for a better world." They are also a commentary on the architectural motives of the host city—its old ambition of height, its new ambition of containment; the difference between aspiration and circulation, between being a pinnacle and being a planet. At a certain point, New York grows so tall that it leaves the earth and enters orbit: then the overreaching Trylon becomes the turning Perisphere. The architecture of the city attests to man's competitive urge to outgrow himself. In "The Lure of the City" (1929), Ferriss set a human figure against the New York skyline. It dwarfs the man, but he tenses and stretches himself, determined

New York World's Fair, 1939. The Trylon and the Perisphere (Harrison and Fouilhoux, architects; Henry Dreyfus, designer) with the Fountain of Victories of Peace by John Gregory.

to equal it. When in 1936 he sketched the anchorage of the Triborough Bridge, Ferriss placed a diminutive stick-man at its base. The homunculus is there to measure the height of the bridge, but he doesn't acquiesce in that lowly function. Ferriss has equipped him with a pole, as if it's his overweening desire to vault above the bridge. The Trylon expresses this longing to surmount: it's a diagram of the skyscraper's celestial aggression, and it's necessary to the Perisphere as a symbolic motor.

Pointing to tomorrow, it tells the world where to go. Ferriss hoped that Hood's globe in the Daily News lobby would provoke people to think about "the situation of their own planet." Left to its own devices, the globe will go on otiosely turning, blithely repeating itself. The Trylon's function is to steer it upward and ahead. But the Trylon is merely a rudder. The future is housed inside the Perisphere, for it was here that the fair lodged its visionary model of tomorrow, the panorama of a pastoral Democracity.

The Perisphere has hollowed out Hood's globe and made it habitable. Now people can enter it and travel within it into the future. Implantation makes the globe an egg. The Perisphere is the womb of time, engendering the future. Its ovoid shape offers us, when we enter it, the safety of regression and the comfort of going round in circles. Everything in it was constructed circularly. Democracity was laid out in concentric rings, its outer edges expanding from a downtown area called Centerton, and visitors saw it from cradling, revolving balconies. The Perisphere has, however, intromitted the present in order to give it rebirth as the future. Inside, we're under one of Hood's Big Tops, removed from reality and abstracted from the earth. The guide to *Your World of Tomorrow* promises that, watching the spectacle of things to come cinematically unfurling across the domed indoor sky, the visitor will have "exactly the sensation of floating in the air." Air conditioning and soundproofing guarantee that "nothing that smells of earth remains to destroy your illusion of flight." Outside, an aquatic illusion held the Perisphere afloat in air. It seemed to be suspended on the fountains encircling it, which evaporated in mist to suggest a sustaining ether. Actually, it had legs to support it, but the water by collaborating with an arrangement of mirrors rendered these invisible. At night passing clouds were projected on it, so it appeared—as the *Official Guide Book* said—to be "revolving like a great planet on its axis." Like the city for which it deputizes, the Perisphere achieves an ultimate abstraction, equalizing inner and outer space, burying you in the earth while in fantasy freeing you to drift weightlessly away from it, moving you through space on electric stairways or revolving ramps and using this automatic progress as a metaphor for movement through time. Democracity is sited in a fourth dimension which, inside the Perisphere, we too can penetrate. It already exists, the brochure tantalizingly pretends, "thirty or forty miles from where you are living today—about half an hour by the new safe-speed boulevard," and you'll be living in it "tomorrow morning." Its position is fixed in both time and space so as to cancel our time and space, to jump laterally into a realm where they unite. The escalators are a passage into that new world. On them, space becomes time; you can arrive in the future without needing to bestir yourself. It's the same illusion that Feininger creates with his telephoto lenses. The Perisphere encouraged Ferriss to dream of cities that didn't only shelter beneath Hood's cerulean umbrella but sought the additional protection of burrowing into the earth, abandoning aspiration for excavation and finding the future underground. In 1942 he proposed the rehousing of New York under the New Jersey Palisades, where vaulted cavities would shield the city in case of air raids. Ferriss's city didn't, in the end, take to the air. Instead, terrified of a nemesis rained from the air, it defensively inters itself. Of this newly inverse and introverted city, the World's Fair was a harbinger. Because of its proximity to New York, it ruled out skyscrapers, as the guidebook explained. It was to be "a 'flat' Exposition, consisting largely of one-story structures." It also prohibited windows. There were practical reasons for this: glass would squander space and overheat the interiors. But the rule also accords with the city of the future, which will recoil into itself and can terminate its contact with the world outside because it has superseded that world.

On the day the World's Fair opened, Mayor La Guardia nominated New York itself as one of the exhibits. At the fair, New York stretched backward and forward through time. The city's Zoological Society had a diorama "representing the New York area of a million years ago." George Jessel reconstructed the New York of another "bygone era," the gas-lit Gay Nineties, with a policemen's quartet warbling at Bowling Green, Bowery newsboys touting antique extras, and Steve Brodie jumping nightly off "a reproduction of the Brooklyn Bridge, 100 feet high." In the city's present, you could embark for the future. At the Theatre of Time and Space, you set out from above "a section of New York's skyline" for a journey by rocket, "which annihilates distance at the fantastic speed of 48,000,000,000,000,000,000 miles per hour." Having been thrust away from the "aerial view of New York" and taken on a tour of "dark cosmic depths," you were redeposited not on earth but in a similacrum of it: as you landed, an explosion of light resolved itself into "a large scale model of the Fair." The Futurama was another such relativistic outing. Just as the Theatre of Time and Space carried you "trillions of miles . . . in fifteen of your brief minutes," so the General Motors midair highway drove you to 1960 and left you there. You descended from the conveyor belt at a traffic intersection in the future, where you could shop for Cadillacs and Frigidaires. Like the city, the fair specialized in time-travel.

Fortune in July 1939 interpreted the city as a replica of the fair.

Though the city is called "the Image of Man," it has passed beyond humankind to arrive at the superman or cybernaut. Its makers, *Fortune* says, "have raised this thing out of the harbor in the likeness of themselves" like a benign version of Frankenstein's monster. The fair's planners similarly raised an ideal hygienic city out of an ash dump in Flushing. The fair was a playground for robots, demonstrations, like Frankenstein's monster, that science had bettered nature. Westinghouse had a genie called Elektro, and the Communications display contained an allegorical Man who was a sapient talking head. Transparent Man at the Medicine exhibit had all his innards on show, while his colleague Mac the Mechanical Man gave a lecture on the organs as engines—the eye was a camera, the brain an instrument panel, memory a library, and the heart a pump. This is how *Fortune* appraises New York. The urban body of Whitman and Sloan, palpitant and perspiring, a fraternity under the skin, is remade with metal, stone, and the adhesion of chemicals. Its integument is brick and granite, its bones are ribs of steel, its eyes dazzling glass. It has a concrete gullet, cemented bowels, and copper nerves. An electronic brain directs the innumerable simultaneous exchanges of its commerce. Peeling away the street surface at Radio City, *Fortune* vivisects the city to expose the tubular networks and alimentary pipes beneath; at 40 Wall Street it X-rays a skyscraper to show how the building fuels, feeds, and laves itself. Statistics detail this office block's consumption of steam and electricity and describe the unending job of cleaning its windows. It can also homeopathically cure its internal ills. A small hospital is installed on its fifteenth floor, where repair men wait in case of an elevator breakdown. In its basement slumber its viscerae, "pumps, compressors, steam gauges, switchboards, meters, transformers, and air ducts." Their mechanical travail is comparable, *Fortune* says, with "the automatism of a beating heart." Forty Wall and didactic Mac at the fair are twins, and both building and robot personify the city.

One dream of New York's architectural projectors was to contain the city within a single building. This the World's Fair ingeniously achieved. The Consolidated Edison pavilion domiciled a scale model of the metropolitan area, "the world's largest diorama, about a city block in length and higher than a three-story building." And because it was electrically activated, it too was a robot: an audioanimatronic New York. The exhibit, designed by Walter Dorwin Teague, was called "The City of Light." The brochure makes it clear that the prototype for the future conjured up at the fair was New York. "No other city has advanced nearly so far along the road that leads to the world of tomorrow," it argued; in contrast, European capitals seem "earthbound"—the aero-

The Con Edison diorama of New York, "The City of Light," at the 1939 World's Fair, from the Official Guide Book. Courtesy of the Consolidated Edison Company of New York, Inc.

dynamic image is noteworthy. One of the brochure's illustrations, computing Con Ed's purchases in 1938, proposes a refabrication of the city. Con Ed had requisitioned enough steel to plate Grant's Tomb six inches deep, enough rubber to swaddle the Woolworth Building, enough cotton to wad the roadway of the Brooklyn Bridge a foot deep, and enough coal to bury Central Park. This presumptive recladding and armoring makes New York an android, its vital signs electrically stimulated. The brochure insists that "it's not just a mass of lifeless masonry and steel—but a living, breathing city with a network of iron and copper arteries and veins under the surface to supply vital heat and energy—a city with electrical nerves to control its movements and transmit its thoughts." The power stations are this robot's beating heart, the telephone exchanges its brain. The electricity that vivifies the urban automaton also consoles human distresses (the commentary to the diorama notes that mothers habitually switch on the light to pacify their squalling infants) and aids the repair of human bodies: "The doctor and the surgeon / Call on Power in a hundred ways / To diagnose and cure the body's ills." Abbreviating and accelerating time to summarize twenty-four hours in twelve minutes, the diorama narrated the life-span of the city and watched it cope with the onslaughts of nature. As an afternoon storm crackles over New York extra generators churn out the emergency kilowatts the city needs to maintain its electrical metabolism. The display begins and ends with nightfall; but the dark goes unheeded by the City of Light. Manhattan is a man-reared "island in the night." Electricity gives it a eugenic immortality: its turbines spin untiringly and will never suffer death. Having vitalized a machine that improves on human existence, electricity advances to supplant nature, creating firmaments of its own. The Great White Way is named, as the commentary points out, after light. Gazing at its neon or at "the dramas of the screen, / Made and seen and heard only by electricity," people are worshiping at the shrine of the urban deity, who is a light-giving dynamo. Above the sky signs the diorama placed a supplementary sky, another of Hood's Big Tops. A note explained that "the thousands of stars that sparkle [there] . . . are tiny spots of flourescent paint . . . visible only when exposed to ultraviolet light." This perfected city has no further need of human inhabitants: the diorama was self-operating, its activities cued by "many miles of complex wiring and robot controlled switches." Because the fair conceived of the future as an irradiation, a cosmic dawn modeled on Roxy's indoor sunrise, its totems were, like Con Ed's electrified Manhattan, pillars of light, buildings whose substance was illumination. Outside the General Electric pavilion, a lightning bolt supported an atom ringed by its orbitals, like a Trylon with the Perisphere balanced on top of it. Westinghouse endowed radiance with a voice in its "Singing Tower of Light," a marvel of lyrical fluorescence, and the American Radiator installation defined buildings as conductors of energy, making columns out of flue lining and setting on them volutes which were copper pipe coils.

Everywhere at the fair this divined future was sealed against the contamination of time and the debilities of nature. Billy Rose's Aquacade boasted of its hydrozonally purified, germless diving pool. Disinfection made it a habitat for amphibious athletic gods: Johnny Weissmuller, on loan from M.G.M., was billed as the revue's "Aquadonis." Purity was also guarded by a clinical refrigeration. In the amusement area, the "Frozen Alive" show exhibited "girls in solid ice"; the Eastern States Ice Association had an Ice Princess whose palace was a freezer; Carrier constructed a modernistic igloo inside which the air was filtered, dehumidified, and crisply cooled. The astronomical clocks of the Elgin National Watch Company conserved their accuracy by insulation. "Hermetically sealed in glass jars to eliminate atmospheric pressure changes and mounted on concrete piers to eliminate vibrations, they are electrically wound every 36 seconds." This is Hood's Big Top, impenetrably closed—for all its transparency—against the interferences of the exterior. The Heinz dome managed an even more arrogant rebuttal of nature inside itself, cultivating vegetables and flowers "in chemically treated water, instead of soil."

All these retentive interiors are, as the fair was and as New York hoped to be, ersatz wombs—laboratories for the insemination of the present and its intact delivery as the future; seed-carrying globes or planetary eggs. The older city had been uprearingly masculine and phallic. The new city, a uterine capsule for generations ahead, who curl up within it like the model of Democracity fetally hatching in the Perisphere, resembles a female body. One of the fair exhibits was an Infant Incubator for premature babies. Dali parodied this exploration of time's interior nursery in his design for the "Dream of Venus" pavilion. He situated the show's box office between the legs of a female kraken. The city's male imperative was height; the fair's symbolic female rhythm was circulation. Inside the Perisphere you rotated while watching Democracity, and you were returned to the present on a spiraling ramp called the Helicline. The Border Dairy Company exhibited nature as a bovine cycle in its "rotolactor," a rotating milking platform to illustrate the "operation of getting clean milk from clean cows." Ford dramatized manufacture with the same maternal circularity. Its Cycle of Production set out the stages in the reproduction of a car, its birth from the elements of copper, coal, and manganese. The display, surmounted by a car, was arranged on a cone whose wooden base revolved on a pontoon; this in turn floated in a circular, pseudo-amniotic moat.

Thus did New York imagine its own rebirth. Eradication of its past would leave it pristine, as laundered and ideally white as Borden's milk or Con Ed's visionary light. In the fair's color scheme, an unstained whiteness was reserved for the Trylon and Perisphere. The rest of the Theme Center had dimmed into off-white. From there, the white radiance of this eternity was fractured into the variegation of the world. Each of the red, gold, and blue avenues that set out from the Theme Center, like rays from a white-hot but also lucidly cool sun, had its own color. At their ends these thoroughfares converged in the prism of Rainbow Avenue. The fair's layout follows the career of light from white immanence on high at its center to the polychrome hues of this world around the edges. This white city prohibited fear, anxiety, and mystery, the incubi of the dark. The Con Ed diorama boasted of their abolition: "This is / The City of Light, / Where night never comes." This confidence was soon daunted. Even before the fair had been dismantled, New York was subscribing to another image of itself—as a defiled and enshrouded place, a guilty city of immitigable night.

14

After Dark

The World's Fair included a preview of this nocturnal, culpable city. In the New York City Building, a drama titled *Murder at Midnight* rehearsed the infallibility of the police. They study a crime, add up clues, and by forensic deduction nab the murderer. All problems are solvable in the laboratory. The fair too glibly refuted the alternative to itself— the night side of its unilluded future, the underworld from which its weightless, encapsulated city had taken off. The actual and unregenerate city remained to parody the fair's anticipated millennium. Whereas the fair used electricity to combat the dark, insisting that night need never fall in the island of light, New York thrived on the extinction of day. While the fair preserved life by sanitary cooling, New York sweltered and began odoriferously to rot. It lay prostrate in a big but fitful and distempered sleep, oppressed by a vindictive big heat.

It's a city exposed, punitively denuded. Realism begins with two acts of disrobing—Manet's girl at the picnic, Eakins's model in Philadelphia. These are pastoral acts, reunions of the human body with an innocent nature. John Sloan thinks of New York as a landscape populated by chubby healthy female nudes, who sun themselves on rooftops or—in a 1933 painting—peep from behind curtains at Washington Square. The city itself is to him a body of frank yet pastorally guileless desire. When Weegee uncovers his city, his act isn't reconciliation but rape. Since the city is so whorishly flagrant in its indecency, how else should it be treated? Before his denudation of New York in *Naked City*, Weegee had been on an assignment in a New Jersey nudist colony and was fond of snapping strippers, one of whom presented him with her G-string as a souvenir of her photographic ravishment. His fabled psychic power (he was nicknamed after the Ouija board, since he had such an instinct for urban catastrophe and would always be at the scenes of murder or arson before the police) was less a matter of premonition than of lecherous intrusion: girls imagined that his camera could X-ray their dresses. Though his business was the disrobing of others, he knew better than to render himself vulnerable, and never (he maintained) took his own clothes off when he went to bed, unless, of course, he had company.

The city surrenders itself to Weegee at night because sleep relaxes its guard. It can then be caught in disarray, like the old man in *Naked City* who struggles to climb into his pants before he is hustled from his burning building. After dark, consciousness is no longer on sentry duty. As the vigil kept by reason ends, the profounder veracity of dreams takes over. This is the biorhythm of the human body; so it is with the city, which at night releases a population impelled, as dreams are, by the savagery of id. Weegee's subjects were the monsters bred by the sleep of the city's reason. In 1950 he publicized the film *The Sleeping City* by photographing missions, flophouses, jail cells, and burning tenements across the country. Sleep is the city's restitution. At night the body is consigned to its own metabolic devices. No longer required to do things for its demanding mental employer, it fantasizes about its longed-for liberty. One of Weegee's sleepers, a fat man seen from the balcony of a movie theater after the show is over, sprawls in his seat, his mouth agape and his belt unbuckled, abandoned to the licentious imaginings that flicker across the psychic cinema screen inside his head. The city at night is taken from those who think they run it and handed over to its amoral aborigines—the sexually hungry, the larcenous, the violent, all of them agents of somnambulistic id. Weegee understood the night to be an exact inversion of the working day. Rather than an uneventful intermission in consciousness, it has an agenda of its own. He dutifully audited its schedule on his police radio. Its crimes were a punctilious mimicry of diurnal routine. Between midnight and 1 a.m., the peeping toms would be out snooping; between 1 and 2, late-night delis would be held up; between 2 and 3 came the auto accidents and fires; at 4 the bars closed, so the police would round up drunkards; from 4 to 5 was the hour sacred to burglaries; after 5 came the suicides of insomniac despairers. Weegee adjusted himself to this nocturnal regime by starting his day at midnight. If he slept, he would leave the police radio playing by his bed. Its babble of accident and mayhem could then insert itself into his subconscious, transmitting directly from the city's dream-life to his own. Asleep, he monitored the city's enfevered slumber and could be relied on to rouse himself if the radio announced a genuine emergency. The cybernetic engineers of the World's Fair donated to the city a brain and a telepathic nervous system of wires, enabling it to marshal—as *Fortune* said of the cranial control room at 40 Wall—"the evolution of industrial man," framing ideas that create "the shape of the future." Weegee deciphered the city differently. For him the installation that told the truth about New York and mapped its labyrinth of complicity was the teletype machine at police headquarters. He called it "the nerve center of the city I knew."

The frontispiece to *Naked City* announces Weegee's notion of photography. Through the dark skyline of lower Manhattan, light erupts. A bleary beam seems to burn through the cables of the Brooklyn Bridge and spills on the water, igniting it. A lightning bolt rends the sky and discharges itself into the Woolworth Building. This is not light's banishment of dark, which was Con Ed's project at the fair. It is light's exposure or anatomy of the dark, like the scenes of love-making on the pitch-black beach at Coney Island which Weegee photographed with "invisible light." Photography is electrocution: that lightning bolt recurs as Weegee's glaring flashbulb, which stuns and deadens his subjects, executing on the spot a rough justice by exploding in the faces of malefactors. Being photographed by Weegee was the equivalent of an arraignment. The criminals cooperated, he noted, by posing as they stepped down from the police wagon. Riis's accident-prone flashes retributively set fire to the dark. Weegee's flash has no such radical intention. It is the carrion cry broadcasting a death, since it mortifies whatever it's aimed at, and it belongs in company with the strobing, wailing siren of the ambulance. To scoop other syndicates after a prizefight, Weegee would sometimes charter an ambulance and speed back to town "with sirens screaming, red lights flashing, and cops clearing the way." Inside, he'd rig up a darkroom to develop his pictures during the ride. His photography could thus cast itself as an emergency service.

Because photographic light is the blaze from a gun barrel, everything Weegee metaphorically shoots—not only those tagged and bloodied corpses in New York gutters—looks as if it might be dead meat, even if it's made of wax or plastic or paper. After a robbery in a Harlem dress store he photographs the carnage among some vandalized, dismembered shop-window dummies. There's the same suspicion of fatality when he photographs the 1962 Macy's Thanksgiving Day parade. Sprawled in the street, undergoing inflation from the helium cylinders, Father Christmas could be an accident victim in need of artificial resuscitation. The camera's morbidity allies it with the tabloid newspaper, which relishes brutal deaths and has itself a chronically brief life-span. Those bundled Sunday newspapers strewn on the sidewalk at the beginning of *Naked City* could just as well be corpses, bagged in neat rows after a tenement fire. They contain corpses and will soon be corpses, or refuse. Sleepers in a mission use them for mattresses, and, in Weegee's photographs of a car crash, they double as a shroud: the dead man is sheeted with newspaper until the ambulance arrives.

The scenes of arson Weegee visits are diseases of the city's sleep, the nightmares that relieve its pressured tensions. Fire does so by night, eruptive water by day, in his scenes of tenement children frolicking in the spout from an opened hydrant. A cop appears to shut off the gutter fount: officialdom bottles up the city's collective hysteria. Night is the city's ulterior—hence Weegee's taboo-infringing shots of sleepers on fire escapes, in doorless public lavatories, or bedded down in the street. During the day, his New Yorkers pine for the oblivious dark. He follows them to the cinemas along West 42nd Street where they go to make love. The movies sell them an artificial night: many of them go to matinees, Weegee comments, just to sleep. And the films they drowse through are themselves nocturnal reports on the city, for Weegee is one of the sources for film noir and its narrative of the urban night. The producer Mark Hellinger bought Weegee's title and applied it to Dassin's *The Naked City* (1948); Weegee himself appeared in several specimens of the genre, among them Robert Wise's *The Set-Up* (1949), in which he played a boxing time-keeper, Joseph Losey's remake of Fritz Lang's *M* (1951), which cast him as a murder suspect, and Stuart Heisler's *Journey into Light* (1952), where he was another of his own photographic characters, a Skid Row derelict.

The inverse New York of *The Naked City* includes and reviews the different city of Whitman and O. Henry. Hellinger praised the scriptwriter Malvin Wald for the "romantic Walt-Whitman-type narration" he'd provided. Hellinger himself, who had been a columnist for the Hearst press in New York before moving to Hollywood, read it on the sound track. It's interesting that he should have thought the voiceover Whitmanesque. If so, it's the monologue of a changed, dispirited Whitman, grieving over the city rather than exulting in it. The narrator in film noir is condemned to re-enactment of his own existential errors. Orson Welles in *The Lady from Shanghai* (1948), Fred MacMurray in *Double*

Indemnity (1943), John Garfield in *The Postman Always Rings Twice* (1946) don't experience the action but broodingly recapitulate it, looking back over their shoulders at themselves. Narrative is their unsparing self-examination and self-execution. William Holden in *Sunset Boulevard* (1950) narrates his own life posthumously. These voice-over tale-tellers are locked in the past historic tense of their helplessness. In limbo, having failed to learn from their history, they must repeat it. Though the impersonal narrator of *The Naked City* isn't a victim of the action, he shares the existential weariness of these noir re-tellers. Instead of a Whitmanesque bard orating on the tribe's behalf, he's the city's therapist, hypnotizing it so he can penetrate its intimately revelatory sleep. His colloquy with it is psychological, and he's impatient with the pedantry of detection. He taunts the cops, telling them that a murder investigation in New York is like a game of "Button, Button"; he sarcastically inquires about their fallen arches as they pound the beat; and during the final chase on the Williamsburg Bridge he takes sides with the frantic killer Garza, soothingly telling him not to lose his head when he shoots a blind man's dog. Perhaps he's a god too disheartened by the human beings he has created to care about the exact apportioning of blame, since all are guilty. At the end of the film, he sends another naked and innocent creature into the naked city, where it will be led astray: what will this child be, he asks as the infant is delivered, when it reaches the age of twenty? (This incident, specified in the script, doesn't occur in the release print. Since there are many divergences between script and film, I refer, in what follows, sometimes to one and sometimes to the other.)

The voice in *The Naked City*, as paralyzed by the city's plight as the other narrators are by their own misadventures, is the commentary of an absent, nameless god, hovering above Manhattan as the film begins, in a plane whose engine hums on the sound track. The city is unclothed by his gaze, as it is by the X-ray eye of Weegee. An aerial view at night discloses its "lighted arteries and veins." Nakedness doesn't, as in Whitman, vouchsafe idyllic physical health. The patient has been undressed for surgical examination. The principal exhibit is the city's battered, singed, misused body: the corpse of the girl killed at the beginning of *The Naked City* has been bruised at the throat and burned by chloroform (which is how the police know she's not a suicide). The city's sleep is also unhealthful—an anesthetic experiment with death. "Does money ever sleep . . . ? Do the machines in a factory ever need rest?" asks the narrator at the beginning as he surveys the deserted banks and factories of New York at night. The insentience

Filming the climactic chase in *The Naked City* (1948) on the Williamsburg Bridge. Courtesy of National Film Archive/Stills Library, London. Copyright Columbia-EMI-Warner Pictures.

of objects is desired and wooed by the New Yorkers of the film, who try desperately to purchase the luxury of sleep. The murder victim keeps a bottle of Seconal beside her bed, and the druggist who sold it to her tells the detective, "half the people in this city can't sleep without pills." Their chemical inducement of sleep flirts with their own demise, the big sleep of death. Yet the surcease they appeal for will itself be a purgatorial waking. It will be haunted by dreams. The dead girl's mother laments that "her kind of dead don't rest." Is crime perhaps a bad dream of the city's perturbed sleep? After a clattering chase down a fire escape and an exchange of gunfire, the lieutenant leans out the window to pacify the agitated tenants, telling them, "Get quiet now and go back to sleep." The law is a sedative, reassuring lullaby.

Though night may bring somatic phantoms onto the streets, it's also the time when reparation is made for the exhaustion of the day. As *The Naked City* begins, a cleaner vacuums a carpet in the lobby of Radio City. She rehabilitates by night a city sullied during the day. So do the cops: the first shots of the Homicide Squad office on West 20th Street include a glimpse of the room "where men on night duty sleep." The wife of one officer objects to his night work. He makes it sound like a renegade sexual outing, and when she asks where his rendezvous is to be, he tells her it's at the morgue—another dormitory for urban sleepers. The crimes committed at night disinfect the city's consciousness, evacuate germs and pustules from its body. The film cuts from the immersing of the girl's body in a bathtub to water gushing out of a street-cleaning truck before dawn. The second corpse appears among the city's effluents in the East River. *Fortune,* anatomizing the street outside Radio City, pointed to the city's concrete bowels: the robot is unembarrassed by its bodily functions. But in the messier nighttown of *The Naked City,* those bowels must be flushed. One of film noir's projects is the irrigation of the city's colon. In a previous collaboration of Dassin and Hellinger, *Brute Force* (1947), the prisoners—themselves society's ostracized waste—work on a dank drainpipe, excavating the institution's anal canal; Orson Welles in *The Third Man* (1949) navigates the sewers of Vienna; and in Roman Polanski's *Chinatown* (1974) the sluices of Los Angeles are its foul conscience, a lavatorial shame which, because of the graft that controls the water supply, "half the city is trying to cover up." Weegee had tracked a cleaner like the one in the film, for whom "this world's made up of nothin' but dirty feet," on her nocturnal tour of duty in a skyscraper. She's a surrogate for him, a detective dealing in the matter we discard or excrete. His photographs define the dead as the city's rubbish. They litter and stain its pavements, or (in one of his crime shots taken in a restaurant) lie under tables on which the chairs have been stacked, waiting to be swept up by the janitor.

The film legitimizes Weegee's peremptory, accusing flash as an item in the equipment of the forensic scientist. "Every murder," comments Hellinger when Niles's business premises are raided, "turns on a bright hot light, and a lot of people . . . have to walk out of the shadows." The police train an ultraviolet lamp on the victim's room to expose clues; the lieutenant orders a pair of pyjamas X-rayed. He also has the bedroom sprayed with iodine vapor: the city's deposit of grime and dust is its membrane of complicity. He is taking New York's fingerprints. "What are you doing to the furniture?" asks the cleaner. "Investigating it," the detective replies. In a contemporary film noir documenting Nazi espionage in New York, Henry Hathaway's *The House on 92nd Street* (1945), suspects are filmed by the FBI in a Columbus Circle office through "specially treated X-ray mirrors" which enable the G-men to "see without being seen." Weegee's prurient spying in the dressing rooms of strippers or up the flaring skirts of old ladies being helped down fire ladders has been ordered by Herbert Hoover and declared to be in the national interest.

The Naked City finds Whitman's corporeal New York dead and conducts an autopsy on it. At the same time, it marks the redundancy of O. Henry's anecdotal city. Mrs. Astor's social quota of four hundred had been multiplied by O. Henry into four million. *The Naked City* doubles that number. Hellinger's narration estimates that there must be eight million stories in New York, of which he tells just one. Earlier, Hellinger had extended the franchise even further, titling a collection of his newspaper stories *The Ten Million*. Whereas O. Henry's extension of the quorum asserts the value of each individual existence, Hellinger's is an inflation which devalues the single integer. There are now so many stories gabbling simultaneously in New York that none of them can be made audible. There are now so many people in the city that the detectives can't identify the one they seek. When they establish that the suspect is a big man, the narrator mocks them with an instant multiplication: he computes that there are "only a half million big men in New York." The murderer can go into hiding simply by mingling with the anonymous throng of look-alikes, and he actually strolls past the investigating cops several times during the film. The arithmetic of *The Naked City* is a shorthand for dealing with a too prolific city, where individuals figure only as compounds of numbers and digits. In the script, the police radio room dispatches cars 206 and 159—symbolized by metal discs on a map of Manhattan—to 198 West 69th Street, Apartment 4-D. The film changes the location of the crime to 52 West 83rd Street and instigates the investigation by showing a switchboard making a sequence of consecutive connections, first to Roosevelt Hospital, then to the Medical Examiner, then to the Technical Research Laboratory, next to Homicide (extension 72). The entrapment of Garza is also a mathematical exercise. Signal 32 sends squad cars 702, 509, and 110 to Rivington Street between Essex and Norfolk streets; officers from the Fifth and Seventh precincts hunt Garza, who's wanted by police in the Tenth Precinct for a murder committed in the Twentieth. The victim's second and more miserable death is her contraction to a statistic. Alive, she was one of "eight million people struggling for life, for food, for air, for a bit of happiness" (on the sound track Hellinger less eloquently comments that she was "just another pretty girl"); when the morning papers report her end, she serves as "marmalade on ten thousand pieces of toast." Her nemesis is numerical. The detectives confront a city where things happen entirely at random, where human fates are no more than variant, unfixed numbers, and their task—in contrast with O. Henry's cult of coincidence and its epiphanic union of strangers—is to devise a logic that connects chance associations. Muldoon dares Halloran to show him that the discovery of the two bodies is "more than a coincidence." He's sure that "these two cases are miles apart." He means it geographically as well as figuratively: Niles and Dexter robbed from East Side socialites; Backalis operated from a pawnshop in Queens. Detection is the proof of a relation—a proximity of intent—between these separate parts of the city. O. Henry's anthological form indexes the failed efforts to reason out such logical demonstrations. The city's sad collection of short stories is the file of unsolved cases at Manhattan Homicide, where Malvin Wald began searching for the anecdote he expanded into *The Naked City*. O. Henry can redeem the city by blessing it; the detectives assume it to be irredeemable and wish merely to know it.

Custodian of this incriminating knowledge, the detective during the 1940s supplants the gangster as the city's homegrown hero. Gangsters like Edward G. Robinson's in *Little Caesar* (1930), James Cagney's in *Public Enemy* (1931), or Paul Muni's in *Scarface* (1932) were moral innocents, raging for self-betterment. Crime for them was a career open to the talents, and their illegalities were social climbing by other means. They desired the city as a peak of privilege. Scarface believes in the sign advertising Cook's Tours, which promises that the world is his; Rico in W. R. Burnett's novel *Little Caesar* (1929) is mesmerized by an electric sign announcing dancing at the Club Palermo. Such characters accede to the city as an extension of the backyard or slum block where their reign was first established: the Big Boy, supervisor of the rackets, assures Rico that "if a guy stands in with me, he owns the burg." Rico prizes mementos of his ascent, keeping a scrapbook on his crimes, and Cagney's Tom Powers treats the urban pavement as the stage for an improvised ballet of nimble-footed glee when, in *Public Enemy*, he succeeds in picking up Jean Harlow. These hoodlums were folk heroes who disputed ownership of the city with the impersonal corporations. H. I. Brock in *New York Is Like This*, published the same year as Burnett's novel, extols the gangster's challenge to a city where loot is accumulated inside arsenals and money has its own army of mercenaries, recruited by the banks, to defend it. The bank robber forbears to threaten the life or property of a private citizen, Brock says. Cagney's film correctly defines him as a public enemy—an opponent of the city's financial system. The banks swindle us by mystifying money, telling us that our savings are "out at interest," as if at stud. The robber, demanding cash, denounces such sleight-of-hand and inaugurates a redistribution of the wealth which the banks keep under armed guard. The public enemy is close to being a model citizen: an archetype of plucky free enterprise and ambitious mobility. When Rico has to flee Chicago and go back to the provinces, where he'd learned his trade by stealing from filling stations, someone marvels, "you sure went up fast over in the big burg."

The detective has outgrown this desire to conquer the city. Nor does he hope for its reform. His professional duty is analysis of it; his fictional task is its unplotting or decoding. Raymond Chandler claimed that the official institutional city is the façade for a nocturnal economy, where the respectable grandees have "made their money out of brothels" and "the nice man down the hall is a boss of the numbers racket." The detective has unriddled these enigmas and evasions. He's a deductive technician who patiently takes the urban machine to pieces. Dashiell Hammett's investigators exchange their participation in the city for this detached decipherment of it. Nick and Nora Charles in *The Thin Man* (1934) exist at an oblique angle to New York, commuting in taxis between their hotel suite and the bars they frequent, engaging a bellboy to walk their dog, telephoning an all-night deli for food. Their skill is their capacity to operate in this city from which they're disengaged and to make connections within it. Nick, drinking on West 52nd Street, knows at once how Dorothy Wynant can get news of her father. He advises her to call his lawyer, whose office turns out to be just around the corner. Guild the policeman keeps all his suspects in putative detention by assigning them to self-elected prisons in their own areas of the city—Jorgenson can always be found dallying extramaritally on West 73rd Street, Dorothy at Bergdorf's, her brother at the Public Library, Morelli "in a joint over in the Forties." Using the city is an expertise, like mental arithmetic. Macaulay in *The Thin Man* evades pursuit by issuing rapid contradictory directions to his cab driver, ordering him "south at Third, east again on Fifty-sixth, and south again on Second Avenue"; Ned Beaumont in Hammett's *The Glass Key* (1931), arriving in New York to collect his gambling winnings, plans his moves by learning which liaisons his quarry has made. At his hotel he picks up a message that locates the girl he's tracking, who "did some phoning from the depot and connected with"—slotting herself into the city's intricate circuit—"a man and a girl who live on E. 30th." Later one of his hirelings supplies another bulletin: "They went to the Buckman, Forty-eighth Street. That's where Despain is holing up—apartment 938—name of Barton Dewey." The detective confronts and derides his predecessor the gangster in *The Maltese Falcon* (1930). Sam Spade despises Wilmer, the Seventh Avenue punk who imagines he can bluster and bludgeon his way to success. The most proficient of Hammett's urban intelligencers is the nameless Op, whose only identity is as an operative and who works by collating information, persuading postal clerks, switchboard girls, and bank cashiers to part with evidence, matching meteorological records against taxi receipts to find out whether his suspects used cabs on rainy days, cultivating sources in the transport industry since these people will be the witnesses to getaways.

The detective at least has the authority of this technical command. Spade tells Brigid that "most things in San Francisco can be bought, or taken." Failing those appropriations, they can be known, and that's Spade's way. But increasingly, in the novels by Dorothy B. Hughes and Kenneth Fearing which are the sources for film noir, the city is an insoluble mystery and the detective is himself pursued through it. After Raymond Chandler's demonstration that its commerce is managed by criminals comes the worse revelation that the city's commonality is a deceit. Dorothy Hughes's characters are alone in New York with their persecutors—alone perhaps with themselves, since they wonder whether they're being stalked by their own shadow, menaced by the echo of their own footfall. Griselda in *The So Blue Marble* (1940) trembles at the sound of her heels on the Fifth Avenue pavement at night. Kit in *The Fallen Sparrow* (1942), filmed with John Garfield, arrives at Grand Central from Chicago and steps into a city peopled by his private terrors. He has entered it through a railway tunnel: "That," he reflects, "is the way you ought to come into Manhattan. See the black heart before you were dazzled by the chromium-plated wings and turrets." On 56th Street he hears behind him the lame shuffle of his tormentor from the prison camp. Aghast, he realizes that the city can't protect him. "Momentarily he was craven, shrinking, here in New York." For him the tunnel to Grand Central is a rite of passage in reverse, transporting him away from rational adulthood and back to infantile trauma; another Hughes hero, Piers in *The Delicate Ape* (1944), emerges from Pennsylvania Station into streets from which "all living, moving things . . . had . . . scuttled into hiding." From the station he walks to his hotel in Times Square, and he sees this journey as an evolutionary advance from the underground into light. The novel is set in 1956 during preparations for a peace conference at which Germany may be permitted to rearm. Reaching the incandescence of Times Square, Piers recalls the blackouts of the last war and swears to keep the city illumined: "the lights of the world, the lights of Broadway must not be put out again." He too debates as he walks whether it's his echoing tread that frightens him or the stealthy pace of someone following. His paranoid alarm turns into a schizophrenic commission for the hero of Fearing's *The Big Clock* (1946), who is retained by his employer to hunt through New York for a witness who can prove the employer guilty of murder. He is that witness: he has been set to harry and exterminate himself.

Like the detectives, the pleasure-seekers of New York in the 1930s and 1940s are noctambulists. Each has his own route through the dark, a beat he polices nightly. During his period as a columnist, Hellinger made a systematic tour of the clubs where he might uncover copy—the Lido, Texas Guinan's, the Silver Slipper, the Cotton Club in Harlem, Barney Gallant's in Greenwich Village—before clocking off at dawn. He would then sleep until 2 p.m., have himself barbered, eat breakfast, and get ready to resume his travels after dark. His colleague Walter Winchell began at the Stork and ended at Lindy's, coinciding with Weegee at an all-night drugstore.

As gossips, the columnists are researchers of the city's dark, comic counterparts to the detective. The motto of the Pinkerton Agency, for which Hammett worked as a detective, was "We never sleep," its logo a staring eye. The detective uses that eye to X-ray the dark, like Weegee with his infrared light. The gossip inserts it, more scurrilously, into a keyhole: a 1933 musical with a Winchell voice-over was titled *Broadway Thru a Keyhole*. To the detective's prying eye, the gossip adds a snooping ear, which like a microphone interviews the city's undertones ("Alert, the Winchell ear hears all," said *Time* in 1931), and a trained, trail-sniffing nose. In one of the photo caricatures Weegee made with his trick lenses, he prolongs Winchell's nose into an erectile beak, the tool of his trade. The gossip's profession is tainted, like the detective's, with an ambiguity deriving from their compact with the nighttime city. The private eye works at a tangent to the law and must reconcile himself to using duplicity and violence in the service of a cause he may not believe in. The gossip also bestraddles the law, maintaining an acquaintance with those who enforce it and those who break it. Hellinger was a habitué of the night court on West 54th Street, where he found material for his stories, and his friendships with the police enabled Wald to research *The Naked City* in the files of the Homicide Squad. He was also the associate of gangsters and racketeers, who often elected him as a mock-magistrate to settle their territorial disputes. One of them, murdered on the job, willed to Hellinger his armor-plated limousine. Winchell also referred admiringly to the mobsters as underworld nobility, and was once compelled by a grand jury to divulge his sources when he reported all too accurately on a gangland killing. The gossip's aim, like the detective's, is incrimination. But he can secure it by innuendo or falsification. Al Jolson once punched Winchell for traducing his

Mark Hellinger, Ted de Corsia, and Don Taylor on location on the El platform for *The Naked City* (1948). Courtesy of National Film Archive/Stills Library, London. Copyright Columbia-EMI-Warner Pictures.

wife Ruby Keeler. The gossip column is notes from the underground, a smirking almanac of the city's bad conscience.

At different times in New York's history, different parts have symbolized the whole—Fifth Avenue for James and Edith Wharton, Harlem for the 1920s, Canal Street (as the next chapter will show) and its treasuries of mechanical junk for the 1960s. When in the 1930s and 1940s New York becomes a night-town, its center shifts to Broadway. As a straight line, Fifth Avenue can be a social arbiter. Broadway is deleterious because diagonal, straying across Manhattan from east to west, and because nocturnal. Winchell called it New York's hardened artery. In Damon Runyon's stories, Broadway secedes from New York. Although Runyon's people are society's idle or criminal rejects, he punctiliously refers to them as citizens. Their citizenship is their presence on the street: joining its shiftless after-dark world, they have opted out of workaday New York. Runyon says of Nicely-Nicely Johnson, "what he does for a living is the best he can, which is an occupation that is greatly overcrowded at all times on Broadway"; the scalper Blooch

Bodinski "comes up out of Essex Street to Broadway and he does this and that, and one thing and another, to make a living." Frequenting the street suffices, for these people, as an occupation. They foregather on it to pass the time, and Runyon's stories begin by placing them—and himself—on its map, which means on set: "it is maybe eleven-thirty of a Wednesday night, and I am standing at the corner of Forty-eighth Street and Seventh Avenue." If the street is their scene, anywhere else is backstage. Madame La Gimp, for instance, lives in a cellar on Tenth Avenue, but journeys to Broadway to conduct her social life. With an exclusivity that mimics the delimitation of terrain in the genteel New York of James and Howells, Runyon is whimsically specific about the foreign, unintelligible areas beyond his beat. Handsome Jack "comes up out of what they call Hell's Kitchen over on the West Side," and he notes that "Princess O'Hara is driving north on the street that is called Central Park West because it borders the Park on the west." Adhering to their local turf, his characters derive from it their motive for being. Dream Street Rose and West Side Willie are named after sections of it. The most civically versatile and ubiquitous of them is Nathan Detroit, whose floating crap game is his mobile home. He is the elusive, omnipresent spirit of the place: his deputies wander up and down Broadway informing its citizenry where he can be found that evening. The rumor-rife street functions as a bourse, helping Runyon compute the odds on a rich marriage for a red-headed chorine; arriving at Columbus Circle, it doubles as a parliament. The Circle, Runyon says, is "a kind of public forum." Rupert Salsinger the shoe salesman incites a small revolution there by haranguing the crowd from atop a box, then leads his followers back down Broadway to loot a store. Economically and politically, the blocks between Times Square and Columbus Circle have declared themselves an autarchic city-state.

Broadway's secession is linguistic too. As a nocturnal alternative to the toiling city, it speaks an after-dark argot. Instead of names, Runyon's people have nicknames, and instead of language, Broadway has lingo, a dialect devised for purposes of conspiracy, like the passwords that admit you to Nathan's itinerant crap game. The first task of this Newspeak is the rechristening of Broadway. The street's clannish sense of itself demands a redenomination, since it won't answer to the title New York presumes to know it by. Hellinger called it Buzzard Boulevard; the columnist Louis Sobol invented a lexicon of pseudonyms for it—the Illuminated Thoroughfare, the modern Appian Way, the Rue of roués, the Gay Lit-Up Canyon, Golden Gulch, and Mazda Lane. His renamings often rely on puns, which are language's smutty basement of implication.

Because of the burlesque dancers in its clubs, Sobol called West 52nd Street "Stripty-Second Street." As well as being illicit, the pun verges on the illegal—Dr. Johnson, after all, likened it to the picking of a pocket —and this too fits it for use on Broadway. Sobol sees it as a concealed weapon and compliments Milton Berle as a "two-pun assassin" of fool-hardy hecklers. On Broadway words can kill. Runyon brands the drama critic Ambrose Hammer a murderer because his job is the slaughter of newborn plays. Broadway's rejection of the city's official, law-abiding language explains Runyon's avoidance of the past tense. That tense is our admission of accountability, our memory of our misdemeanors; there's a unique freedom from reproof to be enjoyed if you can slither along indefinitely in the improvisatory present.

No matter how devious these natives of Broadway may be, they always acknowledge their duty to the street. In the civic terms of Runyon, they see themselves as public servants. Hellinger in his valedictory column, written in November 1937 as he was leaving for Hollywood, solemnly terminated his contract with Broadway: "The street was good to me," he wrote, "—but I was as good to the street." The gossip here echoes the detective's ethical accord with the streets he patrols. In those mean thoroughfares, the detective must comport himself honorably; the gossip likewise testifies that he has kept faith with his constituency. Runyon in 1946 settled a last debt to Broadway by requesting his son to scatter his ashes "over the island of Manhattan, the place I have truly loved and that was so good to me." His son hired a plane and decanted Runyon's remains above Times Square.

By the time Runyon drifted down onto the street in sooty benediction, his Broadway was, in any case, obsolete. Its end is announced by Ben Hecht in the newspaper columns he collected in 1941 as *1001 Afternoons in New York*. He still calls the street people citizens, but the designation is sarcastic. The derelict and dispossessed anger Hecht because they have reneged on their citizenship. They're safe from the promptings of polit-ical conscience, unconcerned about the world war, at ease in their deso-lation, like the scabrous elderly streetwalkers he encounters on Allen Street, "Riviera of the bums," or the three tramps who expire in bliss on the Bowery after imbibing antifreeze from a parked car. Moral probity is exemplified by the old jeweler Hecht writes about in one of his columns who, sauntering down Broadway in the spring, feels death near and, knowing "it's not good to lie dead . . . in the street," hurriedly buys a ticket for a movie and quietly seats himself inside to await his fatal seizure. His act, like the wartime browning out of the Times Square neon, signals the closing down of Runyon's street theater.

There had been other premonitions. Although the musical is the form in which Broadway mythologizes itself, the finales to three Busby Berkeley musicals of the 1930s are skeptical about the myth. *Golddiggers of 1933* concludes with the listless, shuffling breadline in Times Square, a defamation of the Broadway musical's expensive swank. The form the finale takes is sadly parodic: it's a march gone into reverse. The men advanced optimistically to war. Returned to an impoverished peace, they no longer step lively. The camera tracks down the length of their line, enumerating not a parade of identical Berkeley girls but a file of grim-visaged men. Here Berkeley marshals the crowds of Broadway into a sullenly patient welfare line; in *42nd Street* (1933) he choreographs the congestion of Times Square as a frenzied ballet. The finale begins in a traffic jam, with Ruby Keeler tap-dancing on the roof of a taxi. She dismounts to find the whole street jiving. Even a cigar-store Indian struts and swings, while a platoon of goose-stepping chorus girls blocks the roadway. The tap dance here is madly spasmodic, an epilepsy of pleasure which infects the skyline. The chorus girls jerk cutouts of the skyscrapers to and fro and make the city twitch in restless ecstasy. After the doleful march-past of survivors in *Golddiggers of 1933* and the dithyrambic palsy of *42nd Street*, Berkeley composes a deathly lullaby for Broadway in the astonishing finale to *Golddiggers of 1935*. The sequence treats Broadway's nocturnal regime as an insomniac penance. The street needs the song to soothe it to sleep. As the episode begins, Winifred Shaw's face—a blanched oval on the dark screen, like a sickly moon in the night sky—dissolves, while she sings "Lullaby of Broadway," into an aerial view of Manhattan. The cigarette between her lips mutates into a smokestack: she becomes, like the "Broadway baby" she is singing about, an image of hedonism as joyless self-consuming industry. Creeping upstairs to bed at daybreak, the show girl is greeted by the milkman and the cleaner, who recognizes her as a fellow worker. Like them, she's a slave to time. Outside her window, a rooftop clock speeds up to abridge her day of rest. When its hands have spun themselves to exhaustion, her sun—a neon sign—blinks on to hustle her out of bed. She sets off on her usual dutiful tour of the nightclubs with Dick Powell as her escort and ends in a blank cavern where a troop of stomping revelers, militaristically tapping as they approach, summon her to dance. When she recoils, they pursue her onto a high ledge. She staggers and plunges into the street. As she falls, the clockhands whirr in their haste to speed up and have done with her frantic life. The refrain returns as a dirge. Now she can "sleep all day"—and much longer. Broadway's white nights can be obliterated only by the big sleep.

Ruby Keeler and the dancing skyline in Busby Berkeley's *42nd Street* (1933). Courtesy of National Film Archive/Stills Library, and Metro-Goldwyn-Mayer.

The strident lullaby is keened by O. Henry's voice of the city. That voice no longer maintains a blessed silence: it's a primal scream, a feral rage which can be heard only at night. "Just listen to it roar!" said Runyon to Gene Fowler. Eavesdropping—like Weegee with his police radio—on the city's troubled slumber, Runyon claimed that each precinct had its own idiosyncratic cry, voicing its collective unconsciousness. The Lower East Side gave out a subdued, suffering "Oh-h-h, O-h-h. O-h-h," Broadway a shriller "Eeee-eee-eee," Harlem a throaty, ululating "Ooo-ooo-ooo." The asphalt paves a jungle. In the period of film noir, New York is represented as an atavistic lair, home to the phantasmagoric offspring of King Kong: Dorothy Hughes's delicate ape, who symbolizes the warmonger in man, or the *Cat People* of Val Lewton's 1942 film, in which the beasts in the Central Park zoo growl through the night to taunt their feline cousin Simone Simon. The cabaret siren in Ben Hecht's story "Crime Without Passion" describes Broadway as "the world's leading water hole for human beasts of prey."

As well as a jungle, New York is the dragon-haunted forest of Germanic imagination. Fritz Lang's *Metropolis* (1927) exists halfway between the haunted primeval underground of his *Die Nibelungen* (1924) and the different underworld of the American city, where the monsters aren't avaricious gnomes and reptiles but the sadistic enforcers of *The Big Heat* (1953) or the psychotic killer chased by Dana Andrews through the tunnels of the New York subway in *While the City Sleeps* (1956). The affluent superstructure of Lang's metropolis, with aerial highways connecting horned skyscrapers, is a vision of New York. Lang had seen the skyline from a ship docked on the West Side in 1924, and recognized in it his proleptic future. Down below, his city reverts to the Germanic antiquity of the *Nibelungen*, with catacombs, a charnel house, a cathedral, and a woodland cabin for the sorcerer. Steely New York has a Gothic cellarage, into which the industrialist's son descends to find his enslaved brothers. And just as Lang's towering metropolis is sustained by these subterranean toilers, or his Valhalla raised by the labor of Alberich's miners, so New York has a convenient depth beneath the floor to which it consigns its secrets. At the 21 Club during prohibition a button was pressed when the premises were raided, and all the bottles in the bar would at once crash through a trapdoor and shatter on rocks. A sandpit absorbed the spillage. The culpable truth about the city is to be discovered, literally, downstairs.

With the other German directors who fled to Hollywood during the 1930s—among whom Billy Wilder, Robert Siodmak, and Otto Preminger were also specialists in film noir—Lang dedicated the American city to night. In German romanticism night betokens an end to rational timidity, a state of sensual arousal consummated in easeful death. The soulful or sexual German dark, welcomed by Isolde who douses the torch to summon Tristan, becomes the unlawful New York night. Like Tristan and Isolde obliterating day, the denizens of Broadway subsist in a permanent dimout. Jim Bishop, Hellinger's biographer, says that the street's regulars excluded the day "with heavy drapes and eye pads" while they waited for nightfall, when the city would once more be theirs. One of the bogeys of German romanticism acclaimed New York in 1945. Peter Lorre, gliding about in defiance of the wartime curfew, paid it a vampirish compliment. He saw it as a place frequented by the errant undead, those insomniac fiends who shun the dawn. "At midnight New York is dead—deadd—deadd," he told Louis Sobol, who transcribed his grisly consonantal relish; "it is won-derr-ful." In Lang's metropolis, the sleek efficient machines are apt to dissolve into a rabid hell. The factory metamorphoses into a dragon engorging workers, the cabaret into a grim, scything dance of death. The New York of film noir likewise points people toward infernal restitution. A Greenwich Village signpost in Lang's *Scarlet Street* (1945) sends Edward G. Robinson directly to his doom. The elevator shaft in John Farrow's film of *The Big Clock* (1948) is Charles Laughton's shortcut to the pit. The murderer in *The Naked City* tries to evade the police by clambering up the girders of the Williamsburg Bridge, from where he satanically surveys the city which was his domain; John Garfield in Abraham Polonsky's *Force of Evil*, also released in 1948, plumbs a personal Hades under the George Washington Bridge. The racketeers have discarded the dead body of Garfield's brother at the water's edge "like rubbish." Garfield must acquaint himself with that depth before he can rearise to personal salvation. He scurries down monumental steps which look like the entry to hell, "going down and down there—it was like going to the bottom of the world." People in film noir believe their damnation to be as relentlessly scheduled and as mechanically automated as urban transport. Fred MacMurray, in Chandler's script for *Double Indemnity*, says he's on a streetcar which goes only one way, and he must ride it to the end of the line, which is the cemetery. In *Sorry, Wrong Number* (again 1948) the murder of Barbara Stanwyck is planned to coincide with a train's crossing the Queensboro Bridge outside her Sutton Place window at 11:15 p.m. The precision suggests hell's regime of torments. Each excruciation has its appointed place in the daily scheme; her death, like the train's journey over the bridge, will be repeated nightly, exactly on time. In the same film, the telephone exchange—the single recourse for the bedridden Stanwyck—is an incompetent clearinghouse for last judgments. Crossed lines are its snarled, inextricable fates. Martin Scorsese's *Mean Streets* (1973) takes that field of honor where Chandler's detective goes bravely about his business and makes of it another inferno. The lurid, red-glowing bars of New York's Italian quarter are Harvey Keitel's cauldron. He trifles there with his inevitable perdition, thrusting his hands into the fire to test in advance the pains of hell. Down streets where the manholes exhale fumes from the pit, Robert de Niro as Travis Bickle in Scorsese's *Taxi Driver* (1976) ferries his fares to the agonies they've elected for themselves. Travis moonlights in his taxi because he can't sleep; by staying awake he qualifies as New York's avenging and exterminating angel.

The novels Cornell Woolrich published under the pseudonym William Irish—*Phantom Lady* (1942), filmed by Siodmak in 1944, or *Deadline at Dawn* (1944), filmed in 1946 by Harold Clurman with a script by Clifford Odets—interpret detection as a voluntary descent into this New York hell. The girl in *Phantom Lady* suborns a drug-addicted drummer whose testimony she needs by spending two hours in "a sort of Dante-esque Inferno": she attends a raucous jam session in a cellar, where demons wail instrumentally and the air is a smog of gin and reefers. In *Deadline at Dawn* cigarette smoke turns the harlot into a fiend: "smoke suddenly speared from her nostrils in two malevolent columns. She looked like Satan." Detection is pursuit through hell by the hound of heaven, who creates in his victims a moral panic that goads them to self-destruction. The girl in *Phantom Lady* stalks the bartender through the night with lethal resolve until in his frenzy he's run over by a car; Quinn in *Deadline at Dawn* terrorizes a gibbering sinner who decomposes in despair—a false arm of wadded newspaper collapses when Quinn grabs it. To chase and to be chased are the twin vocations of these distraught beings ("Quinn could have kept running straight through the night, straight through the city") because the chase is the soul's race to outrun its own guilt; and since we're all guilty the pursuer is running to capture himself, which he can never do. The sailor and the taxi dancer in *Deadline at Dawn* are harried by New York itself. She loathes the city as her "personal enemy" and accuses it of having brutalized her but is incapable of leaving it. She gets as far as the bus terminal only to be detained by "the vapor, the fumes— . . . the miasma given off by the city." When Quinn goes indoors to undo his crime, she stations herself outside as a sentry, "keeping the city out." The single friendly auspice in New York, so far as she's concerned, is the clock on the Paramount Building, and she prays to it for a remission of her sentence. That compassionate recording angel contrasts with the other clocks in the novel, hastening toward a punctual doomsday, and with the perverse, reversed metabolic clock of the New York nocturnal world. She arrives at the Perroquet at 4:30 a.m. to find it "dead, but not quite cold" because "this was the five o'clock in the afternoon of the nightclub workers." Like Lorre's vampire, these people are revenants roaming a cemetery.

Into this blackened realm, light leaks as a defamation. Woolrich describes illumination as a stain or wound. The bar on 59th Street in *Phantom Lady* sheds a red neon dye on the sidewalk "as though someone had spilled a bottle of ketchup," and in *Deadline at Dawn* the mirrored ball on the ceiling of the tawdry dance hall is a spirochete, smearing the walls with its plague. Light is cosmetic palliation of a discolored body. At evening, for the hour of get-togethers, the sky puts its bleary "make-up on in the west," and the lampposts briefly talcum Quinn and the girl as if with powder from a shaken container as they pass on into obscurity.

The big sleep of New York's zombified night conspires with its big heat. Summer in New York, in this understanding of the city, is a season passed in hell. *Deadline at Dawn* happens during a suffocating summer night. Crime raises the temperature of Weegee's torrid city, which perspires through opened hydrants. Some of Weegee's most acrid puns concern the city's fever. On the side of a blazing warehouse in one of his photographs is a proud advertisement for the food products manufactured therein: "SIMPLY ADD BOILING WATER." And the fire occurs, to make the joke even crueler, on Water Street. A Broadway movie house which he also photographs as it burns happens to be playing *The Heat's On*, a 1943 Mae West musical. If crime is the city's lustful heat, then law is repressive freezing: Weegee calls the lockup a cooler, and its inmates, whom he photographs piled behind bars in 1942, have been put metamorphically on ice by arrest. Battling the city's itchy flames, which rage even during winter, Weegee's firemen change into anthropoid icicles. As they aim their hoses, stalactites harden on their helmets and the collars of their uniforms. Weegee also sought out people being treated for sunburn or heat exhaustion under the boardwalk at Coney Island—casualties of the city's grilling.

Summer's asphyxiation of New York determines the mood of Vera Caspary's *Laura* (1942), filmed by Preminger in 1944. The novel begins with a dual autopsy, for the debilitated city and the defunct Laura. "The city that Sunday morning was quiet," and those trapped there gasp in foul humid air "that smelled and felt like water in which too many soda-water glasses had been washed." Laura's aunt returns from Long Island to her mausoleum on Fifth Avenue where the furniture is in mourning under shrouds of pale linen. Lydecker and the detective McPherson eat in a garden restaurant on MacDougal Street beneath a skinny catalpa that dangles over them "the black bones of skeleton hands." In this urban graveyard, love—like the detective's infatuation with Laura—manifests itself as necrophilia. Lydecker considers McPherson's obsession with a corpse "the perfect O. Henry story" because "so typical of New York." Leaving the restaurant, the men re-enter a sulphurous climatic hell: "the heat hit us like a blast from a furnace. The air was dead. . . . The town smelled like rotten eggs." The weather germinates pestilence and warns of apocalypse. This is wartime New York when brownouts legally enforced the dominion of night, and McPherson hears the thunder "like a squadron of bombers above the roof." Laura reappears, as if resurrected, during this cataclysm, and while the ground trembles and the sky rips, McPherson remembers his grandmother's assurance "about meeting in heaven all those whom he

Weegee, "Simply Add Boiling Water" (1937). Courtesy of the Weegee Collection, Wilma Wilcox, Curator.

had lost on earth." In Odets's screenplay for *Deadline at Dawn*, where summer storms also crackle across the city, the weather supplies the characters with their alibis. They're behaving as befits the inferno they inhabit. Susan Hayward explains her irascibility to Bill Williams by saying, "this heat makes me boil. And so do you," while Paul Lukas

Refrigerating the overheated city: a Greenwich Village sidewalk in Fritz Lang's *Scarlet Street* (1945), with Dan Duryea and Joan Bennett. Courtesy of National Film Archive/Stills Library, London. Copyright UIP.

uses it as a mitigation of his murder: "Anything can happen in this heat. That woman's heart was made of ice." Killing defrosted her, claimed her for the company of the inflamed and damned. In Hitchcock's *Rear Window* (1954), based on a Woolrich story, the New York summer is a hallucinogen. Immobilized by a broken leg, James Stewart spends the season spying on the lives of his neighbors across a Greenwich Village courtyard. One of the tenants in the building opposite has, Stewart deduces, committed a murder. Or is this his heat-induced delusion? The film plays with the possibility that the suspicion may be a wishful delirium, the erotic excitation of the voyeur. He is asleep or dozing much of the time and is first seen sweating feverishly. We imagine him to be ill; then a thermometer is shown registering 92 degrees. When his nurse arrives, she takes his temperature and says he's gotten overheated watching the cavortings of the bikini girls outside. If crimes are the city's bad dreams, the murder may be Stewart's unhealthy invention. Woolrich's story, set in a nameless city, locates the crime at a fictional address, 525 Benedict Avenue. Hitchcock, adapting it to New York, specifies an address slightly beyond the edge of actual-

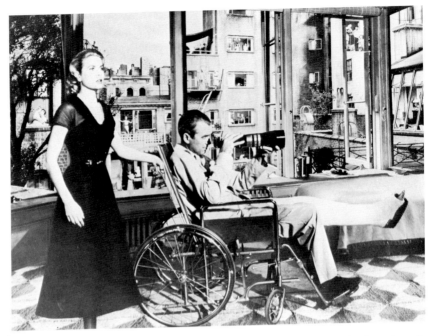

Grace Kelly and James Stewart in Alfred Hitchcock's *Rear Window* (1954).
Courtesy of National Film Archive/Stills Library, London. Copyright UIP.

ity, not so much fictional as fictitious—125 West 9th Street, nonexistent because West 9th has a career of only a single block—so as, perhaps, to imply that it's imagined, a reverie of the distracted Stewart. By the end, Stewart's and the city's febrility have abated: the same thermometer now reads 70 degrees.

The heat afflicting New York sours and rots it. At the same time, it's an agency of benefit. It cauterizes, immunizes, insures the city. Heat disintegrates but also disinfects. Cooking its inhabitants, the sweltering city leaves them with that unfeeling rind which is the existential bravado of the 1940s: they become, as New York already is, hard-boiled. Laura distinguishes between hard-boiled detectives and those who rely on forensic logic. The hard-boiled persona has been annealed in the city's sultry hell. Hard-boiling is a torture of matter, a chemical inducement of molecular disorder, altering a physical state from liquid to solid. It's an experiment that can preserve by a calculated self-extermination. The detective is made insensitive and invulnerable by heat. Mickey Spillane's synonym for hard-boiled is "kill-toughened." His hero in *The Deep* (1961) has been toughened by killing others and by having killed off

294

that part of himself that is sentimentally feeble. Thugs in Spillane's *The Big Kill* (1951) try to break open Mike Hammer's head. He—whose name announces him to be a weapon, burnished in the city's smithy— laconically comments on his resistance: "I got a hard head." McPherson's techniques of interrogation in *Laura* apply the heat he can withstand to those who are unprepared for it and wither under its assault. Laura thinks he's contriving a "hysterical climax" to extort a confession from her. In Lang's *Clash by Night* (1952) Barbara Stanwyck says to Robert Ryan, when calculating the grief they have caused her husband, "we're so hard-boiled, everyone else is soft." They can't be hurt, and this empowers them to hurt others. Lang's *The Big Heat* is about the transformation of actual heat, which sears and scars flesh—the cigarette burns on the back of the murdered girl, the scalding coffee hurled by Lee Marvin in Gloria Grahame's face, the dynamite blasting Glenn Ford's car and incinerating his wife—into a symbolic ire, a vindictive mania which hardens flesh and readies Ford to exact restitution. Both New York's combustible summer and its libidinal night are laboratories for such a metamorphosis—of staid daytime citizens into savages of uncontrollable id; of the city, which the World's Fair promised would be an electronic heaven, into our mutual hell, where the dark is aglow with flame, not light.

Once newly fortified by heat, the detective can reassume power over the city, and can even corporally punish it. This is Mike Hammer's mission in New York. In *Kiss Me, Deadly* (1952) he is "hot" because hunted by the mobsters, yet he thrives in the heat, testing "the temperature of the underworld cauldron" by appraising the looks of nervous dread he gets. He has been hardened by boiling; the city, like its people, remains "soft, pulpy," and can be reduced to its squashy essence by fisticuffs. Hammer trains heat on it to speed up its putrefying. He imagines the Mafia men popping "like ripe melons" and voiding their innards. Thinking for Hammer is mastication and urban clearance evisceration. He gnashes and gnaws at a mystery in *The Big Kill* until its hardness yields and it can be solved by softening: "I wanted . . . to chew my way through it slowly until I found the tough hunk that didn't chew so easily and put it through the grinder." The grinder mechanizes his massacre of substance. Hammer's New York has mashed and defaced its own body, as he bludgeons the bodies of his victims. In *The Deep* 52nd Street has had the guts torn out of it, and Benny-from-Brooklyn hides in a brownstone off Third Avenue that is due for demolition, among houses already pulverized by bulldozers and jackhammers. "The old Dutch district" has repaired the damage by plastic surgery, undergoing "a face change when they tore the tenements down."

From Weegee's ravishment of the city, we arrive at Spillane's sentencing of it to a heat death. Weegee exposes its body; Spillane scorches that body with what he calls his gun's "tongue of flame" until, like the woman he shoots in *The Big Kill*, its countenance melts into "a ghastly red mask that was really no face at all." Hammer calls this his "horrible vengeance," and it works like Weegee's exploding and electrocuting flash. The avenging hoodlum in *The Deep* is warned that "the first time you put the heat to somebody, even if it's a Bowery bum, you'll get fried." This is the sadistic victory of urban paranoia, purgatively setting fire to the city which has schooled us in our evil, foredooming the world in an anticipation of apocalypse. James Cagney rehearses that excoriating blaze when, at the top of the world, he blows up the gas tanks in *White Heat* (1949), and in Robert Aldrich's film of *Kiss Me, Deadly* (1955) the radioactive black box opens to unleash a fury brewed in the desert at Los Alamos but named, as the detective's comment makes clear, after New York—"the Manhattan project."

Spillane's city is a body mortally ill, patrolled by ineffectual phagocytes. He hears the sirens of the police cars in *Kiss Me, Deadly* as "white corpuscles" reconnoitering at the site of an infection. After 1939, travel writers, whose concern is the mental temper of places, concur. They treat New York as a psychiatric patient, suffering from the anxieties of modernity, and their commentaries on the city are advance reports on the contagion which will sooner or later overtake the world. Felix Reisenberg in *Portrait of New York* (1939) estimates the nervy, toxic toll of the city on its people, who inhale poisonous air, are squeezed and stifled in the subway, and have their organs nauseously rearranged in elevators. Reisenberg interprets every object in terms of its strain on the observer. He comments, for instance, on the "headaching repetitions" of the fenestration at Rockefeller Center. And he describes places as diseased lesions—West 42nd Street is the "inflamed appendix" of Broadway, while Bryant Park with its inexplicable excavations is a carious mouth. New York's two medicinal industries cater to the extremities of the long-suffering human body, selling pills for throbbing heads and, on a cross street in the 30s between Fifth and Madison, rectifying fallen arches. Cecil Beaton in 1947 portrays New Yorkers as besieged by a tornado of static electricity, which makes sparks start from doorknobs or shaking hands. This storm incites an emotional instability. New Yorkers veer between love and despair, while their city lunges from boom to crash. The overcharged atmosphere begets constriction within: "One's entrails become tight and metallic," Beaton reports. "Blood and guts change to ethyl and duralumin." In E. B. White's essay *Here Is New York* (1949) urban affrays are pathological symptoms. Traffic jams resemble blood clots or coronary obstructions, and the tonic of the street life is an overdose of surplus vitamins to keep the frenetic body working. The city's thoroughfares extend to the limits of rational composure—"a single run of a cross-town bus" is, White says, enough to transport the driver beyond the perimeter of sanity. Bellevue signifies an ultimate urban terminus, "the end of the line" when the artificial hysteria of the city fails. Analyzing the regions which the city allocates to separate social or economic functions—residential, commercial, artistic—White favors promoting the Medical Center to the status of a neighborhood, since it constitutes the inevitable "sickness unit." He sees above the city "a radioactive cloud of hate and rancor and bigotry," which requires New Yorkers to be warily tolerant for fear of reprisals. The metaphor of radioactivity hints at White's subtext. After Hiroshima, the city is the choicest place for the detonation of the new bombs because, like those bombs, it's the product of energy in destructive excess. White's essay concludes with the imagined sound of war planes overhead and the city's prospective annihilation from on high.

Yet while the detective novels and the films based on them are condemning New York to the perdition of night and heat and the essayists are making pessimistic prognoses for its survival, another form intervenes after the war to secure reprieve, pardon, and a cure for the city: the musical. Its obligation to laugh at the clouds and sing in the rain, to relieve our errors and our doubts, makes the musical determined to convert New York to its ideology of optimism. Music offers absolution to Runyon's toughs in *Guys and Dolls* (1950). Sarah Brown brings her mission to Broadway, which she calls "the devil's own street in the devil's own city," and shows its demons to be homebodies who long for love and connubial respectability. At the end, the mugs are delivered to the Salvation Army outpost on West 49th Street for spiritual and musical reclamation.

The pieties of the musical are rural, and its natural location is the small town—down whose main street, for instance, Bobby Van exultantly hops in Busby Berkeley's *Small Town Girl* (1953). As he bounces along, he sings of his ambition to be a performer, pleading "Take me to Broadway." But the Broadway he's imagining will be an extension of this neighborly, affectionate village. Jane Powell in the same film opines in song that "Small towns are smile towns." To such lyrical snugness, the city's a threat: this is why the family in Vincente Minnelli's *Meet Me in St. Louis* (1944) vetoes the father's proposal to move to New York. When the musical returned to New York after the blackouts and eclips-

Jules Munshin, Frank Sinatra, and Gene Kelly in *On the Town* (1949). Courtesy of National Film Archive/Stills Library, London, and Metro-Goldwyn-Mayer.

ing gloom of the war, it sought to win over the metropolis to the emotional and moral virtues of the small town. *On the Town,* directed by Stanley Donen and Gene Kelley, was credited in 1949 with being the first musical to stage its songs on location in New York; its purpose, all the same, is still the sentimental, sanctifying contraction of the city. Three sailors are on leave there for the first time and for just one day. With them they bring winsome small-town expectations, which New York goes out of its way improbably to satisfy. Frank Sinatra, whose home is in Peoria, carries with him as a token of his fond extraterritorial naiveté a guidebook dating from 1905, and he asks to be shown, as the latest wonders, the Woolworth Building, the Hippodrome, and the Florodora Girls. Gene Kelly, whose provenance is the allegorically (and paradoxically) named Meadowville, Indiana, falls at once for a nonentity he imagines to be a celebrity—Miss Turnstiles, girl of the month on the subway. Though she acts the brittle city sophisticate, she's a marshmallowy provincial too, and turns out to be from the same town as Kelly. Together they dance a leisurely celebration not of New York but of the main street of Meadowville, where the cop last made an arrest in 1903. The project of the musical is advertised in its title: to present the bruising, indifferent city as that smaller and more amenable unit, a town. In Minnelli's *The Band Wagon* (1953) Fred Astaire arrives at Grand Central and walks along 42nd Street to Times Square, where he has his shoes shined. The refurbishing of his footwear melodically brightens his mood, and he entices his fellow strollers and loiterers to join him in a joyous, wish-fulfilling dance. Again the street in becoming a stage has become a community, amiable because choral and choreographic. Gene Kelly roller-skates elatedly through New York in *It's Always Fair Weather* (1955); in *Bells Are Ringing* (1960), Judy Holliday like the salvationist Sarah Brown takes her gospel of uplift back to Broadway. Crossing West 45th Street, she dares Dean Martin—the drunken playwright she saves—to greet a stranger. She does so, accosting a scowling passerby with "Hello." He snarls at first but soon moistens into gratitude and tells her that this is the first time in thirty years anyone has spoken kindly to him in the street. Other strangers follow Judy Holliday's example. A love-feast occupies the intersection, but concludes abruptly when the lights change and everyone has to struggle on competitively against the traffic. More recent musicals have made New York the citadel of a new faith. In *The Wiz* (1978) the yellow brick road is rerouted across the Brooklyn Bridge to the World Trade Center, and in *Godspell* (1973) a hippie John the Baptist pushes a handcart across the same bridge and recruits a cadre of followers who then cavort, like unkempt angels of annunciation, on top of the same building. They're washed free of their sins in the Bethesda Fountain in Central Park; Milos Forman's *Hair* (1979) takes over the tunnels near the fountain as the catacombs of its astrological cult. The accursed city has been befriended, made a place in which to sing, dance, and regenerate yourself.

15

An Aleatory Island

The adage says that New York will be a great place when they finish it. No, it won't: it will be an architectural exhibit in a museum, which is what Huneker's aesthetes try prematurely to make it by comparing it with dead, finished Venice. New York is great only while still growing. Of its unending self-revision, the symbol is litter. The economy of art usually equates form with content: nothing is wasted. But the city is prodigiously wasteful. The gutters and overloaded trash cans testify to the vigor of its self-overcoming. In human terms too the city, like Whitman's ferry, is a place of passage, not habitation. As the evicted litter blows or rambles down the streets, so people drift through New York, never to return. You daren't pretend to belong there. Urban wisdom demands that you accept the randomness of your apparition in and disappearance from the city.

This randomness is New York's ultimate test of the artist. Both realism and abstraction are pledged to the denial of the city's aleatory expenditure of lives and of objects. Realism argues that windblown chance is a contrivance of fate. It's this that makes O. Henry's whole New York kin, enabling Franklin to find his Sarah in "Springtime à la Carte," and that fondly unites the city of John Sloan who, looking at people, is longing for a relation with them. Sloan's paintings are excerpts from a narrative that precedes and outlasts them, for narrative with its consoling continuations is realism's comfort in an arbitrary, accidental world. Abstraction tells no tales; it prohibits randomness by its refusal to narrate. With people in retreat, all that remains of the city is axiomatic and eternal geometry—Hopper's angular corners, Shahn's white walls.

At last, in the 1950s, New York acquires an art that can accept its disorder and mimic its messiness, an art that venerates litter and is thus able to understand the purport of its streets, an art that fossicks through the city's castoffs and finds there totems, toys, souvenirs. In 1939 New York proudly cleared the dumping ground in Flushing to erect the ideal city of the World's Fair. By 1960 Jean Tinguely, assembling spare parts for the suicidal combine called "Homage to New York" in a dump at Summit, New Jersey, said he could happily have set up shop there among the city's outworn exotica. At the beginning of his career in New York, Robert Rauschenberg made two series of works which seem to review and revalue the earlier realist and abstract options for the city. His dirt paintings of 1953, packaging the urban muck in crates, take up the realist characterization of the painter as a mess-maker, which spattered Henri's studio with pigment, soiled Shinn's underclothes, and made Sloan admire the greasy doorframes of the Lower East Side. The Ashcan artists treated paint as metaphoric dirt, real because grubby. Rauschenberg literalizes their metaphor, pasting shredded newspaper to the canvas and painting it thickly black. His white paintings, dazzling in their imagelessness, allude to the alternative white city of abstraction, a vacant lot for shadows to pass across, and declare that perfect New York to be a nullity.

Once art reaches this new accommodation with the ordure and irrelevance of New York, the dispersed, disjunct city is again sacred, for the artist picking among its refuse is researching the city's reasons for being and, from its leavings, is reconstructing myths. On its junk heaps he plants monuments to new urban gods: Rauschenberg's emblematic advertising logos, Claes Oldenburg's cuddly deities, the arcanely boxed cinematic Madonnas of Joseph Cornell.

The city's first gift to Rauschenberg is its indeterminancy. He defines New York as a combinatorial mechanism, a device for assisting the entropy which the nocturnal New York of Weegee and film noir—with its disintegrative big heat—so abhors. "New York," he says, "is a maze of unorganized experiences peopled by the unexpected—change is unavoidable." He refuses to believe that its juxtapositions are casual and causeless and declares that the city's "extremely complex random order . . . cannot be described as accidental." Our perception of the streets is a lesson in the complexity of randomness. We tolerate there a visual indiscriminateness which art customarily forbids. Images float across the available space, half-apprehended or left undeciphered, like the faces of people we pass or the signs we don't stop to read. In 1954 William Klein made photographs in the streets of New York which are essays in this visual inattention. At the corner of Broadway and 48th Street, for instance, a crowd churns by, no one looking at anyone else. An urban cowboy stares in the direction of Klein's camera but doesn't register its fingering of him; a black evangelist with a placard purveys salvation to an indifferent, hustled flock. Klein isn't, like Judy Holliday at a nearby intersection six years later, protesting against the callousness of such self-preoccupation. He values it as a unique freedom: the camera eye enjoys the pedestrian's liberty to see without looking.

Rauschenberg set himself in "Rebus" (1955) and "Street Throng" (1959) to reproduce the pedestrian's fickle seeing. The streets censure art's strict insistence on hierarchical perception. For his silk screens Rauschenberg often uses photographs of drab diurnal views from the window of his New York studio, obliging the eye to canvas the congestion and distraction of the street. In "Persimmon" (1964) Rubens's Venus sits at her toilet, admiring herself in a mirror. She's a pictorial narcissist, convinced of her sanctity and centrality as an image. But to her demand that we defer to her, Rauschenberg inserts a photographic rebuke. Beyond her mirror is the cluttered indifference of the street. The goddess is unseated by the ocular democracy outdoors. Rauschenberg aims as well to reproduce the tonelessness of what he calls "pedestrian color": the absent-minded smudging of values by the eye in the street, which can't be bothered to differentiate the jarring colors of the scene and smears them into a neutral "no-color." The pedestrian soils the pavement as he walks; his eye likewise stains or fades what he looks at. He uses up images and then discards them. The newspaper is to Rauschenberg an urban symbol of this visual expendability. The papers he added to his "Currents" collage in 1970 are themselves the city's detritus because yesterday's newspaper is a synonym for waste and the city's amnesia; and they too, like the streets, can only be read nonhierarchically, since their columns adjoin stories without relating them, which is how the city randomly orders the lives entrusted to it. Those lives are in turn diminished, consumed and wasted by the paper. The headlines Rauschenberg selects refer to cops stabbed and prison inmates beaten—disasters which will be smirched into erasure tomorrow, for the newspaper, as the title points out, is a means of currency like the streets or like paper money, given over to the users who circulate through it or circulate it between themselves until it's used up or they are.

Robert Rauschenberg, "Estate" (1963). Philadelphia Museum of Art. Given by the Friends of The Philadelphia Museum of Art.

Rauschenberg's artistic procedures are those of a walker in the streets: the idling pedestrian who along the way collects impressions from the visual litter and makes a composite of them; the flaneur who becomes a bricoleur. Bricolage is the assembly of and construction from bric-à-brac. Lévi-Strauss sees it as the mental activity of the savage scientist, who is also a mythographer. He combs through the debris which the world contains and builds a coordinated set from these happened-on items. He makes discarded form newly functional and converts useless function into an appurtenance of decorative form. His inventions are altars. Like myth, they piece together a meaning and a god from the accidental evidence scattered around us. They are also the first machines, structures we think with and which do things for us.

The bricoleur is Crusoe on his island. He is also Rauschenberg in New York, scavenging on the beaches of Staten Island and among the downtown gutters and the junk shops of Canal Street for the urban jetsam which is to be the raw material of his art. The artist's compact with the city requires him to behave as if, like Crusoe, he were the first and only man there. He must adapt to its random order by limiting his range of choices. Lévi-Strauss distinguishes the bricoleur from the engineer by saying that the latter employs substances and tools made specifically for the project he's embarked upon, whereas the former must forage for and improvise those tools and substances, making do with what lies at hand or underfoot. This was the Crusoesque habit of Rauschenberg on his urban beat. He had a rule, when on the lookout for objects to make art from, that he'd go once around the block in quest of them. If that didn't yield enough, he could go one further block in any direction; then no more. He is voluntarily closing off what Lévi-Strauss calls the bricoleur's "universe of instruments," invoking an order to delimit the burgeoning randomness of those gutters. On his forays he picked up ventilation ducts, bicycle wheels, rubber tires, packing cases, cardboard, corrugated paper, and a stuffed angora goat. The damage done to these things constitutes, for him, a narrative of origins and worldly vicissitudes—"a silent discussion of their history," as he calls it—which is mythic, since myth is about the history during which we have all forfeited divinity, our collective prostration as the debris of heaven. From these fragments Rauschenberg re-erects collapsed mythologies, reinvesting the objects with talismanic powers the city, throwing them away, has forgotten.

The titles he gives to his combines speak of this interpretative refabrication. A tin can operated by a faucet handle becomes a "Pail for Ganymede," who was cupbearer to the gods; a wooden makeshift on wheels is "Gift for Apollo," a rude chariot; a radio with a motorized dial is "Oracle." The archeological imagination conjectures uses for the dismembered things its excavations turn up and can then exhibit them in the museum. In parody of this process Rauschenberg takes a snippet of the Manhattan telephone directory, recesses it, frames it in an expanse of paisley shawl, and renames it "Hymnal." The obsolete index is a book of the dead, a thing not to be used—since the bricoleur's art is the transformation of function into form—but to be recited from or worshipped, like a sacred relic. Rauschenberg encourages the items in his trove to couple. A matchmaker among these urban orphans, for "Monogram" he plugs his angora goat inside a tire; later he finds the intercourse of the animal with the retentive muscle occurring, un-prompted, on the New York sidewalk. One of his recent photographs shows the street outside a bar, into which a young man in overalls is retreating. On the curb a tilted fire hydrant has a tire gripped around it—an even fitter image of anal impalement than "Monogram." What Rauschenberg calls the city's "provocative facts" generate an automatic and erotic symbolism. When the litter doesn't orgiastically rut, as here, it sorts itself out into a well-mannered commonality. In another of Rauschenberg's photographs, a New York corner is piled with black-bagged garbage, rising in a mound between a lamppost and a mailbox. There are no people on the pavement. The city seems to belong to the trash. At the corner, angled toward the street, sits an abandoned arm-chair. Some bags of litter repose in it to watch the world go by. Refuse here provides an amenity for its own kind: a park bench for the city's rejects.

The city grows its totems, as on this street corner. They accumulate, like garbage, by haphazard accretion. One such urban emblem—a totem pole raised by New York's own piling-up of bric-à-brac and a model of the absent bricoleur's mutation of significances—was a famous crozier-shaped lamppost on Union Square, dating from the 1890s. Reginald Marsh could see it from his studio and sketched it in 1954. By then it was a signifier which signified so much that it polymathically contra-dicted itself, asking to be read not as use but as ceremonial beauty. Traffic lights, street signs, embargos against parking, warnings against turns, and even a mailbox had been hung on it. Pointing every way at once, it offered itself as an all-purpose guide to the city, which it had transliterated in symbols, signs, and numerals referring to streets, postal zones, and periods of the day. It can cope with one symbol's sudden metamorphosis into another, as when East 14th Street unexpectedly renominates itself as Union Square or (since the pole, like a bemedaled veteran, also bears a highway shield) as N.Y. Route 22. As well as a many armed and all-wise directory, it's a tribal elder, a symbol of the city whose contradictory symbols it regulates. In Marsh's sketch, some-one mails a letter in the box tethered to the post, not so much using it as gravely consulting it and trusting it to care for and relay a personal message, treating it as a clearinghouse for prayers. New York's police-men totemize their bodies in the same way as that lamppost, attaching to their sagging belts an armory of guns, whistles, truncheons, and hand-cuffs, with their clanking bunches of keys announcing their right to open every door in the city. Walkie-talkies crackling, they are human radio stations, absorbing and giving off information like the plurally gestur-ing lamppost. Rauschenberg relishes these urban techniques for totem-izing yourself by wearing T-shirts that exhort passersby or by sewing patches on your clothes: he has photographed a display of embroidered emblems—Superman, the Big Apple, the Statue of Liberty. By such self-advertising, you share in the city's manufacture of deity, for its gods are commercial logos. The bricoleur unearths them as shards from the fragmented sky and returns them heavenward. The gasoline-powered Pegasus of Texaco leaps (in a Rauschenberg photograph) up a brick wall; a spread-eagled Olympian youth floats on a billboard above Times Square, his rump squeezed into a pair of Calvin Klein jeans. In 1981 Rauschenberg exhibited a sequence of photographs arranged in cruci-form shapes or layered or skewered. He called them "Photems"—anti-hierarchical totem poles, no longer upright, with some of their images sideways and others (including a few skyscraper summits) upside down; totems pro tem, uneternal monuments made from the city's ephemera, its rusty neon signs and fire escapes, its scruffy sidewalks and wrecked autos, with no logic to their partnership except the pedestrian one of crazy contiguity. These are the bricoleur's toppling, unsteady ladders to the sky, his backyard towers of Babel.

In sifting through the city's unwanted objects and experimentally combining them, assembling—with the adhesion of glue—collaged, shakily integral wholes, Rauschenberg is intimating new tactics for the urban narrator. Can one assemble people in the same way, out of the scraps salvaged from disconnecting randomness? The plaintive adver-tisers in the *Village Voice* think so. Hence two such gambling throws as these: "Woman eating at 2nd Ave Deli (E 10th St) Fri aft at 4. You had small Barnes & Noble bag w/ you. I'm the man you saw getting his check when you turned around. Call 777-5291 anytime after 2 pm" or "11/11/80, 8:45 PM, Times Sq RR. You were boarding train, we smiled, you seemed interested. Wearing blue jacket, tan pants, brown hair, beard. Tel: 201-648-2306. Mark." Like the artist recycling objects the city has forgotten, these petitioners are cultists of the urban find, and they enlist the city, which endlessly circulates and recombines goods and people, as a broker of sexual possibility. Each coincidence is a tantalizing latency. The correspondents accept the perhaps irreversible realities of passage and transit. They can identify their prospective partners only by attaching them to places as speedily forgetful as the fast food deli or the RR subway or by associating them with commodities as infinitely duplicable as a Barnes and Noble carrier. But they believe that the chance which ordained that initial intersection of glances may, after reshuffling all the people in the city, reunite them. They're appealing to the aleatory opportunist who controls New York and devises its happy collisions. As the bricoleur raises improbable ideological temples from the remnants of a disintegrated order, so they extrapolate an erotic adventure from a conversation that never occurred. The narrator in Truman Capote's *Breakfast at Tiffany's* (1958) knows his New York neighbors by a similar stratagem of imagination. He has no information about them; therefore he speculates. And he confects the character of Holly Golightly, as Rauschenberg makes his combines, by assemblage. Rauschenberg's castoffs engage in "a silent discussion of their history." Similarly, the contents of Holly's trash basket, when interrogated by the narrator, confess the habits of their former mistress. She reads tabloids and travel brochures, smokes Picayunes, eats cottage cheese and melba toast, and dyes her hair. Convinced that city dwellers reveal themselves in what they discard, literally giving themselves away in their garbage, Capote in April 1979 tested his expertise at trash decipherment by accompanying his cleaning lady on her rounds. In the empty apartments she services, he guesses at the character of the occupants. Fatty snacks cram the freezers of the rich Jewish couples. An airline pilot has strewn through his apartment a flotsman of miniature vodka bottles; between his seamy sheets is impasted a gooey collage of mayonnaise, chocolate, chewing gum, cigarette butts, and lipstick. As a gossip, listening in on the talk at adjacent lunch tables in *Answered Prayers*, Capote is a bricoleur of another kind, fantasticating histories from the chance crumbs people let fall and preserving innuendos as urban objets trouvés. Not for nothing is a suspected liaison referred to, by those who construct columns out of gossip, as an "item": it's information or inference as a building block, a fact or factoid to be tried out in combination with others as the structure is pieced together.

Collage, unless greasily lubricated like the meal in the pilot's bed, is inherently expedient, as unlikely and unlasting as the connections the advertisers in the *Village Voice* seek to make. It's named after the glue that is its medium, and glue's frail achievement is the temporary affixing of constituents that have nothing in common. This is why the composer Karlheinz Stockhausen calls New York a "social collage," where the conjoining glue is "mainly the knife and mutual exploitation and hatred."

New York can't fuse the items it contains; it makes do therefore with manacling them into coexistence. Oldenburg defines it as a palimpsest, piling up narratives and compressing them, with no apparent agent to bind them as glue cements the collage: "The city is overlay upon overlay of incident," a jarring simultaneity of happenings. Beyond this untrustworthy state, Stockhausen envisages a "real mingling and symbiosis." This would be "metacollage": a globe hugged into a village by brotherly love; a city harmonized and spiritualized by the bricoleur and his gluing generosity. Failing that, New York remains the shakiest of combines, a totem (as Rauschenberg's pun suggests) just for the time being. The New Yorkers of Norman Mailer's *An American Dream* (1966) thrill to the existential precariousness of the collage. The cop believes that "there's a buried maniac who runs the mind of this city. And he sets up the coincidences." Given that maniacal logic, Mailer's characters must tiptoe above the abyss—as Rojack, edging along the parapet of the Waldorf Towers or spending the night in Harlem on a dare, does—holding the insecure structure together by force of will. Studying the precinct map in the station house, Rojack reflects that "the secret to sanity" is "the ability to hold the maximum of impossible combinations in one's mind." The collage now must be cemented by the mind's unaided effort, without glue; the Rauschenbergian recombiner has to be a tense and agile dialectician. Mailer rejoices in New York's trial of one's psychic strength. Human bodies will all at last be torn apart by the city's stresses. Rojack's wife intends to keep his ashes in an urn and scatter them, a handful a day, from her tenth-floor balcony over the East River Drive; after he kills her, he considers feeding her into the kitchen Disposall and packaging the long bones to hurl across the highway into the river, but instead he simply throws her out of the window onto the traffic. One way or another, the city will eventually destroy us. Meanwhile we must keep alert and try—by making our own soiling mark on it—to damage it as much as we can. In a 1974 essay Mailer cheers the existential pluck of the graffiti daubers in the subway. Defacement is their faith, and Mailer finds in their slapdash virtuosity the same idolatry of gesture that excited the critics of Abstract Expressionism. The angry adolescents with their spray cans are mute, inglorious Pollocks, whose dribbles, flicks, and whorls of paint scribble psychic signatures. They willfully affront the blank theater of the canvas or the impersonal metal of the city's surface. They're prepared to risk their lives to make art. They climb along a cliff above the Harlem River to get to the A train yard at 207th Street, paint through the winter with frostbitten fingers, and triumphantly decorate inaccessible areas of wall on the wrong side of the electrified rail.

As the critical myth of Abstract Expressionism demands, Mailer sets the solitary artist's defense of his name on the carriages against the threatening society which conspires to expunge that name. The arcane scrawls jinx the political repressors. Mayor Lindsay's bid for the presidency was ruined, Mailer supposes, by the defilement in the subways. Oldenburg also considers action painting a kind of graffiti. The style looked to him "as corny as the scratches on a NY wall." The "Street" drawings he began on the Bowery in 1959 take as their medium the city's trampling and rending of us. They were made on torn paper, which represents "irrationality, disconnection, violence and stunted expression—the damaged life forces of the city." The paper must be as sordid and persecuted as the urban pavement.

When its fixative won't hold, collage cobbles together a schizophrenic, self-torturing machine. If you can entertain at once all those impossible contradictions, the machine may work. If not, it won't heed your efforts to restrain and order it and will fly derangedly apart. This is New York as Mailer or, more gently, Capote—watching Holly Golightly assemble an implausible persona for herself when she comes from Texas to the city—see it: a willed collage. In 1960 Jean Tinguely built and, in the sculpture garden of the Museum of Modern Art, encouraged the suicide of such a frenetic engine, his "Homage to New York." Tinguely is the bricoleur as mad scientist, unleashing the energy which in the city is harnessed to human uses. What would happen if that electric motivation were allowed to riot out of control? The city would destroy itself. Tinguely's invention burned through a short happy life, smoking, blazing, exploding, and stinking until it left a rusting corpse in the museum's trash cans. At the time, Tinguely's studio was on Walker Street, near Canal Street, the city's graveyard of industrial mechanism. Here in secondhand shops he found motors, an electric fan, and an Army surplus meteorological balloon, which were to be the monster's organs. Its skeleton he exhumed from New Jersey dumps. Here his discoveries included abandoned baby carriages, bicycle wheels, drums, oil cans, and a child's chamber pot, on which the machine beat out a funereal tattoo for itself with a nut. Tinguely fitted it with the gougings of a piano, from which only three doleful notes, repeating themselves in a ritualized lament, still played. It had a radio in its gullet and for a percussive heart an Addressograph machine. Tinguely was perhaps remembering John Cage's orchestration of the urban dump. Cage had enrolled tin cans, brake drums, and flowerpots as instruments, and prepared a piano—with metal, wood, and rubber inserts between the strings—by rubbishily wrecking it. The medium of Tinguely's ephemeral collage was fire, not glue. He welded the scrap metal together with an acetylene torch. That heat, rather than permanently coupling unlike objects, begins their dissolution. A burning candle on the piano was inundated with gasoline; the piano's built-in fire extinguisher failed to work, so it flared up. Near the end of the demonstration, the metal began to melt and the machine sagged into semi-liquefaction. The incendiary doom of the surrealists, which makes Dali's New York rot and twists the girders of Guglielmi's bridge, had overtaken the city. Nevertheless, Tinguely's was a jokey suicide. His monster enacted its death as a model of polite technocratic deportment. It was a kamikaze toy. Once the rubble has been cleared up and the vile smells it gave off have drifted away, its version of the city is benign, for it arrives at ecological peace. Tinguely carried his machine's members back to the dumps of Plainfield and Summit: earth to earth, garbage to garbage. The city has come to terms with its own planned obsolescence. Oldenburg devised an equivalent to Tinguely's docile, self-eliminating meta-matic. Everywhere in the streets he'd pick up angular fragments of metal, pipe, wood, or wire, which he classified with a stockade of plastic pistols as ray guns. These found objects anagrammatized New York. Playing games in 1961 with the words "Ray Gun," he noticed that if you reverse them they make "Nug Yar." He at once predicted that "the name of New York will be changed to Ray Gun." There's no violence to that prophecy. Oldenburg's guns are playthings, unwounding mockeries. When they shoot, no one dies. The pop city is becoming a kindergarten.

It's a city also of an antic consumerism, a big store supplying fantasies for free. Its gutters are emporia, where the trinkets don't have price tags. It's a place where commodities, surfacing again after death, have their second coming in the bazaars of Canal Street. The spendthrift imagination buys things with wishes. Rauschenberg made a mascot for "Homage to New York," and in it expressed this prodigality: it was a money-thrower with springs that catapulted silver dollars through the museum garden, egging on the self-destroyer with its tips. Tinguely had set himself up as an omnivorous consumer, ambitious to guzzle all the city's goods. He planned to take over a department store window where he'd install machines which, on his behalf, would rip and smash the merchandise. A sign would rouse a last panic of consumerism in the passersby: "Come In and Buy before Jean Tinguely Destroys Everything!" Again, there's no threat here. The city's economy defines us as consumers, which means that we destroy—metaphorically engorge—whatever we purchase, clothes, gadgets, and other durables as well as food. And as consumers, we are all producers of garbage. In his *New York: A Seren-*

dipiter's Journey (1961), Gay Talese sees the whole city as engaged in this famished consumption and excretion, ridding itself daily of tons of trash, leaving unclaimed umbrellas in the lockers of the Port Authority bus station, and distributing dead animals through the streets. Talese's is a necrotic consumerism: the genii of his city are the sanitation men who dive into the muddy East River to fish up bodies and even recycle the corpses in the potter's field when space is short, or the A.S.P.C.A. officials who kill 100,000 stray cats every year. But the process remains benevolent. Consuming the city's goodies, we accept its right—like Deborah, in Rojack's imagination, victualing the Disposall—eventually to consume us. Oldenburg in 1966 marveled that "the chief production of New York is garbage." The economical city ensures that our wastes are never wasted. Tramps—one of whom Oldenburg admiringly impersonated in an early happening, dressed in rags and snug in a gallery furnished with collectibles from a garbage lot—construct shacks from our refuse. Our thrown-away plastic bags are their suitcases, and the heat we expel from our buildings provides them with hearths: they curl up to sleep over warm outdoor gratings. They're parsimonious feeders on the city's second helpings.

In the city of consumerism, art is a search for the recondite treasures New York has randomly buried. The most intrepid scrutineer of New York's hand-me-downs, and the most devout recycler of found objects, was Joseph Cornell, who located the oddments he reverently boxed in the shabby arcades of Times Square, the musty bookstores of Fourth Avenue, the flower stalls on West 28th Street, and the curiosity shops above Madison Square. The notion of making containers for the trinkets he picked up was itself an urban coincidence, an alogical combine like those Rauschenberg tacks together. Cornell remembered passing a shop window displaying compasses, then, two blocks farther, a window full of boxes. "It occurred to me to put the two together." He is the bricoleur as an elegiac wanderer in memory, a votary of the souvenir. He collected old postcards, for instance—epitaphs for a defunct happiness; experiences which, having been used up, are put on sale to someone else. Like Rauschenberg carpentering a pail for Ganymede or a cart for Apollo, he reinvests profaned objects with spirit and proves the recurrence of god in the mechanical city. His boxes harbor absences, evaporations as fleeting as memories or scents. As reliquaries, they commemorate a loss by enshrining a fragment: a feather deposited there by a bird or a wing by a butterfly or a snapshot by a movie star. Sometimes by accident these migratory gods could be sighted in New York, but they were always in flight. In 1944 Cornell briefly captured—with his eye only—

Marlene Dietrich, who was waiting for a cab at the curb of Jay Thorpe's. He explored the city in quest of such signs. They were his aleatory epiphanies, accidents which, like Rauschenberg's findings in the gutter or Capote's in Holly's wastebasket, express affinities.

If Cornell boxes the images he worships in the city, Christo—in another modality of consumerism—wraps them. During the 1960s he planned the packaging of three New York buildings, 2 Broadway, 20 Exchange Place, and the Allied Chemical Tower in Times Square. His wrapping muffles and softens, preventing the economic activities otherwise conducted in these buildings: as bricolage, it reads function as form. Tinguely argued that, because his manic engine wasn't made to do a job, there was no way of telling whether, when accidents like the failure of the fire extinguisher occurred, it was working or not. Christo similarly frees the business district from dour, laboring capitalism by proposing to gift-wrap 2 Broadway and 20 Exchange Place. Packaging is part of the rite of purchase, as Cornell realized. It turns whatever we've bought into a surprise or a trouvaille. Yet the wrapping is expendable. Like foreplay, it flirtatiously delays access and teases us with its elaboration; it knows that it will be discarded. Christo, suggesting that the outer garments matter more than what's beneath them, has fetishized the skyscrapers. We enjoy them by dressing them up, not by unclothing them. So long as we don't violate their casing, they'll guarantee us that joy forever. Without satiation there can be no wearying. Christo accepts that his dreamed-of investiture of the city can only be coitally brief. He's reconciled to the consumability of his projects, which he calls temporary monuments. Their very temporariness is to him a gratification, a festive respite in the city's routine. Better an ephemeral monument, which exists only while it delights, than one granitically fixed for all time in grim remonstrance. Packaging buildings makes children's toys of them. Christo, restoring infancy to New York, has repastoralized it. His most recent plan was a ceremonial outfitting of Central Park. He hoped to build there, over twenty-five miles of pathway, a gilded passage flanked by steel doorframes from which yellow nylon banners would flap. The wrapping here would simulate a series of gates, to be undone or opened by the rambler through the park. Being temporary, the portals would re-create themselves around you, canopying you under a sky of cloth of gold if caught by wind, reaching down to ruffle you—so you would have to grope between them—if there were no breeze. Christo has imagined a package that would permit you to unpeel it but could repair the damage by wrapping itself up again. The banners you'd open would close again behind you. Contained inside the gift, you'd never exhaust it.

Richard Estes, the photorealist, sheets New York in cellophane or protects its wares behind spotless plate glass. For Estes the picture, like the city, is a shop window for the display of commodities—food in cool cubicles along the walls of a Horn & Hardart automat, candy glossily boxed and on parade, blooms bunched and wrapped on tiered platforms outside the establishment of the florist Helene. Photorealism is the style of an idyllic consumerism. It duplicates things so exactly that they seem to be there, on the other side of the picture's glass, owned by you. Times Square, in Estes's "Canadian Club" (1974), is an alfresco supermarket where even litter—a 7-Up can in the gutter—qualifies as an item in the stock. The painting takes its name from the promotional sign, not from Times Square. Estes prefers to paint New York on Sunday mornings when it's purged of traffic and human users. People sully it, and he wipes them off the gleaming glass of his pictorial surface. Cars and neon signs reflected in the window of the automat or on the panels of a row of phone booths efface the customers inside; in "Bus Window" (1968–73) a slanting reflection of the buildings opposite Klein's in Union Square obliterates the driver. Newly cleansed and emptied, New York has attained that mood which, in Warhol's meditation on the Empire State, is the sanctity of pop—a beatific blandness. The shops and offices of Estes are conventually quiet and pristine. His is, in its dehumanized way, a holy city, populated only by intact and vacuum-sealed soda cans, unpopped corn, and the identical wax virgins who congregate like an angelic choir in the shop window on West 38th Street in "Bridal Accessories" (1975). "Central Savings," also painted in 1975, is about this cloistering of commodities. Despite the title, it shows a Chock full o' Nuts on Sixth Avenue, closed on one of Estes's Sundays. Backward on its window is printed the Central Savings banner from the bank on the opposite corner. The title comments aptly on the empty Chock full o' Nuts, with its dazzling laminated counters and glistening refrigerated cases: it too is a safety-deposit box, a bank vault for pies and sandwiches, a sanctuary of consumption where—now that it's closed—things are protected from our appetites and permitted to earn interest. The consumerist city of Estes has dispensed with consumers and practices self-delectation.

Oldenburg's shopkeeping is more liberal. The store is for him an enclosure of the street, and the street is the sum total of the refuse it contains. In 1960 he installed at the Judson Gallery behind Washington Square an environment he called "The Street," which he had anthologized from the street's informal self-unwrapping—paper bags, cardboard cartons, burlap sacks, cast-off clothing. The members of his audience were solicited for their own rubbish as a donation to the show. This

Richard Estes, "Central Savings" (1975). The Nelson-Atkins Museum of Art, Kansas City, Missouri. Gift of the Friends of Art.

street, where objects happen along and are gradually embedded in the composite, is coterminous with the field of art. Writing in 1961 about a novelty shop on the Lower East Side, Oldenburg equates it with the wealthy museums uptown. The store is a "place full of objects," and thus a demotically livelier version of the art mausoleum. "A refuse lot in the city," he argues, "is worth all the art stores in the world." His dream is to inhabit the street as a studio and to define the pavement as a canvas. Such a reinterpretation of the urban turf had been one of Rauschenberg's first acts in New York. For his "Automobile Tire Print" in 1951 he glued together twenty sheets of paper, then inked the pavement on Fulton Street. John Cage drove a car through the ink and along the paper. Unrolled, the work measures 16½ inches by 264½ inches. Its horizontal extent is its enfranchisement of the street—since making a painting is for Rauschenberg analogous with smudging the street, and the wheel is his motorized painter's brush—and its gesture beyond the city to the untracked infinity of the American landscape. This experiment on Fulton Street also levels the pictorial plane. In easel painting, it's upright before us like a window. Rauschenberg flattens it beneath us: we don't look out through it, employing it to frame and distance the view, but travel across it and dirty it as we go. The car driven along the paper embarks on an exploration of ground-level America. Its inky imprint might be Man Friday's spoor in the sand. Oldenburg continues this unfurling of the canvas along the street. Rauschenberg's paper, though it could have continued until it had circumnavigated the world and returned to its point of departure, traveled only twenty-two feet. Oldenburg roofed over an entire block as his arena of operations: in 1965 he found a studio a block long on 14th Street at First Avenue.

Setting up shop there, he reconstituted the frugal and dexterous economy of Crusoe's island. The improvisatory engineering of the bricoleur became a house rule for him. The artist must make his tools before he can use them. If the pieces of a broken compass were found in the street, they had to be taped together before being put to work. The fanciful presumption of these artists is that they're the sole subjects in a city which, like Crusoe's solipsistic fief, comprises only objects. Sometimes they seem to be the first man in the world, as when Rauschenberg enlists Cage as his Friday to leave a mechanized footprint on the pavement and inaugurate the trek of exploration; at other times they behave like the wistful last man on a dead earth, shoring up souvenirs, like Cornell, against its ruin. Does Estes's Times Square represent New York on an Edenic Sunday morning or at Armageddon, when only soda cans and passengerless autos remain? Oldenburg reads the city as a landscape, of which he, like Crusoe, is the sole proprietor. A note in 1963 effects a sequence of beautiful metamorphoses, seeing urban objects as flora and fauna—people, Oldenburg says, are single trees, vehicles are animals, stores are collective forests, streets are plains or rivers. Rendered harmlessly vegetative, the city's humans, machines, and institutions assent without demur to Oldenburg's ownership of them. He can arrange them throughout his landscape or shelve them in his shop. Both as commercial cataloguer of the city's warehouse and as traveler through its imitation of nature, he resembles Crusoe. Oldenburg in 1966 called the landscape artist "the only living person in the world." This monopolistic solitude can be either the innocent joy of Adam or the anxious survivalist self-reliance of Crusoe. The difference between Eden and Crusoe's island inflicts an ambiguity on Oldenburg's New York. All Adam in Eden needed to do was attach names to the world, as Whitman does in his odes christening New York. His next obligation was the self-multiplying furnishing of that world—also accomplished by Whitman, who populates New York with sibling selves. Crusoe's tasks demand a more desperate ingenuity. Instead of being born into a premade world, he's cast away in a splintered, unmade world, which he must fit back together by the exercise of skill. Although Oldenburg's New York often has the appearance of an infantile paradise, a Disneyfied Arcady with cuddly, consumable toys as its monuments—a teddy bear in Central Park, a Good Humor bar gooily obstructing Park Avenue—it's also a wrecked place, an apocalyptic dump, a bombed big store. In 1965 he planned a colossal monument for the Battery. It was to be a collapsed vacuum cleaner, lying on its side "without an explanation of why it was fallen (or thrown) as if a skyscraper had been constructed on its side, like a fallen tree." This is the city ravaged, its forests felled: Eden razed by Paul Bunyan. Crusoe destroys the innocent garden in which Adam lives. The teddy bear Oldenburg proposes setting in Central Park can remain there in its peaceable kingdom only as long as it's disabled for work, because the moment it acquires manual crafts it will begin the Crusoesque war against nature which at last builds the city. Oldenburg, explaining his choice of the bear as the spirit of the park, said that he wanted "a toy with the 'amputated' effect of teddy paws" because "handlessness signifies society's frustrating lack of tools." The bricoleur's inefficacy is a safeguard. Armed with the tools he devises for himself, Crusoe turns the garden into a plantation, the island into a factory. Oldenburg's metamorphosis switches into reverse: the landscape once again becomes a city. Resisting this evolution, Oldenburg reveres—and in his New York monuments exemplifies—a craftsmanship that is amateurish and joyous. He redeems Crusoe by making him manufacture toys, not tools or weapons. Oldenburg's boldest ambition is to have New York as his plaything. He wants to fondle it, as he says in some notes written in 1965–66, "in the palm of my hand." He would like to be an unimperial Crusoe, whose island is a playpen, not a sovereign territory.

From that studio coequal with the street, Oldenburg proceeded to treat the entire city as a studio in his schemes for New York monuments. He was reassuming the perquisite of Adam, embracing the city as a private preserve he can gambol in, infantilely parodying the constructive projects of Crusoe. He calls New York "my favorite 'room,'" and as its happy resident he dreams of laying out both the natural landscape and the urban simulacrum of it as circuitry for pranksome delight. He would love to pad Central Park and the slope of Park Avenue with green baize, in homage to the grass of the former and the merely titular vegetation of the latter, and to use them as pool tables. Colored balls would be sent

Claes Oldenberg, "Proposed Colossal Monument for Central Park North, New York: Teddy Bear" (1965). Courtesy of Mr. and Mrs. Richard E. Oldenburg.

bumping through the park to roll down the declivity of the avenue. They'd be collected at Grand Central and shipped back uptown on the underground railroad tracks. At 96th Street they'd pop into view again, ready to resume the game. A city built at right angles now goes around in larking, endlessly repetitive circles. Like a childhood game it can be played over and over without boredom or fatigue. These circles are also the reliable recurrences of pastoral, seasonally renewed. Oldenburg's monuments are often animals, tamed pastoral creatures that have consented to be pets or playmates—the teddy bear in the park, or the gigantic rabbit he wanted to erect in midtown, its ears cocked at skyscraper height to cheer the distant suburbs. He calls his monuments anti-heroic and lyrical. The heroic monument embodies a hard civic value. The statue is a body petrified, fixed in a postmortem attitude which makes it, like Mozart's stone Commendatore, bode retribution. The city resurrects its dead as authoritarian bogies on pedestals. Cornelius Vanderbilt surveys Park Avenue from the ramp outside Grand Central, George Washington lectures to the brokers of Wall Street, Father Duffy preaches to Times Square. Even the Statue of Liberty with its spiky crown and muscular arm is more a forbidding father than a soothing mother. Oldenburg exorcistically ends this reign of statuesque terror. His monuments aren't male aggressors but female sustainers; instead of celebrating power, they disburse companionship and solace. The substitution is summed up in the lipstick he mounted on a caterpillar tank at Yale. The male engine flaunts, as its retractable phallus, a female cosmetic appliance. The city too will be shielded and ceilinged by the monumental mother. Her deputy in one of the 1965 projects was an ironing board, canopying the Lower East Side. The board replicates the shape of Manhattan and with its shadow blesses the former ghetto. Its baldachin testifies to the "million miles of devoted ironing" done beneath it by immigrant mothers sprucing up their off-spring. Oldenburg's monuments are lyrical because they have loosened the hieratic stiffness of the ancestral statue. They're not heroically armored: their substance is furry or fleshly, yieldingly infirm. They're at ease with vegetative nature, in which the rabbit dwells as a mild-mannered herbivore, and with the human body. For we too are squashy, cushioned things, bony only within, hard only when dead. As Olden-burg puts it, we're an architecture of "soft columns—fingers, penis, legs," and he determines to design a city in our corporeal image. Hence his representation of granitic Manhattan as a softly bodily machine. In 1966 he remade the island as a dangling, overstuffed pillow, mapping its postal zones as canvas pads and its subway lines as fraying ribbons. Softening Manhattan, he has disarmed it. The trailing subway extremi-ties have been worn threadbare, like a balding teddy, by the long in-sistence of affection. Surreal softness—which warps Guglielmi's Brooklyn Bridge—is decomposition; Oldenburg's is detumescence, a lyrical relaxa-tion like the Yale lipstick's recoil into its sheath.

Rather than paternal autocrats, Oldenburg's monuments are hospi-table wombs. Entry into them is a return journey to the corporeal inner city of soft warm comfort from which we were long ago evicted. His freeway tunnels for Los Angeles were to travel up into a human nose, and his Broome Street expressway was a tube for traffic in the form of a cigarette extending across Manhattan. Cigarettes and cars both befoul our innards, especially our lungs. Oldenburg's conduit maternally insu-

Claes Oldenburg, "Soft Manhattan #1 (Postal Zones)" (1966). Stencilled canvas, kapok. 80 x 30 x 8 inches. Albright-Knox Art Gallery, Buffalo, New York. Gift of Seymour H. Knox, 1966.

lates us against these twin dangers, since, as he says, "you would be driving inside a cigarette and wouldn't even know it was a cigarette." You'd assume instead that you were traveling through the human viscerae, circulated inside the body as its blood or fuel are. Oldenburg apprehends cities physiologically, using his body "to feel and come to know" a place which it itself a "body image." His monuments are provisions for the city's alimentary and excretory functions. They permit the enjoyment of effluents. Oldenburg has designed a toilet float for the Thames, an elephantine drainpipe for Toronto, an electric fan for Staten Island to dwarf the Statue of Liberty and disperse the city's odors, and—to cope with more solid wastage—that vacuum cleaner for the Battery. The only time when we can guiltlessly dabble in and maybe even make art from our messes is infancy. Oldenburg's New York is an indulged infant, gobbling a diet of fast food. He plans to set up at Times Square an overripe, wilting banana, and on Ellis Island a colossal frankfurter with a tomato on top, impaled by a toothpick. A supplementary island of pizza will bob in the bay; the blades of the fan that unseats the Statue of Liberty are made by unpeeling and softly mechanizing the Times Square banana. If the monuments themselves can't be ingested, Oldenburg locates restaurants inside them. Visitors would alight from helicopters on top of the East Side ironing board and eat in a cabin hanging beneath it. He allows his structures to boast of the ravages of appetite. A bite has already been chewed from the Good Humor bar on Park Avenue; through the gap, cars could be driven. The city's catastrophes are to Oldenburg soft tragedies, like the fate of our provender inside us. His eating isn't a murder of matter, such as occurs in Lorca's surreal abattoirs. The apocalypse he has imagined for New York is an appetitive luxury. He wants to place at the intersection of Canal Street and Broadway—which is the putative site where the atom bomb will be dropped—a premature funeral pile of concrete. The block would be so crushingly heavy that it would subside through the pavement and crush the subway tunnels underneath. But for Oldenburg this disaster is a soft, edible expiry, a delicious molten death. He first thought of the concrete slab as a pat of butter. Its sinking through the street, foreknowing the end of New York, would be the butter's trickling and seeping into the crevices of a hot baked potato.

The oral urgencies of childhood have been prolonged into adult life by consumerism. Fast food, to which so many of Oldenburg's objects and Estes's paintings pay homage, is a synonym for instant gratification. Oldenburg's monuments accept that it's their destiny to be eaten. He wants, he said in 1961, to make things that will be squeezed, licked,

kissed, gobbled up, and then, after all these loving depradations, abandoned "like a piece of shit." The monuments offer their flesh to us
regeneratively. They're gods we can suckle—or goddesses rather, since
consumerism is matrilineal. The mother allows us the consummation of
consuming her. Even when, later in our lives, she's cast as the home-
maker who assembles the commodities we need and cooks up food for
us, it's still her we're symbolically making a meal of. Everything she
lays before us is a substitute for herself. Oldenburg has taken a city of
forbidding masculinity and made a motherland of it. He deflates its
masculine pretensions (as when the recoiling lipstick or the peeled banana deride the penis) and then reinflates it, watching it distend like a
fertile female body to give house-room to new lives. He loves inflatables.
There's a photograph of him blowing up one of the airplanes used in
early happening. And because the gift of breath is, as it was when
Whitman in-spired the city, an impregnation, the offering of a spirit
and life to unloved things, it's answered with a correspondent breeze.
The objects plumped by Oldenburg's breath will themselves respire. In
1966 he designed a pie with a concealed pump which would make it
inhale and exhale. He's especially fond of toys resembling cakes and
cheeses which have built-in squeaks, enabling them to voice their recip-
rocal glee when bitten into. Since his gods are balloons, the event which
sacramentalizes Oldenburg's New York is the Macy's Thanksgiving Day
parade. Weegee in 1962 photographed Father Christmas sprawled in the
gutter like an accident victim. Oldenburg raises that capsized divinity,
puffing out his envelope with warm air and restoring him to the sky
until, with his colleagues, he nods and dances above New York in greeting and reassurance.

That parade, to which Oldenburg is devoted, is a seasonally recurrent
miracle. Otherwise, Oldenburg's schemes for a nursing and nurturing
maternal New York haven't, of course, been realized. Red Grooms,
however, a participant in the first Oldenburg happenings, took over in
1975 the lobby of an office tower on Pine Street and constructed there
a playful walk-through model of the city called *Ruckus Manhattan*.
He cobbled it together with burlap, vinyl, polyester, and plexiglass
bought on Canal Street and sprayed it with a skin of acrylic paint.
Grooms's environment is a genial anarchy—a terrorist bomb has exploded in a Wall Street bank, scattering customers in a havoc of falling
masonry—and perhaps a hell, since the devil himself breathes flame in
the smokestack of the Staten Island ferry. But the monsters inside its
corral are as friendly as Oldenburg's herbivores. An avaricious dragon
coiled round the Woolworth Building flaps its scaly wings, while albino

alligators frolic in the sewers beneath Rector Street. The jaundiced cooks of Chinatown leer as they slice off the heads of fishes or the snouts of pigs. On the subway, papier-mâché derelicts bump and swivel into the laps of horrified fellow passengers. Outsize Texans wearing loud plaid trample the skaters in the Rockefeller Center ice rink. In all this mayhem, there's a saving comic grace. The only tragedies are soft ones, easily undone, like the death by compression of the riders in the elevator at Grooms's World Trade Center. Because their bodies are made of foam, they bounce back into wholeness as soon as the doors release them, models—like Oldenburg's seasonally reinflated balloons—of comic resurrection.

A city that has been either whitely perfected (as at the World's Fair) and anti-gravitationally abstracted from the earth, or else darkly condemned to perdition underground (as in the novels and movies of the 1940s), can now be delighted in for its very accidents and uncohering riot. So far as pop and photorealism are concerned, whatever New York is is right. There is no longer a compulsion to confront the city, like those adversary, distorting modernists or like Stieglitz worrying whether the contents of his gallery could outface the commercial legions on the other side of the window. This new truce with the city frees the artist to play games in and with it, even, like Tinguely, to stage its extinction as a jest. And New York's artistic career ends here—for the time being only—where it began, under the sponsorship of Whitman. It is he who presides over Oldenburg's welcoming of the refuse of New York into his big store or over those monumental projects which are soft and cradling versions of militaristic epic. In "Year of Meteors (1859–60)" Whitman ventures to catalogue the contents not only of New York but of the capacious nation. He will sing "your census returns of the States, / The tables of population and products." The census to him is a native mode of epic because it's a roll call of the species and a convocation (such as he achieves by begetting all the inhabitants of New York) of the tribe. The list is as unhierarchically generous as the Brooklyn ferry, housing all comers. Oldenburg a century later rehabilitates the Whitmanesque census and uses it to restore value to the despised and cast-off victims of the city. In 1961 he wrote a statement for an exhibition in which he declared himself in favor of an art made from spillage, shavings, losses and leavings, from hair clippings and knife parings, from bodily wastes and from organic ferment; an art which bandages these hurt or worn or unwanted things and offers maternal succor—"I am for an art of mama-babble." He is for an art which shops promiscuously in the city's big store, impartially reuniting inimical brand names. He announces that he's for both Kool and Menthol, both 7-Up and Pepsi, for Ex-lax and San-o-med art. He's gluttonously ready to enroll any commodity that promises to aliment us: "I am for U.S. Government inspected art, Grade A art, Regular Price art, Yellow Ripe art, Extra Fancy art, Ready-to-eat art, Best-for-less art, Ready-to-cook art, Fully cleaned art, Spend Less art, Eat Better art . . ." and so on indefinitely, the lines bulging (in imitation of Whitman's free verse) into paragraphs in their inventive enthusiasm.

What now is the container of multitudes? A gormandizing maw, able to ingest all those edibles; an overstocked store; a groaning garbage truck. The city swells to offer bodily hospitality to all the things which chance to be in it at the moment. The epic motive of the city's founder was to prove the necessity of the place. Now, however, the city is content to seem a product of happenstance. Art used to be offended by such whimsical, alogical formlessness. Henry James called it New York's "irrelevance," and his closed doors, like the blanched, vacated walls of the abstract painters, are a critique of it. So is the poetic desperation to wed, in a symbol, the contingent objects out there with one's subjective self—the impossible union responsible for those egotistic skyscrapers or for Crane's neurotically tensile bridge. Not even Whitman could admit the city's utter arbitrariness. But an art that has learned to do so has managed the most arduous formal feat of all—opening itself to contradiction, combining incompatibles like Rauschenberg and thus (as Mailer's hero believes) staying sane. It has also enunciated the most quietly wise rule of living, especially of living in cities: the acceptance of all those other existences, human and mechanical, which clash with and seem to devalue ours; the benediction of strangers; the understanding, forfended by James, of our own irrelevance.

Index